ISLAND OF THE SETTING SUN

In Search of Ireland's Ancient Astronomers

Anthony Murphy and Richard Moore

The Liffey Press

Published by
The Liffey Press Ltd
Ashbrook House
10 Main Street
Raheny, Dublin 5, Ireland
www.theliffeypress.com

A catalogue record of this book is
available from the British Library.

ISBN 978-1-905785-05-6

Printed in Spain by Graficas Cems.

contents

ACKNOWLEDGEMENTS

The number of people who helped us in the creation and completion of *Island of the Setting Sun* is far too great for us to hope to name them all. Throughout the eight years of this project, dozens of people have contributed in some way, whether large or small.

Primarily, we would like to thank our families, for putting up with us and bearing with the project which, at times, might have appeared as though it would be never-ending. On Anthony's side, thanks to Ann, Amy, Luke, Joshua and Tara, and on Richard's, Marita and Elizabeth, and to members of our extended families who provided encouragement over the years and who always believed in us.

The depth of exploration of this book was helped enormously by members of the Irish-Stones e-mail group, past and present. In particular, we'd like to thank Victor Reijs, Gillies MacBain, Anne-Marie Moroney, Martin Byrne, Charles Scribner, Jo Coffey, Hank Harrison, Seán Gilmartin, Philip David, Toby Hall, John Gordon, Michael O'Callaghan and Searles O'Dubhain.

We are extremely grateful to Clare Tuffy, Leontia Lenihan and all the staff at Brú na Bóinne and to everyone in the OPW who have always been courteous and helpful. To the archaeologists who assisted and gave us advice, in particular Matthew and Geraldine Stout, Victor Buckley, George Eogan, Gabriel Cooney and Tom Condit.

There were dozens of people who helped retrieve source material and advise us about where to find information. Foremost among these was Anne-Marie Moroney, who was of constant assistance throughout the project. We are thankful to the County Louth Archaeological and Historical Society and the Old Drogheda Society for advice, assistance and source material. Thanks go to Dermot Foley, Munich Reilly and all the staff at Drogheda and Dundalk libraries.

Thanks also to all the land owners who allowed us access onto their properties during site visits; to Michael Byrne for bringing his binoculars to Baltray!; to Conor Newman, Brian Lacey and The Discovery Programme;

to Larry Lenehan for information about swan counts at Newgrange; to Michael Holohan for his copy of the very valuable Dowth paper; to Chris Finlay for surveying assistance; to Jim Smith for literally bringing us closer to the sky; to Una Sheehan for information and encouragement; to Áine ni Chairbre, Andrew Kieran and Seán Collins for help with source material and information; to Mary McKenna, a consistent source of advocacy and help; to David Moore and all the astronomers who are keeping the very ancient sky watching tradition alive and well; to Tomás de Faoite for allowing us to publish his poem, "Spirit"; to Paul Maher, Seamus Counihan, Colin Bell and all the staff at Maher's Chemist in Drogheda who provided huge photographical assistance and advice throughout the years.

We'd like to thank all the people at the *Drogheda Leader* who have provided unfailing encouragement, and in particular to Andy Gates and Des Grant who were very understanding as the deadline for the book approached.

In bringing this book together, we stood on the shoulders of giants. Due acknowledgement must be bestowed on all those whose painstaking work has been of huge benefit. *Island of the Setting Sun* would not have been possible without massive projects such as the Schools Folklore Collection, the Ordnance Survey Letters and the publication of English translations of numerous ancient manuscripts such as the *Dindshenchas* and the *Annals of the Four Masters*. The exhaustive *foclóirí* and Joyce's place names in three volumes were referenced extensively. So too were the archaeological journals.

While Richard's beautiful paintings adorn the opening pages of each chapter, and most of the photography is by Anthony, we are grateful to the following for use of copyrighted photographs and illustrations, as credited: the Office of Public Works; Geraldine and Matthew Stout; Victor Buckley; Dave Appleton; The Discovery Programme; Michael O'Callaghan; Cambridge University Collection; Mike Fleenor and the Volunteer Observatory, Knoxville, Tennessee; GSB Prospection and Margaret Gowen and Company Ltd..

A word of gratitude to David Givens of Liffey Press who made the process of finding a publisher straightforward by offering us a contract within a day of receiving our proposal; and to our editor, Brian Langan, who has been thorough, constructive and congenial throughout the different stages of preparation of this book.

Go raibh míle maith agaibh.

Anthony Murphy
Richard Moore
November 2006

ABOUT THE PAINTINGS

Richard Moore's paintings, which appear on the title pages of each chapter, are an integral part of this book. They are evocative of the people who built the great monuments of the Boyne Valley 5000 years ago.

Anthony Murphy:

Dedicated to my wife Ann,
and my children Amy, Luke, Joshua and Tara,
the real stars in my life

Richard Moore:

Dedicated to Marita and Elizabeth

SPIRIT

By Tomás de Faoite

On the edge of town in the forest
There grow five tall trees
In a circle. A Druidic temple
Once stood there. I go there
Now and then, hang
No tokens from the branches,
Make no wish, just sit still,
Banish you from my mind
And begin to miss my ancestors.

We cling to anything in loss,
Even bring the dead back
From the grave, resurrect
Heroes out of myth,
Like Ferdia and Cúchulainn,
To try and not hate,
To take no sides
In the fight;

Self doomed Ferdia by the ford.

*Tomás de Faoite is a local poet who was born and raised at Dowth. Some
of his poetry has been inspired by the ancient myths and landscape of
the Boyne area.*

PROLOGUE:
CROSSIПG PAȚHS

The history books tell us astronomy began with the Babylonians, the ancient Chinese and the Chaldeans. Peering out at the winter sky, dominated by the brilliant man-like constellation Orion, I often wondered as a child if the people who inhabited Ireland long ago had their own constellations. Over time, I learned to mark the places where the bright stars would rise on the horizon using manmade and natural markers. In the crisp cold nights of winter, I would watch alone in the dark as Orion, the giant man of the sky, climbed up out of the east over the Boyne Viaduct from my back garden in Drogheda. I knew precisely where Sirius would appear, just at the extremity of a row of trees near the railway station. I would later discover that using horizon markers is a very useful form of astronomical surveying, a practice which was, almost literally, as old as the hills. It seems now, looking back, that I was carrying on a very ancient tradition which had been alive in the New Stone Age, and probably much earlier.

Island of the Setting Sun would probably never have happened if Richard Moore's path hadn't crossed with mine. In 1998, Richard, a lifelong artist, was devising some sort of grand sculptural project which would involve placing large megaliths in alignment with certain sunrises and star risings. The idea was inspired by the ancient astronomers who had constructed their giant monuments by the Boyne. One difficulty he faced in bringing this artistic project to completion lay in the fact that he did not know much about astronomy, and couldn't identify the constellations. His friend, the photographer Michael Byrne, who was also an amateur star gazer, told him about me. Apparently, Michael believed I knew a fair bit about the stars so Richard decided to approach me with a view to learning more about the sky. Caroline Kavanagh, a journalist colleague of mine, had heard about Richard's project and told me to expect a visit.

So when Richard walked into the office in Drogheda where I worked in January of 1999, I thought I had an idea what he wanted from me. He wished to learn about the stars, surely? Well, yes, but during his visit he started showing me drawings of some markings on stones at Knowth. He was particularly interested in finding out if I thought some markings on a Knowth orthostat resembled the constellation Cygnus.

Thus began the eight-year adventure that has culminated in *Island of the Setting Sun*. We were both immediately hooked on the quest to find out more about Ireland's ancient astronomers. In December of that year, Richard, Michael and I discovered another major astronomical alignment in the Boyne Valley, at Baltray. By the next summer we had confirmed a seemingly intentional alignment of a huge henge near Dowth on the summer solstice. Also in that year we first revealed the "Cygnus Enigma" to the world, a theory which holds that the myths and architectural design of Newgrange were inspired by the swan constellation, Cygnus, and the migrating whooper swans which come to Newgrange every winter.

As time went on, we made more and more discoveries, and began to see that ancient mythology and place names could be interpreted in an astronomical context. We were particularly excited about the fact that some of our discoveries tied in very closely with archaeological information and dating, which in our view strengthened our ideas and theories. At one stage, we both took part in an archaeological dig in order to get a taste of real field work. When you want to learn more about a field in which you're not a specialist, there's nothing like getting down and dirty!

There were many times also during our research work where we discovered things as the result of extraordinary coincidence and sheer luck. Some of this is detailed in the book. An immense amount of work was put into creating and maintaining our website, www.mythicalireland.com, which is a handy companion to this book, containing hundreds of pages and images where you can explore ancient Ireland even further.

Island of the Setting Sun is neither an academic nor a non-academic work, but hovers somewhere in between the two. We are, necessarily, dealing in the realm of speculation, but with a healthy dose of fact thrown into the mix. The true unlocking of the secrets of the past lies, we believe, in combining the study of astronomy, mythology and archaeology. Only where the stones, the stars and the stories cross can we begin to see the big picture emerging.

While I have committed to doing all the writing, Richard's contribution has been fundamentally important as well as immense. Two of our major theories, the Cygnus Enigma and the High Man, were both his discoveries. I merely put the "meat on the bones", so to speak. He is an artist of enormous talent, and as a human being he is indefatigably generous, patient and displays tremendous humility. I have come to regard him as a very close friend and hope to work with him for many years into the future.

We are, all of us, children of the cosmos. It is unlikely that astronomy, whether in the form of pure scientific study of the heavens or associated with ritual and spiritual practices, began at any one location. But what is clear from our study is that the people who inhabited Ireland over 5,000 years ago were accomplished sky watchers. Their ritual astronomy appears to have been intrinsically connected with their belief in the afterlife, a stellar otherworld where the soul journeyed after death. The evidence for such knowledgeable stellar study, encoded into mythology, place names and the archaeological remnants scattered throughout Ireland, is widespread and overwhelming.

People often say Ireland's Neolithic builders didn't leave us any writing, a form of textbook from which we can learn all about their culture and the reasons and methods behind their vast works. But the truth is they have left us an expansive record, deeply ingrained into their megalithic structures, carved onto their very stones, rooted in our extensive body of myths and stories and embedded in Ireland's place names.

We invite you now to join us in examining that vast record on this incredible journey through the Island of the Setting Sun.

Anthony Murphy
Drogheda
November 2006

CHAPTER ONE

BALOR'S STRAND:
DISCOVERIES AND
BEGINNINGS

Near the mouth of the river Boyne, in a village called Baltray, County Louth, are two ancient standing stones, erected by megalithic builders five thousand years ago, which can be found at the northern end of a field used as pasture for cattle. The stones are little known, and although recorded in an archaeological survey,[1] are not documented in detail elsewhere. Very few people visit these stones. In fact, there are people living in Baltray who do not know they exist.

Access to the stones is gained by driving up a narrow laneway from the village and mounting an iron gate leading into the field, where the stones are located about 100 metres away at the high end of the field, perched overlooking the sea.[2]

Strategically placed on top of a bluff overlooking marshy grasslands and sand dunes towards the sea,[3] they have a serene majesty, a beauty and a power for the interested visitor who cares to seek them out.

The larger of the Baltray stones with a waning quarter moon

The stones are large slabs of shale, and are set in the ground about nine metres apart. The large stone is 2.9 metres high, while the smaller stone, which is located to the north of the larger, is 1.8 metres high, and there may once have been a third member of the group.[4] Their form can, in certain light conditions, resemble that of two people, caped and murky, watching over the coastline like frozen sentinels.

It is here, at the entrance of Inbher Colpa, where the waters of the Boyne and the Irish Sea meet, that we begin our encounter with the wonderful ancient sites of the Boyne Valley region, and their associated mythology, astronomy and art. After this book, we hope, the Baltray stones will take on a new significance, and their importance in the wider landscape will be understood.

Baltray seems such an inconsequential place to begin an exploration of the ancient sites of Ireland's most celebrated river. What can a pair of menhirs say about the people of a long distant age, especially when we have such monumental expressions of their endeavours further upriver in the Bend of the Boyne, where Newgrange, Knowth and Dowth still stand, silent but potent reminders of what our primeval ancestors were capable of in a far-removed era of enlightenment?

Despite having attracted little attention from academic explorers or casual visitors, the pair of standing stones at Baltray constituted a highly significant part of the ancient Boyne landscape. Although hardly outstanding in archaeological terms, the Baltray stones are the only remaining stone pair in the whole of County Louth,[5] and have a huge strategic, astronomical and mythological importance.

Standing beside the stones, an observer can take in a breathtaking sweep of coastline which stretches all the way from Northern Ireland as far as County Dublin. From Baltray, one can see the Mourne and Cooley Mountains, and Clogherhead to the North, and as far south as Skerries and the Inis Pádraig and Rockabill islands. The Baltray stones, situated less than half a mile from the Boyne estuary, probably would have served as a border marking[6] between the ancient provinces of Ulster, which reached as far south as the Boyne, and Leinster, which was on the other side of the river.[7]

This was the setting, we are fairly certain, where in the mythological epic the *Táin Bó Cuailnge*, the hero Cúchulainn met with his son, Connla, for the first time, and killed the boy after a battle in the shallow waters on the strand of Baltray, known in various sources of the story as Tracht Eisi (Strand of the Track or Footprints), Trá Tracht (Strand of Strands) and Baile Trá – its modern name, supposedly meaning the town (*baile*) of the strand (*trá*).

It is probable that *Baile Trá* is another form of *Traig Baile,* Baile's Strand, which according to tradition was located at Dundalk: "Traigh Bhaile . . . as every County Louth schoolboy knows, is the strand upon which Dundalk is now built".[8] In other sources, Baile's Strand was said to be located in Ulster, near the foot of the hills of Sliabh Breagh. Sliabh Breagh is a range of hills extending from Rathkenny in County Meath, as far as Clogherhead on the coast at County Louth.[9] The Baltray standing stones are located just four and a half miles south of Clogherhead. Dundalk, on the other hand, is over 15 miles north.

Another historical writer has said that "the Strand of Baile must therefore have extended well to the south" and, in fact, said the strand continued from Dundalk "unbroken to Dunany, resumes beyond that, with one interruption at Clogherhead, as far as the mouth of the Boyne".[10] So it seems Baile's Strand was the beach along the whole coast of Louth.

"There is a Baltray on the coast near Dromiskin, and there is the better-known one further south . . ."[11] This "better-known" Baltray is the village at which the standing stone pair is located. Its Irish name, *Baile Trá*, is identical to *Traig Baile*.

In the *Táin Bó Cuailnge* legend, Connla came to Ireland to seek out his father at the tender age of seven. He had been born to a princess, Aife, whom Cúchulainn had left pregnant after being trained in arms by Scathach in Letha (Scotland). Connla came across the sea in a bronze boat, and taunted the Ulstermen who had gathered at Baltray.

Connla would not name himself to two of the Ulstermen, Condere and Conall, so eventually Cúchulainn challenged the boy. Still refusing to give his name, Connla sealed his fate and Cúchulainn wounded him mortally with the *gae bolga,* a magical barbed spear which Cúchulainn used in ford water.

The story describes how Connla tried to reach Cúchulainn's belt, and climbed up on two stones, which are described as "pillar-stones",[12] and "thrust Cúchulainn three times between the stones" while the boy did not move either of his feet from the stones until his feet sank into the stones up to his ankles. The story says that Connla's footprints are still on the stones. We know the standing stones of the Connla story are located on a height above the strand, and Thomas Kinsella's *Táin* translation tells how Cúchulainn and the boy "went down into the sea" from the stones to try to drown each other.[13]

The Baltray stones are located on a ridge about 20 metres above the "tidal lagoons"[14] between there and the sea, so when one is standing at the great stones, one is looking down towards the sea. The comments of geologist and archaeologist Frank Mitchell about the Baltray bluff are interesting in this regard. He says:

> . . . it is probable that in early post-glacial time waves reached the base of the bluff. The coast then retreated, and the dunes were thrown up, leaving between them and the bluff tidal lagoons which have since been drained.[15]

Today, there is a substantial swath of land between the stones and the sea, some half a mile or so in width. Presently, it is occupied by a golf links, the home of the County Louth Golf Club.

Perhaps the story of Connla's death reflects a time when the tide was located directly beneath the stones. After he was killed by his father

Cúchulainn, there was a lament for Connla, and for three days no calves were let go to their cows by the men of Ulster, in commemoration of the boy.[16] This interesting gesture was to have echoes in another story relating to Baltray, about Balor and a cow and a calf.

Given the astronomical nature of ancient sites in the Boyne Valley, we deemed it possible that the standing stones at Baltray could have an astronomical significance. In May of 1999, Drogheda man Michael Byrne, on a visit to the stones with Richard Moore, discovered that if he placed his binoculars on the side of the long axis of the larger standing stone, he could see Rockabill, two small islands out in the Irish Sea, in his eyepieces. This led me to speculate that the long axis of the stone could have been intentionally aligned with Rockabill for an important astronomical event, and after taking compass measurements, I predicted that winter solstice sunrise would occur at Rockabill as viewed from the standing stones.

On winter solstice 1999, I was at Newgrange, taking photographs at the sunrise which that year was a big media event, labelled "dawn of the new millennium". Richard and Michael were dispatched to Baltray to see if the solstice theory was correct. Arriving at the standing stones just as dawn was breaking, they were both surprised and delighted to see the orb of the sun rising very close to the Rockabill islands – as it was halfway up above the horizon of the Irish Sea, it was located just two sun widths

Winter solstice sunrise comes up directly in line with the larger standing stone at Baltray

to the left of Rockabill. Although it was not photographed, the event was captured on video tape by Michael Byrne. Those few minutes of footage, when we viewed them the next day at Michael's house, aroused a great sensation of discovery and fascination. The Baltray discovery was significant. It was further proof that Newgrange did not exist alone in the Boyne Valley as an astronomically aligned monument.

Baltray bears striking similarities to another solstice-aligned standing stone monument in Scotland. The site was studied by a man who dedicated 40 years of his life to the study of hundreds of stone circles in Britain. Alexander Thom, a Professor of Engineering, discovered that the megalithic builders used a common unit of measurement, which he termed the "megalithic yard".[17] Of those sites which Thom referred to as "solstitial sites", two were "the most important".[18] One of those "important" sites is at a place called Ballochroy, which is located in Argyllshire, Kintyre. There is an alignment of three stones at Ballochroy (one more than the alignment at Baltray but, as stated already, there may have been a third stone),[19] and the centre of the three is very like the larger monolith at Baltray – tall, thin, with a straight edge, and a very similar lean.

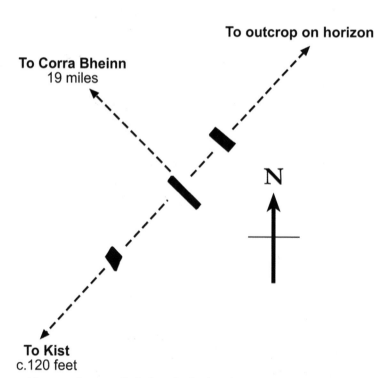

Alignment of stones at Ballochroy, Scotland, as discovered by Alexander Thom

The similarities don't end there. The two sites both have a tantalising name beginning with "Bal", a reference perhaps to the ancient Balor of the baleful eye, the ancient sun deity, of whom we will hear more later. The long axis of the large central standing stone at Ballochroy points towards an island too, which is just over 19 miles away. The stone has the same south-east to north-west axis as the Baltray stone; however, the significant astronomical event marked at Ballochroy is not winter solstice sunrise, but rather summer solstice sunset in the opposite direction.

Thom's careful examination of the site showed that the most northerly peak in the Paps of Jura,[20] pointed out by the flat axis of the standing stone, was the exact location of the summer sunset. In fact, the upper limb of the sun setting would have "just grazed the top of the slope" as viewed from the stone.[21]

Interestingly, Thom was convinced that, at an early stage, people living on the shores of the ocean must have been aware of the connection between the tides and the moon. He suggested this may have been one of the factors that led megalithic people to study the movements of the moon.[22] In this regard, it is perhaps fitting that the Baltray stone pair has been described by one prominent archaeologist as "a prehistoric mariner's guide".[23]

Arriving at a date for the erection of the Baltray stones is a matter of speculation right now. Standing stones in Ireland were erected over a broad time span, beginning in the Neolithic period at the time the great passage-mounds were built and continuing into the Iron Age.[24] Our suggestion that they could date to the early Bronze Age, or perhaps even the late Neolithic, cannot be ruled out, and at least one prominent archaeologist has told us we would "not be considered mad" to make such a suggestion.[25] We will have to leave it to the archaeo-astronomers to do the precise calculations, but the sun's rising position, located about two sun-widths to the left of Rockabill, suggests a period of up to 5,000 years has elapsed since the alignment was formed, assuming the stones were erected when the sun rose directly over Rockabill.

It was becoming apparent that the seemingly innocuous Baltray stones were perhaps much more crucial to the Boyne megalithic culture than had been assumed. Some time after our discovery that the stones were aligned with Rockabill for winter solstice, we happened upon a folk tale which contained what we considered to be an elucidation of the astronomical occurrences which were marked at Baltray.

BALOR AND ROCKABILL

The following is the story as it was told by Mary Halligan, of Strand Street, Skerries, who died in 1906 aged 89.[26]

"There was a very famous cow called *Glas Gablin*[27] belonging to Ulster. No matter how large the vessel used to milk her, she could fill it immediately with rich creamy milk. She lived about the time that the Dé

Dananns were in Ireland. Balor of the Evil Eye, one of the Dé Danann Chiefs,[28] was anxious to get this wonderful cow for himself.

"He and his servant went to the Mourne Mountains where *Glas Gablin* was grazing with her calf. He got the servant to drive the cow and her calf to the province of Leinster – to Wicklow, where he had his stronghold.

"He told the man to keep the calf in front all the time so that the cow would not look back and that she would not know that she was leaving the province of Ulster. The servant did as he was told and everything went well until they crossed the River Boyne.

"Then the servant got careless and allowed the calf to walk behind the cow. Soon after, the cow missed the calf and she looked behind her to see where she had gone. Looking back she saw the Mourne Mountains far away to the north, and knew that she was very far from her native Ulster, so she gave a terrible scream the like of which was never heard before.

"Balor heard the roar and he understood there was something wrong. Now Balor had only one eye and that was in the middle of his forehead. When the giant was talking to anyone he had to keep his eye covered. The eye was evil and had the power of turning to stone whatever was seen by it – animals, people and so on.

"When Balor turned to see what was wrong he forgot to cover the eye and immediately the cow and calf were turned into stones. The two rocks stand to-day as Balor left them – the cow on the south side and the calf on the north side."

The story does not mention Baile Trá, or Tracht Eisi, but we can pinpoint Baltray from the story using astronomy. Balor, although stated by the storyteller to be one of the Tuatha Dé Danann, was in fact the leader of the Fomhóire, or Fomorians, a "sea-pirate race . . . who oppress the

Rockabill viewed from Skerries . . . the larger island now has a lighthouse perched on it. This photo illustrates how there are two islands, a smaller one to the north and the larger to the south.

Winter Solstice sunrise from Baltray . . . note how the sun rises to the left of Rockabill today. 5,000 years ago, it would have been rising directly over Rockabill. Due to refraction, only the larger island is visible in this image.

divine race Tuatha Dé Danann".[29] He had the nickname "Balor of the evil eye"[30] because his gaze could turn his foe to stone, and was also known as "the flashing one".[31]

To us, Balor is very much a kind of solar deity. The lifting of his great eyelid could be compared with the sunrise, and one source refers to the image of Balor as "having eyes that shot out rays like the setting sun".[32] The Welsh version of this deity is Beli, who has many solar attributes.[33]

The critical moment of the Balor story occurs when the servant crossed the Boyne with the cow and calf. At this point, the tale relates, the servant became careless and the calf walked behind the cow. Balor looked with his opened eye and, immediately, the cow and calf were turned to stones in the form of the Rockabill islands, which are, incidentally, situated, according to the story, with the larger island (containing a more modern lighthouse) to the south of the smaller island.

So what does the story mean? Does it have a meaning? We think it has a meaning, one related to astronomy, and this is our interpretation. We understand Balor and his baleful eye as being the rising sun, viewed from the east coast. References to Ulster, the Mourne Mountains (which are visible from Baltray), Rockabill and the Boyne allow us to identify the coastal area, and specifically the Boyne Estuary and Baltray, as being a key location of the story. A corruption of the place name Traig Baile could involve Balor, the sun deity who has important links with Baltray; perhaps the original form was *Traig Balor* – Balor's Strand?[34]

In order to explain how the astronomical and mythological elements combine, let us assume the cow, called *Glas Gablin* in the story, but also known as the *Glas Ghoibhneann,* or literally "the grey of Goibhniu"[35] to be the moon, and the calf Venus.[36] Let us furthermore assume a position at Baltray and watch the story unfold.

It is just after nightfall, around the time of winter solstice, and the full moon is rising out of the Irish Sea. The moon rises in the north east, and spends a good deal of the night high in the sky. The next night, the moon rises a little bit later, and still in the northeast. The night after, as the full moon wanes towards its gibbous (three-quarters full) phase, it rises a little further south, and again later in the night. If we wait until early morning on any of these nights, we watch as the sky begins to brighten, and the stars begin to fade. In the southeast, not far from the Rockabill Islands, we see a particularly bright "star" – brighter than all the others – rising from the sea. This is Venus, the calf of the Balor story. Some time later, the sun rises, and because it is the time of winter solstice, it rises at Rockabill. This is Balor, opening his malignant eye.

On the night of the full moon, the moon sets in the northwest as the sun is rising at Rockabill. They are opposite each other in the sky, and the long axis of the large standing stone points out both objects. But as each day progresses, and the moon travels on its course through the stars, as the ancient astronomers would have seen it, it lingers longer each morning in the west as the sun rises, moving as each day passes closer to the sun. And, it rises and sets further south. At waning quarter (which we see as the waning half-moon), it rises roughly due east and sets due west. This is the *Glas Gablin,* the magical grey cow, of the Balor myth, moving each day from its northernmost position, the Mourne Mountains, towards its meeting with the sun, Balor, at Rockabill.

The full moon at summer solstice rising over the Irish Sea in the same position as winter solstice sun

By the time the moon reaches its crescent phase, we must wait until the pre-dawn light has filled the eastern aspect before we even see her. By this time, she is rising close to Rockabill, and alongside her is the calf, Venus. On the last day of the crescent phase, the moon has moved beyond Venus, to the south of the calf, and as they rise they are swamped in the growing, strengthening light of the new day.

By the next day, the moon has disappeared, apparently turned to stone by the malignant eye of the rising Balor. Venus soon follows, moving closer to the sun each morning, and speeding up as it does so. The legend tells us that the calf lagged behind, that the cow got in front of it, and that when this happens Balor opened his eye and turned them into the Rockabill islands, the smaller "calf" island to the north and the large "cow" island to the south.

What's so special about the meeting of the crescent moon with Venus? Well, they do meet on a regular basis, sometimes as an evening pairing when Venus is the "evening star", and sometimes in the pre-dawn sky when Venus is the "morning star". When Venus is at its maximum elongation[37] from the sun, either in the east or west, the moon will pass it once every lunation – once every 29 days.

But the regularity with which they meet as morning objects, with the moon in a more southerly declination than Venus, is a rarer occurrence. Five synodic periods of Venus[38] is equal to eight of our solar years, the period of time it takes Venus to return to exactly the same position relative to the stars as a morning object. Even rarer still is the meeting of the crescent moon with Venus at winter solstice.

We have watched moonrises at Baltray, particularly full moon rises at the time of summer solstice. Because the full moon is always opposite the sun,[39] at midsummer the rising of the full moon occurs in the direction of Rockabill.

We have interpreted the mythology, with the help of the astronomical alignment, in a way that shows a significant astronomical event was being marked at Baltray, one that was to have echoes right up the Boyne Valley. Understanding the eight-year Venus cycle is important to the decipherment of the movements of the moon and planets. The eight-year period of Venus ties in neatly with the moon's metonic cycle,[40] and we will later show how the Venus and moon cycles were recorded on the stones of the magnificent Boyne Valley passage-mounds, less than ten miles upstream from Baltray.

It is highly probable that the Baltray astronomers were aware of the link between the moon and the tides. Alexander Thom believed this was one of the factors which led the megalithic people to study the movements of the moon.[41] The tidal link was undoubtedly an important factor in the location of the stones, which sat overlooking the seashore and the Boyne Estuary.

Connecting the cow with the moon is an important but somewhat tentative link at this point. But we were to see time and time again that the symbolism of the cow in the Boyne Valley was very persistent, and that it could be tied strongly with the moon and the heavens.

One writer has said that the different colours of cattle symbolised "various phases of the moon".[42] The gestation period of a cow is strongly tied to lunar time.[43] In fact, the cow's pregnancy is 283 days long, which is almost exactly nine and a half lunar months.[44] In other words, if a cow becomes pregnant at, for instance, new moon on the day before St Patrick's Day, she is likely to give birth at the time of full moon around winter solstice. The traditional cow breeding calendar, still used by cattle breeders in the Boyne Valley region, is based on the phases of the moon.[45]

BÓANN AND DABILLA

For more cow lore, and a tale involving a mother earth/river/moon goddess, we turn to another story involving the Boyne River and the Rockabill islands – this one a very famous legend, preserved in the Books of Lecan and Ballymote,[46] and known far and wide. It is the story of how the Boyne was formed, and how the goddess Bóann was washed out to sea with her lapdog.

We first heard it from a prominent folklorist in Drogheda, the late Caitlín Bean Uí Chairbre, who told it accurately and fluently to us one night as we sipped our pints of Guinness in the pub which she owned and ran until the time of her death in 2001.

The source of the Boyne at Necchtain's Well

The story begins at a place called Carbury, which is in County Kildare, and the well which is known as the well of the Blessed Trinity, called Nechtain's Well in ancient times. It is located at the foot of the hill of Carbury,[47] which was said to be the Sidh, or fairy hill, of Nechtain, king of Leinster. Nechtain, or Nuada as he was also known, was said to have been Bóann's husband, and had this secret well in his garden, and no-one was allowed approach it except his three cup-bearers, who were called Flesc, Lesc and Luam. But Bóann was curious of her husband's secret well, and she became determined to test the mystical powers of its waters.

So she approached the well, and passed round it three times "to the left".[48] But when she had completed her third journey round the well, the spring rose and three huge waves burst forth over her, "mutilating her sadly", and, says the original, "breaking one of her eyes".[49] In some versions, Bóann's foot and hand were injured,[50] but in all accounts the water rose up from the well and she fled in the direction of the sea, in order to hide her deformity, but the waters rushed forth from their source and followed her all the way to Inbher Colpa, the mouth of the river Boyne. She, along with her lapdog, Dabilla, was washed out to sea. The dog was transformed into the Rockabill islands. The exact whereabouts of Bóann's drowning was not precisely recorded, but it seems she was drowned somewhere in the Irish Sea.

We can connect Bóann with both the moon and the Milky Way galaxy, and also help to interpret this great legend which recalls an ancient time when people looked to the heavens and, with great imagination, recorded the happenings which they saw played out on the great vault of the cosmos.

Bóann means, literally, "illuminated cow"[51] and was derived from a primitive Irish form "bou-vinda". Folklore scholar Daithí Ó hÓgain says the following about her:

> "The name of the river is one of the earliest cited Irish toponyms, occurring in Ptolemy's geography in the form 'Buvinda'. This dates from the 2nd century AD, but may be based on sources somewhat earlier still. The original compound would have referred to a goddess in bovine shape, and would have meant literally 'illuminated cow'. The Celtic word 'vind' covered a semantic range from the colour white to brightness and wisdom."[52]

Our connection with the moon will, for now, remain tentative, but the translation "illuminated cow" could be a reference to the fact that the moon does not shine by its own light, but rather by the reflected light of the sun. We will see later how the ancients would have known this from their many years of observations.

THE ROAD OF THE ILLUMINATED COW

One very strong cosmic link with the Boyne Valley has been overlooked, forgotten almost, and can help prove an astronomical link to the ancient river-cow goddess.

In the Irish language, the Milky Way – the bright bands of our galaxy which can be seen in the night sky – is called *bóthar/bealach na Bó Finne*, which translates as the "way/road of the illuminated cow".[53] So the Boyne River and the Milky Way, the cosmic river, share a similar name and the same meaning. As a singular discovery, this may seem somewhat tentative, but in the context of many of the ancient sites along the Boyne and their astronomical alignments and symbolism, it was to prove a watershed in our research.

Ireland is not unique in having a river which was possibly considered to flow "from heaven to earth".[54] In fact, "one faces a frightening confusion between the rivers in heaven and those on earth, and the names which were given to both kinds of streams . . ."[55] The ancient Egyptians regarded the Milky Way "as a kind of celestial Nile".[56]

To speculate further, Bóann's lapdog Dabilla could be equated with one of the dog constellations. These are Canis Major and Canis Minor, the big dog and the small dog. Sirius, the Dog Star, the main star of Canis Major, is the brightest star in the entire night sky. In the Irish Stone Age, the Dog Star shared the same rising place as the winter solstice sunrise, which can be demonstrated using computer software which simulates the night sky. As well as the fact that the two dogs straddle the Milky Way, one on each side, Sirius, which we are tempted to call Dabilla, would have been rising at Rockabill in the Stone Age, as viewed from Baltray.

For the moment, until such time as we can explain the story in full later in the book, we hold that Bóann was a representation of the moon, and that the Milky Way, the "road" of the illuminated cow, formed the backdrop for her movement through the heavens. Our encounters with Bóann's husband Nuadu, custodian of the mystical well, were to continue at Tara, and we will later see how Nuadu is in fact one of the night sky's most famous constellations.

Balor, too, proved interesting in the context of disentangling some other Irish sky myths.[57] As a Fomorian, Balor was a member of a kind of pantheon which, according to one writer, "were held to be more ancient than the gods":[58]

> "Offspring of 'Chaos and Old Night', they were, for the most part, huge and deformed. Some had but one arm and one leg apiece, while others had the heads of goats, horses, or bulls. The most famous, and perhaps the

A flaming red sky greets the dawn of Winter Solstice at Baltray

    most terrible of them all was Balor, whose father is said to have been one Buarainech, that is, the 'cow-faced' . . ."[59]

Balor may be a variant representation of Bile, the god of death, who was said to have been married to Dana, or Danu, both of them being the "primordial parents" of the Children of Lir,[60] and perhaps of the ancient pantheon of the Tuatha Dé Danann. Etymologically, the name Bile has been said to have been derived from a word that means "tree", especially in the sense of a sacred tree.[61] It has been said that the lore of places "frequently mentions the trees that marked the centres of the provincial divisions",[62] like the tree at Uisneach, which was said to be the centre of Ireland in ancient times, and marked the division of the land into five provinces.[63]

    We have seen already how the Baltray standing stones marked a division of the provinces of Ulster and Leinster, and it should be no surprise to read, in "The Wooing of Emer" from the *Táin* epic, that there was a yew tree "at the head of Baile's strand",[64] the strand which we have identified firmly with Baltray, and the place in the "land of the mortals" where Cúchulainn promised to meet the otherwordly lady Fand, with whom he had spent a month in paradise. Cúchulainn's wife, Emer, found out about the proposed meeting at Baile's Strand, and went there herself with 50 of her maidens. If Baltray is the Traig Baile or Baile's Strand of myth, then a sacred tree marking the provincial boundaries probably would have been in place there in ancient times.

The tree at Uisneach was called "dor nime", or the "door of heaven",[65] suggesting that it was a means of gaining access to other worlds, most likely the heavenly world. It was said that Tír na nÓg, the land of eternal youth and beauty, lay in the direction of the setting sun.

Another connection between Bile (Balor) and the Boyne occurs in the *Metrical Dindshenchas* (lore of the eminent places) where, we read, "the son of Gollan without darkness of dishonour was the white Bile of the plain of Brega".[66] The plain of Brega, which contains Brú na Bóinne, was said to be the great plain lying eastwards of Tara between the Boyne and the Liffey,[67] and so it can be seen that Baltray is not an isolated example of a monument which has the lore of Balor, or Bile, attached to it.

The *Glas Gablin*, or *Glas Ghoibhneann*, the cow whom we met in the Balor-Rockabill legend, is also known across Ireland, and a legend which is known widely "describes how she filled with milk every pail put under her . . .".[68] Could this be the milk of the Milky Way, the way of the illuminated cow? The story continues: "However, a jealous woman claimed that she had a vessel which the Glas could not fill, and accordingly she brought a sieve and began to milk the great cow. The Glas yielded a continuous stream of milk, enough to fill a lake, but it all ran through the sieve."[69] The milk, we can assume, turned into a spray of milky droplets after running through the sieve, perhaps reminiscent or symbolic of the appearance of the Milky Way, which, in clear conditions, can be seen to contain a myriad of stars, almost as if someone sprayed the heavens with sparkling white dots. Daithí Ó hÓgain says also: "Variant accounts of the Glas state that she was a fairy cow which came in from the sea . . ."[70]

The magical cow is further remembered at Baltray in a field near the standing stones where, according to local tradition, there is a well called the Cowan Well. Cowan is most likely a corruption of Gabhan, which itself is a corruption of Gobhán, as in the Gobhán Saor, also known as Goibhniu, the archetypal smith of the Tuatha Dé Danann. Ironically, it has been argued that "as a god of thunder and lightning, Goibhniu may be identified with Balor, as both derive from a conception of the sun".[71] Furthermore, although there is some dispute over the matter, the magical cow *Glas Gablin* is said to have originally been owned by the Gobhán Saor (Goibhniu).[72]

Balor's identity as the sun is further confirmed in an account from County Mayo, which tells us:

"He had a single eye in his forehead, a venomous fiery eye. There were always seven coverings over his eye. One by one Balar removed the coverings. With the first covering the bracken began to wither, with the second the grass became copper-coloured, with the third the woods and timber began to heat, with the fourth smoke came from the trees, with the fifth everything grew red, with the sixth it sparked. With the seventh they were all set on fire, and the whole countryside was ablaze!"[73]

We were to see many more examples of legends concerning the sun and moon at the ancient sites of the Boyne Valley, and our encounter with Balor and the *Glas Ghoibhneann* at Baltray was not to be the last.

SOME OTHER INTERESTING ALIGNMENTS AT BALTRAY

Apart from the fact that the large stone at Baltray seems to be set in position so that it points to Rockabill, and the winter solstice sunrise, there are some other interesting alignments at Baltray which are worthy of mention.

If we stand to the south-east of the stone and look along its axis from the opposite side of where we would be positioned to watch winter solstice sunrise, we are looking at the setting place of the summer solstice sun. This is because winter sunrise and summer sunset are located diametrically opposite each other on the horizon. There is no visible marker, though, for summer sunset – certainly not one like the Rockabill islands, but if we take an Ordnance Survey map, and draw a line along the winter solstice axis, from Rockabill through the Baltray stones, and backwards towards the place of summer sunset, something very interesting can be seen.

The line continues northwestwards towards a hill called Carnanbreaga, in a townland called Drumshallon, and passes directly through a standing stone located on the slopes of that hill. From here, the line can be traced in the distance towards a place east of Ardee town called Barnaveddoge, where it intersects another standing stone – this one the largest standing stone in County Louth, standing at 3.2 metres in height.[74]

Both of the stones sitting on the extended Rockabill-Baltray line are part of a group. At Drumshallon, there are a total of four standing stones in the environs of Carnanbreaga hill, while the Barnaveddoge example has a companion stone a few hundred metres further up the hill.

Of greater interest is the fact that the Drumshallon and Barnaveddoge stones may have crude astronomical alignments. The stone at Drumshallon is oriented east–west, and may roughly point out the rising and setting place of the sun on the equinoxes. The stone at Barnaveddoge has a smaller companion on the peak of the hill which is roughly diamond-

The larger of the two Barnaveddoge monoliths, which is the biggest standing stone in Louth, in silhouette against a summer evening sky.

shaped in section, and its straight sides crudely point out the solstice positions.[75]

On a visit to this stone at the time of summer solstice 2000, we watched as the sun set in the northwest, directly in line with one straight edge of the stone. We speculated that another surface marked summer solstice sunrise, although we were unable to witness this event, and that the large 3.2-metre tall stone a couple of fields northeast of here, which sat on the extended Rockabill-Baltray line, probably lay in the direction of summer solstice sunrise from here. We did take a photo showing the sunset from the smaller stone, which interestingly has an Ogham marking on one edge which reads "Branogeni".[76]

Another alignment of interest was connected with the ridge containing Fourknocks and associated mounds. The two standing stones at Baltray line up, as accurately as can be observed, in the direction of Fourknocks, a Neolithic passage-tomb located on a hill in County Meath some 16 kilometres or so roughly south of Baltray. Fourknocks, as we will see in Chapter 7, has an important astronomical connection with Newgrange.

It seemed strange that the two stones at Baltray should point out the exact location of Fourknocks, because the latter is not actually visible from the former.[77] Neither are the standing stones at Drumshallon and Barnaveddoge, which seem to form some kind of intricate alignment with Baltray and Rockabill. But Alexander Thom says there was evidence that the megalithic builders were not only good surveyors, but that they "could 'range in' a straight line between mutually invisible points".[78] We would find plenty of evidence of this in the Boyne Valley.

In addition to lining up with Fourknocks, the Baltray stones can be used to point out another mound, on the same ridge, but further east of Fourknocks. The alignment is achieved by first lining up the two stones, facing approximately south, and then moving to the right slightly so as to allow a v-shaped gap appear between the stones. When this happens, the second mound on the Fourknocks ridge is actually visible beyond the easternmost edge of the smaller stone. This second mound has on its summit a more modern feature commonly called a "folly", evidently used by someone with too much money and too much time to peer out upon the landscape at a more recent juncture in history.

This mound, in all probability, dates from the same time as the two excavated mounds at Fourknocks, which have been dated to between 3000 and 2500 BC.[79] We wondered if it was coincidental that this mound, pointed out by the

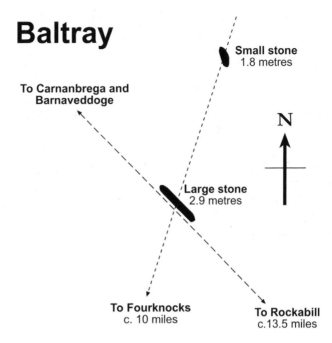

Summary of the alignments at Baltray

Baltray standing stones, was located on an elevated site overlooking the Irish Sea, and positioned directly due west of the Rockabill Islands. Could it be that the Fourknocks mounds were part of an equinoctial alignment using the same islands as the Baltray standing stones?

If so, this would constitute a three-way triangular configuration of sites incorporating astronomical alignments, and an impressive feat of ancient engineering. There was more, it seemed, to the "inconsequential" Baltray stones than first impressions would leave one to believe. Balor's Strand proved to be an "eye-opener" in more ways than one, and the interpretation of such a seemingly trivial monument provided by myth and sky was to have echoes right up the Boyne valley, the valley of the Milky Way . . .

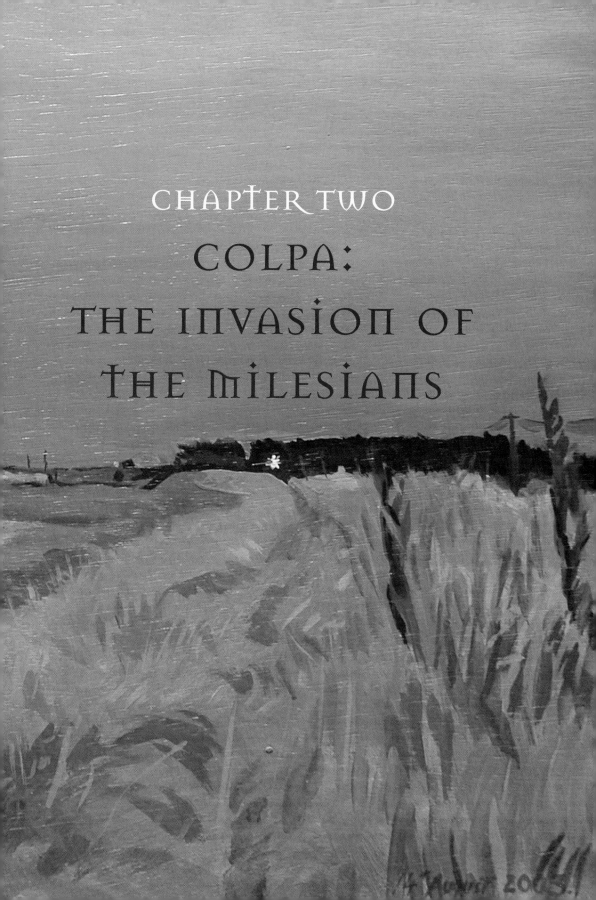

CHAPTER TWO

COLPA:
THE INVASION OF
THE MILESIANS

Inbher Colpa, the Boyne Estuary, is part of an ancient and venerated landscape. It is here that the sacred "way of the White Cow", the Milky Way of the Boyne, meets its destination, the Irish Sea. As would be expected of the entrance to Ireland's most celebrated river, this place had great eminence in ancient times, and is rich in archaeology, myth and legend.

The river at this point widens considerably, and as it flows towards the sea, it is flanked on the northern side by the village of Baltray, with the village of Mornington to the south. There is a strong sense here that the ancient has been replaced by the modern, the landscape having

Sunset on the River Boyne

been altered considerably in recent times, now displaying such prominent features as a nineteenth-century railway viaduct, a port development, a periclase factory, a municipal sewage treatment plant and other such paraphernalia cluttering the scene. The Inbher Colpa area, which included the town of Drogheda, is now the most developed part of the Boyne Valley, but thanks to a rich tradition of writing associated with its enormous history and folklore, we know much about its glorious past.

Inbher Colpa seems to have been the name used in former times to describe the whole estuary, from the town of Drogheda, as far as the sea. It is derived from *Inbher* (also written *Inver*), a word which means "meeting of the waters",[1] and *Colpe*, a name which, we will see, has more than one meaning. Inbher Colpa is remembered in the names of a parish and townland on the southern flank of the river. The parish of Colpe covers 5,785 acres, and is divided into 12 townlands. This parish extends all the way to the sea at Mornington, and so covers much of the southern hinterland of the Boyne between Drogheda and the sea.

There are two distinct and very different stories which tell how Inbher Colpa got its name. One, from the *Metrical Dindshenchas*, a collection of folklore stories about important ancient places, recalls how a mythical monster, called the *Mata*,[2] was slain at Brú na Bóinne, and his bone (the story says specifically his shinbone (*colptha*)) was washed out to the estuary, "whence pleasant Inber Colptha is named".[3]

The story about the monster is repeated in the ancient lore about how Ireland's capital city, Dublin, or Áth Cliath, got its name, although the spelling of the monster's name varies:

> "When the men of Erin broke the limbs of the Matae, the monster that was slain on the Liacc Benn in the Brug of Mac Oc, they threw it limb by limb into the Boyne, and its shinbone (colptha) got to Inber Colptha ("the estuary of the Boyne"), whence "Inber Colptha" is said, and the hurdle (cliath) of its frame (i.e., its breast) went along the sea following the coast of Ireland until it reached yon ford (áth); whence "Áth Cliath" is said."[4]

The great monster was said to have had a hundred legs and four heads, and was killed by the Dagda, one of the chiefs of the Tuatha Dé Danann, at the "Liacc Benn", the Stone of Benn, which was said to have been located near the Boyne.[5]

What meaning could possibly be taken from a story relating how a monster's shinbone gave its name to an eminent estuary?[6] One possible interpretation of this legend will be explored in Chapter 12.

THE SONS OF MIL

Another account of how the Boyne estuary came to be named is derived from a much more illustrious and well-reported episode in ancient mythical history – the arrival of the Sons of Mil from Spain. It was in the year 1694 BC,[7] according to the *Annals of the Four Masters*, that the Milesian bard Amergin, on placing his right foot on the shore at Inbher Colpa,[8] pronounced:

> "[Who knows] the place in which the setting of the sun lies?"[9]
> "Who can tell you the age of the moon but I?"[10]
> "What land is better than this island of the setting sun?"[11]

These were lines from his famous "rhapsody", which included Amergin's exclamation that he was "a ray of the sun".[12] So who was this mysterious Spanish bard? An account of the invasion of the Milesians is necessary to explain who Amergin is, and how their arrival here gave Colpe its name. The story will throw up a few astronomical surprises as well.

Mil[13] was a legendary king of Spain, and was said to be the "ancestor of the gaels",[14] although there is some debate as to whether Mil and his offspring were "an invention of the historians, patterned on the Latin term 'miles Hispaniae' (soldier of Spain)", or a genuine character of Celtic mythology.[15] Some scholars believe the Milesians were totally fictitious; others that the Milesian epic is a pseudo-historical narrative. Some authors have attempted to link the Sons of Mil with the Celtic race or even the Phoenicians. Folklorists generally believe the characters of these epic tales existed in real life, although some aspects of the narrative are greatly exaggerated or invented. Our belief is that the invasion myths may be "star stories", tales inspired by events in the cosmos and the slowly changing position of the sun in relation to the constellations over long periods of time.

In Spain, which was given the unattractive title "the land of the dead",[16] there was a great tower, built by a man called Bregon,[17] who had two sons called Ith and Bile.[18] It was this watch-tower from which, "one winter's evening, Ith saw, far off over the seas, a land he had never noticed before."[19] Ith had been "contemplating and looking over the four quarters of the world", and Breg son of Bregan told him "that it was no land he had seen but the clouds of heaven".[20] He resolved to sail to this land and decided he would go there with a large number of warriors; some sources put the number at 90, and others "thrice 50".

Ith, on arriving in Ireland at Mag Itha, was said to have found the land largely uninhabited[21] and made his way to Aileach, in the far north of the country, where a stone ring-fort stands to this day.[22] The ruling kings, Mac Cuill, Mac Cecht and Mac Gréine, who were of the Tuatha Dé Danann, were grandsons of the Dagda, and had succeeded Nuadu of the Silver Hand who had been killed in battle with the Fomorians.[23] Nuadu had been buried in a tumulus at Grianán Aileach. The three kings were unable to decide how Nuadu's kingdom should be divided among them, and it seems Ith arrived just in time to act as arbitrator in the matter.[24] Ith counselled the kings to act with morality, encouraging them to "do just righteousness", and reminded them of the great land they inhabited, with its plentiful harvest, and its moderate climate. His last words to them were "all that is sufficient for you is in her" and he left them to return to his ship.[25]

It was Ith's kindly words of advice to the Dé Danann kings that were to prove decisive in bringing the Milesians to Ireland, and Inbher Colpa. For the Dé Dananns concluded that because of his lavish praise for Ireland, Ith had some ulterior intention, that perhaps he had designs on the country.[26] So they seized him and killed him.

His companions brought his body back to Spain, and there Mil, Ith's nephew, vowed to go to Ireland with his sons and avenge the death of Ith on the Tuatha Dé Danann. Along with Mil's eight sons and their wives, there were hosts of other chiefs, and the total number of ships gathered for the expedition was 65.[27]

The expedition first arrived in Ireland, at a place called Inbher Sceine (Kenmare Bay in County Kerry), although some sources say Mil never arrived in Ireland, having died in Spain of unknown cause.[28] They arrived in Ireland, we are told, on the 1st of May, or the evening beforehand, the day on which was celebrated the feast of Bealtaine, or the "fires of Bel". Bel is another name for the god Balor whom we met first at Baltray.

Whether or not Ith's brother Bile (the father of Mil) is another representation of this deity is a matter for discussion, but it is stated that this Bile is one of the names of Balor, who is describes as being a god of Death and the Underworld.[29] The evidence emphasises the importance which the sun deity held at the Boyne Estuary in ancient times.

The Milesian expedition made towards the Hill of Uisneach, said to have been the ancient centre of Ireland. On their way, they met the wives of the three Dé Danann kings. First they met Banba, wife of Mac Cuill, then Fodla, wife of Mac Cecht, and finally they met Eriú, wife of Mac Greine, at Uisneach. Mac Gréine, "son of the sun", was said to have received his name because he worshipped the sun.[30] At the centre of Ireland, Eriú told them their coming had been long prophesied, and told them the island would be theirs forever. "From the setting to the rising sun there is no better land," she told them.[31] Eriú was to become the principal name of Ireland, in its genitive form Erinn.

When finally the Milesians came to Tara, the "Beautiful Hill" (later we will see that Tara has strong astronomical connections to the Boyne Estuary), they were met by the three Dé Danann kings, who insisted that they had been taken by surprise with the Milesian invasion, and this was not in keeping with the "courtesies of chivalrous warfare".[32] The kings proposed that the Milesians leave Ireland for three days to allow them to decide if they would put up a fight, but the Milesians did not trust them and felt that they would use their magical powers to keep them from making another landing. Charles Squire tells what happened from here.

In the end, Mac Cuill, Mac Cecht, and Mac Gréine offered to submit the matter to the arbitration of Amergin, the Milesians' own lawgiver and bard, with the express stipulation that, if he gave an obviously partial judgement, he was to suffer death at their hands. Donn asked his druid if he were prepared to accept this very delicate duty. Amergin replied that he was, and at once delivered the first judgement pronounced by the Milesians in Ireland:

> The men whom we found dwelling in the land, to them is possession due by right.
> It is therefore your duty to set out to sea over nine green waves;
> And if you shall be able to effect a landing again in spite of them,

You are to engage them in battle, and I adjudge to you the land in which
you found them living.
I adjudge to you the land wherein you found them dwelling, by the right
of battle.
But although you may desire the land which these people possess, yet yours
is the duty to show them justice.
I forbid you from injustice to those you have found in the land, however
you may desire to obtain it.

The judgement was considered fair by both parties.[33]

When the Tuatha Dé Danann saw the Milesians out at sea, they raised
a fierce tempest with their druidical incantations, and the Milesian fleet
was dispersed.

The bard Amergin lifted up his voice against the tempest, and was
said to have "invoked the Land of Ireland itself, a power higher than the
gods it sheltered".[34]

I invoke the land of Eriu!
The shining, shining sea!
The fertile, fertile hill!
The wooded vale!
The river abundant, abundant in water!
The fishful, fishful lake![35]

For a time, his invocation worked, but the Dé Danann lord of the
sea, Manannan, lifted up another tempest. The ships of the fleet were
scattered, and many sank. Donn, one of the sons of Mil, was among the
fatalities, which included three more of his brothers, as well as many of
the boats' crews.

*A boat at Inbher Colpa, not far from the point where
the Milesians are said to have landed*

In the end, only a
portion of the ships made
land, after being beaten on
the seas around the coasts
of Ireland. They landed at
Inbher Colpa, the mouth
of the Boyne, which
derived its name, according
to some accounts, from
another Milesian brother,
"Colpa the Swordsman",[36]
who was drowned while
"attempting a landing
nearer its mouth. [He]
gave his name to the

haven Inver-Colpa, as well as to the point where he proposed to land, still known by the name of 'Colpe'."[37]

Colpa the Swordsman was one of the brothers of Eremon, the leader of the Milesian invasion band. Amergin himself, the poet warrior, was another brother, and he was the first to land. Most accounts say he planted his right foot on the shore, before he chanted his famous poem:

I am the wind that blows upon the sea;
I am the ocean wave;
I am the murmur of the surges;
I am seven battalions;
I am a strong bull;
I am an eagle on a rock;
I am a ray of the sun;
I am the most beautiful of herbs;
I am a courageous wild boar;
I am a salmon in the water;
I am a lake upon a plain;
I am a cunning artist;
I am a gigantic, sword-wielding champion;
I can shift my shape like a god.

In which direction shall we go?
Shall we hold our council in the valley or on the mountain-top?
Where shall we make our home?
What land is better than this island of the setting sun?
Where shall we walk to and fro in peace and safety?
Who can find you clear springs of water as I can?
Who can tell you the age of the moon but I?
Who can call the fish from the depths of the sea as I can?
Who can cause them to come near the shore as I can?
Who can change the shapes of the hills and headlands as I can?
I am a bard who is called upon by seafarers to prophesy.
Javelins shall be wielded to avenge our wrongs.
I prohesy victory. I end my song by prophesying all other good things.[38]

The Milesians buried Colpa the Swordsman near the Boyne. His resting place is said to be a low, flat-topped mound known locally as Rath Colpa,[39] less than a mile south of the Boyne, near St Columba's Church in Colpe.

Having buried their brother, they marched on the Tuatha Dé Danann. Two battles were fought between the Milesians and the Dé Dananns, one in Glenn Faisi, a valley in the Slieve Mish Mountains, near Tralee, and the second at Tailtiu, or Teltown, located not far from the ancient stone sites at Loughcrew. The three Dé Danann kings were killed – Mac Cuill by Eber, Mac Cecht by Eremon, and Mac Gréine by Amergin.[40]

"What land is better than this island of the setting sun?"

IΠVADERS OF THE SKY?

It is perhaps fitting, and certainly more than coincidental, that Amergin, who claimed to be a "ray of the sun", should kill the king who had received his name because he worshipped the sun. Amergin had landed at Inbher Colpa, not far from "Balor's Strand", where the rising sun was marked by people who erected large menhirs there in far-off times.

Again the line from Amergin's rhapsody, quoted in various sources, is recalled: "[Who knows] the place in which the setting of the sun lies?" The fact that the Milesians first landed in Ireland on the celebration of the festival of Bealtaine (the fires of Bel or Balor) further underlines the memory of the sun's importance in this landscape. And it was Amergin, after all, who described Ireland as the "island of the setting sun", echoing similar sentiments to those of the queen Eriu who said at Uisneach: "From the setting to the rising sun there is no better land." Uisneach was at one time known as the "Hill of Balor".[41]

But there are other astronomical intricacies in the epic tale of the Milesian conquest. Amergin's claim to be able to tell the ages of the moon is suggestive of knowledge of lunar cycles, such as the 19-year metonic cycle of the moon, so named because it was supposedly discovered by a Greek, called Meton, in the fifth century BC.[42] The year of Amergin's landing was 1694 BC, according to the annals, over 1,000 years before Meton existed. Complicated lunar knowledge probably existed long before Amergin's time in the Boyne Valley, as we will see in the chapters on

Dowth, Newgrange and Knowth. It may have been crucial to the naming of the river Boyne, which as we saw in Chapter 1 means the "river of the White Cow". It is likely that one of the native Irish concepts relating to the Milky Way considered it to be the milk of the magic cow.[43]

Amergin's mention of the bull is important astronomically, because at the time of the Milesians' arrival at Inbher Colpa, the sun's vernal point had moved out of the bull constellation, Taurus, into Aries. The bull is present in many myths and stories, and both the cow and bull are symbolic remnants of an astronomically adept society which originated, we believe, in the Stone Age. The bull constellation, which includes the Pleiades or "Seven Sisters" star grouping, was located in a hugely important part of the sky in ancient times, and it shall be seen that this area of the sky was to feature centrally in our exploration of many sites and myths along the Boyne Valley.

In one translation of Amergin's rhapsody, there is a line: "Who brings his cattle from the house of Tethra?" If the word cattle is a reference to our cow and calf, or moon and Venus, it is obscure indeed. But the word Tethra is very curious.

Tethra was a Fomorian chief, and a consort of Balor. He was known as a sea god, but was also a god of the otherworld,[44] and we are told that after being killed in the first battle of Mag Tuireadh (Moytura), he went to *Mag Mell,* the "Pleasant Plain" to rule there. But what is this Mag Mell, and why is Tethra named by Amergin?

For the answer, we turned to another translation of the "Song of Amergin", which gives further clues as to what Tethra is. This translation has a line about the cattle of Tethra which seems to qualify their context:

> Who calls the kine from Tethra's house,
> And sees them dance in the bright heavens?[45]

The "kine", or cattle, are called from Tethra's house to "dance in the bright heavens". Now we have the vital clue as to the identity of the cattle and the location of Tethra's house – *Mag Mell.* The "Pleasant Plain" could be, we think, a region of the sky,[46] and the cattle are indeed the cow and calf, or the moon and Venus, who we met at Baltray. One translation of the "cattle of Tethra" is given as "the stars rising out of the sea".[47] There is a place in the landscape also with links to Mag Mell, located not far from the Boyne Estuary – just a few miles inland in fact. It is recalled today in a Drogheda townland called Mell and also at a place a few miles out the Collon Road called Mellifont, the site of an old Cistercian abbey dating back to the 1100s. Mellifont was an important site in ancient times too.[48]

A further clue as to the identity of the cattle is entwined deeply into the whole story, in the name of Inbher Colpa, the very place where Amergin set down his right foot and began chanting the arcane words. The old Irish word *colpa* has a number of meanings, two of which are very relevant to the story. *Colpa* can mean "a three-year-old calf" and it can also mean the "calf of the leg",[49] or shinbone, as already discussed. Is Colpa a reference to Venus, while at the same time representing the leg, or calf of the leg, of Amergin, who planted his foot on the shore at Colpe?

The fact that Amergin sees the cattle "dance" in the sky is suggestive of movement, so we are inclined to think of the planets, which move among the static stars, as possible candidates for his "kine of Tethra".[50]

Another astronomical dimension is added if consideration is given to what happens at sunset on spring equinox. The "vernal point" – the position of the sun on the spring equinox – was housed in Aries after the arrival of the Milesians. Just after sunset on the 1st of May in 1694 BC, the stars of the constellation Taurus, including the Seven Sisters cluster (perhaps the "seven batallions" of Amergin's poem?), would begin to appear low in the twilight of dusk in the west. Is this why Amergin says "I am a strong bull"? The Taurus constellation is located such that the horn stars are touching the bright band of the Milky Way – the heavenly "road of the white cow" which stretches through that part of the sky. Later, in Chapter 6, it will be demonstrated how the Seven Sisters grouping was probably once referred to in the sky myth relating to how and why the mound at Dowth was constructed.

The word "house" is important in an astronomical context. The constellation that contains the sun at a given time of year is said to "house" the sun. It could well be that modern astrological terminology is derived from ancient times. The house of the vernal point has always been very important, because it defines the zodiacal "age". Hence, the current age is called the "Age of Pisces" because the vernal point is housed in that constellation. In Neolithic times, the vernal point was housed in Taurus, and around the time of the arrival of the Milesians, it had moved into Aries.

The area of the night sky featuring Taurus, Orion and the Milky Way will feature strongly in our investigation of other ancient Boyne Valley sites, and it will be seen later how Orion was at the centre of astronomical mythology in ancient Ireland. It is tempting to identify Orion with the immortalised Amergin, who claimed in his chant that "I am a gigantic, sword-wielding champion". Orion could indeed be described as a giant, a huge hero of the night.

Mag Mell, one of a number of ancient Irish otherworlds along with Tír na nÓg, Tír na mBeó and Hy Brasil, is identifiable with the night sky. The route to the otherworld was said to open at the setting sun, a concept present in the legends attached to these magical realms, which were often visited by mortal heroes.[51] There is a consistent theme in the ancient astral lore which suggests that at the moment of sunset, in which the sun appeared to touch the ground, the route to the stars was opened and, in the growing darkness after the sun disappeared, the stars of the netherworld appeared. One of the rulers of Mag Mell was Labraid Luathlám ar Claideb, whose name meant "swift sword-hand",[52] a figure who may have been one of the many representations of the constellation Orion present in the Irish star stories.[53]

COLPA'S MOUND

Rath Colpa, the place where Amergin's beloved brother was buried after drowning at the Boyne Estuary, is a monument with a strange appearance. It is a low, wide mound with a very flat top. It almost looks like a kind of circular platform, something one would perhaps expect to be used as an outdoor stage for orators or musicians. One could imagine the bard Amergin speaking solemnly here about the death of his brother over 3,500 years ago.

The fact that a fosse and ditch are determinable around much of the site suggests settlement here during later times, and there is a curious linear trough running east–west across the field to the south of the mound. A considerable growth of trees and bushes around the western, northern and eastern sides of the mound renders the view from the top disappointing. Looking eastwards, half expecting to see the sea, or Rockabill, or Mornington, we could see only fields, trees and the rooftops of a nearby housing estate.

Measurements of the site show that, somewhat surprisingly, it is not exactly circular, as the immediate visual impression would appear to suggest. The top platform of the mound is 29.5 metres across from north to south, and 35.5 metres east to west, so the site presents a distinctively oval shape.[54] The platform is elevated by 2.69 metres above the level of the surrounding field, so given the mound's diameter, it is quite shallow.

The mound is located less than three-quarters of a mile from the southern shore of the Boyne at Inbher Colpa, and less than two and a half miles from the Millmount at Drogheda, where Amergin himself was later said to be buried, and which will feature in the next chapter. The Lady's

The visually unimpressive Rath Colpa, said in folklore to be the burial place of Colpa the Swordsman, one of the Milesians

Finger, a curious monument described later in this chapter, lies exactly two miles north-east of here.

The road to the river from St Columba's Church at Colpe, adjacent to the mound, is extremely straight, leading us to imagine that it might have been constructed by the Milesians as a ceremonial roadway on which to bear their brother Colpa to his resting place, or maybe to serve as a pathway for visitors wishing to pay homage to the famous Milesian who gave his name to the estuary. Interestingly, straight roads adjacent to ancient sites are not at all uncommon in the Boyne Valley. The name of that "ceremonial" straight road is interesting too. It is called the Mill Road. We are tempted to link it with the sons of Mil. Perhaps it was originally known as the "Mil Road" after the sons of the Spanish king? There is a tradition that the grave of Colpa had a "rude stone over it" and that this stone had engraved on it "the Coat of Arms of Spain".[55]

Inbher Colpa later became the setting for another great and famous landing. St Patrick was said to have put his boat to shore at Colpe in the year 433 AD, and from there made his way up the Boyne River towards Slane.[56] It is said that the church of Rath Colpa was founded by St Patrick, although "this is by no means certain".[57] Later folklore stated that the area was named after St Colpa, "a fellow countryman of St Patrick".[58]

Colpe also marked the division of territories of the ancient Fir Bolg rulers, and we are told that Slane (or Sláine), the eldest brother, "had the province of Leynster for his part, which containeth from Inver Colpe, that is to say, where the river Boyne entereth into the sea, now called in Irish Drogheda, to the meeting of the three waters, by Waterford . . ."[59] Rorye, the fifth and youngest brother, had the province of Ulster, from Easroe to Inver Colpe.[60]

It is clear that although the seemingly insignificant size and shape of Rath Colpa suggest it was not an intrinsic component of the ancient landscape of the Boyne, the legends associated with Inbher Colpa, which are among Ireland's most illustrious stories from former times, mark out the area as one of the most important places in the ancient landscape. It is probable people were landing on the shores of the Boyne Estuary since the very earliest periods of human activity in this country:[61]

> "Ireland is one of the most ancient kingdoms of Europe, so Drogheda is one of the most ancient towns in Ireland. Its original name was Colpa or Colpe, which took its rise from Colpa, who, entering the Boyne, landed at Colpe. Being killed, he was buried where the church of Colpe now stands."[62]

LADY'S FINGER

Further downstream from Colpa's mound and the landing place of the Milesians, near the village of Mornington, right at the mouth of the Boyne River, there is a curious monument which could have links with this ancient exploration.

Called the "Lady's Finger" locally, this "phallic symbol of date unknown"[63] is made with stones and mortar, and forms one part of a unique navigational system along with the nearby "Maiden Tower". The tower, and evidently the Finger, were erected long before lighthouses were in use in Ireland[64] and in latter times when ships were approaching the river mouth, they could find the correct navigational channel for entry to the river by first lining up the Maiden Tower and Lady's Finger. This function of the monuments is still well known and related in stories locally.

Our curiosity was aroused by the phallic nature of the Lady's Finger, and the fact that, as Henry Boylan says, "it does not at all resemble a finger".[65] Its strikingly phallic nature leads us to speculate that it is probably pagan in origin, but there is no record, written or otherwise, which can point us to its date of construction.

Phallic stones were symbolic of fertility in ancient times, and there was a distinct connection with the festival of Bealtaine, which was not merely a celebration of the beginning of summer, but a celebration also of new growth and fertility. The "maypole", a feature of ancient May Day and modern Bealtaine celebrations, is often considered a wholly sexual symbol,[66] and perhaps the phallic stone (like the one called the Lia Fáil at Tara) were the early precursors. A symbol of Bealtaine, located not far from the place where the astronomer Amergin landed in Ireland on the ancient festival of the sun, is not conclusive evidence of its antiquity, but there may be further astronomical details to support the notion that the Lady's Finger may be quite old – pre-Christian at least and perhaps much older.

The Lady's Finger (foreground) with the Maiden Tower behind at Mornington

The ancient fire festival of Bealtaine has an astronomical basis, being tied very closely with the cross-quarter day which marked the sunrise at the half-way point, measured in days, between the spring equinox and the summer solstice. According to one expert on the ancient festivals: "fire seems to have been a male attribute and would thus have been associated with phallus/pillar stones. As gnomons,[67] their lengthening shadows have quite an obvious analogy with the masculine role in the union of elements."[68] Although Bealtaine is said to be a Celtic festival, and therefore rather late in the context of our 1694 BC Milesian conquest, there is more than sufficient evidence to suggest that the cross-quarter astronomical dates were first considered important back in the Neolithic, more than 5,000 years ago, and that the division of the year on the cross-quarter days was much older than the Celts.

There is a fascinating little story told of the Maiden Tower which may echo the astronomical explorations and tie in very closely with the river Boyne itself. The story is nicely recalled by William Wilde, father of playwright and novelist Oscar Wilde:

> "There are many 'old stories' related about this tower – tales of love, of maiden faith and knightly honour, and, in latter days, of mystery also. Tradition says it was erected by a fair lady, to watch the return of her

betrothed from a far-distant country, whither he was obliged to journey upon the eve of their nuptials. It was agreed beforehand that, if her lover returned successful, he should hoist a milk-white banner; but if the contrary, a red flag should float from his mast-head. The preconcerted signal was forgotten, and the knight, seeing the tower – which his true love had erected during his absence to watch his return – and mistaking it for the watch-tower of an enemy and an invader, instantly displayed the blood-red flag, whereon the disconsolate maiden precipitated herself from the top of the tower, and was dashed to atoms."[69]

Some versions of the story say the preconcerted signal was to be a white flag but Wilde's version details exactly what the signal is to be – a "milk-white banner". Here, at the entrance to the ancient and great "river of the Milky Way", we wondered if this was perhaps the remnant of an ancient story connected with the bright bands of the Milky Way galaxy. Ultimately, the flag raised by the returning knight was "blood-red", a possible reference to a total eclipse of the moon, during which the moon is said to turn blood red.

The moon and the Maiden Tower

The Maiden Tower and Lady's Finger are located at a place called Mornington, and the local church is called the "Star of the Sea". Are these names the vague remnants of the Boyne astronomy culture, referring perhaps to Venus, the morning star? Was the rising of Venus out of the Irish Sea once observed here, on the flank of the mouth of the Boyne opposite Baltray? Further, a small river, which could be considered no more than a stream, runs down into the Boyne at Mornington. It is called the Calf River, another vague reference perhaps to Venus, and is located about a mile east of Rath-Colpa.

The rising of the moon and the morning star Venus may have been observed simultaneously by astronomers at the Baltray stones and whatever stone may have existed at Mornington, whether it be the currently standing phallus or an earlier monolith. By carefully watching the rising position of Venus in relation to the Rockabill islands, it was likely that the early astronomers were able to directly observe its eight-year period – the five synodic periods it takes the planet to return to exactly the same position against the stars.

In ancient times, with little technology other than stones, sky observers might have been able not only to observe the moon and Venus, but to see that they moved in cycles and patterns, and to record key moments in these cycles so that their seemingly complex movements among the stars could be predicted by those with the appropriate level of knowledge. In context, Amergin's claim, "Who, save I, knows the ages of the moon?",[70] seems to make perfect sense.

The eight-year Venus interval was definitely recorded by the people of the Stone Age in the Boyne Valley, carefully inscribed into the huge megaliths at Brú na Bóinne over 5,000 years ago, as we will see in Chapter 8. Evidence of this will be presented in due course, but before we leave the Mornington area to move upstream to Drogheda, there is one more site in this area worthy of mention.

BURIAL PLACE OF CÚCHULAINN'S CHARIOTEER

There is a well-known mound, or motte, at a place called Ninch near the village of Laytown, less than three miles from Colpa's mound. This mound is situated on a bluff and overlooks the Nanny River. In local folklore it is said to be the burial place of Cúchulainn's charioteer, friend and messenger, Laeg. Here we find another connection to the calf, because the name *Laeg* could be connected to an Irish word *laogh,* which means a "young calf".[71] Laeg's mound gave its name to Laytown. There is an old sacred well on the western slope of the Hill of Tara called *Láeg,* the "Calf Well",[72] and a whole raft of ancient symbolism and mythic motifs involving cow and calf, and other imagery associated with the moon and Venus in the Boyne Valley, as we will see.

There was "limited archaeological excavation"[73] carried out at the site in 1979, and two burials were found near the base of Laeg's mound. Radiocarbon dates obtained from the site gave it an Iron Age date,[74] making it much later than some of the stone sites of the Boyne Valley. However, as archaeologist David Sweetman points out, "it might be suggested that Ninch can be paralleled with the small earthen mounds of the Boyne Valley but until these are excavated no valid comparison can be made."[75]

Sweetman said Laeg's mound was "unique", and that the burials had been "articulated and extended whereas those of the other sites were often disarticulated".[76] Could he have uncovered the remains of the real Laeg, someone who existed in the real world rather than just in mythology?

THE LEG AND THE CALF

The megalithic culture which reached its zenith in the Boyne Valley over 5,000 years ago would more than likely have had a significant presence in the Inbher Colpa area. The estuary would have constituted a convenient landing point for boats, something pointed at in the area's folklore, and in the earliest period the stone-erecting star gazers would likely have become adept at predicting the tides using their proficient lunar knowledge. It is likely that the stones at Baltray are contemporary with the great monuments of the Bend of the Boyne, and on the southern bank of the Boyne Estuary there may have been a further stone observatory, marked today by the Lady's Finger.

Whether or not Rath Colpa was a component of the original Neolithic Boyne system remains to be seen, but examination of the myths pertaining to Colpa's mound, and the wider estuary area, suggest a very early genesis and a definite concern with the sun, moon and stars.

There is an unswerving premise in the Inbher Colpa myths which state that the Boyne and its estuary formed divisional boundaries in different mythical epochs, something that will be explored in more detail in the next chapter.

The Colpe mythology also consistently refers to a calf, although it is not immediately clear whether this is the calf of the leg, or a young cow, given the parallel etymologies of both meanings of the modern English word. Because we are only in the early stages of our investigation of the sites of the Boyne Valley, it is not yet possible to present a complete picture of what these apparently vague references might mean. However, for the time being, it is sufficient to state that both meanings have enormous relevance to the ancient astronomical studies carried out in the Boyne area, for reasons that will be seen as we progress through the chapters.

For now, we will leave Rath Colpa, lost among the trees and hedgerows of modern day Colpe on the outskirts of Drogheda, and move upstream to a mound which would have commanded a spectacular, sweeping view of the Boyne from a point on the west of the town all the way down to the sea, a striking vista of five miles: the last "leg" of the Milky Way.

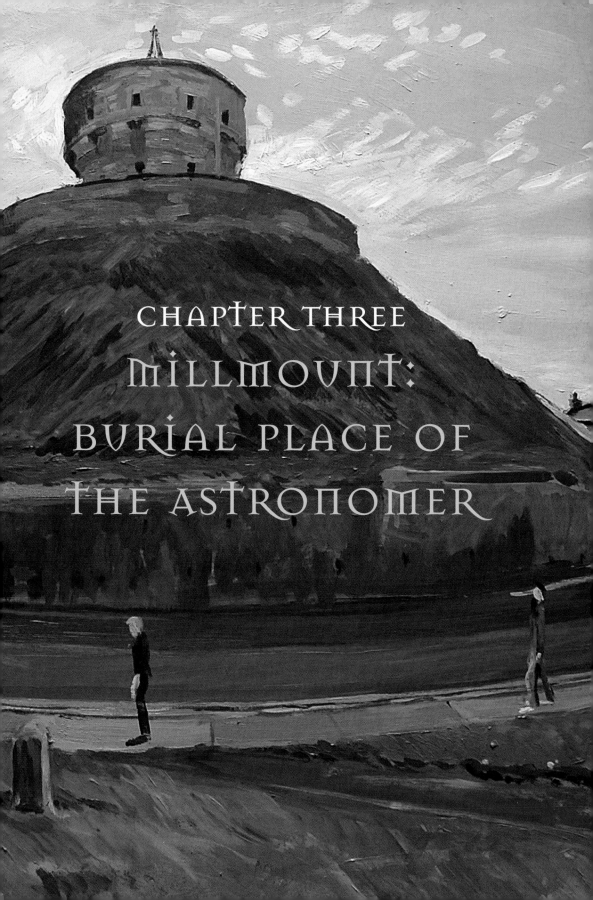

CHAPTER THREE

MILLMOUNT:
BURIAL PLACE OF
THE ASTRONOMER

The Millmount is the most remarkable monument in Drogheda, dominating the skyline above the ancient town from its lofty position on a high bank overlooking the River Boyne. The steep-sided mount, with the striking Martello tower sitting on top, can be seen for miles. It is visible from most of the approach routes to the town, and its position on one of the highest points above the Boyne gives it a special prominence, a stately presence above the many steeples and other buildings of the town.

The Millmount has a varied and fascinating history. Different sources tell different stories about its origin and various purposes over the ages. Some accounts say it was raised by Turgesius the Dane in 830 AD;[1] others that it was built as a fort by the Vikings;[2] some attribute the construction of the motte-and-bailey to Hugh de Lacy, who established a borough on the south side of Drogheda after the Anglo-Norman invasion of the twelfth century.[3]

The Millmount has other claims to fame. In 1649, when Oliver Cromwell laid siege to the town, the mound was said to have offered strong resistance. In 1808, it was known as Richmond Fort, and it was at this time that the famous Martello tower was constructed on top of the mound by the British. This same Martello tower was later shelled during the Irish Civil War of 1921–22.[4]

The Millmount as seen from the Boyne shore

However, we are not interested in Millmount's recent history. There are other sources which push Millmount's origin way back, considerably earlier than the 830 AD of Turgesius's invasion. In fact, as investigations were to reveal, Millmount conceals a hidden legacy, a wonderful, awe-inspiring genesis which has been lost to the passage of time, garbled and confused by successive layers of myth and history, and revealed only by a diligent and intuitive study of the various elements which form part of this elusive legacy. These elements, including astronomy, mythology, the ancient landscape, local folklore, combine to bring to life the story of this wonderful true heritage of the Millmount, and its place in the grand scheme of things in the ancient "Valley of the Milky Way".

It is important to point out that the name Millmount is locally considered to be quite modern. There was a mill on the top of the mound in the seventeenth century, owned by a man called Delahoyde, who was said to have supplied the Cromwellian army with meal.[5] The ruins of this mill, according to L.C. Johnston's 1826 *History of Drogheda*, "were to be seen prior to the building of the present tower on its site".[6] Of the Martello tower, Johnston says: "The military tower was erected a few years ago, on the summit of this fort, by Government, which rendered Drogheda a garrison town. Its utility is of little worth, it is 'more fit for ornament than use'."[7] We have a tendency to agree with some of this sentiment, because it is what lies under the mound, not on top, which is of fundamental importance.

A DEEPER HISTORY

Back in the summer of 2000, Richard and I listened as the folklorist Caitlín Bean Uí Chairbre was engaged with us in one of our many conversations about the ancient lore and history of the Boyne Valley. During that conversation, she emphasised to us that the Millmount's true history was often overlooked, and that it was a greatly important place in ancient times. She was the first to assert to us that Millmount was "one of the ancient mounds of Brú na Bóinne". And she informed us that Amergin, the astronomer-poet of the Milesians, who knew the ages of the moon and the place of the sunset, was said to be buried at Millmount. The idea that Millmount might be truly ancient was captivating to say the least, but in reality it came as no surprise given some of the things we had already learned about the place, such as the fact that even the more modern written accounts of its history attribute its origins to ancient times.

> Mill-mount fort is, as well as the town walls, ascribed to them [the Danes]. But may it not as well be ascribed to the Irish? Such places as this, which are found through the kingdom, are called by the Irish, Danish Raths or Forts; may they not as well be called Irish Raths, for in the opinion of many, such they are. That Raths were in early use among the ancient Irish cannot be doubted, for "according to an old Brehon law, it appears that particular chiefs alone were permitted to build them as a mark of distinction".[8]

John D'Alton, in his 1844 *History of Drogheda*, said about Amergin:

> This warrior bard fell in battle in Meath, and is supposed to have been here buried on the southern shore of the river Boyne, where, according to the

fashion of the time, the funeral pile, now known as the Mill-Mount, was then elevated over his body . . .[9]

Millmount's link with Dowth, Newgrange and Knowth could be found tentatively in some historical sources, which said: "The monuments ascribed to the Tuatha Dé Dananns are principally situated in Meath, at Drogheda, Dowlet, Knowth and New Grange."[10]

Millmount is the only obvious site in Drogheda which fits the bill. But it is on the south side of the Boyne, unlike Newgrange, Knowth and Dowth, which are located on the north side of a spectacular loop in the Boyne some four miles upstream of Drogheda. And none of those Bend of the Boyne mounds can be seen from Millmount. Why? The answers would come, but first a fuller account of the written and spoken lore about the Millmount is needed.

Some time after the arrival of the Milesians at Inbher Colpa, the island of Ireland was divided into two kingdoms, and the Boyne river marked the division between those kingdoms, with Millmount acting as a kind of boundary marker between the kingdoms. The story of how the island came to be divided is recalled in the *Lebor Gabala Erenn*, the Book of Invasions, which is preserved in *The Book of Leinster*, a manuscript which dates from around 1150 AD.

After the Tuatha Dé Danann were crushed and expelled by the Milesians, the sons of the King of Spain took control of Ireland. At this time there was an argument about the kingship between Eremon and Eber, and Amergin was called to make peace between them.

> He said that the inheritance of the eldest, of Donn, should go to the youngest, to Eremon, and his inheritance to Eber after him; Eber did not accept that, but insisted on dividing Ireland. Eremon agreed to do so. Accordingly Ireland was divided in two between them, the northern half to Eremon, from Srub Brain to the Boyne, the southern half to Eber, from the Boyne to Tonn Clidna.[11]

The Millmount itself may have acted as a boundary marker: "Old bardic tales tell us of a mound having been fashioned in the plain of Magh Breagh, where the kingdoms of Heremon and Heber met at the Boyne."[12]

Just as the Mill Road at Colpa's mound might have been an echo of the sons of Mil, we wondered too if the name Millmount was more ancient than the seventeenth-century Delahoyde Mill after which it was apparently named. Is the name Millmount a remembrance of its ancient heritage? Perhaps it was once known as the Mil mound, or Rath Mil, after the famous sons of Mil who used the Boyne as their boundary marker?

The division of Ireland into two parts, each one ruled by one of the Milesian brothers, did not last long. After just one year, each brother wishing for unlimited sovereignty, the two met in battle at a place called Géisill to decide who would rule the entire kingdom. Eber and his chiefs fell in battle, and Eremon assumed the sole government of the island.[13] After defeating Eber, Eremon established his capital at the hill of Temair (Tara), named after his wife Téa. This link with Tara was to become fundamental to the interpretation of Millmount's ancient origins.

The Milesian invasion occurred, according to the annals, in 1694 BC. But there was some evidence that Millmount was contemporary with Newgrange, Knowth and Dowth, which were far older than that. If it was truly that old, there would be very few ways to prove its antiquity. One of those would be an archaeological dig, which has been ruled out in the near future because of the large Martello tower which sits atop the mound. Presumably, any disturbance of the mound material beneath might cause a subsidence and the possible collapse of the tower.[14] Besides, Millmount, unlike the Bend of the Boyne sites, is in an urban area.

If there were astronomical alignments involving Millmount, this might suggest it was contemporary with the Brú na Bóinne complex. There are an abundance of astronomical alignments in the Bend of the Boyne, as we will see in later chapters. Many of the smaller mounds are aligned with the larger ones for specific calendrical purposes. If Millmount shared the same age as the great Bend of the Boyne sites, there would be alignments there too.

LINES ON MAPS

The very first indication of something astronomical was back in 1999, at the very beginning of our research project, when Richard recounted a story told to him by a Drogheda folklorist, Dermot Fairclough. The story recounted how Bóann, the illuminated cow, lived beside Millmount and had a white bull that was her protector. One time the white bull, while grazing upriver, went slightly out of sight over the brow of the hill when a black bull came in from the sea and made to attack Bóann. The white bull came back in time and a fight ensued with the white bull driving the black bull back into the sea. (The tale bears similarities to the *Táin*, in which the brown bull, Donn Cuailnge, and the white bull, Finnbennach, battle to the death, although in the *Táin* it is the white bull that is killed. The significance of the *Táin* will be discussed in later chapters.)

One evening, while standing at the Martello tower on top of Millmount, gazing towards the east, that story began to make some sense to us. Towards the east there is an old area of the town which was called Black Bull. It is commemorated today with the name of a local public house and

Was the Black Bull that was driven into the sea in fact Taurus?

restaurant, called the Black Bull Inn. This area stretched down to the Boyne, according to the late Mr Fairclough, who had told us the story of Bóann and the bulls. A few miles further east, there is an area at Donacarney called the Black Hills, which affords a beautiful sweeping view of the Boyne Estuary and the coastline from Mornington to Clogherhead and as far as the Cooley and Mourne Mountains in the far distance.

There is a small mound not far from Millmount across a place known today as The Dale, a valley which runs from south to north towards the Boyne just to the east of Millmount. This mount is known locally as "Cromwell's Mount",[15] probably because Oliver Cromwell's army pitched there in 1649 before he besieged and sacked the town of Drogheda.[16] Cromwell's Mount is believed by archaeologists to be a "denuded passage grave" dating to the Neolithic.[17] The presence of such an ancient mound less than half a mile from Millmount suggests that the ancient mound-builders of the Boyne Valley were busy in this area and their activity was not just confined to the Bend of the Boyne upstream. It was additional evidence supporting the idea that Millmount is much more ancient than widely believed.

Closer to Millmount, there was once a stream running down through The Dale which was called the "Dove Stream", originally "Dubh" in Irish, meaning "Black". How do the Black Bull area and the mound on the other side of the "Black Stream" tie in with the story of Millmount and the two bulls? There could be a connection with the constellation Taurus. The bull was a very important constellation in the Stone Age, because it contained the vernal point during that period. The story could be a reference to the spring equinox, which as we will see was crucially important at Millmount.

On the morning of spring equinox, in the time leading up to the construction of the passage-mounds of Brú na Bóinne, the sunrise would be presaged by an unusual astronomical event. Before dawn, the star cluster in Taurus known as The Pleiades, or Seven Sisters, would rise due east.

Shortly after their rising, the sky would begin to brighten and eventually the sun would rise, swamping the stars in light and eventually making them disappear. In astronomical terms, this event is known as a "heliacal rising", and was crucially important in determining the sun's position among the stars at certain times of the year. By watching the stars before dawn, and by recording the heliacal risings which occur, early astronomers were able to determine the movement of the sun's vernal point through the zodiac, a slowly changing position which was caused by a wobble in the tilt of the Earth's axis. The effect, called "precession of the equinoxes", causes the vernal point to move westwards through the constellations of the zodiac, completing one entire revolution once every 25,800 years.

It is possible that this rare astronomical event is commemorated in Millmount's folklore. Such an event was, we are fairly sure, recorded also at Dowth in the Bend of the Boyne, something we will discuss in Chapter 6.

Because both the Colpe mound and the nearby "Cromwell's Mount" are not exactly due east of Millmount, it is not possible to tie them precisely with this heliacal rising event. However, the direction of Black Bull townland is east of Millmount. If Taurus is the black bull of the legend, what then is the white bull, and where does Bóann fit in?

Well, if there was a full moon at the time of the spring equinox, it would be located diametrically opposite the sun. It is an interesting fact that the full moon is always located exactly opposite the sun. This can be observed very easily on any of the 13 occasions during the year when there is a full moon. If the sun is setting in the north-west, the full moon will rise at the same time as the sunset, in the opposite direction, south-east. Hence, when the sun rises due east and the moon is full, the moon will be setting due west, and vice versa. It was when we turned our attention to the west that pieces of the puzzle began to fall firmly into place.

Millmount floodlit at night

We began by simply drawing a line on an Ordnance Survey map. We traced a line due west of Millmount, as far as the map would allow. That line passed through the Hill of Slane, just south of the peak, a very prominent and eminent location on the landscape about eight miles inland from Drogheda. It was at the Hill of Slane that St Patrick was said to have lit Ireland's first paschal fire.

On the peak of the Hill of Slane, there is another ancient site, a mound, or motte. This motte is somewhat smaller than Millmount. While Millmount measures 27.6 metres at the summit and 62.5 metres at the base,[18] the Slane motte is 19 metres wide at the top and 45 metres at the base.[19] Today, it is surrounded by a "wide ditch" and a "tree-ring bank"[20] and hardly visible from the Christian buildings and cemetery which dominate the eastern side of the hill. In folklore, this motte is said to have been the burial place of the Fir Bolg King, Sláine.

Sláine was leader of the Galióin, a division of the Fir Bolg, in pseudo-history, who divided Ireland with his brothers, taking the largest province for himself.[21] The *Dindshenchas* tells us how Slane got its name:

> Sláine, whence the name? Not hard to say. Sláine, king of the Fir Bolg, and their judge, by him was its wood cleared from the Brugh. Afterwards, he died at Druim Fuar, which is called Dumha Sláine, and was buried there: and from him the hill is named Sláine. Hence it was said:

The snow-covered mound at Slane, said to be the burial place of Sláine, king of the Fir Bolg

"Here died Sláine, lord of troops, over him the mighty mound is reared: so the name of Sláine was given to the hill, where he met his death in that chief abode."[22]

Like the Milesians, the Fir Bolg also used the Boyne to divide the kingdom of Ireland. *The Book of Invasions* tells us that the Fir Bolgs divided Ireland into five provinces, each governed by one of the five brothers, of whom Sláine was the eldest.

Sláine, the eldest brother, had the province of Leynster for his part, which containeth from Inver Colpe, that is to say, where the river Boyne entereth into the sea, now called in Irish Drogheda, to the meeting of the three waters, by Waterford, where the three rivers, Suyre, Ffeoir, and Barrow, do meet and run together into the sea.[23]

The Fir Bolg division had echoes of the Milesian episode, because it was recorded that Sláine "soon enlarged his dominions", so that he became king of the whole country.[24]

The Boyne, the river of the Milky Way, was a very important boundary marker for both the Fir Bolg, and later the Milesians. Previous invaders, the three sons of Nemed, had also divided the country between them, making the Boyne the southern boundary of the realm of Beotac.[25]

From this time forward the mouth of the Boyne at Drogheda – named by the annalists from a later event at Inber Colpa – was made a boundary line in almost all divisions of territory, becoming in fact the most frequent and important line of demarcation in use.[26]

We saw how the line due west of Millmount could be traced in the general direction of the mound of Sláine. We wondered if there was some possible astronomical connection between Millmount and Slane, tying in with the equinoxes. A visit to Millmount on the spring equinox in 2000 confirmed to Richard that indeed there was something very special going on. He found that on the day of spring equinox, the sunset, viewed from the top of Millmount, occurred in the direction of the Hill of Slane.[27]

Of further interest is the fact that a few days after the equinox, the sun sets in the direction of a range of hills much further inland than Slane. These are the hills of Loughcrew, which are the site of dozens of Stone Age passage-tombs. There appeared to be a reasonably accurate equinoctial alignment formed between Millmount in Drogheda, through the Hill of Slane, towards Carnbane West in Loughcrew, more than 32 miles away.

Waiting for another couple of evenings after the sun sets directly over the Hill of Slane, it has moved a further two sun-widths north of due

Sunset from Millmount over the Hill of Slane, 22 March 2004

west. This line from Millmount, traced on a map, passing north of Sláine's mound, intersects the hill called Carnbane East at Loughcrew, the site of a very famous passage-cairn known as Cairn T. And this Cairn T is a very special equinoctial site.

DISCOVERIES AT CAIRN T

To recap, the sunset on spring equinox viewed from Millmount, the burial place of Amergin who claimed to know the setting place of the sun, occurs slightly to the left of the Hill of Slane. Two days later, the sunset viewed from this point sets directly at the Hill of Slane, over the mound of the Fir Bolg king Sláine. Another two days later, with the sun setting two sun-widths to the north of the Hill of Slane, the direction of the sunset is towards the equinoctial site Cairn T at Loughcrew.

Was this another example of how the megalithic builders (if we assumed Millmount to be Stone Age in origin) were able to "range in" mutually invisible sites just as Alexander Thom had said they were able to do?[28] It was certainly interesting that both the Slane mound and Cairn T lay within days of the equinox viewed from Millmount – at a time when the sun would have been housed in Taurus, the bull constellation, perhaps recalled in the ancient folk tale about Bóann and the two bulls. This tale of the two bulls recalled how the white bull had partially disappeared behind the brow of a hill, perhaps more evidence of astronomy linking up with landscape. It is likely that the white bull was in fact the Bó Finn, the white cow, which is the moon, and that the story related to the full moon at the time of the equinox. At this time, the full moon would set in the direction of Slane while the sun was rising due east in Taurus.

If there were any lingering doubts about the apparent equinox alignment between Millmount, Slane and Cairn T, these were firmly put to bed during a visit to Cairn T itself during September 2001.

Cairn T has been made famous by an important discovery there by an American artist and writer in 1980. Martin Brennan, who visited there on St Patrick's Day in that year with his research colleague Jack Roberts, revealed that Cairn T had an important astronomical alignment:

> The lock on the modern door leading to the passage had frozen during the night, and as we struggled with it the rising sun was already above the horizon. When we drew back the door a narrow chink of light streamed down the passage and flashed into the end recess of the chamber. On the upper left of the backstone a rectangular patch of light was rapidly beginning to take form, brilliantly illuminating the entire chamber in a glowing splendour of shimmering golden orange light.[29]

The "clearly defined geometric shape" projected onto the upright rear chamberstone of Cairn T appeared to move diagonally across the face of the stone, "tracing the path of the sun against a mural of prehistoric art".[30] Some of the symbols carved onto the chamberstone looked like images of a rayed sun.

It was clear to Brennan and Roberts that they had discovered a solar observatory which, they said, was "capable of defining an individual day

The "equinox stone" of Cairn T at Loughcrew on a misty equinox morning

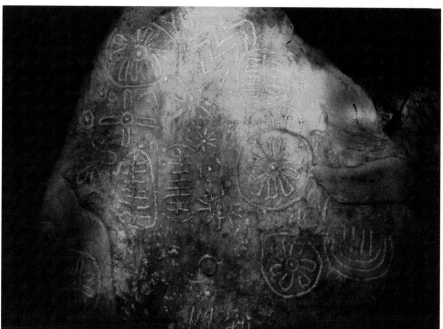

with far greater precision than Newgrange. The wider differences in the sun's apparent movement at equinox made it considerably easier to define the actual day of equinox at Cairn T than the day of winter solstice at Newgrange."[31]

Given the spectacular nature of his discovery, it seemed our own visit to Cairn T could hardly provide any new information beyond what Brennan had disclosed. In fact, the event has been observed and photographed by a growing band of academics, writers, photographers and assorted enthusiasts every year since Brennan's discovery. What new information could we glean for our quest?

My particular interest in visiting Cairn T was to obtain some good quality photographic prints and slides of the ancient artwork of the passage and chambers. With some assistance from Richard, along with author Anne-Marie Moroney and artist Raymond Balfe, I succeeded in getting some very nice photographs. We were particularly interested in getting good photographs of the ceiling stone of the end recess (the one into which the equinox sun shines), which appeared from Brennan's drawing to be some kind of star map or astral guide.

I carefully placed the camera on the floor of the recess pointing upwards towards the ceiling stone and took some exposures. After taking the exposures, I decided to climb into the small end recess to take a photograph looking out of the chamber towards the passage and beyond into the daylight.

When I crouched down carefully, with my back facing the famous equinox backstone, I peered down the passage out the entrance, and noticed immediately that there was a hill on the distant horizon. It was

The passage of Cairn T at Loughcrew

as if the passage of Cairn T was deliberately oriented towards that distant landmark. Taking up the camera, I zoomed in and very quickly I realised I was looking at the Hill of Slane. I excitedly told Richard and the others of this apparent "discovery".[32]

It was to have far-reaching implications. This stone site, at least 5,000 years old, and possibly older than Newgrange, was pointing to a very important horizon marker for the equinox event – the same horizon marker which seemed to have an equinoctial link with Amergin's mound of Millmount.

One interesting feature of the Cairn T passage is that it does not point directly towards due east. Its orientation is skewed somewhat south of east, as Brennan himself observed in 1980. He said that at equinox, the sun is rising due east on the horizon. However, Cairn T was oriented to the south of the sunrise point. It was constructed in such a way "so that the beam does not enter the mound until the sun rises to the proper altitude".[33]

The Cairn T alignment, which Brennan clearly stated had tracked down the sun on the day of equinox with great accuracy, was not pointing due east, as might be expected of an equinoctial alignment. In fact, Brennan says the alignment is skewed nine degrees to the south.[34]

Our Millmount–Slane alignment was also skewed, but only by a single degree or so, to the north of west. Both Millmount and Cairn T appeared to have equinoctial alignments involving the Hill of Slane, which was the site where St Patrick was said to have lit the Easter Fire within days of the spring equinox in 433 AD.[35]

The existence of a passage in Millmount is hinted at in the *Annals of the Four Masters*, which recounts how some of the ancient Boyne Valley sites were plundered by foreigners in 861 AD:

> The cave of the Achadh Aldai, in Mughdhorna Maighen; the cave of Cnoghbhai; the cave of the grave of Bodan, i.e. the shepherd of Elcmar, over Dubhath; and the cave of the wife of Gobhann, at Drochat Atha, were broken and plundered . . .[36]

The reference to a "cave" at Drochat Atha, while not proving the existence of a passage, is a tantalising hint nonetheless. The *Annals* also mention caves at Cnoghbhai, which is Knowth, where there are two "caves", or passages, one opening towards the eastern aspect and one towards the west.

In his 1826 *History of Drogheda*, L.C. Johnston says there were underground chambers in Millmount until the time the nearby barracks were built. He said of the mound: "Mill-mount fort is similar in its construction to the rest which were raised by the early Irish. It seems, like them, to have been dug out of the ground upon which it stands, and contains vaults or subterraneous chambers and sally-ports, the entrances to which were open until the building of the present barracks close by the rath."[37]

The only way to prove Millmount's antiquity beyond a shadow of a doubt is through archaeological investigation, specifically some sort of dig. This is something we would not encourage, mainly because of the weight of the Martello tower above. There has been a limited archaeological investigation on top of the mound, carried out before the Martello tower was reconstructed during restoration work in the year 1999.[38] A thorough archaeological probe, with the sinking of at least one trench into the mound, would be required to obtain datable material from the mound. Until that occurs, if it ever does, we are armed only with fragmentary mythological and legendary evidence, and whatever supportive astronomical data can be put forward.

ST PATRICK AND THE MILESIANS

We were encouraged by the Cairn T discovery, and so, on Midsummer's Day in 2001, ventured to the top of Millmount once again to see where the sunset occurred on summer solstice, and to see if it had any significance to our research. At that time of year, the evenings are long, and, if the sun is shining, warm too. That's how it was on this particular occasion.

I had previously traced the line of summer sunset from Millmount and found it to intersect a place called, interestingly, Black Hill, in the village of Collon, some seven miles away.[39] The name Black Hill is of interest because it may signify the coming of the darker evenings after the turn of the year at summer solstice.[40]

On the longest day in 2001, I photographed the sunset, and found that the sun set over a gently sloping hill northwest of Drogheda called the Hill of Rath. Some ancient monuments, including some Neolithic remains, were unearthed on the hill during archaeological work carried out as part of the construction of the new M1 Drogheda by-pass motorway.

Even more interesting was the fact that the line of the direction of summer solstice sunset from Millmount passed over the townland of Mell, which we met in Chapter 2 as Mag Mell, the Pleasant Plain, the probable otherwordly Tethra from which Amergin called the cattle to dance in the bright heavens. Amergin's words come to mind again, "Who but I knows the place in which the setting of the sun lies?"

It was at this location, in the townland of Mell, in the year 433 AD, that St Patrick was said to have met the people of Drogheda on his way into the town. "On the Collon Road, there is a large pock-marked boulder or weather worn stone, outside a labourer's cottage . . . He is also reputed to have performed baptisms at a nearby well, St Patrick's Well, now closed up. This event and the stone gives the placename Cloghpatrick, the stone of Patrick."[41]

The summer solstice sun setting over the Hill of Rath, as viewed from Millmount

Was St Patrick following a path laid out 2,000 years earlier by the Milesians, and probably by the Stone Age builders another 2,000 years before that again? He had landed at Inbher Colpa, the same place where Amergin and his brothers set foot, and followed the course of the Boyne westwards to Slane, where he lit the first paschal fire at Sláine's mound. Richard described this journey of Patrick as "an equinox journey". Now, we found Patrick again on another astronomical pathway, this time a summer solstice journey, which seemed to echo a much earlier alignment.

We decided to take the research of Millmount's summer solstice line a step further by looking at the position of the sun in the zodiac at specific times, namely the Neolithic, at the time Newgrange, Knowth and Dowth were being built (assuming that Millmount was contemporary with those sites), and then at 1694 BC, the date which the annalists gave for the arrival of the Milesians at Colpe. The astronomical evidence told an important story.

In the Neolithic, the sun was positioned in the constellation we know today as Leo, the Lion, at the time of summer solstice. However, this distinctive group of stars was not known as a lion in old Ireland. It was instead listed in the zodiac as *Cú,* meaning "hound".[42]

Immediately, a link with the great Irish hero Cúchulainn was evident. We had the sun positioned in the hound, Cú, setting in the direction of Collon, the name of which may have some connection to the hero of the *Táin Bó Cuailnge.*[43]

What made the Cú–Collon summer alignment even more interesting was the fact that it seemed to be marked out by a very straight road on the map. This road is marked on the Taylor and Skinner map of 1778,[44] and was the main road to Collon from Drogheda in earlier centuries. The straight stretch, which closely matches the Millmount–Collon line, goes over the Hill of Rath.

This Cú–Collon road is the one at the side of which lies St Patrick's stone, which is still there to this day. There is a well at the roadside too, called St Patrick's Well. The exact location of the well was "directly opposite Clogh Patrick stone, which is situated on the street in front of Miss Maureen Morgan's residence."[45] "St Patrick's Well and the Clogh Patrick Stone are situated at Waterunder in the townland of Mell.[46] It has been stated that the "carved impression of his [Patrick's] knees is still plainly visible" on the stone.[47]

A LIGHT AT BEALTAINE

There is a folk tale told in Drogheda which links Mell and a mysterious "light in Millmount". It goes like this:

> About a mile from the centre of the town is a townland of Toberboice. It is at the cross roads of Mell on the main Slane Road. The biggest house in that townland was called "Toberboice Cottage". The story is as follows. A long time ago a man lived there by the name of Mr. Didmond. One of his ancestors was supposed to have hidden a bag of gold but nobody knew where it was. One day he was out shooting on a place called Firry Hill, so many fir bushes grew on it. While shooting he saw a little man with a red cloak on him. He knew this little man was a fairy and he also knew that the fairy knew where the gold was hidden. He ran up all of a sudden and before he knew what was happening the fairy was captured and brought to the cottage. The man invited many of his friends to see the fairy. They kept asking him questions and pinching him, but to no avail. On the third day the fairy began to get tired so he said "Look at the light in Millmount" but someone was clever enough not to look at Millmount, so the fairy did not escape . . .[48]

There is an archaeo-astronomical link between the Hill of Rath, where the summer solstice sunset occurs, and Millmount. In a public lecture in November 2001, ironically held at a lecture hall adjoining Millmount, archaeologist Coilín O'Driscoll outlined a very interesting site which had been excavated at Balgatheran, on the Hill of Rath. A circle of post-holes, with an associated find of "Dundrum Longstone" type grooved ware pottery dating to 2,600–2,500 BC, around the end of the Neolithic, was found to have an entrance oriented towards what the archaeologist described as "a narrow east–southeast window", which he said "suggests a concern with the rising sun".

Mr O'Driscoll said that just because a site could have been astronomically inclined, does not prove that it was, but he raised the possibility that it could have been "a sophisticated solar observatory, a temple dedicated to the sun, with offerings made such as pottery and bone fragments". Such a site on the Hill of Rath, with its entrance opening towards the southeast, would have pointed in the direction of Millmount for winter solstice sunrise.

The investigation of Millmount's summer solstice sunset line had yielded some valuable results. With an astronomical link firmly established in the Neolithic, some time around 5,000 years or so ago, it was now time to examine a more specific date, given in *The Book of Invasions* – the day the Milesians first set foot in Ireland.

> They encircled Ireland three times, till at last they took the harbour at Inber Scene; a Thursday as regards the day of the week, on the day before the first of May, the seventeenth day of the moon . . .[49]

The Milesians arrived in Ireland on the eve of the feast of Bealtaine, a very important date in the pagan calendar. It marked the end of the dark half of the year and the beginning of the bright half.[50] It was a feast associated with fires, and the ritual eating of certain kinds of food.

Astronomically speaking, the information given in *The Book of Invasions* is very important. Bealtaine was one of the four "great Celtic calendar feasts",[51] which are known today in archaeo-astronomy as the "cross-quarter days". Each of these feasts is located halfway, measured in days, between the solstices and the equinoxes. Hence Bealtaine is half-way between spring equinox and summer solstice. The *Lebor Gabala* says that the Milesians arrived on the "seventeenth day of the moon", indicating again that the moon was indeed used in the calculation of days in the ancient calendar.

However, it is when we simulate the heavens on the eve of that date, 1 May 1694 BC, that a whole correlation of astronomical and mythological information occurs to give a much bigger picture. Using SkyMap to zoom back in time to 1694 BC, an epoch known by archaeologists as the Bronze Age, we see that the sun is located near the horns of Taurus, a little to the east (left) in fact, above the very human-like form of the constellation of Orion. The line of the ecliptic, which is the imaginary line the sun follows through the zodiac, passes very close to the raised arm of Orion. One could say it looks like the sun is actually in the hand of Orion.

The mythic iconography of the giant sky hunter with the sun, moon and planets passing above his head would prove very important in our decipherment of the myths and sites of the Boyne Valley. But for the moment, there are two primary reasons for its importance.

The first is that Orion is one of the constellations which, down through time in different countries across the globe, is identified almost universally as a large human figure, a giant of the night sky.[52] Orion is a great hunter of classical legend. We believe he features strongly in what we call Irish "sky myths".[53] Amergin himself proclaimed, "I am a gigantic, sword-wielding champion."[54]

The second reason this point in the sky is important is because it is one of only two places in the entire night sky where the ecliptic, the sun's path among the stars, intersects with the bands of the Milky Way, the heavenly river of the illuminated cow, the Boyne of the cosmos.

On the date of the mythical arrival of the Milesians to Ireland, the sun was positioned in the raised hand of Orion, in the Milky Way river. The other point where the ecliptic crosses the cosmic Boyne is located in the gap between the zodiac constellations of Sagittarius and Scorpius, and occurs six months after Bealtaine, on the first day of November, the Celtic feast of Samhain, the beginning of the dark half of the year.

The division of Ireland into two kingdoms by Eremon and Eber, one taking north and the other south of the Boyne, the earthly Milky Way, began to make sense taking the astronomical evidence into account. Their rule over the land did not last long before their contentions began, as mentioned earlier. Their joint rule lasted only a year. Could this tale be interpreted astronomically?

The year began at Bealtaine, when the sun crossed the heavenly Boyne, the way of the white cow, and ended after a year at the same time again, when the sun was back in the Milky Way in the hand of Orion. It was clear that Eremon's and Eber's division was to be interpreted in the physical sense, with each taking a half of the actual country divided by the Boyne river, but also in the astronomical sense, with each taking a half of a year, one half which began with the sun crossing the cosmic Boyne at Orion and the other half crossing back again in the gap between Sagittarius and Scorpius.

The whole idea of divisions being represented physically and astronomically began to make sense with regard to Millmount and Slane, too. Millmount was a boundary marker, located overlooking the Boyne, separating the kingdoms of Eremon and Eber. Slane mound was another, earlier boundary indicator, marking out the territory of Sláine, the eldest brother, who had the province of Leinster to himself.

Although Millmount and Slane are almost due east and due west of each other, one is located north of the Boyne (Slane) and one to the south (Millmount). In 1694 BC, when the sun was in the hand of Orion, it was on its way north, towards its maximum northerly declination on the summer solstice. Hence the reason Bealtaine was seen as the beginning of the bright half of the year. When the sun was in the gap between

Sagittarius and Scorpius, it was on its way south, towards the maximum southerly declination which occurred on winter solstice.

If we assume that Millmount is Neolithic, and contemporary with Newgrange, and that Slane's mound may have the same antiquity, then one original intention of the sites seems to have been to halve the year at the equinoxes. By the time the Milesians arrived, a different division of the year was suggested, involving the so-called "fire festivals" of Bealtaine and Samhain.

The accuracy of the annals in pinpointing the astronomically important date of the Milesian arrival would be considered without question, according to Ireland's first president, Dr Douglas Hyde, who wrote:

Moonrise behind Millmount

> The numerous Irish annals in which the skeleton of Irish history is contained, are valuable and ancient . . . The illustrious Bede in recording the great eclipse of the sun which took place only eleven years before his own birth is two days astray in his date, while the Irish annals give correctly not only the day but the hour. This proves that their compiler had access either to the original record of an eye-witness, or to a copy of such a document. These annals contain, between the end of the fifth century and the year 884, as many as eighteen records of eclipses, comets and such natural phenomena – and modern science by calculating backwards shows that all these records are absolutely correct, both as to the day and hour. From this we can deduce without hesitation that from the fourth or fifth century the Irish annals can be absolutely trusted.[55]

One major question is whether the Milesian invasion actually happened at all, and whether the supposedly historic events recorded in the invasion myths and the annals were actually complex myths created as a means of relating changes that were happening in the sky.

COW AND CALF, MOON AND VENUS

Returning to our Cú–Collon summer solstice alignment, it is interesting to note that Cúchulainn's territory, known as Mag Muirthemne, stretched across much of County Louth from the Boyne river as far as Dundalk. Yet again the Boyne was acting as a boundary. And we saw how, at Baltray, the stones where Cúchulainn slew his son Connla were another form of boundary marker at the southern extreme of Cúchulainn's realm.

In order to effect a full and thorough investigation of Millmount's possible alignments, a return to the Ordnance Survey maps was made. We investigated the summer solstice line, but this time, instead of just running it from Millmount to Black Hill, we also ran the line backwards, in the reverse direction, towards winter solstice sunrise. This line intersects another Neolithic site, a mound by the side of the N1 Dublin–Belfast Road, at a place called Knocknagin, which means the "Hill of the Heads". This mound overlooks the estuary of the Delvin river, and there were once numerous mounds here, some of which were reportedly washed into the sea due to coastal erosion in the nineteenth century.

If the people who built Millmount were the same people who built Newgrange, Knowth and Dowth, and we're fairly sure they were, then they would have studied the movements of the moon. Of this, there can be no doubt. Newgrange, Knowth and Dowth all have lunar functions, which will be explored in coming chapters.

There is some mythological evidence of a lunar link between Millmount and Baltray. Millmount is said to have been the burial place of the wife of Gobhann, also known as Goibhniu, in the *Annals*, as previously mentioned. This Gobhann was the divine smith, an articifer, who was one of the five chiefs of the Tuatha Dé Danann. Interestingly, the Tuatha Dé Danann arrived in Ireland on Bealtaine also, and their descent from the clouds was said to have resulted in a three-day eclipse.[56] The fact that Gobhann was one of the five chiefs – the others being Nuadu, Dagda, Ogma and Diancecht – makes him an important character in ancient myth. He was the archetypal master craftsman. And he helps establish a link with Baltray and the moon.

The Glas Ghoibhneann (Glas Gablin) who was linked with the moon in Chapter 1 as the "Grey of Goibhniu", was supposed to have been originally owned by Gobhann.[57] The Gobhann's wife, whose cave is at Drogheda, could be linked with the Glas Ghoibhneann – both are female, and both have a strong association with Gobhann.[58]

There could be a further Millmount–Collon link through this famous smith, Gobhann, because there was another smith, in the *Táin*, whose name was Culann. This is the man who owned the hound which Sétanta killed, after which he became known as Cúchulainn, meaning "hound of Culann".

The old crest of the town of Drogheda features a star emblazoned above a crescent moon. Today, the symbol is used widely throughout the town, and is known locally as the "star and crescent". On the Mayor's ceremonial chains, the star and crescent are engraved onto the central medallion, with the words "Inbhear Colpa" underneath. This star and crescent symbol was said to have been adopted as Drogheda's symbol when the town was granted its charter by King John in 1194 AD.[59] It is featured on John's own royal seal.

It is possible this symbol has a much more ancient origin, possibly dating right back to the New Stone Age, when Newgrange, Knowth, Dowth and Millmount were being constructed by the ancient builders who had a keen interest in all matters relating to the heavens. Does this "star and crescent" symbol represent the Glas Ghoibhneann and her calf, the moon and Venus, which perform a graceful dance through the heavens passing across the Road of the White Cow, the cosmic Boyne?[60]

The moon and Venus, the crescent and star, the cow and calf

If all of the evidence so far unearthed did not complete the astronomical jigsaw of Millmount, then the final piece of that jigsaw fell into place when we investigated the line of winter solstice sunset from Millmount. That critical calendrical event, which is so important at Dowth and the Bend of the Boyne sites, must have been considered with huge importance by the builders of Millmount too, because on the shortest day of the year, the sunset, viewed from Millmount, occurs in the direction of the Hill of Tara, the ancient capital of Ireland, seat of the High Kings and the setting for epic stories and romances and tragedies.

The Millmount–Tara alignment, when we discovered it, proved beyond a shadow of a doubt in our minds, that Millmount was indeed very ancient. And, as we would discover, there were great mythological links between these two ancient sites which proved they both had significant strategic importance to the astronomical plan set down by the stone builders.

CHAPTER FOUR

TARA:

SEAT OF THE

SKY KING

S tanding on the Hill of Tara, it almost feels like you can reach out and touch the heavens. The great prospect afforded by Tara's height, combined with its relatively wide and reasonably flat summit, gives one the feeling of being detached from the sweeping countryside below. It is said that as many as 16 counties can be discerned from Tara's summit.[1] Here, in ancient times, five great roads reached out across Ireland, with their epicentre at Tara, like the roots of a great tree snaking out into the soil all around.[2]

There are many hills in Ireland, some of which yield even greater prospects than Tara, but there are none which equal this, the old capital of Ireland, in terms of historical eminence, romance, myth and cultural importance. Tara embodies the heart of ancient Ireland and was at the centre of civilisation in this country in remote times.

Author Elizabeth Hickey introduced her book about Tara with the words "some places on this old earth on which we dwell seem always to have had a history and Tara is one of those places."[3] They were simple words that made a profound statement. That statement affirms that, as another author on Tara has written, the place was "prominent in our oldest myths and legends". The hill has "been at the centre of things Irish since the earliest times."[4]

Snowdrops in the churchyard at Tara on a winter evening

Archaeologically, Tara contains a diverse cornucopia of monuments. There is one small passage-tomb, much smaller than the huge mounds overlooking the Boyne at Brú na Bóinne. It is located near two conjoined embanked structures, which from the air look like concentric rings in a sort of figure-of-eight pattern. All this is enclosed by another, huge ringed structure. To the north of these is an extensive linear earthwork, while there are other circular enclosures to the northeast. In the churchyard on Tara are two stones, said to be ancient standing stones. On one of these is a carved female figure, possibly a *sheela-na-gig*[5] or a goddess. There are a number of ancient wells on the hill, and another strange, phallus-like standing stone called the Lia Fáil.

The oldest structure identified at Tara is a "large, probably palisaded enclosure around the summit of the hill that was built during the Neolithic."[6] The majority of the visible monuments at Tara are barrows, most of which are likely to date from the Bronze Age.[7] The Mound of the Hostages (*Duma na nGiall*) was constructed around 3000 BC,[8] making it a probable contemporary of Newgrange, Knowth and Dowth.

In recent years, another huge circular enclosure, invisible today, has been discovered under the turf at Tara using sophisticated archaeological techniques.[9] At least 100 new monuments have been discovered at Tara thanks to "non-invasive exploratory techniques".[10] More recently, even more sites have been identified around Tara through aerial reconnaissance.[11] While there are many monuments dotted throughout the landscape around Tara, the "greatest concentration . . . is on and around the summit of the hill".[12] It is clear from the sheer number and range of types of monument that the hill was important in ancient times.

On the morning of the summer solstice, the longest day of the year, at around 5.00 am, the sun creeps above the far northeastern horizon and sends out its warm rays upon the land. Although it cannot be seen from Tara, the Millmount, Amergin's

Ground-probing radar techniques have revealed an enormous circular enclosure underneath Tara (Image: © The Discovery Programme)

resting place, lies in the direction of that sunrise. You may not be able to see Millmount from Tara, but at dawn on the longest day of the year, you are able to pinpoint the direction in which it lies simply by watching where the sun appears on the horizon.[13]

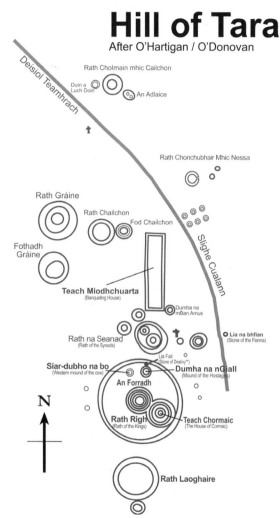

Hill of Tara
After O'Hartigan / O'Donovan

Deisiol Teamhrach

Rath Cholmain mhic Cailchon

Duin a
Luch Doin
An Adlaice

Rath Chonchubhair Mhic Nessa

Rath Gráine

Rath Chailchon
Fod Chailchon

Slighe Cualann

Fothadh
Gráine

Teach Miodhchuarta
(Banqueting House)

Dumha na
mBan Amus

Rath na Seanad
(Rath of the Synods)

Lia na bhfian
(Stone of the Fianna)

Lia Fail
(Stone of Destiny")

Siar-dubho na bo
(Western mound of the cow)

Dumha na nGiall
(Mound of the Hostages)

An Forradh

N

Rath Righ
(Rath of the Kings)

Teach Chormaic
(The House of Cormac)

Rath Laoghaire

Map of the major sites on the Hill of Tara as they were depicted in the nineteenth century

At Tara, which was the "place of the setting sun" as viewed from Amergin's mound in Drogheda, the visitor unwittingly finds themselves at the core of a great astronomical masterplan, set down by distant ancestors whom time has almost forgotten. What has become of these prehistoric forebears?

They have passed like rain on the mountain, like a wind in the meadow;
The days have gone down in the west behind the hills into shadow.[14]

A great many days have waned in the west since the Stone Age astronomers first laid out their grand scheme. A great many moons have walked the road of the white cow. And yet, despite the enormous span of time which separates us from them, fundamental aspects of the achievements of those people have come down to us, fixed and embedded in the landscape, immortalised in the very soil of the Boyne region. Their monuments, many denuded, damaged or partly destroyed by time, speak out to us across the centuries.

The Millmount–Tara solstice alignment was a crucial ice-breaker in our interpretation of the ancient Boyne landscape, and how the heavens were brought down to earth by the ancient astronomers.

When the alignment was discovered in 1999, quite early in our research, and almost by accident, it raised more questions than it answered.

As previously mentioned, Richard and I had a habit of marking lines on maps from one old site to another. It became almost an obsession for us. There was good reason for this obsession – these lines regularly yielded interesting results.

Because of people like Alexander Thom, and other authors like Michael Dames,[15] we were aware of the fact that many ancient sites seemed to form imaginary lines across the landscape. Earlier researchers including Sir Norman Lockyer, H. Boyle Somerville and Lieutenant Devoir "had all noticed the phenomenon of aligned megalithic sites, which they believed to have had an astronomical function".[16] Was this the case with the Millmount-Tara alignment?

Further inquiry revealed that some of these lines across the Irish landscape coincided with significant calendrical events. Eventually, we would reveal a complex pattern, or what we termed a "grid", of these imaginary "straight tracks",[17] criss-crossing the landscape in a labyrinth-like structure which, we believed, could only be the result of an extremely convoluted set of coincidences, or else a cleverly crafted master plan.[18]

Initially, we had believed that Tara might mark the position of winter solstice sunset as viewed from Dowth, one of the three great mounds of the Bend of the Boyne. Because there is a Neolithic mound on Tara, we figured any solstitial alignment involving that mound would involve another Stone Age site. At that time, we knew little of Millmount's antiquity; hence the reason for assuming it was Dowth.

Anne-Marie Moroney, an artist and author who spent five consecutive winters studying the winter solstice phenomenon at Dowth,[19] was able to tell us that winter solstice sunset as viewed from the top of Dowth occurred some distance north of Tara along the horizon. We would have to look elsewhere for a possible viewing site, if it existed at all.

Only much later in our research – in 2003 in fact – did it transpire that anyone who had seen summer solstice sunrise from Tara was able to report that the sunrise occurred in the direction of Drogheda. Midsummer sunrise occurs in the northeast, exactly opposite the position on the horizon where midwinter sunset occurs. They are said to be "diametrically opposite" each other. So if the midsummer sun viewed from Tara rose over Drogheda, it made sense that the midwinter sunset from Drogheda went down over Tara.

A QUEEN'S BURIAL

The first and most obvious link between the sites was provided by mythology, and the epic story of the Milesian conquest of Ireland which was preserved for posterity in the ancient *Lebor Gabala,* the *Book of Invasions.*[20]

Amergin, the poet, astronomer and judge of the Milesian brothers, was, according to folk stories recorded in historical accounts, buried at Millmount.[21] His brother, Eremon, who had achieved sovereignty over the whole country after the death of Eber, went on to establish his capital at Tara, which was named after his wife, Téa.

Amergin was the poet and judge, Eremon the king. These brothers, just two of a total of eight, were the principal figureheads in the supposed Milesian conquest of Ireland. And the places with which they are associated were important keystones in the ancient ground system. Eremon was king of Tara. Amergin was buried at Millmount. Both sites are connected astronomically.

Reading back through the myths, we learned that Amergin was directly involved in ensuring Tara was the place from which the descendants of Eremon would rule, on the strict instructions of the princess Tea, Eremon's wife. Before the sons of Mil had arrived in Ireland and defeated the Tuatha Dé Danann, the Spanish princess had insisted that she be buried on Ireland's most beautiful hill when she died.

According to the *Book of Invasions,* ". . . therein should she be buried and her rampart and her lair dug; and that therein should be every royal dignity and every assembly that should be convened, of the progeny of Erimón, for ever. This is the mound which she chose, Liath-druim; because it was the fairest sod by far which she saw in Ireland. And therein was the dignity of Ireland; and from her it is named, Temair, from her being therein habitually. And she was buried afterwards, and her rampart was raised over her, namely, Múr Téa, Téa-Múr."[22]

Such was her intent to be buried on this hill of eminence, Téa asked Amergin and Eber to act as guarantors to ensure her will was fulfilled.[23]

So Amergin, whose site is Millmount in Drogheda, helped chose for Téa the hill originally called *Liath-druim,* and later to be named the Hill of Tara. The two sites were connected both through astronomy and mythology.

But there was more still. Indefatigable as we were in the joyful pursuit of drawing lines on maps, we soon found that an extension of the Millmount–Tara line took us in the direction of County Kildare, and a seemingly innocuous little place called Carbury.[24]

Hadn't we been there before? Indeed we had, in Chapter 1, where we learned that the story of the origin of the Boyne River began at Nechtain's Well, at Carbury. It was at this magical well that Bóann defied her husband's orders and met her watery fate. The waters burst forth from the well and rushed after Bóann, following her all the way to the sea, where she was drowned and her dog was transformed into Rockabill Island.

What was the significance of a solstice line from Millmount through the Hill of Tara towards Carbury and its magical well?

The major implication is that Tara was placed directly between the source of the Boyne river and its estuary. Amergin set foot at Inbher Colpa, the estuary, and guaranteed that Tara be the place where Téa should be buried. And the myth about how the Boyne was formed tells us that Bóann's tragic demise began at Carbury (source) and ended at the meeting of the waters at Inbher Colpa (estuary). The actual source of the Boyne is very close to the well at Carbury, less than three kilometres to the north. The Boyne passes within feet of the Carbury well as nothing more than a streamlet.

Nechtain's Well, the mythical place where the Boyne river is said to rise. The well is located at Newbury House near Carbury, Co. Kildare. The Boyne, which is just a trickle at this point, passes within feet of the well.

Although it does not sit perched upon the rolling banks of the Boyne like many of the megalithic sites in the valley region,[25] Tara is unique because it sits at the centre of a source-to-estuary alignment system, fixed on specific astronomical events. The astronomical alignments of Millmount–Tara–Carbury were not confined to the sun either, as we soon learned.

A mythical connection between Tara and Carbury is made through Nechtain, who as we mentioned in Chapter 1 is also known as Nuadu of the Silver Arm. As the Tuatha Dé Danann king of Ireland who reigned before the Milesian invasion, Nuadu ruled Ireland from Tara. In one famous story, "The Coming of Lugh",[26] Nuadu was holding a great feast at Tara when Lugh came knocking on his door, pronouncing himself as the "*Ildánach*", the "Master of all Arts".[27]

So impressed was the king by Lugh's abilities, and lured by the thought that with Lugh's help "the country might get free of the taxes and the tyranny put on it by the Fomor",[28] Nuadu came off his throne and allowed Lugh to sit in his place for the length of 13 days.

So Nuadu owned the sacred well at Carbury and he ruled Ireland from Tara. With this firmly established, could we learn anything more from his story to connect him with the Millmount–Tara–Carbury alignment? We think so.

GIANT WITH A SILVER ARM

The story of Nuadu's silver arm[29] is a curious one indeed. Nuadu was a central figure in the Tuatha Dé Danann conquest of Ireland, and their first king. The Tuatha Dé Danann were said to have brought four great artifacts to Ireland with them. They were the *Lia Fáil*, the "Stone of Fal", brought to Tara, which was said to shout when touched by the rightful king of Ireland; the Spear of Lug (Lugh), against which there was no victory because it was said no battle was ever won against either the spear or the person who wielded it; the Dagda's Cauldron, from which no-one ever left unthankful; and the Sword of Nuadu. "When it was drawn from its deadly sheath, no one ever escaped from it, and it was irresistible".[30]

The Tuatha Dé Danann formed an alliance with the Fomorians, the giants of the sea, in which the Fomorian king Balor, whom we met in Chapter 1, gave his daughter Eithne to Cian, son of the Tuatha Dé Danann healer, Diancecht. Through the union of Cian and Eithne, the gifted child Lug (Lugh Lámdfhada) was born.[31]

It is worth noting at this point that, in one version of the Balor myth which we explored in Chapter 1, the magic cow which Balor took possession of belonged to Cian, the father of Lugh.

In the first battle of Moytura, the Tuatha Dé Danann routed the Fir Bolg, killing a hundred thousand of them. It was in this battle that Nuadu's hand was cut off, by Sreng son of Sengann. The Tuatha Dé Danann healer, Diancecht, is said to have fashioned a new hand, made of silver, which was said to move like any other hand.[32] Thus the epithet *airgetlámh*, "silver hand", was given to Nuadu.

Because his hand had been chopped off, Nuadu was stripped of the kingship and deemed disqualified from holding the position[33] and was replaced on the throne by Bres. Eventually, through episodes too lengthy to recount at this juncture, Nuadu regained kingship of Ireland and "held sovereignty over the Tuatha Dé".[34]

It was at this time Nuadu held a great feast at Tara, during which Lugh Lamhfadha declared himself the *samildanach,* the "many-gifted".[35]

During the course of our research work, Richard and I often found ourselves looking towards the heavens to help with the interpretation of the myths. In the case of Nuadu, we had been beaten to it by William

Síth Nechtain at Carbury, County Kildare

Battersby, author of *The Age of Newgrange*, who was the first to propose that the mythical Nuadu silver hand might have been inspired by the constellation which we know today as Orion. Our reasons for connecting Nuadu with Orion might have been somewhat different to those of Battersby, but nonetheless, he is to be credited for what was a significant statement.

Battersby proposed that Nuadu was a "walker god". Citing Stonehenge author John North as his inspiration,[36] Battersby equated Orion with the "walker god" Nuadu, who would be seen to walk along the ridge across the River Boyne from Newgrange in the Neolithic.[37] He furthermore stated that North's discovery "reveals a feature of Newgrange and Loughcrew likely to play a big part in the ultimate decipherment of the two sites and indeed the whole period".[38]

And we are inclined to agree, but before we reach Newgrange we must explore Nuadu's links with Tara.

It is a matter of extraordinary coincidence that, at the time the Boyne monuments were constructed, the brightest star in the sky, Sirius, the "Dog Star", shared the same declination as the winter solstice sun, and therefore rose and set at the same place on the horizon as the sun did on the shortest day of the year. Viewed from Amergin's mound at Millmount, Sirius would set precisely in the direction of the Hill of Tara. This is interesting because of an episode involving Cúchulainn, another giant warrior who could easily be equated with Orion, in which he attempted to woo Emer.[39] Emer told him, "I am a Tara of women . . . the whitest of

73

maidens, one who is gazed at but who gazes not back, a rush too far to be reached, an untrodden way . . ."[40]

Throughout the ages, Sirius has been connected to Orion by astronomers and star gazers because Orion is seen to herald the rising of the Dog Star. Canis Major, the large dog, has "from the earliest times" been known as the "Dog of Orion".[41] In fact, the three stars of Orion's belt form an imaginary line which points in the direction of Sirius. In Greek legend, the two dog constellations, Canis Major and Canis Minor, were the hunting dogs of Orion.[42]

With Sirius setting over Tara in the Neolithic, could this event have been presaged by something Orion did? Surely if the rising of Sirius is preceded, or announced, by Orion, it follows that Orion sets before Sirius does. Using astronomy software widely available for the home computer,[43] we can take ourselves back in time to the Neolithic and recreate what the sky looked like back then. And it did look somewhat different.

Due to a phenomenon called precession of the equinoxes, the sun's vernal point – that is the point where the sun's path crosses the celestial equator at the vernal equinox, is slowly drifting westwards through the 12 zodiac constellations. One complete cycle takes 25,920 years.[44] Back in the

In the Neolithic, Orion set directly over Tara viewed from Millmount in Drogheda.
Is this the king touching the Lia Fáil?

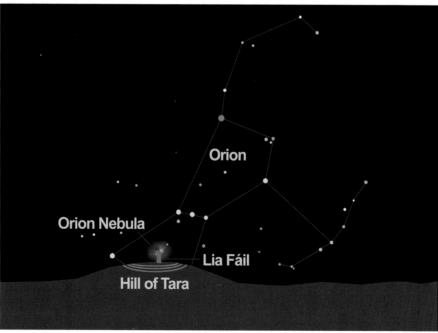

Neolithic, the vernal point was in Taurus, the bull constellation, a possible explanation for the persistence of bull mythology in Ireland.

With our computer locked on the date 3200 BC, the epoch for the construction of Newgrange, the other Boyne mounds (including Millmount) and the Duma na nGiall on Tara, we can take a clear look at how the constellations were behaving in the Stone Age.

Looking towards the southwest, we see that Sirius, the Dog Star, shares the same setting place as the winter solstice sun. If we work backwards in time from the setting of Sirius, we see that the Orion constellation, our Nuadu, does something very interesting. After "walking along the ridge", he appears to set over the Hill of Tara, with Millmount as our viewing location. Specifically, the famous "Orion Nebula" sets at the winter solstice point. This would mean that astronomers would have viewed three important settings over Tara – the winter solstice sun; Sirius, the brightest star in the night sky; and the "walker god" constellation, Nuadu, the King of Tara.

Leafing through our old *Foclóir*,[45] we found that one way of referring to Orion in Irish is "*slat an ríogh*", which, literally translated, means the "sceptre of the king".[46] In another *Foclóir*, we find that *Slat an Rí* specifically refers to Orion's Belt.[47] We read also that the belt and dagger were known as "an tSlat agus an bhannlámh".[48] *Bannlámh* is a unit of measure, the equivalent of a cubit, also called a "bandle", but one must wonder in the case of Orion if *Bannlámh* was a corruption of *Bán-Lámh,* which would mean "white hand". *Bann* on its own can mean a belt, a chain, or a band,[49] reminding us of "Lug's Chain", which, according to Charles Squire, was the Milky Way.[50]

If all of this seemed a bit circumstantial, our guess that Nuadu could be Orion was cemented through the association of his nickname with the Milky Way. *Airget* (the first component of the name *airgetlámh*) is an old Irish word for "silver", and is also used to describe money, presumably because of its metallic composition. The fixing of a silver hand for Nuadu by Diancecht seems to fit better in a Hollywood film than it does in an old Irish myth.[51] But if we take a closer look at the typical representation of the Orion constellation, we see that his upraised arm sits amidst the bright band of the Milky Way galaxy, which, in this area of the sky, runs past Orion's left shoulder, marked by the red giant star Betelgeuse.

Nuadu's sobriquet, "Silver Hand", was probably derived by the myth makers from the fact that the Nuadu constellation's upraised hand is embedded in the silvery Milky Way.

TOUCHING THE STONE

In the collection of placename lore, the *Dindshenchas*, we see that the River Boyne, which we have already linked with the Milky Way, is described thus:

> From the well of righteous Mochua
> to the bounds of Meath's wide plain,
> the Arm of Nuadu's Wife and her Leg
> are the two noble and exalted names.
> From the bounds of goodly Meath
> till she reaches the sea's green floor
> she is called the Great Silver Yoke
> and the White Marrow of Fedlimid.[52]

These metrical verses describe the origin of place names on the ground, but could this also be a description of the heavenly Boyne, the *Bealach na Bó Finne?* The "Great Silver Yoke", besides its obvious link with Nuadu's upraised silver hand, also brings to mind "Lug's Chain", the Milky Way, because the word "yoke" can mean something which binds, or forms a bond, like a chain. But the verse explicitly states that the river's two names were the "Arm of Nuadu's Wife and her Leg". Leg is translated from *Colptha*, so we see again a possible connection on the ground at Inbher Colptha, the meeting of the waters in the Boyne Estuary. And that's where we meet Amergin the astronomer and his burial mound, the Millmount, which is the crucial keystone for the interpretation of Tara's astronomical myths.

In the course of our investigations, we were continuously seeing a strong connection between the sky and ground, through the astromyths. If Nuadu was the Orion of the ancients, there are other elements of the star stories which make sense in the context of a sky–ground connection.

The *Lia Fáil*, as we stated earlier, was one of the four great treasures of the Tuatha Dé Danann. This stone is currently located atop the "Forradh", the "King's Seat", but had been moved there from a location beside the Mound of the Hostages after the 1798 Irish rebellion.[53]

There is some debate as to whether this stone is the true Stone of Fal, but its phallic shape would suggest it is.[54] Its form reminds us very much of the Lady's Finger, which was discussed in Chapter 2. The *Lia Fáil* is ten feet in length, with only about half of its total length protruding from the ground. It has also been referred to as the "Penis Stone".[55]

According to tradition, the *Lia Fáil* would "roar under the foot of each king that took possession of the throne of Ireland".[56] That tradition furthermore states that the name of the stone is derived from *Fo-Áil,* which means the "under-stone", that is, the "stone under the king".[57] The *Lia Fáil* is commonly referred to as the "Stone of Destiny".

If we imagine ourselves perched atop Amergin's Millmount back in the Stone Age, the "Nuadu constellation" would set in the direction of the Hill of Tara. In other words, the king appears to be touching the *Lia Fáil.* Is this what the legend of the *Lia Fáil* is about? Orion's setting over Tara could be encoded in the astro-myth as the king touching, or sitting on, or even putting his foot on, the *Lia Fáil.* Remember that after the invasion of the Milesians, Eremon became king, ruling from Tara, a place chosen for him by, among others, Amergin, whose nickname was "bright knee". The bright foot, or knee star, now known under its Arabic name "Rigel",[58] which may have signified the "left leg of the giant",[59] would appear to set in the general direction of the Hill of Tara viewed from Millmount.

It is tempting to think of another link, this time between two of the great Tuatha Dé Danann artifacts, which could be said to come together through the interpretation of the myths. In its typical configuration, the constellation Orion is shown as a mighty hunter or warrior, with his sword hanging in its sheath beneath

The Lia Fáil

his belt. Specifically, the Orion Nebula is said to represent the hilt of his sword. If we think of Nuadu in this typical configuration, the hilt of his sword, Nuadu's Sword, "touched" the *Lia Fáil,* the "stone under the king", as the constellation set over Tara.

We can take the interpretation of the myths even further still. Nuadu (also known as Nechtain), owned the mysterious well of Carbury, which he kept closely guarded by three cup bearers. It was this well which, as we described already, burst forth when his wife, Bóann, disobeyed him and approached it. Another name for Nechtain's Well was the "Well of Segais". The word *segais* can mean both "pleasure" or "joy" and "a wood" or "a wooded height".[60] The well was said to be the source of supernatural knowledge, and around it grew nine hazel trees, the nuts of which fell into the water.[61] The hazel tree is traditionally associated with wisdom, fertility and kingship in Ireland.[62] Incidentally, Tara was described as a "pleasant hazel wood" in the *Dindshenchas*.[63]

It's possible that the ancient astronomer builders thought of the mysterious Orion Nebula, that hazy, milky patch beneath Orion's Belt, as the well from which the waters of the Milky Way emanated.[64] In the Stone Age, about 500 years before the completion of Newgrange, the Orion Nebula set directly over Carbury when viewed from Millmount (remembering that neither Tara nor Carbury are visible from Millmount.)[65] Could it be that the ancients were commemorating a previous time when the Nechtain's Well of the sky set over the Nechtain's Well on the ground, something which no longer happened due to the effects of precession?

One indigenous concept involving the belt stars of Orion may have equated them with the hazel nuts, the nuts of wisdom. The Arabs were said to have known Orion's Belt as the "golden nuts".[66] There are esoteric connections with the hazel nuts which can be made through the

The Orion Nebula (photo: © Mike Fleenor)

sky–ground legends. Hazel trees are traditionally noted for growing beside water, and a forked rod of hazel is used by diviners in this country to find sources of underground water.[67] Did the ancients make this connection in their sky myths, with the hazel rod (Orion's belt) divining for water in the mysterious Well of Segais (Orion Nebula)?

There could be a fertility or sexual significance involved in the Millmount-Tara-Carbury alignment also, suggested by the idea that there was a gushing forth of water from Nechtain's Well, his sceptre. The Nechtain's Well of the sky did, at the likely time of Millmount's construction, set over the *Lia Fáil*, the "penis stone". Michael Slavin connects the "obvious phallic symbolism" of the stone with the ritual marriage which the true king underwent with the "goddess of sovereignty".[68]

We could also think of the three belt stars of Orion as the three cup bearers. These three characters are named in the *Dindshenchas* as Flesc, Lam and Luam.[69] The meaning of their names can all be connected to the Nuadu constellation. *Flesc* means a "rod", *Fleasc Ríoghda* meaning "a sceptre".[70] We saw earlier how the Irish phrase for Orion's Belt is *Slat an Ríogh*, "sceptre of the king". *Lam* is probably from *Lámh*, which means "hand", bringing to mind Nuadu of the silver hand. *Luam* means a "leader" or "champion",[71] bringing to mind both Nuadu, the king or leader, and Amergin, who described himself as a "gigantic, sword-wielding champion".

Esoteric connections aside, it is clear that there is a strong body of circumstantial evidence to connect Nuadu with Orion, and to indicate probable associations between the sky and the ground, through myths, monuments and astronomy, in ancient times.

We picture Lugh of the Long Arm in a similar light to Nuadu.[72] He may well be a later Orion. "It was claimed of Lugh, the Superman of these wonder-tales, that on a morning when he stood on the rampart of Tara, people thought the sun had risen in the west, so bright did his countenance shine. The Milky Way he wore as a silver chain around his neck . . ."[73] Charles Squire goes further, telling us explicitly that, "the Milky Way was called 'Lugh's Chain'."[74]

THE SALMON OF KNOWLEDGE

Another giant hero of Irish Lore is Fionn Mac Cumhaill, and yet again we see a connection with Orion. He lived, we are told, in Almhuin of Leinster (Hill of Allen), "where the white dun was made by Nuada of the Tuatha Dé Danann . . . and that got its name from the great herd of cattle that died fighting one time around the well . . ."[75]

His name, Mac Cumhaill, is the same as that of one of the three Tuatha Dé Danann kings killed by the Milesians at Teltown. Literally, it means "son of the hazel".[76] Fionn Mac Cumhaill's great wisdom came from the famed "Salmon of Knowledge", which was said to have swam in the well of Segais. The nuts from the hazel trees growing over the well fell into the water and the salmon ate them, thereby gaining the "knowledge of all things". While helping the druid Finnéces to roast the Salmon of Knowledge on a spit, Fionn burned his thumb on the salmon and immediately placed his thumb in his mouth to relieve the pain. From that moment, Fionn would only have to suck his thumb to see into the future.

The tale of Fionn Mac Cumhaill is rich in symbolism, but there is a common thread with the Nuadu and Amergin tales. Amergin had, in his famous poem, declared "I am a salmon in the water", sometimes translated "I am a salmon in a pool". Nuadu, of course, was the original owner of the well in which the Salmon of Knowledge ate the hazel nuts.

In one tale connecting Fionn with Tara, we are told that he volunteered to guard Tara alone one night against attack from a troublesome goblin known as "Aillen of the flaming breath", who had caused chaos at the Tara assembly every year by burning it down.[77]

Alone on Tara after dark, he was joined by an elderly warrior called Fiacha, who produced "an enchanted spear, wrought in the Otherworld by Len of Loch Lene, who beat into it the heat of the sun and the light of the moon and all the stars".[78] He was told to press the tip of the spear against his forehead to keep him awake. The rest, as they say, is history – Fionn defeated the goblin.

Fionn's home, the Hill of Allen, is located less than ten miles southeast of Nechtain's Well in County Kildare, lying somewhat to the east of where Orion was setting in the Neolithic.

Another king of Tara, Conn Cétchathach, "Conn of the Hundred Battles", was said to have seized power from Cathaír Mór. He closely guarded Tara for fear of it being seized by the people of the Sídh (the Tuatha Dé Danann or the "people of the otherworld") or the Fomorians.[79] "Conn was in Teamhair one time, and he went up in the early morning to the Rath of the Kings at the rising of the sun . . ."[80] The reason for his daily observations? – to guard against any attack by "aerial beings".[81]

On the day of his first observation, he stood upon "a stone that was in the rath" and it screamed under his feet, a scream heard "all over Teamhair and as far as Bregia".[82] This is a slightly different rendition of the Nuadu–Lia Fáil sky myth. Incidentally, *Conn* means "dog" or "hound", a connection, perhaps, with the Dog Star which also set at Tara from Millmount in the Neolithic.

The kings of Tara were often referred to as the *Ard Rí*, the "High Kings". The word *ard* can mean "high, lofty" or "above the ground, elevated".[83] This could be a hint at the astral context of many of the myths. The word *ard* meaning "high" would ultimately become central to our eventual decipherment of many things connecting sky and ground.[84]

MOUND OF THE HOSTAGES

The myths, as we have demonstrated, speak volumes about the heavens, but what of the actual monuments? Is there anything in the physical remains at Tara which can tell us of an ancient interest in the sky at this ancient seat of the High Kings?

The Duma na nGiall (Mound of the Hostages) is one of only two monuments remaining on the Hill of Tara which can be definitively linked with the Stone Age, along with the earlier mentioned palisaded enclosure. Everything else, we are told, came later. The Mound of the Hostages is the only example at Tara of the "passage-tomb" type of monument, and is minuscule in comparison with the great Boyne Valley passage-tombs, which are, in some cases, four times larger in diameter.[85]

There is a single passage in the Mound of the Hostages, which is undifferentiated,[86] measuring four metres long. There is one single engraved stone in this passage, on the southern wall. The main motif on this stone is a central series of concentric circles with a large dot in the centre. Martin Brennan found that the short undifferentiated passage of Duma na nGiall was aligned towards sunrise on the so-called "cross-quarter days" of November and February.[87] He decribed how the beam of light entering the mound was formed by a sillstone, a lintel and two uprights at the entrance.[88] The resulting light beam leaves a 48-inch wide stream of light on the back stone of the chamber. The cross-quarter sunrise is precisely pinpointed when this patch of light is centred on the backstone. Brennan compares the Mound of the Hostages with two cairns at

Decorated stone in the passage of the Mound of the Hostages

Loughcrew, Cairns L and U, which he says are also both aligned on the February and November cross-quarter day sunrises.

Brennan points out a connection between the Samhain (November) alignment of the Mound of the Hostages and the great Samhain *feis* said to have been held at Tara. Samhain marked the beginning of the winter season, the "dark half" of the year, in ancient Ireland. This "first half" of the year began with a great November feast, which was marked by the lighting of great fires.[89] Samhain was the most significant of the cross-quarter celebrations because it marked the Celtic new year.[90]

At Tara, the winter *Feis* was an "important institution".[91] At this great festival, "the kings of the provinces and their chieftains, together with the *ollamhs* and law-makers, met under the High King to settle matters of national importance . . ."[92] We are furthermore told the assembly lasted for "three days before Samhain and three days after".[93]

There could be further astronomical significance to some of the other monuments at Tara. Just to the west of the Mound of the Hostages, there once stood another mound, called the *"Siar Dúbho na Bó"* on O'Donovan's plan of the monuments at Tara.[94] Translated, this means the "Western Mound of the Cow called Glas Teamhrach",[95] echoing the magical cow *Glas Ghoibhneann* which we met at Balor's Strand in Chapter 1.

Regrettably, the Western Mound of the Cow has been destroyed since O'Donovan compiled his charts and records of Tara's monuments for the Ordnance Survey in 1836. There are some indications of the location of this mound in certain aerial photographs, but the mound itself has all but disappeared. It was still there in 1839, when historian George Petrie described it as being six feet high and 40 feet in diameter at the base.[96]

The "Mound of the Cow" is described in the *Dindshenchas* as being "west of the Mound of the Hostages". Perhaps it too, like the Duma na nGiall, once had a passage orientated towards the sun – and, most likely, the moon too.

A short passage such as that of the Mound of the Hostages would naturally admit a range of sunrises, except where those sunrises are blocked by some intervening landscape feature, such as a hill. In the case of Duma na nGiall, there are no such obstructions.

Using SkyMap Pro to take us back to the Neolithic period, we can calculate that the declination of the sun at the November cross-quarter day (half-way between autumn equinox and winter solstice measured in days) was approximately −16.5°.[97] This would place the sunrise on the horizon at an azimuth of 118°.[98]

Another feature of SkyMap Pro allows us to examine the declinations of the moon over the 18.6-year term during which it completes one cycle of extremes. Minor standstill south[99] rising position for the year 3200 BC was 121.5°, based on a declination of –18.75°. This is just 3.5°, or the equivalent of about seven sun widths, away from the rising position of the November cross-quarter sun.

Brennan does not provide us with exact data about how a moonbeam at minor standstill might behave in the passage. A precise range of dates during which the sun penetrates the Duma na nGiall at the time of cross-quarter would be enormously helpful towards the process of identification of how and if the moon might illuminate its interior.[100]

We know that the megalithic astronomers would have watched and recorded each sunrise for a couple of weeks either side of an event such as the cross-quarter sunrise in order to ensure the maximum accuracy of the final structure. If, as Brennan states, the patch of sunlight at Samhain is centered on the back stone in Duma na nGiall, it is likely that the "patch of moonlight" at minor standstill would be somewhat to the right of centre, perhaps striking one of the orthostats[101] on the northern wall of the passage. Again, because of the short length of the passage, it is highly likely the standstill moon would shine in. Whether or not this was the original intent of the builders – to capture both the cross-quarter sunrise and the minor standstill moonrise – is a matter of conjecture at this point.

All the minor standstill events are similarly close to the cross-quarter horizon points. There is limited evidence, some of it presented by Brennan, that there could be more than one target involved with certain passages. The proximity of cross-quarter and minor standstill azimuths would be central to our investigation of Dowth, and later we will show how Newgrange was probably built to accept light from numerous heavenly targets.

The moon-Venus conjunction theme we met at Baltray and Drogheda continues at Tara, where there are two wells called the "Well of the White Cow" and the "Well of the Calf".[102] These wells are located on opposite sides of the hill, the White Cow Well being on the eastern slope, and the Calf Well on the western incline.[103] The *Dindshenchas* refers to the "*Tipra Bó Finne*" (well of the white cow) as having numerous names, including "the well of the numbering of the clans" and makes succinct reference to the geographical separation of the cow and calf wells by saying of the latter, "calf is its name, though it never sucked a cow".

Just to the north of the Mound of the Hostages is the Rath of the Synods, in Irish *Rath na Seanad,* which was vandalised during the "excavations" carried out by the British Israelites in 1899. "Seanad" is a word which can mean "a synod", or "a union" and "a reunion".

To the north of Rath na Seanad is the linear monument Teach Miodchuarta, known as "The Banqueting House". It is here, according to legends, that the five great roads of Ireland had their junction.[104] Brennan notes that the Great Hall appears to form a north-south alignment with the Mound of the Hostages, and therefore would mark the position of the midday sun.[105]

A precise north–south alignment of such an extensive linear earthwork, which is 180 metres long,[106] would indicate a keen knowledge of astronomy, and suggests an insight into the movements of the stars around the northern pole of the sky. This alignment could be connected with the star Deneb, which is the brightest star of the swan constellation, Cygnus. In his epic work on Stonehenge, John North said, "It will shortly be noted in connection with tomb architecture that an approximate north–south line was associated with the behaviour of the star Deneb . . ."[107] Such an alignment with the swan constellation is also interesting because the banqueting hall points towards the distant peaks of a range of hills known as Slieve Breagh, part of which was called *Sliabh na gCearc,* the "Hill of the Hen".[108] In Chapter 7, we will examine the swan constellation and its apparent link with ancient Newgrange.

Just before we leave Tara for Brú na Bóinne, we must make mention of a few interesting alignments, such as the fact that Fourknocks lies exactly due east of Duma na nGiall.[109] Fourknocks is the location of a "passage-tomb cemetery",[110] and was the target of an alignment of the two standing stones at Baltray. The main tomb at Fourknocks[111] contains an interesting array of megalithic motifs on its chamber stones, and overall, the mound is almost identical in diameter to the Duma na nGiall at 19 metres.[112] This small but significant passage-tomb is, like the others along the Boyne and at Tara, a crucial piece of the sky-ground jigsaw, as we will see in Chapter 7.

The sunset from Tara on the summer solstice occurs over the town of Kells, just to the right of the Hill of Lloyd, as witnessed by Richard Moore on 21 June 2003. There is a "late prehistoric hillfort" on the Hill of Lloyd,[113] along with a small cluster of other sites consisting of three enclosures and two tumuli.[114] The river which runs to the north is called the Blackwater, "Abhainn Dubh". To the south are townlands called Newrath Big and Newrath Little. A townland to the northwest of Kells is called "Moat", where there is a motte and a nearby enclosure,[115] while southeast of Kells is a townland called Gardenrath.

Contemplating the summer solstice sunset on the warm June evenings of the year, we must now depart towards another place at which the summer solstice was important. The best way to leave Tara – if you can afford it – is by helicopter, because the only place from which Tara can truly be appreciated is the sky. As we lift off on our imaginary flight, we begin to visualise the monumental scale of the earthworks on its summit. There are large ringed embankments encompassed by an even bigger circular monument which appears to surround the entire hill. As we ascend towards the clouds, our view takes in the huge Banqueting Hall, and farther to the north east are more rings on the edge of the western slope of the hill. As we turn towards Brú na Bóinne, we peer down on the enormous Rath na Ríogh and it brings the heavens to mind. With its small circles set inside a much larger ring, it could almost be a sort of moon map. Contemplating the purpose and meaning of the giant rings, we turn swiftly away from Tara, home of the "high" kings of old, and head towards another huge ring in the landscape overlooking the Boyne, and to another piece of the complex, and ancient, sky–ground puzzle.

Aerial view of Tara

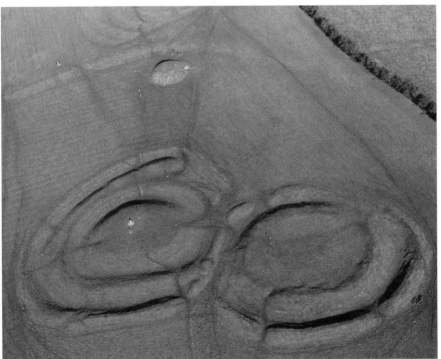

CHAPTER FIVE

COSMIC CIRCLES:
THE GIANT RINGS

The hill of the hound became a mountain of fire as dawn broke and the sun spilled its warm light across the Boyne Valley.

It was just after 5.00 am on St John's Eve.[1] There was a fresh breeze blowing and, up until the moment of daybreak, Richard and I had been wishing we had stayed in bed. "The ancient sky watchers must have had unusual sleeping patterns," I thought to myself as the rush of the wind set the branches above our heads dancing and rustling as if it were October, not June.

Such is the difference in the length of day at this latitude, you can watch sunrise at 9.00 am at Newgrange on winter solstice, but on the summer solstice, the sun announces the day shortly after 5.00 am. In winter, the nights are eternally long, and the light of the brief day seems like that from a candle which burns only for a moment. During summer, in contrast, there is no such thing as a black night. For about five weeks

Map showing the main sites at Brú na Bóinne
(adapted from Eogan (1986); O'Kelly (1982); Cooney (2000))

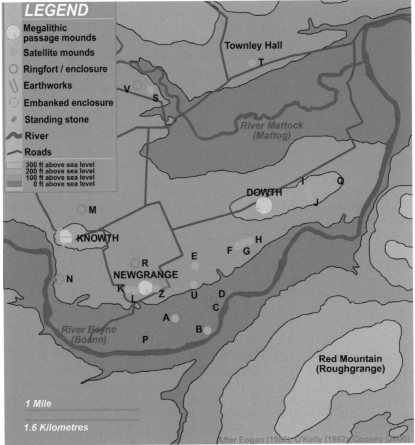

either side of the longest day, there is a constant blue glow on the northern horizon, giving off enough light to see clearly in the dark.

Standing as we were at an ancient circular amphitheatre-like monument, unglamorously named "Site Q" by some archaeologist of old, we were about to experience a trip through time. We were hoping to witness a dawn of the Bronze Age. At last, we were promised the chance to test our own theory. If we were right, and if the cloud broke in the right place at the right time, we would witness something which had not been seen for a very long time.

Site Q is what archaeologists call a "henge" or an "embanked enclosure". Sir William Wilde, the noted antiquarian, who wrote about the Boyne Valley in the mid-nineteenth-century, reported that Site Q was said to be the second-largest "ring-fort or military rath" structure in Ireland, after the Giant's Ring near Belfast in Antrim.[2] Standing there at five o'clock in the morning, its giant banks looming before us, it certainly seemed like the biggest monument we had ever seen.

This egg-shaped enclosure sits on a gentle slope not far from the great megalithic cairn of Dowth, one of the three great passage-mounds of Brú na Bóinne, the so-called "Bend of the Boyne" assembly. The banks of Site Q are at their highest on its southwestern end. It is here, on the higher end of the slope, that there is a large break in the embankment, like a great opening into this quasi-circular amphitheatre, an entrance of sorts into a monument so different from the great passage-mounds, yet having many similarities. There are four of these embanked enclosures in the Bend of the Boyne, and a further nine in the lowland river valleys of the wider area.[3] Dowth henge measures some 175 metres across at its widest point,[4] but although other henges in the region are larger,[5] none is as visually impressive and well preserved as Site Q.[6]

Standing outside the sacred space of this giant ring, peering in through the 20-metre-wide "entrance" on the south-western side, we can clearly see, on the opposite end of the monument, another, similar opening. Our theory (and our reason for being at Dowth Q at 5.00 am on a June morning) was that the two breaches in the henge wall were lined up intentionally with the rising of the summer solstice sun.

We had arrived at 4.40 am and for 20 minutes or so we waited under a tree, trying to shelter from the wind, only emerging to set up my camera on its tripod and to take compass measurements. Suddenly, there was a small break along the north-eastern horizon in that belly of fast-moving cloud which had threatened to ruin our morning. The distant hill of Castlecoo – *Caislean Có* – "fort of the hound",[7] at Clogherhead, was crowned with a

Anthony Murphy witnesses summer solstice dawn at Site Q

rim of blazing red below a thick black blanket of broken stratocumulus. Sunbeams reached upwards from beneath the horizon. It was clear the sun was going to rise in the right direction. That fact allowed us to breathe a slight sigh of relief.

But the weather was determined to spoil our show. At the critical moment, cloud blocked the instant of sunrise. We waited anxiously for what seemed like an eternity, and then, just as hope was fading, the sun broke through and cast its long arms across the fields.

We felt a warm joy in our hearts and the struggle to get out of bed at 4.00 am was finally justified. The two entrances or gaps of the henge lined up towards the rising of the midsummer sun. But what was the significance of this, and were we the only ones to have witnessed it since the monument was built?

SUMMER SOLSTICE AT SITE Q

One major significance linking Site Q with our other discoveries is the involvement of a placename meaning "hound". It brought to mind the "Cú-Collon" alignment outlined in Chapter 3. Here again we had a place, an eminence or horizon feature, seemingly connected to a constellation housing the sun on the solstice in former times.

But the large henge structures were not built at the same time as the passage-mounds, according to archaeologists. They came a number of centuries, possibly even a millennium, after the passage-tomb phase, in the early Bronze Age.[8] The giant rings are not contemporary with the great mounds. They mark a later phase of activity, and a shift in the type of monument constructed.

That said, the astronomical link still stands. Throughout the thousand years following the construction of Newgrange, Knowth, Dowth and Millmount, the sun remained housed in the constellation of the hound (Leo) during summer solstice. In the late Neolithic, it was located under the middle of the hound. Around the year 2000 BC, the slow process known today as "precession of the equinoxes"[9] had caused the summer solstice sun to drift westwards, placing it just above the hound's forepaw, not far from the bright star known as Regulus or Alpha Leonis.

Another major significance of the "discovery" was the realisation that there must have been a continuity of influence from the cosmos on the construction of monumental structures in the Bend of the Boyne over a period of time, perhaps as much as a thousand years. It is widely known throughout the world that Newgrange features an alignment homing in on winter solstice sunrise, while the nearby passage-mound at Dowth also featured a winter alignment, this time on winter solstice sunset.[10]

This fresh revelation about prehistoric astronomy seemed to indicate that the extent to which the sky was a factor in the ancient architecture was perhaps wider than believed. But archaeological opinion on the matter of the Site Q openings is somewhat divided.

Some time after we witnessed the St John's Eve sunrise at the Dowth henge,

Diagram showing the summer solstice alignment at Site Q

Site Q
After Stout (1991)

Summer Solstice
sunrise

Northeast gap

Scarped area

Southwest gap

Scarped area

N

Henge embankment   Top of bank

which was in the summer of 2000, archaeologist Geraldine Stout sent me a copy of her paper on the Boyne region henges. It was a comprehensive and fascinating study of the 13 "rings", and provided us with a broad archaeological insight into the structure and size of the henges.

But there was one niggling detail. In the section relating to the Dowth henge, the archaeologist brought attention to the gap at the northeast end of the monument, suggesting that it was not contemporary with the construction of the site.[11] Stout said the following of the Dowth Henge: "The second opening, in the north-east . . . was marked by a dotted line on the OS first edition map. Today the bank at either end of this break narrows considerably and there are traces of a narrower bank continuing across part of the break, leaving a gap of 5m. A slight rise and a definite fall to the exterior along this opening in line with the bank make it highly probable that this opening is not contemporary with the construction of the enclosure".[12] If there was only one gap originally, that which looked like an entrance on the southwest, then it follows that there may have been no intended alignment towards Summer Solstice built into the structure of the rampart. So the place name "Hill of the Fort of the Hound" would no longer make any sense from an astronomical perspective.

Henges are sometimes found to have contained post-holes or stone settings within their enclosed spaces,[13] something which has not yet been confirmed to be a feature at Site Q because of lack of conclusive archaeological data obtained from digging or other methods, such as those used to find the giant circle of post holes at Tara.[14] If Site Q did have posts as part of its integral structure, perhaps these featured some alignment to Summer Solstice which would make sense of the Hill of the Hound. With no hard facts to hand, we could not say either way.

For the time being, it became a grey area, something which was only exacerbated by the writings of another eminent archaeologist, Professor Michael J. O'Kelly, the man who excavated Newgrange. O'Kelly pointed

Summer solstice sunrise looking through the two gaps of Site Q

out that the first edition Ordnance Survey map and a field survey of the time marked the north-east gap as a dotted circle and symbols representing "bushes and scrub".[15] He continued: "Even today this opening is narrower than the other and one is led to the belief that it was breached in modern times to facilitate the movement of farm machinery, as the enclosure has been constantly under tillage."[16]

Even William Wilde, Oscar Wilde's father, referred to only one of the openings in his 1847 book. Having said this, he does not categorically state that there was just one entrance, but simply says, "It [Site Q] is about 300 paces in circumference, round the top of the embankment, and has a large opening on the south-western side."[17]

Geraldine Stout suggested to me in a telephone conversation that perhaps the site was concerned with the winter solstice sunset, and that an observer situated in the centre of the site, looking out through the entrance, would see the sun set in that direction on the shortest day of the year. If this was the case, the site mirrored the nearby passage-tomb at Dowth, where one of its chambers is illuminated by the sun at winter solstice.[18] Such an alignment, with an observer placed in the centre of Site Q looking out of the southwestern gap, might involve the Hill of Tara, which lies in that approximate direction.[19]

Without further evidence, we could not ascertain whether or not the design of this great site had any inspiration from the heavens. In any case, connecting earthen henge monuments with the heavens is a contentious issue. While alignments involving circles of standing stones can be clearly defined, usually involving two or three stones aligning to a rising or setting point on the horizon, with embanked enclosures the question of definitive alignments becomes an area of ambiguity. Newgrange excavator Michael J. O'Kelly said: "Some are assumed to have served ritual and ceremonial purposes, others are sepulchral and some of the stone monuments in particular are nowadays being hailed as solar and/or lunar observatories".[20]

With the archaeological evidence to hand, and with so many other sites and myths and place names to investigate, Richard and I shelved our summer solstice theory for Site Q, or at least left it hanging, so that we could concentrate on other work.

SYNCHRONICITY

It was a long time before we would get excited about Site Q again. When it finally did happen, it came about by the most extraordinary coincidence, which must be detailed to be believed. A whole five years to the day after our 5.00 am "discovery" visit to the enormous egg-shaped enclosure, we found ourselves in delightful company at the Millmount in Drogheda. We had just been introduced to Ronald Hicks, a world expert on henges and Professor of Anthropology at Ball State University, Indiana, a man who was very familiar with henges, and with Site Q.

Our paths should probably never have crossed, but for a remarkable chance which came about in a rather extraordinary fashion. Richard and I had longed to start an annual festival of sorts at Millmount to commemorate its ancient mythical and astronomical links. We came up with the idea of a summer solstice festival, and had begun to organise an event which would include music, poetry reading and art. I flagged the event on our website. In the meantime, we both became waylaid and found ourselves with lots to do, so we were forced to abandon the idea of hosting a festival.

I was sitting at home on the longest day of the year when I received a phone call from Millmount. The woman on the phone asked, "Is this Anthony Murphy from Mythical Ireland?" "Yes, it is," said I. She informed me that there were two people up at the monument who were there to enjoy the "summer solstice festival" and who were asking why there was nobody around. They had read about it on our website. I had forgotten to provide an update saying the event was cancelled. Not wishing to disappoint them, I agreed to go over to Millmount and at least give these visitors some information about the place and the astronomical connections we had found. The couple were travelling through Ireland together and intended visiting the summer solstice festival at the Hill of Tara the next day.

While I was at Millmount, they introduced me to another young man, an American called Randy Wooldridge, who was apparently waiting for his university professor to turn up. Randy and his professor had agreed previously to meet in Drogheda on their way south to Cork. The professor, when he eventually turned up, was none other than Ronald Hicks. Randy introduced me to Professor Hicks, whose name I was very familiar with. In fact, I think I blathered out something like "You're Mister Henge, aren't you?" while shaking his hand.

We spent a good hour and a half atop the mound at Millmount, looking out over Drogheda and the Boyne Valley and the distant hills, talking excitedly about the things Richard and I had been discovering and the interesting parallels with Professor Hicks's own work. Professor Hicks and Randy were on a tight time schedule, so we reluctantly parted, but we agreed to continue corresponding via e-mail, something which later proved very important to our investigation of Site Q.

It was during that electronic correspondence that Professor Hicks made the following statement, which immediately grabbed my attention: "I think that there can be no question that the axis of Site Q was intentionally oriented on the solstices".[21] He referred to the solstices, in the plural. Furthermore, he had written about this 20 years previously, in a 1985 article in the US version of *Archaeoastronomy*. The place name myth from the *Dindshenchas* about Dowth, which will be discussed in Chapter 6, and which seemed to point to the summer rather than the winter solstice, supported that conclusion, he maintained.

In his 1985 article, he said the following of Site Q: "In Dowth Townland there also stands an impressive henge enclosure whose axis, and entrances, correspond to the summer solstice sunrise / winter solstice sunset line".[22] The article also referred to the Dowth legend, which he concluded appeared to be a "solstice legend, or at least a legend meant to explain why the almost endless days of summer are replaced by the darkness of winter."[23] Here was an internationally renowned expert who was not only supportive of the idea that Site Q was built with both solstices in mind, but who said the matter was beyond question.

But what about the ambiguity surrounding the north-eastern gap? Surely its condition could not be overlooked in the overall evaluation of the site? Professor Hicks said he understood the scepticism of archaeologists regarding the north-east entrance. "It certainly appears to have been mucked about in some ways. This is very evident on the aerial photos. But that doesn't necessarily mean that there wasn't an entrance there originally."[24]

The monument is situated on a gently sloping bank, which has the effect of putting the top of the embankment below the actual horizon when viewed from outside the south-western entrance looking towards the direction of the north-east gap and summer sunrise.

Viewed from the opposite side, the pinnacle of the bank acts like a false horizon. Perhaps this was an intentional and integral component of the structure's design?

Professor Hicks indicated that it would be difficult to ascertain whether the sloping location of the site was an essential part of its layout, but said, "I have certainly come to believe that the builders of these monuments had carefully thought out just about every aspect of the design, but sometimes it's hard to tell about specific elements."[25]

He had his own thoughts on the "mucked about" north-east gap: "I've wondered if the odd, built-up look of the northeast entrance may have been intentional to create a sort of artificial horizon or to make it clear that the proper 'entrance' (at least for people/viewers) was the one in the south-west."[26]

In this scenario, observers wishing to see the sunrise on the longest day would situate themselves outside of the "sacred space", so to speak, of the interior. In the absence of further archaeological data from Site Q, we cannot speculate on what structures may have been incorporated into this sacred space, whether they were used for astronomical purposes or for some ritual function.

What we do know is that a large circle of post-holes, perhaps some form of "woodhenge", was found during archaeological investigations just south of Newgrange. This woodhenge, or pit circle, produced Beaker and Grooved Ware pottery, indicating a date of "c. 2000 uncal BC for the building of a large ritual circle in the Boyne Valley."[27] Two much smaller pit circles were found, one at Knowth, near the entrance to the eastern passage,[28] and another a short distance to the west of Newgrange.[29] The Knowth post circle has been reconstructed as part of the archaeological

The reconstructed timber circle at Knowth

and restorative work there. It has been dated "towards the end of the Neolithic" and the structure had an opening on the east side.[30] Another pit circle, found at Balgatheran on Hill of Rath near Drogheda and discussed in Chapter 3, may have featured a winter solstice sunrise alignment.

Of the other large ring-shaped monuments present in the Bend of the Boyne assembly, little can be said of entrances or possible alignments. One, labelled Site N, sits on the edge of a steep bank overlooking the Boyne below. This site is like a viewing platform, offering breathtaking views down the Boyne valley towards Slane. One could easily imagine watching the stars from this elevated site. Another of the Boyne rings, Site P, which is situated at the edge of the Boyne River on its alluvial plain, may have had opposing entrances facing roughly towards the east and west.[31]

But none of the other rings was as well-preserved as Site Q, and there was further interesting data which might indicate that some cosmic connection was intended there. From the air, the Dowth enclosure is very obviously oval-shaped, but specifically like a squashed oval, wider towards the south-west. In fact, the most fitting description of its shape is that of an egg. This makes it similar in shape to Newgrange. Both the Dowth and Newgrange passage-tombs have entrances which appear to be oriented towards the winter solstice sun. Site Q's "main entrance" is also apparently oriented in the direction of the winter solstice.

SKY CIRCLES

Were there any lingering clues in the mythology and folklore of Brú na Bóinne that could tell us anything more about this great enclosure's cosmic connections?

There are plenty of mentions of the principal monuments of the Brú in early Irish literature. The passage-tombs of Knowth, Dowth and, particularly, Newgrange, feature prominently, as one might expect given the obvious scale and importance of the assembly in former times.

Mention of the other monuments is a bit more obscure. There is a "splendid-sounding list of monuments in the area" outlined in the *Book of Ballymote*,[32] according to the archaeologist Claire O'Kelly, who excavated Newgrange along with her husband, Michael J. O'Kelly. However, O'Kelly said the sites described in the *Book of Ballymote* "cannot be identified" and added that experts in Irish literature and tradition maintain the stories are founded on imagination.[33]

Another archaeologist who has worked extensively in the Boyne Valley is Geraldine Stout, whom we have met already. She has been able to identify at least some of the monuments from the lists given in both the *Book of Ballymote* and the *Dindshenchas*,[34] which itself contains two poems about *"Brug na Bóinde"*.

The first *Brug na Bóinde* poem in the *Dindshenchas* is described by Stout as "the first historic survey of the Brú in which individual monuments are interpreted in the light of traditional mythology".[35] One monument, called "The *Mur* (wall) of the great Queen (of the Dagda)" is said to have been among the monuments visible at the Brú "in the days of Kineth O'Hartigan", the man who composed the *Dindshenchas* poems about the Brú.[36]

We are tempted to think this "wall of the queen" is Site Q. The "great Queen" of the Dagda would refer to Bóann, who was often considered to be wife of the Dagda in the old myths,[37] even though in other myths, such as the Nechtain's Well story, she was married to Nechtain. Another ancient place described in the *Dindshenchas* is Tara, which was said to have been derived from *Téa-Múr,* meaning the "wall" or "rampart" of Téa,[38] and the *Dindshenchas* describes how:

> Round her house was built a rampart
> by Téa daughter of Lugaid;
> she was buried beyond the wall without,
> so that from her is Temair named.[39]

The *Dindshenchas* appears to accurately describe the large earthen enclosures atop the Hill of Tara. Perhaps the "wall of the great queen" was Site Q. Bóann, as a personage representing the moon, has strong connections with the Boyne Valley megaliths.

As we will see in Chapter 6, the old *Dindshenchas* story about how Dowth got its name seems to have a strong solstice and eclipse influence. Ronald Hicks alludes to this when he says the Dowth legend is a "clear example of a solstice legend, or at least a legend meant to explain why the almost endless days of summer are replaced by the darkness of winter."[40] Whether we are supposed to view both the Neolithic passage-mound and the later enclosure within the context of the *Dindshenchas* poem about Dowth, we cannot know.[41] What we do know is that both sites share a solstice connection.

The "illuminated cow" goddess, Bóann, is intrinsically associated with the Milky Way, a "giant ring" of sorts which arcs across the vault of the heavens. In some parts of Ireland, the Milky Way was known as *Ceann Síne.* While *ceann* is a word that can mean head, top, roof or even finish,[42] *síne* specifically means "chain".[43] This chain, which is no doubt of similar derivation in the oral sky-lore tradition to "Lugh's Chain" discussed in Chapter 4, was undoubtedly viewed as a complete loop encircling the Earth. Perhaps it is from this giant ring that Dowth Q takes inspiration for its design, its shape and its sheer scale. We will see in Chapter 7 how the Milky Way and the horizon were uniquely linked and how this may have contributed to the inspiration behind the design of Newgrange.

Bóann, the "great goddess of the winter sky", is also represented by her birth-giving aspect or the splitting of an egg into halves.[44] Looking down at Site Q from the air, we see this image starkly imprinted onto the Boyne landscape. One study which examines the astronomy underlying Celtic and Greek mythology suggests that the "cosmological idea of the splitting of the primordial egg finds its roots in the Paleolithic Era where images of water, a water bird, eggs, a doe, and a woman are found."[45] In the later Neolithic era, vase paintings and frescos also depict the world forming from this primordial splitting egg.[46]

Aerial view of Site Q

Poet and author, Robert Graves, in his singular exploration of the "White Goddess", says the "world-egg", which was laid by the "Great Goddess", was split open by the Demiurge, whom Graves identifies as Helios, the Sun.[47] Perhaps this is the vision which unfolds at Site Q at the solstices – the giant world egg being split into two by a beam of the sun? Whatever its inspiration, the circular (or almost-circular) shape is seen in ancient architecture with fairly unbroken continuity right from the Neolithic through to the Early Christian era, a period covering over three millennia.

Ronald Hicks is intrigued by the fact that, although there are some rectangular houses in the early Neolithic (including at least one example in County Louth), later the circular shape for houses and enclosures "becomes the dominant form, continuing into the Early Christian period when monastic enclosures also take that shape".[48]

A shift from the study of stars to the recording of the movements of the sun and moon would doubtless have led to the use of "more strictly circular ditch systems", as seems to have happened in Britain, where the single-ditched long barrow was replaced by circular shapes.[49] Henge expert and Stonehenge author John North explains why this change came about: "The reason is that their [sun and moon] rising and setting positions mark out nearly symmetrical arcs in their cycles . . . with a circle this will allow observation in *all* possible directions, given the right observation point."[50]

Matthew Stout, who has collaborated with his wife Geraldine on various archaeological work in the Boyne Valley, is a renowned expert on ringforts. He says there are 45,000 known ringforts in Ireland,[51] a truly staggering number. These structures, which are generally "fairly circular", date in the main from the Early Christian period, and are considered to have been enclosed farmsteads.[52]

Apart from a continuity of shape, there is little to link the ringforts of early Christian Ireland to the giant ceremonial enclosures of the early Bronze Age. Stout says, "There's quite a gap between henges and enclosed farmsteads, something in the region of 2,200 years".[53]

Despite the apparent difference in purpose between the early henges and the much later ringforts, the ring shape was, as Hicks calls it, the "dominant form" for three thousand years, and it has its origins in the Neolithic. Because of the association of some monuments, both Neolithic passage-tombs and the ringed enclosures, with alignments involving the sun and moon, it is not beyond the realms of possibility that their circular shape was in some way a replication of the orbs of those heavenly bodies. One of the Boyne region henges, Rath Maeve, may well have marked the setting position of the sun viewed from Millmount, forming part of the unique estuary–source alignment which included Nechtain's Well at Carbury. It is conceivable that Rath Maeve was regarded as the hallowed spot where the earth swallowed the sun, a concept which may have been developed by astronomers who were such diligent surveyors that Rath Maeve cannot be seen from Millmount due to intervening hills.

Matthew Stout says the rectangular enclosures were introduced by the Normans, and quotes a holy man of the Native American tribe Oglala Sioux, who nicely expressed why there is a sacredness associated with the circular structure. Black Elk, the tribal leader, who was forced to live in a rectangular home built on a government reservation, said that "there can be no power in a square".[54] He added, "You have noticed that every thing an Indian does is in a circle, and that is because the Power of the World always works in circles, and everything tries to be round . . . the *Wasichus* have put us in these square boxes. Our power is gone and we are dying . . ."[55]

Living as they did under the stars without artificial light, it is probable that the ring builders drew inspiration from the ideal of cosmic unity. It was likely that some unique cosmic connection inspired the rings, from the giant enclosures of the Boyne to the circular farmsteads of much later times. Ringed structures, especially the early henges, mimicked the horizon, creating in a sense a nearer, false horizon, over which the risings and settings of sun, moon and stars could be watched.

The Irish term for "horizon" is *bun na spéire*,[56] which literally means "bottom of the sky" or "edge of the sky".[57] An observer performing a 360-degree turn will absorb a view of the entire horizon in a single swift sweep. A clean, uninterrupted, relatively flat horizon will allow for the

Midnight at Dowth

inspection of the rising positions of the heavenly bodies in the eastern sector and the setting positions to the west. We know from evidence already presented that landmarks, whether islands, hills or other monuments, were used as markers for certain risings and settings. Horizon was all-important in astronomical study.

ΑΠ IRÍSH STOΠEHEΠGE?

The vast circular structures set down since early times are not confined to the earthen enclosures which are found in Geraldine Stout's study. In the northern part of County Louth, about 20 miles or so from Newgrange, there once stood a vast "stone" henge, on a scale even larger than the famous Stonehenge on Salisbury Plain in England. Just a few miles northwest of the town of Dundalk, which was in the hero lore said to be the home of the great hero Cúchulainn, at a place called Ballynahattin, there was once a giant astronomical observatory which has been dubbed "Ireland's Stonehenge".[58]

Tragically, nothing remains of this vast monument today. Its loss is one of the heart-wrenching stories of Irish archaeological history. It was present in all its glory in 1748, when the astronomer and draughtsman Thomas Wright recorded it in his survey of County Louth's field monuments.[59] But by 1907, just 159 years later, all signs of this huge ringed structure had vanished. In that year, Henry Morris, writing for the *County Louth Archaeological Journal*, said Ireland's Stonehenge was, "Gone! Cleared away; its very site not exactly known".[60]

Morris bewailed the destruction of the monuments, saying, ". . . it is certainly provoking to find these magnificent memorials of the prehistoric ages swept away and demolished in an age of vaunted civilisation".[61] He reported that some people believed it had been destroyed when the nearby railway line was being constructed, but that a Reverend Father Lawless had assured him it had already disappeared when the railway was built.

A contemporary of Henry Morris, writing in 1911, said: ". . . the circles were there in 1747 and so must have entirely disappeared between that date and about 1855, when the connecting line between Drogheda and Portadown was laid down, and probably some time earlier."[62]

Wright does not give a very detailed description of what was clearly a very massive and comparatively complex site. He describes it as having been a "very great Work, of the same Kind with that at Stone Henge in England, being open to the East, and composed of like Circles of Stones within".[63] His drawing of the Ballynahattin site depicts a very unusual monument, probably unique in Ireland. It shows two concentric circles of standing stones, surrounded by a large earth bank and ditch structure with an opening on the east side, all of which are further circled by a ring of giant monoliths. He judged the number of outer monoliths to have been ten, but showed just six in his drawing, indicating a further three with faint, broken lines.

Thomas Wright's 1748 drawing of "Ireland's Stonehenge" at Ballynahattin

The inner circle appears to number 21 stones, while the second circle on the inside of the enclosure numbers over 40 members. His drawing also seems to detail a number of stones which appear to sit on the embankment, but of these he makes no mention in his all-too-brief description of the site. He supposed the site to be of greater antiquity than England's Stonehenge, saying, "But it appears to be much older, many of the Stones being broke, and others remov'd . . ."[64]

Henry Morris offers us a tantalising insight into what the purpose of Ireland's Stonehenge once was: "I have read or heard it stated somewhere that this place was the site of a school of astronomy. Its position on the plain, with a semicircle of mountains around would enable an ancient astronomer to observe and mark the places where the various heavenly bodies appeared on the horizon at different times of the year."[65] Regrettably, Morris does not tell us where he heard this critically important information, but states that the stone circles in Wright's illustration "may also have been for the same purpose".[66]

That the ancient astronomer builders used landmarks as foresights, we can be pretty certain. We've seen evidence of this at Baltray (Rockabill) and Millmount (Slane, Black Hill). There are many documented sites in Ireland where natural landscape features are used to mark risings or settings. One specific example involving a mountain is the unique alignment of the Boheh Stone with Croagh Patrick in County Mayo. The stone, also known as "Saint Patrick's Chair", is the viewing point for a phenomenon where the sun appears to "roll" down the side of Croagh Patrick twice a year, in April and August, thus dividing the year into three equal parts.[67]

From the site of Ireland's Stonehenge, the mountains sweep across a large portion of the northern sector of the visible horizon in a huge semi-circle, giving the stone-building sky watchers an array of peaks, slopes and notches with which to mark specific risings and settings. Slieve Gullion is almost due north of here, with the Cooley Mountains looming to the northeast and east.

The Scottish engineer Alexander Thom believed the Stone Age sun calendars to be very accurate because, at the latitude of the British Isles, "it is easier to mark a given day in the year by establishing a foresight for the setting sun on that day".[68] Thom explained that the reason for this was because of the larger range between the setting points throughout the year at more northerly latitudes. In Scotland, this range is twice as large as that in tropical countries.[69]

One can only presume that, because the mountains cover much of the northern aspect from Ireland's Stonehenge, observations made on the plains of Ballynahattin in former times were not confined to the rising and setting of the sun, but most probably included the moon and the stars as well.[70] Indeed, distant foresights, such as the "notches" between mountains, would provide a very precise indicator with which to mark the slow drift of the stars caused by precession.

Whatever its purpose, Ireland's Stonehenge, the ancient "school of astronomy", appeared to have vanished from the face of the earth. Its giant stones were removed and its earthen bank flattened. Nothing was thought to exist of the site until 1988, when the archaeologist Victor Buckley found it – or at least its footprint – in an aerial photograph of the area. It was not located in the townland of Ballynahattin, but in an adjoining townland to the southwest called Carn Beg.[71]

The only discernable remnant of the Irish Stonehenge was a cropmark, which showed up in an aerial photograph taken in 1970.[72] It wasn't until 1988 that Buckley identified that this cropmark was none other than the site of the "Ballynahattin Stonehenge". The triple-ringed cropmark was

The original aerial photograph of Carnbeg from which Victor Buckley discerned the "Ballynahattin Stonehenge" (Photo: Cambridge University Aerial Photograph)

only visible from the air, indiscernible from the ground. "On the ground, all you can see is a field," Victor Buckley told me when I first asked him for directions to the site.

The importance of his discovery, or rediscovery, was not lost, and in 1988 it made the front page of the *Irish Times*. The diameter of the large earthen bank was estimated by Buckley to have been 130 metres, or over 430 feet, which is about 90 feet larger in width than the outer embankment at England's Stongehenge.[73] And at the Ballynahattin Stonehenge, the huge bank was further surrounded by enormous megaliths.[74]

Further excitement was stirred in January 2006 when an archaeological survey of the Carn Beg site revealed the remains of an enormous triple-ringed embanked structure beneath the surface. Geophysical resistivity imagery showed the remnants of a massive circular monument (see image on right). The imagery excited Victor Buckley immensely. It was the absolute proof, he said, that this was indeed the monument which Henry Morris had said had been "swept away and demolished".

Intriguingly, there is a legend that states that England's Stonehenge was "moved" from Ireland. Geoffrey of Monmouth, in his *Historia Regum Britanniae* (History of the Kings of Britain), records that Merlin, under instruction by the king to erect an "everlasting monument" to the murdered consuls and princes buried at Salisbury, called for the king to "send for the Giant's Dance, which is in Killaraus, a mountain in Ireland."[75] "For there is a structure of stones there," Merlin told the king, "which none of this age could raise, without a profound knowledge of the mechanical arts. They are stones of a vast magnitude and wonderful quality; and if they can be placed here, as they are there, round this spot of ground, they will stand for ever."[76] The stones, according to Merlin, were brought to Ireland from Africa by giants, and they were "mystical stones" with a "medicinal virtue".[77] The exact whereabouts of this Mount Killaraus was, according to one author, located at Uisneach, the centre of Ireland.[78]

Monmouth's history has been debunked in some quarters as a work of fiction. Nonetheless, the Ballynahattin site recorded by Wright is proof that huge stone circles *were* constructed in Ireland. Whether Ireland's Stonehenge was older than England's, we may never know.

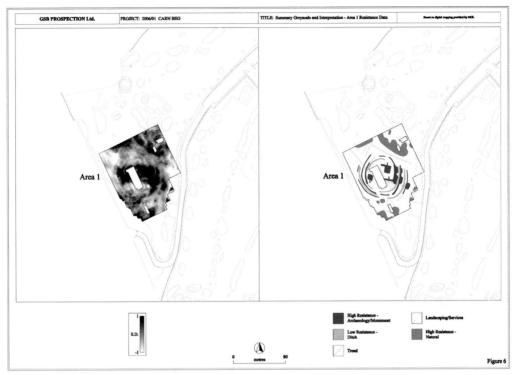

| GSB PROSPECTION Ltd. | PROJECT: 2006/01 CARN BEG | TITLE: Summary Greyscale and Interpretation - Area 1 Resistance Data | Based on digital mapping provided by MGL |

Archaeological survey resistance data plot of the site at Ballynahattin/Carn Beg. (Summary Greyscale and Interpretation – Area 1 Resistance Data. The survey was carried out by GSB Prospection Ltd by F. Robertson assisted by J. Gater and C. Stephens for Margaret Gowen and Company Ltd in 2006. Digital mapping provided by MGL.)

It is clear that the ancient astronomers undertook their observations with great fervour, erecting menhirs and earthen structures, such as those at Ballynahattin and Site Q, on a scale that would be considered impressive even with today's machinery and methods of construction.

Lamentably, the Ballynahattin Stonehenge was not the only stone circle monument to disappear. Two further sites recorded by Wright in the vicinity of Ireland's Stonehenge had also vanished by the time Henry Morris put pen to paper in 1907.

A megalithic complex including a stone circle at Ballrichan, located near the meeting of two rivers within a few miles of the Carn Beg / Ballynahattin circle, was described by Wright as a *"Druid's"* Grove" and included a stone circle containing five members.[79] When Henry Morris visited the site of this complex, which included other standing stones and what appears to be a cairn or stone heap surrounded by standing stones, the stones had completely vanished and all that remained was "a cultivated field". So complete was the site's removal that Morris remarked, "You might walk over it every day in the year, and you would not suspect that it ever was anything but a cultivated field, so diligently has every trace been swept away."[80] Another hill-top stone circle, at nearby Killing Hill, was also destroyed, along with a portion of the hill itself.[81]

Closer to the Boyne Valley, another stone circle which disappeared was located near Monasterboice, nowadays famous for its round tower and two of the finest examples of Irish High Crosses on the island. This circular monument of 12 stones is recorded in the folklore archives, and was said to have been called the "Calya Vera's House".[82] The Calya Vera, or *Cailleach Bhéarra* to give her proper Irish name, was an old hag associated with many ancient places, including the megalithic cairns on the top of the Loughcrew hills in County Meath. The hag was said to have been carrying an apron full of stones and was jumping from hill to hill at Loughcrew.[83] Each time, she dropped some stones which formed the cairns on the hills, which are called *Carn Bán,* meaning "white cairn". Upon trying to leap to the last hill, she fell and broke her neck.[84]

A similar tale is told about Monasterboice, where it is said the round tower was formed in the same fashion, as the result of a hag dropping stones from her apron. In the Monasterboice story, she disappears when she jumps from the top of the tower at dawn, leaving the mark of her heels in the stone at the bottom of the tower. Obviously this story is a remnant of a much earlier association of the *Cailleach Bhéarra* with the stone circle at Monasterboice.

The majority of stone circles in Ireland are concentrated in two clusters, one in south-west Munster and the other in mid-Ulster,[85] but it is clear that there were examples in Louth and Meath. In the Boyne Valley, we suspect that perhaps Site Q once contained posts or even standing stones within its sacred enclosure. Hard evidence of this may come in the future. In the meantime, we can state with certainty that there once was a stone circle in the Bend of the Boyne, yet another of the disappeared stone rings.

In the same field as the huge "cosmic egg" of Site Q, at a place called Cloghalea, there was a stone circle which has all but vanished from existence. It was recorded by Governor Pownall, who had visited the area in 1770, as having 11 stones in position.[86] "The stones are large and massive, and about 5 and 6 feet high. There remain eight of these stones together in one part of the circle; two in another part, and one by itself."[87] Antiquarian George Coffey, who wrote about it in 1912, said the remnants of the stone circle could still be seen, but he could not locate all of the stones mentioned by Pownall.[88]

Darkness settling over Site Q at Dowth

Writing in 1849, William Wilde said only four stones remained standing, with two more "lying prostrate" and a further two lying in the adjoining quarry.[89] He mentioned that some of the stones contained "indentations similar to those in some of the stones of the passage of New Grange."[90]

It is probable that here, on the periphery of the Brú na Bóinne complex, ancient sky watchers once gazed at the heavenly bodies and watched their risings and settings across the tops of stones, recording the slow turning of the seasons, the waxing and waning of the Moon and the gradual drift of the stars caused by precession. Cloghalea may have been the Boyne Valley's "school of astronomy", albeit on a much smaller scale than the huge circle that once graced the plains of Ballynahattin. It breaks the heart to think that both sites are now gone, nothing more than the melancholy memory of a time when the great cosmic circles embodied a powerful unification of sky and ground, a union which has long been broken in the modern age.

CHAPTER SIX
DOWTH:
THE DARKENING
OF THE SKY

The king of Ireland brought all the men of the country together in one place, in order to construct a tower from which he could reach heaven.[1] That great deed, according to legend, was endeavoured at a place which is known today as Dowth.

Standing at the foot of the giant cairn of Dowth, one of the three great passage-tombs of the Boyne Valley, it is not difficult to imagine that the construction of a giant cairn of stones on this magnitude would require every man in the land. Peering upwards from the bottom, the mound takes on the appearance of a small, steep, rounded hill, its precipitous banks giving it the resemblance of some miniature mountain, a quasi-natural feature looming up from the flat field on which it was assembled.[2]

It is another of the colossal structures of the Boyne Valley, a lingering remnant of a great age long since vanished. The immense quantity of material needed to assemble a cairn of this size, measured in tonnes, would number in the hundreds of thousands.[3]

The first time I ever climbed to the top of Dowth, on a school tour in the early 1980s, I felt like I had climbed a mountain. But like my fellow pupils, I was surprised to find that the whole top of the cairn was missing, and instead of finding a summit of sorts, we came across a vast crater in the top of the mound. This, we were told, was the result of an "excavation" which had been carried out years before.[4]

As is repeatedly the case with ancient sites, there is a wonderful panoramic view of the landscape from the top of Dowth. Much of the Bend of the Boyne assembly can be seen from here, and in the further distance other sites such as the hills of Slane and Tara. Martin Brennan said that from the top of Dowth, "one sees in a single panoramic vision the places that have been central to Irish history and culture for thousands of years".[5]

I've often found myself alone on the top of Dowth, drawn by its mystical lure, comforted by its soothing tranquillity, contemplating higher things and greater times, seeking to imagine what it was that made men and women strive to leave such an indelible mark in the landscape. The poet and patriot, John Boyle O'Reilly, who was born near Dowth in 1844, longed for that beautiful landscape which could be seen from the top of the cairn. In a letter to Father Anderson of nearby Drogheda in 1884, Boyle O'Reilly, writing from Boston, said:

> . . . I send my love to the very fields and trees along the Boyne from Drogheda to Slane. Some time, for my sake, go out to Dowth, alone, and go up to the moat, and look across the Boyne, over to Rossnaree to the hill of Tara; and turn eyes all round from Tara to Newgrange and Knowth, and Slane, and Mellifont, and Oldbridge, and you will see there the pictures

Red sky over Dowth

that I carry forever in my brain and heart – vivid as the last day I looked on them.[6]

Boyle O'Reilly wished to be buried at the little graveyard near the mound. He never got that wish, although the spot where he wanted to be interred is today marked by a monument in his honour. But the landscape in which he grew up "fashioned the poet's heart"[7], something that is embodied in his poem 'The Cry of the Dreamer':

> I am tired of planning and toiling
> In the crowded hives of men;
> Heart-weary of building and spoiling,
> And spoiling and building again.
> And I long for the dear old river,
> Where I dreamed my youth away;
> For a dreamer lives forever,
> And a toiler dies in a day.[8]

The river of which Boyle O'Reilly wrote is, of course, the Boyne. It was here, on the banks of the "Milky Way", that the agglomeration of megalithic sky–ground structures was laid out over 50 centuries ago. Boyle O'Reilly shared a unique attachment to the landscape of his home with his ancient ancestors who once watched the stars there.

There is a touch of irony in "The Cry of the Dreamer". One can imagine the men of Ireland who came to build Dowth as the planners and toilers, the builders and spoilers, and the king, who commanded them, as the dreamer who lives forever.

STONE OF THE SEVEN SUNS

At the outset of our research project, back in January 1999, the very first site visit Richard and I undertook together brought us to Dowth. We had set out to wander through the Boyne Valley, looking for "astronomical clues". Over the following seven-year period, we found those clues – dozens of them. On that cold and very wet day in 1999, the very first clue we found was one of Dowth's giant kerbstones, a stone which Martin Brennan has beautifully named "The Stone of the Seven Suns".[9]

On its front surface are etched a total of seven sun-like symbols, five of which are contained within a circle. Each "sun" symbol has a picked-out circle in the centre, although not all these central disks are consistent, some being surrounded with another circle. Radiating outwards from all seven disks are a number of rays or lines, giving one the impression that these icons are representational, not abstract images. They are petroglyphs which remind us of a child's drawing of the sun. These markings are variously described as being flowers, comet symbols and suns. The antiquarian George Coffey was satisfied that they were "suns", and recognised that this stone was "exceptional".[10]

We have directly observed a phenomenon involving the Stone of the Seven Suns and the summer solstice. The stone appears to be wedge-shaped when looked at from above. The rear surface of the stone, which faces inwards towards the mound, is at an angle to the front surface.

Some of the suns on the "Stone of the Seven Suns"

Looking along the rear façade of the stone, facing northwest, we observed that the summer solstice sunset occurs directly in line with it.

The Stone of the Seven Suns is just one of an estimated total of 115 kerbstones, only half of these being visible, and some only partly exposed.[11] A 1969 survey found that the remainder of the kerbstones were "buried beneath the mound and beneath the boundary fence on the west" while "some may have been removed altogether".[12]

Petroglyphs have been found on a total of 15 kerbstones, but none of these matches the Seven Suns stone, which is officially designated as Kerbstone 51, in terms of exquisite finishing and overall appeal. The picking work has been described as "fine and remarkably regular".[13] If Dowth was the Louvre, Kerbstone 51 would be the "Mona Lisa". It's the stone everybody makes sure to see while they're there.

What are these mysterious sun symbols, etched onto this huge slab with intricate care over 5,000 years ago? What do they signify? Are they really supposed to represent suns, or do they in fact symbolise something else? We think we can provide a reasonable explanation, backed up by evidence from both the archaeological remains of the site itself and its associated mythology.

The earliest antiquarian accounts of Dowth tell us it contained a "cove" and "subterraneous passages".[14] George Petrie, writing in 1834, said it was unquestionable that the mound contained "a chamber within it",[15] while William Wakeman, author of *Handbook of Irish Antiquities*, wrote in 1848 that there were two passages contained under Dowth which were "in a very ruinous state and completely stopped up . . ."[16]

There are, in fact, two chambers, or "tombs" at Dowth. The opening of one chamber can be found on the western side of the cairn, while the opening of another is located on the south-western side. Quite confusingly, they are officially called the "North Tomb" and the "South Tomb", which designations, although being somewhat cumbersome, are probably far more helpful and acceptable than the "West-southwest Tomb" and the "Southwest Tomb" which would more accurately describe the directions they face.

These chambers are not at all similar. The northern tomb is cross-shaped, like the tomb at Newgrange, although much shorter. The 8.2-metre passage leads into a chamber containing three side chambers, known as recesses, with a total combined length of 12.5 metres for passage and chamber. The combined length of the Newgrange tomb is 24.2 metres, nearly double that of Dowth North.[17]

A unique feature of the northern chamber is that it contains an annexe, a sort of L-shaped ante-chamber which is accessed by crossing a stile in the

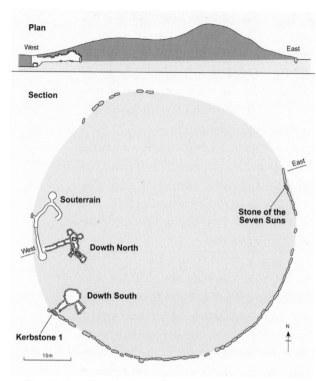

Plan

West · East

Section

Souterrain

East

Stone of the
Seven Suns

West · Dowth North

Dowth South

Kerbstone 1

N

15m

Ground plan of Dowth (Image: © Matthew and Geraldine Stout)

corner of the right-hand recess. Archaeologist Claire O'Kelly reported that "Deane called this outer compartment 'the King's tomb', though on what authority we do not know".[18] It may have been an important feature in the early construction of Dowth, as we will see later.

Dowth South is a completely different structure to its northern counterpart. A short passage of just 3.3 metres leads into a circular chamber which measures five metres across.[19] There are 12 large upright slabs, known as orthostats, forming the wall of the chamber, while there are just six orthostats in the passage, three on either side. This compares with 19 chamber orthostats at Dowth North and 17 passage stones.[20]

LIGHT IN THE CHAMBER

It was here, inside the circular chamber of Dowth South back in the winter of 1980, that Martin Brennan and Jack Roberts discovered something hugely significant which everyone else appeared to have missed – the chamber was illuminated by the light of the setting sun at winter solstice. The rays of the sun entered the chamber for "about half an hour",[21] and moved towards a stone at the rear of the chamber.[22]

The discovery made news headlines in Ireland and abroad. Brennan could not overstate the importance of his great breakthrough, saying that it meant there could be no doubt that the alignment of nearby Newgrange on winter solstice sunrise was intentional, not the result of some accident or chance.[23] Coupled with his discovery that March, when he announced the equinox configuration of Cairn T on Loughcrew (see Chapter 3),[24] Brennan's unearthing of another solstice alignment in the Boyne Valley brought the whole sphere of megalithic astronomy into sharp focus. One alignment towards the sun could be dismissed as accidental. But two or three?

"The discovery confirms that the astronomical alignments were preconceived and intentional," Brennan told the *Irish Press* at the time of his Dowth revelation. "It demonstrates that early man directed attention towards the sun and moon and developed methods for making accurate precision observations that would enable formulating an efficient calendar".

Years later, long after Brennan's time in the Boyne Valley had ended and with his ground-breaking book still in print, a more exhaustive and painstaking study of Dowth South's solstice alignment was undertaken by Anne-Marie Moroney. Her observations in the winters of 1997–98 and 1998–99, documented in her book *Dowth: Winter Sunsets*,[25] showed something very important about Dowth South. The chamber structure was not, like Newgrange, long and narrow, allowing for penetration of the Sun for just a few days either side of the solstice. At Dowth South, the aperture of the tomb allowed for a much greater range of sunsets to penetrate inside, and Moroney observed that the evening sun shone into Dowth South from the beginning of October right through to the end of February, a period of almost five months.[26]

During that period, "the sun sends its rays from the south-west into . . . Dowth South. As the sun appears progressively lower in the sky towards the winter solstice, the beam, entering the passage in the space between the top of kerbstone K1 and under the lintel, travels first over the sill stone, then enters the chamber and finally shines directly onto the stones at the back of the chamber. The beam of the Sun is so strong that the whole chamber is lit up."[27]

Winter Solstice sunset penetrates into the chamber of Dowth South (photo: Anne-Marie Moroney)

The year after Anne-Marie Moroney published her book, in November of 2000, she was given the chance, along with Richard Moore and I, to view cine film footage from inside Dowth South which was shot by Brennan's team in 1981.[28] It was remarkable to view a silent film, and an astonishingly short film at that, which had captured such a momentous and far-reaching discovery.

In the years since Moroney published her wonderful little book about Dowth, she has kept an almost constant vigil at this ancient place during wintertime. I have come to regard her as some sort of unofficial guardian or custodian of Dowth's stones, her silhouetted shape atop the great cairn often the first sight one sees driving up the road from a distance.

Sadly, in that time a row of evergreen trees has grown opposite the south-western side of the mound, all but blocking out the winter light. That said, more and more people are coming here every winter to attempt to see the phenomenon for themselves. Hopefully the authorities will come up with some solution to the problem of the trees.

With no light shining into Dowth South, or Dowth North for that matter, even in the short days of winter, we are reminded of the legend of this place and how it got is name. The name Dowth is anglicised from *Dubhadh*, which means "darkness" or "blackening".[29]

DARKNESS SHALL BE ITS NAME

And thus we turn to the legend about Dowth, the story which relates how the king brought all the men of Erin to build a tower by which he could pass to heaven. Contained within this short tale about how Dowth got its name is a solution of sorts, we believe, which explains the astronomical functions of Dowth and correlates with some aspects of its design.

The legend of Dowth is contained in the *Dindshenchas*. In fact, it's in there twice, once under its own heading, "Dubad", and again, in more detail, under the section relating to Knowth, "Cnogba", one of its sister sites. The *Dindshenchas*, the "lore of sacred places",[30] is contained in Ireland's ancient manuscripts. The twelfth-century *Book of Leinster* details stories of 150 places in Ireland and contains the oldest copy of the *Dindshenchas*, while the 1400 AD *Book of Ballymote*, includes "a much more complete and beautiful *Dindshenchas* than that in *The Book of Leinster*".[31] Place name lore can also be found in other manuscripts, but all of these are comparatively modern when compared with the great age of Dowth and some of the other sites described.

It would be a bold step to suggest that these place name legends are as old as the actual monuments themselves, but that is exactly the conclusion we draw when we take a close look at the Dowth story. We are reminded of the fact that some historians believe the stories come directly from the deepest depths of time, transmitted along the way by word of mouth until they were finally written down during the eleventh century and proceeding centuries. The Dowth story may be a "contrived fiction" of medieval times,[32] but it is rooted in prehistory.[33] The *Annals* place the king who ordered the building of Dowth, called Bressal, in the Iron Age,[34] but it is clear from our interpretation of the Dowth tale that it relates directly to the original purpose of the monument and therefore carries a direct resonance from the Neolithic.

Here is the story as it is told under the heading "Dubad":

> Dubad, whence the name? Not hard to say. A king held sway over Erin, Bressal bó-dibad by name. In his time a murrain came upon the kine of Erin, until there were left in it but seven cows and a bull. All the men of Erin were gathered from every quarter to Bressal, to build them a tower after the likeness of the tower of Nimrod, that they might go by it to Heaven. His sister came to him, and told him that she would stay the sun's course in the vault of heaven, so that they might have an endless day to accomplish their task. The maiden went apart to work her magic. Bressal followed her and had union with her: so that place is called Ferta Cuile from the incest that was committed there. Night came upon them then, for the maiden's magic was spoilt. "Let us go hence," say the men of Erin, "for we only pledged ourselves to spend one day a-making this hill, and since darkness has fallen upon our work, and night has come on and the day is gone, let each depart to his place." "Dubad (darkness) shall be the name of this place for ever," said the maiden. So hence are Dubad and Cnoc Dubada named.[35]

There are a number of things we can deduce from the *Dindshenchas* lore about Dowth. It is obvious that Dowth was a particularly eminent monument, which is evidenced not only from the fact that it was said to have been built on the command of the king of Ireland, requiring men "from every quarter" of the land, but also from the fact that the legend itself is contained twice in the *Dindshenchas*.

This king, Bressal bó-dibad, must have been a very powerful and persuasive individual, if indeed he ever really existed and this is not some sort of pseudo-historical narrative or a symbolic tale fashioned in the recent, and not ancient, past. Bressal was able to draw men from every part of Ireland to assist him in the completion of his task. The king wanted to build a tower from which he could "pass to heaven".[36] Such a tower would probably have been a grand symbol of the king's reign, and he apparently chose this hallowed spot overlooking the sacred river, the Boyne.

This gargantuan undertaking was supposedly instigated at a time of famine, when there was nothing left of Ireland's cattle except a bull and seven cows. Bressal's epithet, *bó-dibad,* means "lacking in cattle",[37] and here again we see reference to cows in the Boyne Valley. Would all the men of Ireland be expected to work on such a massive task without food? Maybe the king had some secret store for the duration of this undertaking?

One of the most striking aspects of the story is the fact that the whole episode appears to have taken place in conjunction with some extraordinary events in the heavens.

This photo was taken at midnight on summer solstice, and demonstrates how the sky does not get dark at this time of year. Is this the "endless day" which the men of Ireland were guaranteed during their construction task?

His own sister said to him,
she would not let the sun run his course;
there should be no night but bright day
till the work reached completion.

His sister stretches forth her hands . . .
strongly she makes her druid spell:
the sun was motionless above her head;
she checked him on one spot.[38]

The hill, or tower, was to be made "all in one day", and in order for that to happen, the king's sister, who goes unnamed in the story, "would not let the sun run his course". This statement, contained in the *Cnogba* version of the legend,[39] establishes a male identity for the sun, which concurs with the Baltray myth where we saw that the sun deity, Balor, was also male.

In performing the magical feat of stopping the sun's course in the sky, the king's sister appears to have made the sun stand still, which is exactly what the word *solstice* means – stationary sun.[40] She promised the king that there would be "endless day" so that he could accomplish his great task.

We have already established that Dowth has at least one passage which accepts the light of the setting sun at the time when the sun is standing still – winter solstice. At this time of the year the days are short and the nights long and dark.

At the time of summer solstice, by contrast, the days are lengthy, warmed by a sun which is visible for 17 hours from the time of sunrise to the time of sunset. During the longest days of summer, when the rising and setting sun is standing still on the horizon, it does not dip far enough below the horizon for astronomical twilight to end.[41] The result is that the June nights do not get fully dark.[42] In fact, during this month there is a distinct brightness in the night sky over Ireland, and it could be said that, although the stars are visible, there is no dark night at this time.

Back in the Neolithic when Dowth was being built, this effect was probably even more pronounced. Due to a variation in the axial tilt of the Earth, the separation of the sun's maximum and minimum declinations from summer to winter was greater in the Stone Age. The summer solstice sunrise and sunset would have been located two sun widths further to the north along the horizon, because of the fact that the sun's declination was over a half a degree higher at summer solstice than it is today.[43]

It is likely that the nighttime was slightly brighter then than it is now. The endless day combined with the standing still sun are the reasons why Professor Ronald Hicks refers to the Dowth story as a "clear example of a solstice legend".[44]

With the promise of an everlasting day, the men of Ireland set about constructing the king's grand project. But something happened then which upset Bressal's ostentatious plan. The king committed the "crime" of allowing lust to seize him, and he committed incest with his sister, causing her magic to fail and a darkness to descend upon the land. With Bressal's pledge of light broken, the builders elect to abandon the task and return to their homes:

> When it was no longer day for them thereafter
> (it is likely that it was night),
> the hill was not brought to the top,
> the men of Erin depart homeward.[45]

"Let us go hence," said the men of Erin, "for we only pledged ourselves to spend one day a-making this hill, and since darkness has fallen upon our work, and night has come on and the day is gone, let each depart to his place." "Dubad (darkness) shall be the name of this place for ever," said the maiden.

ECLIPSE OF THE SUN

The darkness, which seems to have been quite sudden, came about as the result of a union of a male and a female at a place called Ferta Cuile, which could translate as "tumulus of the secret place".[46] There can be no doubt in our minds that this is a legend not only about the summer solstice, but

An eclipse of the sun peers out from behind cloud. The eclipse took place in August 1999 and was visible from Ireland, but was only visible as a total eclipse in Cornwall, England

also about a total eclipse of the sun. The incestuous coming together of male and female represents the joining of the male sun with the female moon, the darkness of night coming mid-eclipse. It is this darkness which gives Dowth its name.

That name, *Dubhadh*, is directly related to eclipses because its precise meaning is "blackening". The word *dubhadh* is very closely associated with the Irish word for "eclipse", which is *urdubhadh*.[47]

It is with the image of a total solar eclipse etched in our minds that we return to the Stone of the Seven Suns, where the petroglyphs resemble suns, but with the subtle difference, as stated earlier, that on some of the symbols the central hub of each sun is picked out, as if signifying that there is another disk in front. Are these carvings, crafted in the remote past, some astronomer's sketchbook, showing the various stages of a total eclipse of the sun which was observed here in far-flung times?

If they are suns, whether eclipsed or not, there is now a definitive four-way collaboration of facts which supports the notion that Dowth was some kind of astronomical observatory:

(1) The legend, which speaks of the sun standing still and a sudden darkness;

(2) The passage: Dowth has a passage aligned on winter solstice;

(3) The petroglyphs: sun symbols, seven of them;

(4) The name: *Dubhadh/urdubhadh*, which is related to the darkening which happens during an eclipse.

But the astronomical interpretation of Dowth is much deeper than this, with abundant evidence of strong sky influences. The legend also speaks of a cattle famine, during which the livestock has been reduced to a meagre bull and seven cows. Our interpretation is that this bull and seven cows are the bull constellation, Taurus, and its associated star cluster, the Pleiades, also known widely as "The Seven Sisters".[48] We have previously identified an association between cattle and heavenly bodies.

Reference to the bull constellation sets a time frame for the origin of the whole story. At the time the great mounds of the Boyne Valley were constructed,[49] the sun was housed in Taurus on the spring equinox. This is the sun's vernal point, the point where the ecliptic crosses the celestial equator on its way north through the zodiac. At this time, day and night are of equal length and the sun rises due east and sets due west. An astronomical assessment of the megalithic ruins at Loughcrew reveals a prehistoric interest in the equinox, and Brennan discloses that the shape and path of the beam of light against the back stone differs from spring to autumn. In springtime, more of the sunwheel symbols on the back stone, which are similar to the suns on Kerbstone 51 at Dowth, are illuminated than at autumn. This may be an indication of a greater importance attached to the vernal equinox.

One of the suns on the Seven Suns stone

In the early days of our research, we were drawn to the idea that the Stone of the Seven Suns could be a representation of what's called a "heliacal rising" of the Pleiades, the Seven Sisters cluster in Taurus. In the centuries leading up to the estimated time of Dowth's construction, the Pleiades would have been swamped by the sun's light as they rose in the east on the day of the vernal equinox. Interestingly, the Dogon tribe in Africa used a symbol similar to the Kerb 51 suns – a star within a circle – to depict the heliacal rising of Sirius, the brightest star.[50] We later came to believe there was perhaps a duality of function encoded onto the seven suns stone. Perhaps it depicted the stages of a total eclipse of the sun *and* an interpretation of the heliacal rising of the "seven cows".[51]

Further exploration of Dowth reveals a high probability that eclipse prediction was at least part of its intent. An examination of the configuration of both Dowth's tombs reveals a sophistication belied by the apparent simplicity of its construction. This passage-tomb is not a mere stone-heap, thrown together at the whim of some megalomaniac king for his simple amusement. It is a precisely tuned astronomical observatory, refined and regulated so that its massive unhewn stones can be used as a measuring device for computing large amounts of cyclical astronomical time.

Proper assessment of Dowth's passages relies, in part, on a survey carried out in 1969 which gave measurements according to the magnetic compass.[52] "The definitive survey carried out by O'Kelly and O'Kelly in 1969 appears to displace the orientation by about 12 degrees . . . What may have begun as a trivial mapping error – failure to correct magnetic to true north – has been copied into later publications enough times to make it seem like the considered consensus of several authorities, rather than a minor matter overlooked by one. In this has lain concealed the secret of Dowth".[53]

ALIGNMENTS AT DOWTH SOUTH

In the summer of 2002, a survey of Dowth confirmed that the original measurements were magnetic. The surveyors pointed out that in 1969, magnetic north was "approximately 12° west of true north".[54] In correcting the original measurements, the new survey found the axis of the southern passage pointed to an azimuth of 217°, which the surveyors acknowledged "points crudely towards the winter solstice sunset, as suspected locally".[55] The reason it is only a "crude" alignment is because of the wide range of azimuths covered by the structure, its short passage allowing it a 'sweep' of the horizon from approximately 207.6° to 231.4°.[56] This wide sweep is apparent from the length of time the sun's light shaft is able to penetrate the passage and into the chamber, as recorded by Anne-Marie Moroney.

The implication of Dowth South's wide angular sweep is that, as well as accepting the light of the sun during winter, the chamber would likely have accepted light from the setting moon at certain times of the year. In fact, this is an astronomical certainty, provided the night is cloud-free and the moon is bright enough. The ability of Dowth South to "capture" or "point out" sunsets *and* moonsets is not unique. It is an easily observable reality that the moon sometimes shares the same declination as the sun, so any passage pointing to a sunrise or a sunset will, at some time, also point to a moonrise or moonset. This duality of purpose, whether intentional or accidental, is an integral element of passage-tombs. Our observations and the evidence we have gathered during our research shows that, in many cases, the Irish passage-tombs were intentionally constructed with more than one heavenly body in mind.

The central axis of Dowth South points to about 217°,[57] which is a whole ten degrees south of the point, roughly 227°, where winter solstice sunset occurred on the horizon back in the Stone Age.[58] Why is there such a large discrepancy? One would imagine that if the winter solstice sunset was the main target of the southern passage, the central axis of that passage would point directly to that sunset. With very long passages, such as those at Newgrange and Knowth, this is not an issue because of the narrow range of azimuths which those passages point to.

Dowth South is a different kettle of fish. Its central axis, if the megalith builders ever thought of their passage having a "central axis", does not point to the winter solstice sunset. It is aligned towards something else.

During a visit to Dowth in November 2003, I met Anne-Marie Moroney outside the entrance to the southern passage. I asked her if she knew what horizon feature, if any, the southern passage pointed to. She was able to tell me that at winter solstice, the sun set behind the hill of Realtoge. But we both instinctively knew that Realtoge, which means "star", was not the central target. As we stood there, wondering what it could be, we decided to partake in a simple experiment which would reveal what horizon feature, if there was one, would line up with the axis of Dowth South.

I told Anne-Marie to stand looking into the passage, placing herself roughly on the axis, imagining herself standing on a line emanating from the passage midway between the passage orthostats. Then I climbed up the side of the mound and asked her to tell me when I was "standing over" this imaginary axis line. "Left a bit. Left a bit more," she said. "Okay, that's it now."

I looked over her head. There, on the distant horizon, was the Hill of Tara. I knew immediately it was Tara because I had become very familiar with a clump of trees which surround the old church up on the hill. Having not suspected this apparent alignment, we were both a bit stunned. This was more than coincidence. Far too often Richard and I had seen alignments between sites, and now, with this new information to hand, we knew there must be something astronomically significant to this Dowth South–Tara line.

The Moroney-Murphy experiment was admittedly rough, giving only an approximate indication of the Dowth South target. But the alignment could be checked more precisely. I later replicated our experiment using sticks, placing twigs on the mound in line with the axis of the chamber and passage. It still appeared that Tara was the target.

The best survey information to hand placed the azimuth of the axis at either 217°, or 219.5°, both approximations. Victor Reijs, an amateur archaeoastronomer of many years who had studied megalithic structures across Europe, was satisfied that the "likely average azimuth" of Dowth South was 219.5°.[59] The 2002 survey, meanwhile, had yielded an azimuth of 217°. I decided to try to establish the azimuth of a line from Dowth to Tara using a JavaScript tool provided by Victor Reijs on his website.[60] This handy tool enables the user to enter grid co-ordinates for two points taken from Ordnance Survey maps and calculates the azimuth – both the map azimuth and the true azimuth (°T). I entered the grid co-ordinates for Dowth and for the Mound of the Hostages on Tara. The result was 218°T, breathtakingly close to the rough central axis azimuth calculated for Dowth South. In fact, it was a degree off the 2002 survey figure, and a degree and a half off Victor Reijs's result, lying between the two.

It appeared as if Anne-Marie and myself had found another site-to-site alignment, one of the many which cropped up in the Boyne Valley area.[61] This one had further significance because it involved two very distinguished sites, one a primary monument of the Brú na Bóinne complex, the other a place which held huge importance in the king-lore of Ireland and was long considered its ancient capital.

If Dowth South had pointed towards some nameless horizon feature, it's possible I may not have done what I did next. I went to the computer, with the specific aim of finding out if there was a particular heavenly body which set around 218°, give or take a degree or so. While not dealing with obsessional exactness, especially given the impreciseness of the figures, I was only prepared to deal with an astronomical body which set within the 217–219.5° range.

But before I had even consulted the computer, I already had a good idea that the Dowth South–Tara line was an important azimuth direction and that it was inexorably linked with the myths, the sky and the supposed eclipse function of Dowth. I was aware from discussions held with other interested amateurs that the setting moon at its standstills was located roughly 11 degrees or so either side of the azimuth values for the solstices. This meant the 218° value was close, given a winter solstice sunset value of 227.5° for the year 3200 BC.

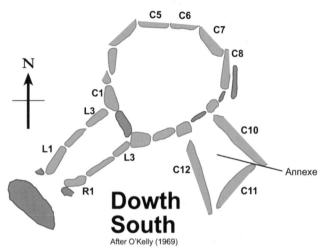

Ground plan of the southern passage at Dowth
(Image: © Matthew and Geraldine Stout)

It transpired from our investigations that the line from Dowth to the Mound of the Hostages at Tara corresponded only approximately to the major standstill moonset.[62] Using SkyMap, one can see the extremes of declination of the moon over a period of time. This feature enabled us to see that the most southerly declination of the moon in the era Dowth was built[63] was –29°20', which corresponds with a setting azimuth at Dowth's latitude of 215.5°. This is outside the 217–219.5° range calculated in the surveys. However, the "central axis" line of Dowth South to Tara (218°) was a very close marker for major standstill, just 2.5° off, while the axis is a whole 9.5° away from winter solstice sunset, so it became apparent to us that there was probably a lunar standstill element to Dowth South's overall intent.

Alexander Thom pointed out that while he termed the maximum and minimum declinations of the moon the "standstills", the moon does not actually "stand still" like the sun does at winter solstice. Instead, he said, "the limiting declinations do not vary by more than 20 arc minutes . . ."[64] The cycle of standstills repeats every 18.61 years.

Perhaps the Dowth South aperture and chamber were used to track the approach of the major standstill? Is this why it is so constructed, with a short passage and circular chamber allowing a range of directions to be observed from within?

The 2.5° difference between the actual setting position of the major standstill moon and the Dowth–Tara axis troubled us because, even with the moon moving around by about 20 arc minutes at the time of standstill, 2.5° is the equivalent of roughly five moon-widths, too much of a margin of error in our opinion. We had seen on our journey up the Boyne that megalithic sky alignments were more precise than this.

So we looked again at the Ordnance Survey maps, and revisited Rath Maeve, one of the giant rings located south of the Hill of Tara, about a mile away from the Mound of the Hostages. Rath Maeve has a diameter of 275 metres, as we pointed out in Chapter 5, and is the largest embanked enclosure in the Boyne region, and one of the largest in Ireland.

The line from Dowth to Rath Maeve yielded an azimuth of 214.8°, closer again to the 215.5° setting azimuth for major standstill than the line from Dowth to the Mound of the Hostages. But we are still indulging in approximations. Suffice to say that the moon at the time of the major standstill, viewed from Dowth's southern chamber, would set in the direction of the Hill of Tara. In any case, the figures yielded by SkyMap are based on a flat horizon at an altitude equivalent to sea level. Local variations in both altitude and horizon features could skew the figures slightly.

Beyond Tara we looked at Carbury and Nechtain's Well to ascertain if there was a similar pattern to what we found at Millmount, where the winter solstice line passed through Rath Maeve and the well at Carbury. Using the Reijs azimuth calculator, we found that Nechtain's Well lay at 221°, which is between the major standstill azimuth of 215.5° and winter solstice sunset azimuth of 227.5°, almost exactly half-way. Whether this is of any significance we do not know.

With all the evidence to hand, the central target of the chamber structure appeared more likely to be the major standstill than the winter solstice sunset, with the southerly major standstill moon setting in the direction of Rath Maeve at Tara.

Another myth holds that Dowth was the burial place of Boadan, a shepherd. "Elcmar's shepherd was named Boadan and Dubad or Dowth was said to be the grave of Boadan (*Fert Boadain*)."[65] Apart from a brief mention in the *Book of Ui Maine*, the manuscripts appear to be almost bereft of references to this "shepherd of Elcmar", except the *Dindshenchas* poem *Brug na Bóinde I*, which refers to:

> The Hide of the Cow of undying Boadan,
> over the cheek of his yellow-white stone:
> the Precinct of the staunch keen warriors
> about the eastern level of a noble sanctuary.[66]

Is it possible that Boadan, who was clearly associated with a cow in the *Dindshenchas*, was a variant of Bóann? There is a *"Firt m-Bóinne mna*

Nechtain", meaning "grave of Bóann wife of Nechtain" in the Bend of the Boyne, according to the *Dindshenchas* in *The Book of Ballymote*.[67] Nechtain also went under the name Elcmar.[68] If Dowth was held as the burial place of Bóann, there is some stark astronomical imagery presented. Bóann, the moon, set behind the Hill of Tara, its orb appearing to be buried in the earth, shining its last faint rays into Dowth South at the standstill.

ALIGNMENTS AT DOWTH NORTH

So what could Dowth's other passage tell us? Did it too have an alignment of significance to the sun or moon? If so, could it help us decipher the overall astronomical master plan of the whole site, if there was one?

The O'Kelly survey of 1969 showed that the central axis of Dowth North, the imaginary line stretching from the centre of the back stone in the rear recess to the midway point between the outermost passage orthostats, was 250°. Again, this is a compass measurement, so we are dealing with magnetic directions. Thankfully, because we know the year the survey was carried out, we can calculate the differential between magnetic and true.

Taking the 11° estimated differential away,[69] we get an approximate true azimuth for Dowth North of 239°. This is just one degree, or two moon widths, to the right of where the moon sets at minor standstill south in the epoch Dowth was built.[70]

Again, because we are dealing in approximations, the figures could be wide of the mark, but a study of the bearing of Dowth North carried out by Victor Reijs indicated that "the O'Kelly measurements sound more substantial due to her defined reference axis: 239°"[71] Reijs concluded that the "sky window", based on the O'Kelly reference axis, would target a sweep of the horizon between 232.8° and 246.6°, with a likely average azimuth, give or take half a degree, of 239.7°.[72]

Given these findings, it is apparent not only that Dowth North targets the southerly minor standstill setting of the moon, but also that it would accept a beam of the sun at the time of sunset on the old cross-quarter days of Samhain and Imbolc (November and February).[73]

The central axis of Dowth North is more closely targeted on minor standstill moonset. This conclusion is based on approximate figures, and on the passage structure as it exists today. It may originally have been longer, allowing for a narrower range of azimuths. Claire O'Kelly pointed out that "at least one and possibly two further orthostats were probably present at each side at the front when the tomb was first built".[74]

The entrance to the northern tomb may have been altered during the construction of a souterrain, an underground chamber which was built "several thousand years after the prehistoric tomb",[75] which links up with the entrance to Dowth North. Added to this difficulty is the fact that the entrance to the ancient passage is now blocked up and the sun and moon can no longer shine in. A concrete shaft was sunk into the ground at Dowth North in the early twentieth century to provide access to the passage and chamber, which was gained using a ladder. It is this concrete structure which blocks Dowth North.

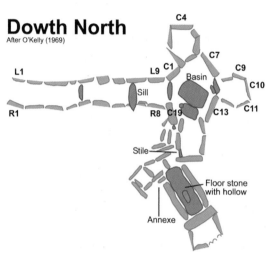

Dowth North
After O'Kelly (1969)

Ground plan of the northern passage at Dowth
(Image: © Matthew and Geraldine Stout)

A narrowing of the horizon sweep resulting from a longer original passage may have made it more likely that the moon was the main target, but we will never know for certain. If the setting moon was being observed from the chamber, it would be visible in the rear recess. The stone at the back of this recess, Chamber Stone 10, contains no ornament.

Martin Brennan appears to have been the first to propose that an imaginary line between Dowth and Newgrange pointed towards the minor standstill moon – rising in one direction, with the viewer at Newgrange looking towards Dowth, and setting in the other direction. What Brennan didn't know is that Dowth North points to Newgrange. He suspected that the southern tomb pointed to Newgrange, even including a drawing of what this might have looked like in his 1980 book *The Boyne Valley Vision*.[76] The view from Dowth South is obscured by trees, so one is unable to see Newgrange from the chamber.

The modern sunset which most closely marks the place where the minor standstill moon set back in 3200 BC occurs on 16 November.[77] An observer standing on top of Dowth will see the sun setting directly over Newgrange on 16 November. Specifically, the sun appears to set over the white quartz façade of Newgrange. When we imagine the megalithic astronomers watching the Moon setting over the brilliant white stones of Newgrange, we wonder if these milky white stones were chosen for that very purpose.

The megalithic art present on some of the chamber stones of Dowth North may help us decipher what was being observed in there over 5,000 years ago. On two faces of Chamber Stone 19, the first stone of the chamber at the end of the passage, are a series of petroglyphs, including some spirals and concentric circles. This stone was regarded by Claire O'Kelly as "the finest stone as regards ornament" in the north tomb.[78] Along the corner of this stone are a series of linear grooves which could well be some sort of calibration mark used to track the progress of the sunbeam at the time of the Samhain/Imbolc cross-quarter days. The actual azimuth of sunset on these dates is approximately 242°, which is four and a half degrees inside the northerly limit of the azimuth sweep calculated by Victor Reijs. It is highly probable that, as well as striking the corner of Chamber Stone 19, the Samhain/Imbolc sunbeam would have penetrated the chamber and shone directly onto Chamber Stone 13. Again, this is a stone which has no decoration.

After the November cross-quarter day, the sun moves along the horizon, its beam gradually moving so that it shines along the centreline of the passage, into the rear recess. Coming towards the winter solstice, the shaft of the sun would move towards the left of the chamber, shining onto Chamber Stone 7. Interestingly, the right-hand side of this stone contains a number of petroglyphs, including some small sun wheels. These engravings mark the place where the sunbeam would last be seen before retreating from the passage coming up to winter solstice – about three weeks or so beforehand. After the solstice, the sunwheels mark the first point where the sunbeam re-emerges into Dowth North on its way north along the horizon again.

At minor standstill, the standstill moonbeam, shining up the centre of the passage, would have crossed two sill stones in the passage, a further sill stone which marks the threshold at the chamber entrance, before crossing a large rectangular stone basin in the middle of the chamber, and on over a fourth sill stone into the rear recess. Whether there was some ritual element to the large stone basin, we can only speculate. Perhaps the ashes of the dead were placed there in order that their souls might travel along the sun or moon beam into the sky? Both the cross-quarter sunbeam and minor standstill moonbeam would have crossed over this basin stone. There could be a hint in the Dowth legend pointing to a funerary purpose to the passage-tombs. The king had instructed the men of Ireland to assemble the structure so that he might gain immortality. Perhaps it was his ashes that were to be placed in the stone basin.

PATH TO THE OTHERWORLD

In old Irish myth, the otherworld, known variously as Magh Mell, Tír na nÓg and Hy Brasil, was believed to lie in the direction of the setting sun. "Mag Mell was the way to the otherworld . . . it consisted of the golden path the sun makes over the ocean between the horizon and the observer. Thus Mag Mell was the route to eternity".[79]

This could be what King Bressal meant when he said the purpose of his grandiose mission was to enable him to get to heaven:

> By him is built the solid hill
> in the likeness of Nimrod's tower,
> so that from it he might pass to heaven,
> – that is the cause why it was undertaken.[80]

This passage brings to mind an image, not of a tower with its top literally touching the sky, enabling the king to reach heaven, but an image of a sacred structure opening a portal to the otherworld at the time of a specific sunset or moonset. This sacred sky–ground architecture would allow the king to become immortalised among the stars, which, as we saw in earlier chapters, is the likely location of the old Irish otherworld.

There is a connection between the king's name and the otherworld. One Irish otherworld is the mysterious sunken island of Hy Brasil, an Atlantis of sorts, said to have been located in the Atlantic Ocean. "Bresal was a mythical High King of the World and the island of Breasal was reputedly where he held his court every seven years".[81]

The island was said to be visible from Ireland once every seven years, and "was depicted as a place of eternal happiness where everyone was immortal".[82] It was said to have been the place to which the Tuatha Dé Danann retreated after their defeat by the Milesians. It may have given its name to the south American country of Brazil. "When sailors landed in South America, they thought that they had reached O'Breasail – the Otherworld. Now it is called Brazil."[83] Journalist and author P.A. Ó Síocháin said, "the story of Hy-Brasil is part of ancient Irish history. It has its roots in the race-mind. It has always told of a lost civilisation; something finer and richer than anything known since."[84]

Although the authority of T.N. Deane's statement that the main compartment of the annexe or antechamber off Dowth North was called "the king's tomb" is not known, it is a fascinating piece of information. On the floor of this compartment is a large flagstone, with a hollow in its middle.[85] This is a unique feature in Irish passage-tomb architecture. So thick is the floor slab that this part of the antechamber is 20 centimetres higher than the inner compartment.[86]

Examination of the bearings of the annexe generates further interesting astronomical results. The central axis of the main compartment of the annexe, the "king's tomb", points towards a true azimuth of 299°, which is very close to the setting place of the sun at the cross-quarter days of Bealtaine and Lughnasa (May/August) in 3200 BC. Once again, because of the shortness of the chamber, the northerly setting of the minor standstill moon (303.5° approx.) could also have been a target. This is all assuming that the annexe was the earliest part of the northern tomb structure, coming before the main passage and cruciform chamber were constructed. As things currently stand, the axis of the king's tomb points towards a wall of stone!

The smaller compartment of the annexe points roughly towards the north-northeast, giving an azimuth of about 20° true. This is too far north along the horizon for any sunrise or moonrise. Its purpose, if any, remains unclear.

Dowth South's side chamber, meanwhile, has an interesting orientation. This wedge-shaped annexe has an opening which would accept a sweep of azimuths from approximately 315° to 341°.[87] The centre of this sweep is at 328°, which is almost perfectly in line with the place where the moon would be setting at the time of major standstill in 3300 BC.[88]

With all this structural, astronomical and mythological evidence to hand, the question begs: was Dowth a solar site, a lunar site or was it more advanced, perhaps concerned with both?

Our conclusion is that it was more advanced. This is obvious. In what manner could the structures at Dowth be used? Does the eclipse element of the Dowth legend point to some function of the site which is concerned with eclipses? We think so.

There is a very high likelihood that someone watching the standstills of the moon, the so-called "moon swing", would become aware of the fact that eclipses happen in patterns, and that eclipses are predictable. We could think of someone watching a clock's pendulum swinging, and then noticing that the swinging of the pendulum is connected with the movement of the second hand on the clock. That said, it is important to realise that the moon swing and the eclipse cycle are not intrinsically connected. An eclipse of the moon happens when the moon is full and located near one of its nodes.[89] The nodes, which are invisible, mark the point where the moon's path crosses the ecliptic, the moon's path through the sky being inclined to the ecliptic by 5.15°.[90] If the moon's path was not

The gate to immortality? The sun setting over Newgrange, as viewed from Dowth

inclined to the ecliptic, "there would be an eclipse of the sun at every new moon, and every full moon would be eclipsed".[91]

There is a key difference between two periods of the moon which results in the full moon happening in a different part of the sky every lunation. The lunar tropical month, which brings the moon back to the same position in the sky relative to the vernal point, is 27.32 days long,[92] while the period it takes the moon to return to the same phase – called the synodic month – is 29.53 days. Thom points out that the reason for the difference is that, in the time it takes the moon to make a circuit of the sky, the sun has advanced, so it takes the moon an extra two days to catch up.[93]

To further complicate things, the time it takes the moon to complete a circuit from a node – i.e. the point where the moon's track through the sky crosses the ecliptic – back to the same node, is 27.21 days.[94]

Thus we see that the lunar movements are quite complicated. But this does not by any means indicate that the prehistoric stone builders could not work out these movements, if they watched the moon and counted its periods over long intervals. Charles Scribner, an American sky watcher who has studied the movements of the moon using the naked eye for over 20 years, maintains that the 19-year metonic lunar cycle, the 18.61-year standstill cycle and the 18-year eclipse cycle (known as the Saros Cycle),[95] could be observed with a bit of patient study and careful recording.

Alexander Thom believed there was an intrinsic connection between the 18.6-year standstill cycle, what we term the "moon swing", and the forecasting of eclipses. He held that if the megalithic astronomers could detect slight perturbations in the maximum and minimum declination limits of the moon, they could predict eclipses.[96] The limits, he said, were "subject to a wobble of amplitude Δ equal to about 9 arc minutes and a period of 173.3 days".[97]

A serious study of the standstills would reveal this wobble, or irregularity, which with devoted observation would lead to eclipse prediction. Having studied the moon for both its illumination in the long nights of winter and its connection with the tides, megalithic astronomers would eventually have seen the moon swing. "The 18.6-year cycle would obtrude itself, if in fact it had not been recognised from time immemorial".[98] Thom claimed that once the technique of using a horizon mark with a backsight was applied studiously, the irregularities at the standstills would have made themselves apparent.

Whether passage-tomb architecture could operate at this level of exactness, we are only in a position to speculate. A beam of moonlight being observed on the rear stones of the Dowth chambers may not have provided the accuracy needed to detect the perturbations at the standstills. A distant foresight would have been required. The fact that Dowth South points towards Tara in the direction of major standstill while Dowth North points towards Newgrange for minor standstill suggests that perhaps more distant foresights were used to track the perturbations more effectively.

While the sunlight penetrating into the southern chamber at the solstice mainly illuminates the bottom of Chamber Stones 7 and 8,[99] the moon at major standstill is likely to have illuminated Chamber Stone 6, a stone featuring markings which could have been used as calibration markers tracking the moon beam at different lunations around the time of standstills.

Another aspect of Dowth's architecture is very interesting in the light of the eclipse interval. Archaeologists have estimated that there are a total of 115 kerbstones. As pointed out earlier, some of these are buried, so in essence this is an educated guess. If there are 115 kerbstones, there is a strong link to eclipses in the number. If you were to go around Dowth twice, counting kerbstones as you go, your total would be 230, which is the number of synodic lunar months (new moon to new moon or full moon to full moon) in the 18.6-year moon swing cycle.[100] It could be one of those extraordinary coincidences which pops up from time to time, but only a full exposure of the kerb around Dowth will tell us for sure.

If the kerb does contain 115 members, then the four-way collaboration of facts we discussed earlier becomes a five-way collaboration, thus:

(1) The name: Dubhad, darkening, eclipse.

(2) The legend: An eclipse at the time of summer solstice.

(3) *The passages*: Homing in on the lunar extremes.

(4) *The petroglyphs*: Eclipse symbols on the seven suns stone.

(5) *The kerb*: 115 stones, half the moon swing cycle in synodic months.

The eclipse symbols on the Stone of the Seven Suns are similar to markings on the back stone at Cairn T, Loughcrew, which have been interpreted as being depictions of an actual eclipse of the sun.[101] Another Irish archaeoastronomer, Paul Griffin, says he has discovered confirmation of the world's oldest solar eclipse recorded in stone at Loughcrew.[102] This eclipse, according to Griffin, happened in the late afternoon on 30 November 3340 BC.[103] Depictions of the eclipse are found on petroglyphs in two chambers, on the back stone of Cairn T on Carnbane East and on stones 19 and 20 at Cairn L, another site which has a chamber structure aligned on the November/February cross-quarter days (sunrise) and probably aligned also on minor standstill moonrise.[104]

While eclipses of the moon would have been both predictable and observable, eclipses of the sun are much more difficult to observe.[105] This is because to see a total solar eclipse, the astronomer would have to be located along a very narrow strip on the surface of the earth, and as Thom points out, "this zone is different for every eclipse".[106]

Thus we see that solar eclipses, particularly total eclipses which bring about sudden darkness, are very rare indeed at any one location on the earth. So rare were they, in fact, that the idea that a great monument such as the Dowth observatory was constructed to commemorate an eclipse is not an outlandish notion.

One interesting observation about a total solar eclipse at the time of summer solstice is the fact that, two weeks beforehand, the full moon would set exactly at the same place on the horizon as winter solstice sunset, and there is a possibility that that full moon was also eclipsed because it would have been located at one of its nodes.

It is clear that the legend of Dowth paints a picture for us of a great undertaking – the construction of a huge monument which not only served as an astronomical observatory but as a sacred structure by which the elect could attain eternal life in the otherworld. It would appear this legend contains echoes of actual events, and thus stories which were weaved into consciousness more than 50 centuries ago survive intact today, with obvious additions, such as the reference to the tower of Babylon (Babel).

> By him is built the solid hill
> in the likeness of Nimrod's tower . . .[107]

Dowth at Midsummer

And they said, Go to, let us build us a city and a tower, whose top may reach unto heaven; and let us make us a name, lest we be scattered abroad upon the face of the whole earth.[108]

And this is exactly what happened to the king's builders in the Dowth legend. They were scattered back to their homes. The king's great plan appears to have been spoilt by the sudden darkness brought about by a total eclipse. The legend tells us that the men of Erin abandoned the project and the enormous sky–ground structure remained incomplete:

When it was no longer day for them thereafter
(it is likely that it was night),
the hill was not brought to the top,
the men of Erin depart homeward.

From that day forth the hill remains
without addition to its height:
it shall not grow greater from this time onward
till the Doom of destruction and judgement.[109]

. . . darkness has fallen upon our work . . .
Dubad (darkness) shall be the name of this place for ever.[110]

CHAPTER SEVEN

NEWGRANGE: THE CYGNUS ENIGMA

D riving towards Newgrange, on the narrow roads leading through the tranquil countryside of the Boyne Valley, we are filled with a sense of wonderment, a feeling of arcane intuition, and the emotions begin to sway. We are approaching Ireland's greatest monument, and one of its enduring mysteries.

As the great dome of Newgrange looms into view, the pathway to the past has been breached once again, and the motorcar and the monolith become juxtaposed in a physical union that transcends the persuasion of time. We are in the domain of the Neolithic. It's like we've crossed a concealed borderline, an imaginary barrier between the present and the past. Behind is the twenty-first century AD. Ahead is the fourth millennium BC.

No matter how many times we have made this journey, each time we go there we feel a lump in the throat, a tingling in the heart, a rush of excitement. The road from Dowth turns sharply at 90-degree angles a number of times on the way to Newgrange. Negotiating the last few of these corners, we perceive the great cairn, with its brilliant white quartz façade and the great monoliths which encircle it, standing like giant silent sentries guarding a castle. We have arrived at:

> . . . that glorious dome that stands
> By the dark rolling waters of the Boyne
> Where Oengus Og magnificently dwells.[1]

Newgrange, the "white brugh",[2] "brilliant to approach",[3] is the centrepiece of the vast scattering of disparate monuments that make up the Bend of the Boyne assembly. It is the quintessential icon of Ireland, its culture and people, an echoing vestige of enlightened prehistory, an embodiment of the inimitable megalithic spirit and the influences that forged it and strengthened it in the ancient epoch when people had arisen out of the obscurity of the ages to celebrate the union of heaven and earth and bring light into dark places.

But it is much more than a patriotic symbol. It represents the zenith of megalithic achievement, when bright human beings walked the fertile lands of the Boyne Valley and with the strength and toil, the zeal and conviction which drove them to greater things, set down on the land immense edifices which they envisioned as the technology and sacred architecture with which they could unify their cosmic beliefs with their chaotic physical existences.

The author Elizabeth Hickey said that Newgrange "retains still a quality which awes us, something greater than the mere materials from which it is composed, and greater than the wonder at its size and age. It

Newgrange, the "white brugh", "brilliant to approach"

retains within its composition the will of a people, who conceived their kings as more than mortal and laboured monumentally to enshrine their immortality in stone."[4]

It is just one of a total of 93 recorded monuments in the "core and buffer zones of Brú na Bóinne",[5] many of which are prehistoric. The great importance of Brú na Bóinne as one of the most outstanding archaeological landscapes on the planet was recognised in 1993 when the area was designated a World Heritage Site by UNESCO.

Today, Newgrange is a major tourist attraction, drawing up to a quarter of a million visitors per year from every quarter of the globe.[6] The mound has been publicly accessible for over three centuries, but the tourist numbers increased dramatically when the site was excavated and restored in the 1960s and 1970s.[7]

THE LIGHT OF FIVE THOUSAND YEARS

In 2006, over 27,400 people – approximately one out of every ten visitors to the Newgrange visitor centre – applied for the annual "Winter Solstice Lottery", which is a yearly draw made in October to select the lucky few to get the chance to be inside Newgrange on the shortest days of the year when the sun penetrates into the chamber.

Since Professor Michael O'Kelly rediscovered the solstice alignment in 1967, Newgrange has captured the public interest. Initially those who wanted to see the solstice phenomenon put their names on a list, but eventually the list became so long that it was abandoned in favour of a draw in 2001. Fifty names are drawn in the solstice lottery, with another 50 as a "reserve list" in case some people don't turn up. The odds of being drawn as a witness to the solstice phenomenon are about one in 550.[8] But

Winter solstice sunrise over Red Mountain, as viewed from Newgrange

that doesn't stop Richard and me entering our names every year, in the vain hope that some day we will see this momentous event for ourselves! In the meantime, we have to rely on the witness accounts of others in order to paint a picture of what happens inside "yonder brugh chequered with the many lights"[9] at winter solstice.

Shortly before 9.00 am on the morning of winter solstice, the first glimpse of the golden orb of the sun reveals itself over the crest of the hill of Red Mountain. For a few minutes the ridge of the hill across the valley from Newgrange is rimmed with golden orange, the fire of the dawn of the shortest day, a reminder of the life-giving heat and light which the sun yields in the cold and gloomy days of Irish winter. There can be little doubt that this hill was given its name by the Stone Age sky watchers, the cunning master builders who perceived that at moments such as this, when the sun's course along the horizon had been stayed, there was a sanctified, visual fusion of sun and earth. The modern townland name connected with this hill is Roughgrange, the "rough" part translated from *rúadh,* meaning "red" or "golden", and the *grange* bit borrowed from the English word *grange,* meaning a farm or a granary,[10] but often associated with the word *grian,* meaning "sun".[11] Thus a place name such as Red Mountain takes on a hallowed and enduring denotation, the signification of a singular cosmic moment.

At around four and a half minutes after sunrise, the light of the sun, which enters into the dark interior of Newgrange through a specially constructed aperture known as the "roof box", shines onto the floor of the chamber 18 metres inside.[12]

For the following 17 minutes, a narrow shaft of light penetrates into the structure, shining onto the floor of the cruciform chamber, bringing a warm glow to the almost permanent darkness of the interior.[13] At present, the solstice sunbeam is just over a foot wide as it enters the chamber, tapering towards the rear recess.[14] It is thought to have been as wide as 40 centimetres when Newgrange was built, the beam being narrowed by the fact that some of the passage stones are now leaning inwards.[15]

It is now thought that when the cross-shaped passage structure of Newgrange was assembled, the shaft of light from the midwinter sun would have penetrated one metre into the rear recess.[16] Carved onto chamber stone C10 in this recess is the famous so-called "triple spiral",[17] which replicates a similar petroglyph on the entrance kerbstone, a twirling coil pattern which has become a universal symbol of Newgrange throughout the globe.

The solstice phenomenon lasts just 17 minutes. It is a fleeting moment of illumination, which happens every day for three days either side of the winter solstice.[18] For the remainder of the year, the chamber remains in darkness. Unlike Dowth South, where the sun reaches into the chamber for months on end, Newgrange is much more focused. It is a precisely tuned astronomical apparatus, a finely regulated machine whose rough, unhewn stones were positioned with such proficiency and expertise that the light of the sunrises on the shortest days was captured with meticulous accuracy.

But the Newgrange apparatus, as we will see, captures much more than winter solstice sunrise, and there can be little doubt that, like Dowth, it was a portal of sorts, designed to forge a bridge between the earth and the

otherworld which lay among the stars. In the story of the "Pursuit of Diarmaid and Gráinne" from the *Ossianic Cycle* of tales, we are told that the deceased hero Diarmaid was taken to Newgrange by Aonghus in order to "'put an aeriel life into him so that he will talk to me every day".[19] In another version of the tale, Aonghus says, "and since I cannot restore him to life I will send a soul into him, so that he may talk to me each day".[20]

In these legends lies a clue that Newgrange and the other passage-mounds may have had a ritual funerary purpose, that the archaeological denotation "passage-tomb", although it describes only one function of these sites, is

The celebrated winter solstice sunbeam entering the passage at Newgrange (photo: © Office of Public Works)

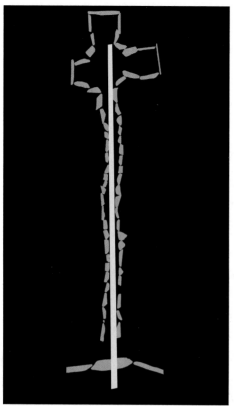

Illustration showing the path of the light in the passage at winter solstice

indeed an important element of this type of monument. Professor O'Kelly, the excavator of Newgrange, found the remains of at least five individuals in the "tomb" during excavations, two of which were unburnt and three cremated.[21] These fragmented remains are the definitive pathological evidence, if it could be considered definitive, of a sepulchral purpose for Newgrange.[22] Beyond this evidence, we must work in the realm of speculation, deduction and supposition. For the time being, our supposition is that if there was some burial purpose to Newgrange, it was connected with the belief that the soul of the deceased could be transported to the otherworld out of the chamber, along the sky beam formed by certain heavenly bodies such as the sun, and on into the plain of happiness, the land of eternal youth of myth.

The fact that there is an indication of a funerary purpose to Newgrange in mythology suggests that the stories about this place come down to us from the remotest times. O'Kelly acknowledged this: "The concept of Newgrange as a house of the dead and as an abode of spirits at one and the same time, was in no way contradicted by the findings of the excavation."[23] He also acknowledged that there was a belief in the vicinity of Newgrange, before he discovered the solstice alignment in 1967, that the rising sun penetrated into Newgrange and illuminated the triple spiral on Chamber Stone 10 in the rear recess.[24] Whether this knowledge was transmitted orally in the locality across the five millennia since Newgrange was built, or whether someone had witnessed the sunlight in the chamber in more recent times, we will probably never know.

Claire O'Kelly, who had worked so closely alongside her husband at both Dowth and Newgrange, accepted that the stories about the Boyne passage-mounds were of great antiquity, saying that the stories showed the Boyne tombs "were known and recognised . . . from a very early time indeed."[25] It was "not at all fanciful" to put the origins of some of the myths into pre-Christian times, she said.[26]

SWANS AT THE BRÚ

There are many myths and legends connected with Newgrange, as would be expected of Ireland's most illustrious monument. Of these, we are very interested in the stories about swans. The swan is a creature which held a very special significance in the ancient tales, and some of the major narratives relating to Newgrange include references to swans.

One example of such myths is the story of the visit of Dechtine, Cúchulainn's mother, to Newgrange at wintertime, where she is visited by the god Lugh who makes her pregnant with the child-hero. Dechtine had arrived at the Brugh after chasing a flock of 180 swans from Eamhain Macha (Armagh) along with Conchobor and the Ulster noblemen.[27]

Perhaps the most famous of swan myths, apart that is from the tragic tale of the Children of Lir, is the romantic tale of Aonghus, the mythical owner of Newgrange, and Caer, the otherworldly swan maiden.

Aonghus was a mythical chieftain of the Tuatha Dé Danann, which was the principal race of the otherworld – the gods – in ancient Irish mythology. He resided at Brú na Bóinne, specifically at the tumulus of Newgrange, and was often referred to as "Aonghus an Bhrogha"[28] or "Oengus of the Brú".[29] His father was the Daghdha, the "good god", a principal deity of the Tuatha Dé Danann, and his mother was Bóann, the

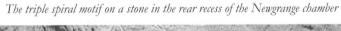

The triple spiral motif on a stone in the rear recess of the Newgrange chamber

moon/Milky Way/river goddess. The story recalls how Aonghus dreamed of a woman and fell madly in love with her. He eventually found her in the shape of a swan and they flew together to Newgrange, where they remained together, presumably happily ever after.

What was the inspiration for this swan story? We wondered if it was an entirely romantic myth, or whether it had contained within it concealed secrets telling a greater tale of happenings from the time Newgrange was built.

It was in the year 1984, while completing one of the many paintings he has done in the Bend of the Boyne, that the artist and co-author of this book, Richard Moore, first took note of the swans on the fields in front of Newgrange. The number of mute swans, the orange-beaked swan, wintering at Newgrange that year was over 30, while at one time in the winter of 1984, there were over 100 yellow-beaked whooper swans.[30]

Newgrange is a very important wintering ground for the whooper swan (*Cygnus cygnus*), and probably the only site in County Meath holding a flock of these birds on a regular basis each winter.[31] The whoopers come to Ireland from Iceland, landing first at Donegal and then dispersing to their various wintering grounds around Ireland. This makes them a particularly difficult species to census. "Their increased use of agricultural habitats not necessarily immediately adjacent to wetland habitats is part of the reason for this. Things become even more difficult in wet years when birds become even more dispersed."[32]

Ornithologists say all the whoopers which visit Ireland are from the breeding population in Iceland. The size of the winter population here has in recent years been estimated to be between 14,000 and 16,000 birds.[33] The whooper swan population was first officially recorded at Newgrange

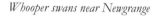

Whooper swans near Newgrange

in the winter of 1966/67, but both whoopers and Bewick's swans were recorded feeding on large open meadows and bogs in County Meath in the last century.[34] The flock at Newgrange varies in size from year to year, ranging from as few as 30 birds to as many as 226, the highest number ever recorded at the site, in the winter of 1987/88.[35] However, it is not known how long the birds have been coming to Ireland as statistics are unavailable for the preceding centuries.

What can be said for certain is that Newgrange is a nationally important wintering ground for the whoopers. During the five-year period from 1984 to 1989, the average number of whooper swans at Newgrange was over the threshold of 105 needed to qualify the site as being of national importance.[36]

We wondered if it was possible that swans have been coming to Newgrange since ancient times, and whether that was part of the inspiration for the swan myths. Tales such as the swan-chase from Armagh and the romance of Aonghus and Caer establish a firm mythical connection between swans and Newgrange. In the case of the latter story, there are wider associations with the heavens and the monument of Newgrange itself that must be explored in further detail.

It is in the text called *Aislinge Oenguso* ("The Vision of Aonghus") that we read the dramatic and romantic swan story. The story tells how Aonghus fell madly in love with a maiden who visited him while he slept. She appeared to him in his dreams for a year, and all this time he could not touch her because she would disappear. The story describes how he becomes sick with love.

His physician called upon Aonghus's mother, Bóann, to help. She searched Ireland for the maiden, but was unable to find the mystery maiden after a year of searching. Aonghus enlisted the help of his father, the Daghdha, who in turn sought out Bodhbh, who was the Tuatha Dé Danann king of Munster. Bodhbh revealed that the maiden was Caer Iobharmhéith, and brought Aonghus to meet her at Loch Béal Dragan (Lake of the Dragon's Mouth) in Tipperary. Bodhbh explained how Caer was from Sídh Uamhain, an "otherworld residence" in Connacht.

Caer's father revealed to the Daghdha that his daughter went in the forms of a bird and a girl on alternate years. He told the Daghdha that Caer would be found in the form of a swan at the Lake of the Dragon's Mouth the following Samhain (November). Aonghus went to the lake and found Caer in the form of a swan, accompanied by 150 (thrice 50) swans, all linked together by a silver chain. Caer herself was said to have worn a silver necklace.

When Aonghus went to Caer, he was transformed into a swan. They embraced each other, flew three times around the lake and then "flew together to Brugh na Bóinne and put the dwellers of that place to sleep with their beautiful singing. Caer remained with Aonghus in the Brugh after that".[37]

So here we had an ancient story relating directly to swans and to Newgrange. The fact that Caer was from an "otherworld residence" was intriguing, given that we have already established firm mythological evidence that the otherworld was located in the sky, among the stars. It is interesting also that there is a constellation or grouping of stars in the sky which is known as Cygnus, the swan. This constellation has its supposed origins in the classical world, representing the Greek God Zeus who has taken on the guise of a swan, flying across the sky "to pay an illicit visit to Leda, wife of King Tyndareus of Sparta".[38]

A group of whooper swans (photo: © Dave Appleton)

Is it possible that the ancient Irish classified the Cygnus constellation as a swan, albeit under a different name, long before the Greeks? We think so, and will outline some evidence to support this claim.

THE CYGNUS ENIGMA

Barry Cunliffe, Professor of European Archaeology at Oxford University, believes that the ancient people of Ireland and Britain were "far more advanced than any of the early Mediterranean cultures" and that our view of the Stone Age in the British Isles had been "skewed by our historical reliance on the Greek and Roman classical texts, which were thick with prejudice and ignorant of almost anything beyond the Pillars of Hercules (Gibraltar)".[39]

Cunliffe said that "for all these years we have been looking at Europe the wrong way round, and the idea that civilisation flowed out from the Mediterranean out to the barbarian edges of Europe has clouded our view that it flowed the other way too."[40] Furthermore, he said, there had been a belief up until three decades ago that Newgrange and the other great megalithic monuments were "influenced from the Mediterranean cultures", but that the evidence from carbon dating had shown that these buildings were being constructed here "long before they began to appear in southern Europe".[41]

British writer and earth mysteries researcher Andrew Collins, the author of six books including *The Cygnus Mystery*, believes the swan constellation was hugely important to many ancient cultures. He reports that Dr Michael Rappenglück of Munich University concluded that Cygnus, along with neighbouring constellations Lyra and Aquila, were represented in an ancient star map in the world famous Lascaux caves in France, dating back to 16,500 years ago.[42]

All of this leads us to wonder if, perhaps, some of the constellations were first envisaged on the periphery of Europe, and later these shapes migrated into the classical world. The Atlantic societies, according to Barry Cunliffe, were far more advanced in their navigation, their solar knowledge and their knowledge of the seasons and the stars. If the swan constellation was visualised by the megalith builders of Ireland, the evidence of this would surely be greater than a few old stories about swans. This led us to examine further connections and to form a theory which we came to call "The Cygnus Enigma".

It is our belief that the layout of the passage and chamber of Newgrange was influenced by the shape of the Cygnus constellation, and that this can be further inferred from the Aonghus-Caer love myth which specifies that they went "into" Newgrange after taking the form of swans. The chamber structure, being cross-shaped, reflects the cruciform figure of the swan star grouping which, as we will see, was an especially important constellation which held a very special significance at the time Newgrange was built.

It is one of a number of such cross-shaped passages known in Irish passage-grave architecture. A preference for cross-shaped tombs was "a pronounced insular trait" of the Boyne passage-mound builders,[43] although examples of cruciform chambers are found on the European continent also.[44]

At Newgrange, though, something very out of the ordinary confirms a far-reaching aspect of the complexity of its design. It is a little-known fact that the passage of Newgrange points in the direction of another group of ancient monuments, on the hill of Fourknocks, just inside the Meath–Dublin border near a village called Naul, about 15 kilometres southeast of Newgrange.

While the chamber actually aligns to a point in the sky where the sun appears above Red Mountain on winter solstice, the range of azimuths covered by the chamber structure is between four and five degrees wide.[45] The old habit of drawing lines on maps came into play again when we realised, very early on in our research, that a small passage-tomb at Fourknocks lay roughly in the direction of winter solstice viewed from Newgrange, even though neither site is visible from the other. On a clear day, the Dublin Mountains can be seen to the south from Newgrange, but nothing can be seen to the southeast beyond the slopes of Red Mountain. It is in this direction, beyond Red Mountain and towards the direction of rising sun on winter solstice, that the Fourknocks mound sits on the ridge along with a number of other ancient remains.[46] Wondering what significance Fourknocks held in the scheme of things, we went up there to have a closer look.

Fourknocks is minuscule in comparison with the huge trio of passage-mounds at Brú na Bóinne. At just 19 metres in diameter, it is less than a quarter of the size of Newgrange. It was excavated in the early 1950s by P.J. Hartnett, who found that it contained a large pear-shaped chamber, measuring 7.5 metres at its widest point. This chamber has three side-chambers or recesses, and 12 of the structural stones at Fourknocks are decorated with intricate petroglyphs.[47] Today, it is topped with a "shell-concrete dome", although there is no clear evidence Fourknocks had a roof on it at the time it was in use. It has been suggested that while part of a roof structure may have been formed of corbelled stones, the remainder of the roof structure may have consisted of a framework of rafters supported by a wooden post.[48]

Approaching the mound of Fourknocks up the long path connecting it with the nearby road, visitors are struck by the fact that the entrance door of the passage is around the northern side of the mound. Not surprising is the fact that Fourknocks sits on a ridge and, standing on the top of its grassy dome, people who come to this tranquil spot are impressed

Fourknocks
After Cooney (2000) and Eogan (1986)

N

The ground plan at Fourknocks (image: © Matthew and Geraldine Stout)

with the views of the landscape which sweeps away towards rolling green hills to the north and south and down towards the sea to the east. Once again, the strategic location on a hill or upland area, an attribute widely seen with megalithic passage-mounds, is repeated at Fourknocks, where the site presently being discussed is just one site in a "large concentration of prehistoric monuments".[49] The feeling of being detached from the earth and closer to the sky is accentuated by the modern dome covering Fourknocks.

Two things which we perceived as immediate connections linking Fourknocks with Newgrange were the cruciform shape that seems to have inspired both chambers, and the squashed oval shape which was inherent in both the outline of the Newgrange cairn and the composition of the chamber of Fourknocks. This shape brings to mind the primordial "cosmic egg" of site Q which we met in Chapter 5. At Newgrange, this egg is pierced, or split open, by the rays of the winter solstice sun, and at that moment the union of male sun shaft and female earth mound inspires the notion that an act of conception leading to the birth of a new

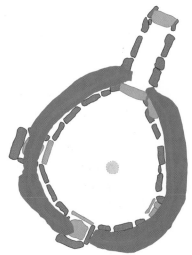

Overlay of the ground plans of Site Q and Fourknocks, showing the similarity of their egg-shaped structures

sun for the year was taking place symbolically. It is possible, according to one author, that the "goal of astral rituals . . . was to magically influence events so as to improve survival and fertility".[50]

At Fourknocks, unlike Newgrange, the sun cannot shine down its passage and into the dark chamber beyond. The stark reason for this is that the aperture of the chamber opens towards a point on the horizon which is too far north to accept light from the rising sun. In fact, due to the fact that the axis of the chamber's alignment points roughly towards 14°,[51] the interior structure of Fourknocks cannot even accept light from the rising moon at major standstill, which would be located a whole 19 degrees further east along the horizon, the equivalent of about 38 moon widths away.

What is particularly notable about the orientation of the Fourknocks passage is that it would appear to point fairly accurately in the direction of the Baltray standing stones which we met in Chapter 1.[52] At Baltray, we had noted that if an observer lined up the two stones, they appeared to align towards Fourknocks. Here, at Fourknocks, the passage points back in the direction of the two monoliths overlooking the Boyne Estuary.

Examining some of the passage alignments we had investigated up to this point, we saw a pattern emerging. Dowth North points to Newgrange. Newgrange points towards Fourknocks. Fourknocks is aligned in the direction of Baltray and Baltray points back again. One is inclined to lean towards the hypothesis that all this was not the result of a bizarre string of coincidences, but was in fact an integral objective of the megalithic astronomer builders. Their passages did not merely point to specific celestial risings and settings; they also pointed towards other star temples and sacred sites. Other examples of this illustrated thus far include Cairn T, which points to the Hill of Slane, and Dowth South, which points towards Rath Maeve and Tara.

Inside the Fourknocks chamber

So what in the heavens, if anything, did Fourknocks point to? Did anything actually "rise" so close to due north? Therein lies the central cornerstone of the Cygnus Enigma, the key that cracks the code and elucidates an abundance of factors which help explain much about the structures and shapes of the monuments, their orientations, the myths and the cosmic connection which has already been potently hinted at.

It is not known exactly when Fourknocks was built, but archaeologists say it was probably in the time period 3000–2500 BC.[53] It is to this epoch we returned to recreate the ancient sky using computer software. With our view centred on 14°, we watched the stars pass by as we progressed through time using 15-minute intervals. The first time Richard and I did this, we were struck with a startling sight – Deneb, the bright primary star of Cygnus, the heavenly swan, came into view as it began to rise off the northern horizon. Moving back and forth using SkyMap's time skip feature, we could see that the swan star appeared to skim the horizon at due north. It became apparent in that moment that the swan constellation of the sky may have held a special significance to the Stone Age astronomers.

What was not immediately transparent to us then was what exact importance Cygnus held. We would see in time the pieces of an enormous jigsaw fall into place and a truly breathtaking picture of the complexity of megalithic sky worship emerged. The picture as it had thus far revealed itself was as follows: swan mythology was central to the story of Newgrange; the fields in front of Newgrange are and were an important wintering ground for swans; the passage of Newgrange points towards Fourknocks; Fourknocks points towards a place on the horizon where Deneb, the swan star, would have been rising after skimming the horizon five millennia ago.

But the Cygnus Enigma runs much deeper than all this. Both Newgrange and Fourknocks have chamber structures which are based upon the cross shape, echoing the cruciform outline of the swan constellation. A comparison of the ground plan of Newgrange with Cygnus is interesting because, even though the two don't make an exact fit, the Newgrange passage is sinuous, with a kink which helps narrow the solstice sunbeam but which also serves as a reflection of the heavenly bird because its axis is also crooked.

The star at the centre of Cygnus, known as Gamma Cygni or *Sadr*, meaning "the breast of the hen",[54] is off axis, so to speak, lying somewhat amiss of the point where imaginary lines running through the wing axis and the body axis would intersect if the cross shape was formed of two straight lines. In addition, the star Eta Cygni, which lies on the "neck" of the bird, is also slightly off axis. Whether Newgrange was intended to

Comparison of the passage at Newgrange and the Cygnus constellation shows the remarkable similarity of the cruciform shape

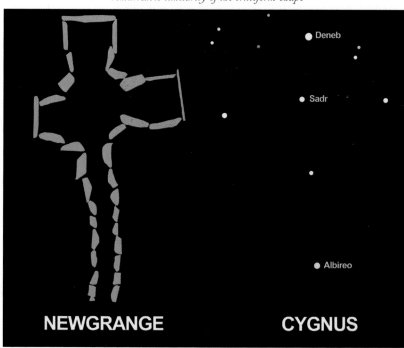

exactly imitate the great bird of the sky or not, it is apparent that the cross was a potent symbol inspiring the construction of the three main Boyne passage-mounds, all of which have a cross-shaped chamber.

Fourknocks, despite having a circular chamber, is also based on a cruciform design, with the three recesses and the passage duplicating the shape of the swan star grouping. Interestingly, the post-hole which is near the centre of the chamber floor provides a ground equivalent for the central star, Sadr. Also interesting is the fact that Fourknocks may not have had a roof. If one purpose of Fourknocks was watching star risings, which happen in the dark of night, no roof would have been necessary.

Newgrange and Fourknocks are not the only monuments displaying an apparent concern with Cygnus. Andrew Collins is interested in the fact that John North determined that a Neolithic monument called Wayland's Smithy in Berkshire, England, a long barrow, "displayed a near-northerly alignment to the setting of Deneb in the late fifth millennium BC".[55] The central chamber of Wayland's Smithy, like Newgrange, is cruciform in shape.[56]

Of significance is the fact that both Newgrange and Fourknocks have, as an integral element of their design, the shape of an egg, the symbol of fertilisation, of reproduction, of new birth. We are reminded of the fact that the primordial cosmic egg has its roots in much more ancient times, and is connected with symbolism which includes water, a bird, a woman and an egg. The woman in this case is Caer. The egg is represented by the stone structures themselves, which are held to be womb-like edifices connected with the rebirth of the sun and the rising of the swan. What about the water?

There are some interesting water features down along the Boyne below Newgrange which are considered to be man made. These circular ponds were "deliberately created",[57] and their circular shape and structure has been interpreted by archaeology as significant with regard to their similarity to the henge structures.[58] There are four ponds in total, one being located a mile and a half north of Newgrange not far from a henge at Monknewtown, the other three sitting on the flood plain of the Boyne in front of Newgrange. Two of these are conjoined, and appear to be clay-lined.[59]

Whooper swans "winter on freshwater lakes and marshes, and, in western Europe especially, on low agricultural land . . ."[60] They feed on shallow water and although they can occasionally be found on feeding arable land, less than 15 per cent do so in winter.[61] Their tendency towards "freshwater habitats"[62] makes the Boyne floodplain the ideal wintering base for the whooper swans, something which may have been further aided by the artificial ponds which may have been created specifically for these birds.

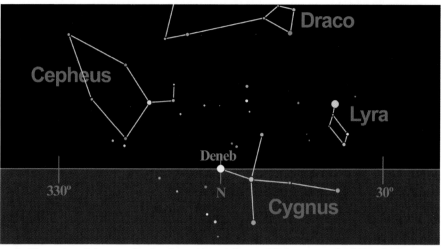

An illustration of the stars showing the position of Cygnus 5000 years ago, with Deneb skimming the horizon due north, and the constellation Draco above it

It is clear that swans were held with great reverence, something which would have been accentuated by the apparent presence of a giant swan in the sky, gliding down the Milky Way. It has been said that Cygnus is one of the few constellations which actually resembles the thing it is meant to represent, "a rare thing among constellations".[63] But this fact alone can hardly justify the creation of a vast sky–ground system such as the Newgrange–Fourknocks harmonisation. What was the great significance of the swan constellation in ancient Ireland, and why was so much effort made to create such an astronomical master plan?

PRECESSION OF THE EQUINOXES

The answer lies in precession of the equinoxes, the slow wobble of the earth's axis first mentioned in Chapter 3. There is little doubt that competent communities of astronomers such as the people who built the Boyne assembly would have perceived the sluggish turning of the wheel of precession, and that over time they witnessed the regression of the vernal point of the sun in conjunction with the fact that the pole of the sky, the apparent point around which everything else appeared to revolve, was occasionally marked by a star. During the epoch in which Newgrange and Fourknocks were in use, the pole was marked by a star called Alpha Draconis, which has the proper name Thuban in modern astronomical use.[64] It is the main star of the constellation Draco, the dragon.

The dragon constellation is woven into the Aonghus–Caer love story, in which we are told Aonghus finds his swan maiden at the lake of the dragon's mouth. Hanging above Cygnus in the sky as it rises on the northern horizon is the head of Draco. The romantic legend appears to divulge some primeval precessional knowledge.

Graham Hancock, author of *Fingerprints of the Gods* and *Heaven's Mirror*, who has been on a quest for an ancient highly knowledgeable civilisation for many years, compares the "luminous dome of the celestial sphere" to a "vast and intricate piece of machinery. And, like a millwheel, like a churn, like a whirlpool, like a quern, this machine turns and turns and turns endlessly."[65]

Hancock acknowledges the "landmark study" by Giorgio de Santillana and Hertha von Dechend entitled *Hamlet's Mill*, declaring that its remarkable contribution to scholarship was "the evidence it presents – compelling and overwhelming – that, long *before* the supposed beginnings of civilised human history . . . precession was understood and spoken of in a precise technical language by people who could only have been highly civilised."[66]

The evidence that the Irish Neolithic builders knew about precession is starkly and stunningly illustrated by the Fourknocks passage-mound, which homes in on Deneb, the bright star of Cygnus and the twentieth-brightest star in the entire sky,[67] at a key moment in the "turning of the millwheel" of precession.

For almost the entire 25,800 years of a single cycle of the precession of the equinoxes, Deneb is a circumpolar star as viewed from the latitude of Fourknocks. This simply means that it does not set below the horizon; that, on any given night of the year in any epoch of time, Deneb remains visible throughout the night. But there is a brief term during this long cycle when Deneb glances the horizon in the north, appearing nightly

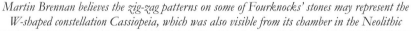

Martin Brennan believes the zig-zag patterns on some of Fourknocks' stones may represent the W-shaped constellation Cassiopeia, which was also visible from its chamber in the Neolithic

to set momentarily behind whatever distant landmark features lie in that direction, before rising off the earth again. This phenomenon probably lasted just a couple of centuries before Deneb became circumpolar again.

An observer inside the southern recess of Fourknocks, looking out through the passage, would have seen Deneb framed by the aperture of the entrance, rising slowly at a shallow angle off the distant hills and mountains. Because of the very slow "rising and falling" of Deneb over time, it is probable that astronomers in Fourknocks might have seen the star through the entrance for as long as a millennium or so.[68]

But despite the slow change in its position, Deneb retains a huge significance at the time of the Newgrange–Fourknocks construction because of the fact that it appears to vanish for a short time below the horizon. From the present day, right now in the early twenty-first century, it will be another 20,800 years before this happens again. The implication is that there was a very profound knowledge of precession and that this was encoded into the Aonghus-Caer love story.

Another astronomical element of the Newgrange–Fourknocks system is the fact that at the time of winter solstice, the "wings" of the swan constellation Cygnus appear to point downwards towards the position of the sun below the horizon, albeit roughly. Thus, Cygnus could perhaps have been used to track the position of the sun during the night preceding the winter solstice dawn. Towards daybreak, the swan stars would vanish in the encroaching light from the sun and thus the swan would "announce" the sunrise on the shortest day. This correlation of swan stars and sun is mimicked in a fashion inside Newgrange on winter solstice, where the light from the sun shines into the heart of the cross-shaped chamber at dawn.

SILVER CHAIN

The inference that Cygnus held a special importance to the stone builders can be further extrapolated from unique astronomical data subtly woven into the narrative of the "Vision of Aonghus". When Aonghus first found Caer, she was with "thrice 50" maidens linked together by a silver chain. In one account, Caer herself was adorned by a silver necklace.[69] It is patently obvious that the silver chain is the Milky Way, which, as a matter of major significance, runs right through the Cygnus constellation in the sky.[70] The giant swan of the sky appears to be flying along the astral river. We have encountered this "silver chain" before – in the chapter about Tara – where we were told that Lugh of the Long Arm wore the Milky Way "as a silver chain around his neck".

The Milky Way and Cygnus as viewed from Newgrange

This silver chain of the Milky Way connects Cygnus with another nearby constellation which has long been considered to represent a bird. That star grouping is called Aquila, the eagle, which contains the bright star Altair.[71] The bird stars of Deneb and Altair are the twentieth and thirteenth-brightest stars in the night sky respectively. The location of two bird star groupings so close together in the sky with the Milky Way as a backdrop suggests the idea that one constellation represented Aonghus and the other Caer.[72]

The Milky Way, the "most spectacular band of heaven"[73] provides a resplendent backdrop for the great swan stars. The Milky Way was regarded by the Polynesians as "the road of souls as they pass into the spirit world".[74] In the ancient Irish mindset, it was held as the "road of the illuminated cow". It figures very importantly in the study of precession, for "once the precession had been discovered", it is "a reference point from which the precession could be imagined to have taken its start".[75]

Ancient monuments in Turkey, dating back to c.9500-9000 BC, "expressed a shamanic worldview that reflected a far older cosmological mindset which saw Cygnus as the bird of creation atop the sky-pole".[76] This "sky-pole" is the Milky Way, along which Cygnus is flying.

The authors of *Hamlet's Mill* infer that this was when the vernal equinoctial sun left its position in the Milky Way in Gemini (or more precisely, above the upraised hand of Orion) and that afterwards, the notion transpired that "the Milky Way might mark the abandoned track of the sun".[77] Similarly, as is probably the case with the Irish astronomers, it was regarded as being the track of the moon, the road of the cow. Interestingly, the East African Turu envisioned the Milky Way as the "cattle track of the brother of the creator".[78]

Today, the huge ring of the Milky Way cannot be viewed as one complete circle. At most, we can see about two-thirds of its bright bands, the rest remaining beyond view below the horizon. Of course, observing the Milky Way in the first place requires dark, unpolluted skies, something which rules out observation of it in the centre of large cities and towns. In former times, before the Industrial Revolution and prior to the invention of the light bulb, observing the Milky Way would have been much easier in many parts of the world where it is today virtually impossible. It is best seen at the zenith, the point in the sky directly overhead, because its faint bands are harder to see when closer to the horizon.[79]

In the Neolithic, it would have been much easier to perceive. It is difficult to imagine in this modern age a time when the night sky would have held a luminous brilliance and a crisp clarity, the stars and planets and bands of the galaxy appearing more vivid and dramatic than they do even in dark unpolluted skies today. In modern times, sadly, "only in remote spots can one still glimpse the grandeur of the Milky Way".[80] In this regard, we are jealous of the ancient star gazers and the sights that they beheld.

Something very unique connects the Milky Way with the Cygnus Enigma. It is the fact that, 5,000 years ago, the bright central band of the galaxy would have been visible as a complete ring, sitting along the horizon all the way around from north to east to south to west back to north again.[81] This is something which, as stated already, does not happen today. It must have been a powerful sight, evoking imagery of a greater connection between sky and ground – even greater than the solstice sunrise celebrated at Newgrange – a moment in which a pathway to the stars was opened up in every visible direction.

In India, the Ganges river symbolised the Milky Way, and in one story we read, "Falling from on high, as she issues from the moon, she alights on the summit of Meru (the World Mountain in the North), and thence flows to the four quarters of the earth, for its purification".[82] Here we see similarities with the Irish visualisation, which ostensibly saw the Milky Way as being the milk of the illuminated cow, the moon.

Observers aware of the slow turning of the millwheel of precession would, by extension, have been aware of the vagaries of that process, including the fact that the regression, or backward progression, of the vernal point would at some epoch result in the Milky Way settling on the whole horizon. That epoch coincided with the time Newgrange and Fourknocks were in use.

Just like Deneb changes its altitude above the northern horizon very slowly over time, so too does the Milky Way gradually skew so that it no longer wraps itself around the whole horizon. In fact, it is probable that the Milky Way phenomenon lasted for a few thousand years at a time. Nevertheless, the next time observers watching the sky from Ireland will be able to see this phenomenon is in the epoch 19000 AD, a whole 17,000 years from now, so it retains a major precessional significance. One fact worthy of note is that the phenomenon coincided with the era of megalithic construction in Europe.

At Newgrange, the Milky Way phenomenon was commemorated uniquely in both the physical landscape in which the monument is set, and the actual design of the monument itself. Visitors to Newgrange will no doubt have been impressed by its visual grandeur, fronted as it is with a giant wall of milky quartz stones. During the course of his work in the 1960s and 1970s, the archaeologist who excavated Newgrange found that there was a layer of "angular pieces of white quartz" located at the bottom of what was termed the "cairn slip",[83] material which was presumed to have slid off the cairn, over the kerbstones and out onto the ground at some juncture in the past. Professor O'Kelly concluded that the quartz must have been at a "near-vertical" surface, and not a natural sloping face as had been previously suggested.[84] He further proposed that the subsidence of the cairn material was a "fairly rapid and clean collapse" and postulates that this falling down may have been precipitated by a sudden thaw after a severe frost or even an earth tremor.[85] Experimentation carried out by O'Kelly demonstrated that Newgrange would have been "drum-like" rather than dome-shaped when constructed.

The fact that the sheer face of white quartz fronting Newgrange is today supported by a concrete wall which must be about 15 feet tall raises the question of how the sheer "near-vertical" face of quartz was held in place when the mound was originally built. That's not a question we're going to try to answer in this book; suffice it to say that the front of Newgrange was decorated with this beautiful stone, with some water or glacially rolled grey granite boulders mixed in.[86]

The fact that the white stones are called "milky quartz" encourages us to connect this element of the Newgrange architecture with the great ring of the Milky Way, the "spectacular band of heaven" settling on the horizon. Was the semi-circular milky quartz wall constructed to mimic the Milky Way?

This interpretation is strengthened by the fact that the Milky Way phenomenon was happening precisely when Deneb was rising off the northern horizon and shining into the chamber of Fourknocks. So we see that the two events – the rising of Deneb during the period of its lowest altitude and the settling of the "road of the illuminated cow" on the whole horizon – are intrinsically connected. For this reason, the Newgrange–Fourknocks alignment is unlikely to have been the result of probability, but rather it is evidently the result of a carefully crafted astronomical blueprint fabricated when these extraordinary precessional events were happening.

The looping river of the Milky Way, mirrored by the looping milky quartz wall of Newgrange, is further mirrored by the Boyne River itself, the "bright cow" river, which encircles Newgrange and the other great passage-mounds of Brú na Bóinne, embracing them in a huge arc. Newgrange is bounded on three sides, to the east, south and west, by the Boyne.

Thus a hypothesis emerges that the architecture of Newgrange and its strategic siting in the landscape could have been intentionally precessional in nature, immortalising a great epoch in which unique phenomena were happening in the sky. It is not beyond the realms of possibility that the astronomer builders comprehended the great lengths of time which separated their exceptional era from the next age in which these events would be repeated. Maybe this is why Aonghus and Caer were said to have gone into Newgrange and remained there. Perhaps the brief disappearance of Deneb, when it seemed to connect with the ground, is also why Aonghus was said to have sometimes become visible in the physical world:

> And as to Angus Og, son of the Dagda, sometimes he would come from Brugh na Boinn and let himself be seen upon the earth.[87]

CHAPTER EIGHT

NEWGRANGE: WOMB OF THE MOON

The astronomer and writer Carl Sagan once said that the ancient mythmakers knew "we are the children equally of the sky and the Earth".[1] There is something about the sky myths and archaeology associated with Newgrange which suggests its builders understood that concept, the notion that all that happens on earth is influenced by all that happens in the sky. They engaged in a mammoth effort to immortalise their cosmic beliefs, creating a dedicated astronomical structure which continues to function today, more than 5,000 years after it was set down in the Boyne Valley.

> Something in us recognises the Cosmos as home. We are made of stellar ash. Our origin and evolution have been tied to distant cosmic events. The exploration of the Cosmos is a voyage of self-discovery.[2]

The architects of the sacred stone observatories of Ireland were among those who, in ancient times, asked the question, "What is in the Great Beyond?"[3] Were these stone builders adherents to "an ancient rebirth ritual – wrapped up in sophisticated astronomical observations and descended from a worldwide cosmological system that also left its legacy in Egypt and south-east Asia"?[4]

> This system, which taught the duality and interpenetration of ground and sky, earth and heaven – matter and spirit – urged the initiate to shed attachments to the sense-world . . . and to ascend upwards, through self-sacrifice and the quest for knowledge, to the celestial realms.[5]

This idealism is certainly present in ancient Irish folklore. In one tale, Connla of the Red Hair asked a messenger from the otherworld where she came from: "I come from Tir-nam-Beo, the Land of the Ever-Living Ones, where no death comes". When Connla's father enquires of the boy who he is speaking to, the woman says:

> He is speaking to a high woman that death or old age will never come to. I am asking him to come to Magh Mell, the Pleasant Plain where the triumphant king is living, and there he will be a king for ever without sorrow or fret.[6]

The entrance to the Pleasant Plain, as we saw in Chapter 6, was believed to have opened when the sun was touching the ground, particularly at sunset. And the Tuatha Dé Danann, of whom Aonghus, the owner of Newgrange, was a principal, were "certainly gods of the sky".[7]

How much did the cosmos influence Newgrange, its design and layout, its myths, its megalithic art, its very essence? Enormously, we think, and the evidence for this transcends the connections already established with winter solstice sunrise, Cygnus and the Milky Way.

BRUGH WITH THE MANY LIGHTS

In the old literature, there is a tale in which Newgrange is referred to as the "rath with the many lights".[8] There is an abundance of folk stories connected with a profusion of ancient sites scattered across Ireland which speak of these prehistoric monuments as having lights inside them.[9] We outlined one example of this in Chapter 3, where we read about a fairy who said "look at the light in Millmount".

The description which portrays Newgrange as "yonder brugh chequered with the many lights" could be interpreted in a number of ways. It could be that the milky quartz was considered a sanctified reflection of the Milky Way. On bright moonlit nights, the brilliant façade of Newgrange reflects light in such a way that it can be seen from a distance.

It could be a reference to something else. A little-known effect of rubbing two pieces of milky quartz together in the dark – called triboluminescence – results in the emission of light,[10] which can be blue or orange-yellow in colour. I saw this process demonstrated on television once and was fascinated. The light is produced by friction and pressure. It is likely the people who fashioned Newgrange knew of this property of quartz. After all, they went to great effort to bring quartz to the Boyne, all the way from the Wicklow Mountains, 50 miles away. All it would have taken for this glowing effect to become obvious was for one person to accidentally rub two pieces of quartz together, or to drop one onto another.

The reconstructed quartz façade at Newgrange

The Irish language words for quartz are interesting too. There are a number of aboriginal Irish phrases used to describe quartz. They are *grianchloch* or *cloch ghréine*, which means "sun stone"; *clocha scáil*, which means "shadow stone" or "reflection stone" – it could refer to the reflection of an astral body[11] – *clocha geala*, which could mean white, shining or glowing stone.[12] It is this word, meaning shining or white, which gives rise to the word *gealach*, meaning "moon".[13] More about the moon later.

The "many chequered lights" of Aonghus's abode is equally likely to be a reference to the number of heavenly objects which could potentially have been seen from within its stony vault. Any object roughly sharing the same declination of the winter solstice sun would have been a potential target of its design. We know for sure that the sun was a target, but other prospective objects would include the moon, the planets and some stars. Whether any of these was a definitive preordained target is the issue under examination here.

CAILLICHÍN NA MOCHÓIRIGHE

It has been suggested that the bright planet Venus, the calf of the Baltray story, shines into the chamber of Newgrange during its eight-year cycle. Christopher Knight and Robert Lomas, authors of *Uriel's Machine*, suggest that the light of Venus would have penetrated into the chamber before sunrise at the winter solstice just once during its eight-year cycle.[14] They point to markings on the lintel which forms the top of the roof box as evidence of this. The markings consist of a series of eight "rectangular boxes with a line joining each corner to form a cross".[15] These diagonal crosses, according to Knight and Lomas, seemed to be the megalithic signification of a year; thus, eight symbols is eight years, the cycle of Venus. Brennan had reached a similar conclusion, saying that each unit of four triangles "probably" made a "year sign".[16]

Knight and Lomas say the Newgrange roof box was a specially constructed apparatus which was designed to "trap" light from certain objects, such as Venus, while minimising scattered light from the sky. This is why the chamber interior is almost permanently in darkness, as stated in Chapter 7.

Further to the evidence in *Uriel's Machine* is the fact that there was a folk tradition alive in the Newgrange area which indicated that Venus would do exactly as Knight and Lomas postulated. Joseph Campbell, the American writer who worked extensively in the field of comparative mythology, recorded that there was a local story which stated the morning star cast a beam of light into the chamber of Newgrange directly onto a stone which contains two worn sockets.[17] This "stone" is a stone basin, which was originally located in the centre of the chamber floor but which was later moved into the eastern recess.[18] Campbell notes that if the folk story were found to be true, it would be a "good example of the durability of local tradition".[19] Like the story about the sun shining onto the triple spiral in the rear of the chamber, the "morning star" folk legend may be an enduring memory of something five millennia old.

Based on their findings, Knight and Lomas concluded that Newgrange was used for "astronomical ritual", not for burying the dead. This ritual, they say, involved the belief that the souls of the deceased were transferred into the bodies of the newborn by the light of Venus.[20]

Speculation, projection and postulation aside, the Venus event has been witnessed in recent times. Hank Harrison, a member of Martin Brennan's research team in the early 1980s, says he saw Venus "transit the roof box from the centre of the chamber".[21] Harrison described how the morning star could be seen for "several days before and after solstice", and how he adopted a different viewing position in the chamber as its position in the roof box changed.[22]

The "caillichín na mochóirighe", Venus

This is not how the folk tradition outlined by Campbell described the event. According to Campbell, the story stated that the Venus phenomenon happened on "one day in eight years" and that it occurred "precisely at sunrise".[23] Such a description is astronomically naïve because it would be impossible for the faint light of Venus to cast its light into the chamber just four minutes before the sun comes in. It is also highly improbable that Venus was seen inside Newgrange on just one day, as its declination would have to change very rapidly for it to disappear from the roof-box in such a short space of time. Harrison's observation, during which he saw it for "several days", better fits the actual reality.

Even in the one year during the eight-year Venus cycle when the morning star would appear in the sky window according to Knight and Lomas, it rises just 24 minutes before the sun, so clearly this phenomenon would have occurred when there was strong twilight.

An analysis of Venus's position at winter solstice around the year 3150 BC using SkyMap yields results which differ from those given in *Uriel's*

Machine. Here are the winter solstice declinations and positions relative to the sun of Venus during an eight-year cycle:

- *Year 1*: Declination –25° 15' 35.6"; Venus is just 1° 17' beneath the sun, and would be completely swamped by its light.

- *Year 2*: Declination –13° 24' 47.9"; Venus is a morning star, rising 265 minutes before the sun and located about 46° west of it.

- *Year 3*: Declination –19° 50' 34.0"; Venus is 36° east of the sun, not rising until two hours after it in daylight.

- *Year 4*: Declination –23° 20' 12.4"; Venus is 18° west of the sun, rising 1 hour 23 minutes before it. This is the winter solstice morning star which would shine into Newgrange.

- *Year 5*: Declination –16° 22' 20.5"; Venus is over 10° above the sun, and way out of line with the Newgrange passage.

- *Year 6*: Declination –24° 2' 12.7"; Venus is near 20° east of the sun. The declination is right for it to be visible from inside Newgrange, but it would be rising in daylight, so only an experienced observer would be able to see it.

- *Year 7*: Declination –18° 56' 47.8"; Venus is nearly 35° west of the sun, but its declination makes its altitude too great to shine into Newgrange.

- *Year 8*: Declination –15° 11' 47.1"; at 46° east of the sun, this is Venus's maximum easterly elongation at the time of the winter solstice. Again it is bright day when Venus rises, way too far north along the horizon to be visible from the Newgrange chamber.

The actual year closest to 3150 BC when Venus shone into Newgrange was 3147 BC. The declination of the "morning star" is almost identical to that given by Knight and Lomas, but the time separating the rising of Venus and the sunrise is almost an hour out.[24] Any object with a declination between –22° 58' and –25°53' would be seen from the central chamber.[25] Venus, at a declination of –23° 20' in 3147 BC, would have been visible from the chamber provided the weather conditions were clear.

Venus would have been rising in twilight, and there is some question as to whether its luminance would be strong enough to cast light across the basin stone in the chamber of Newgrange. It has long been said that Venus is bright enough to cast a shadow in very dark conditions, but whether this could be true in a twilight situation is a matter of conjecture.

What is certain is that an observer sitting on the floor of the chamber would have been able to see Venus through the roof box.

The Irish for Venus, or more precisely the Irish for "morning star" is *"caillichín na mochóirighe"*,[26] which means "early-rising little hag".[27] In Chapter 5, we met the Cailleach Bhéarra, the hag with the apron full of stones who was said to have formed the cairns on Loughcrew and the round tower at Monasterboice. This "veiled woman" is a variant of the illuminated cow/moon goddess, Bóann. Antiquated lore suggests that the hag's name was Boí, which was a variant of the old Irish word for cow, Bó.[28] Other research suggests that because she appears in triplicate, she is a triple moon goddess.[29] Her apron, from which she dropped the stones, was considered by one author to be "the divine womb, translated into the language of dress".[30]

If the Cailleach Bhéarra was the moon, we can infer that the Caillichín, the "little hag", was Venus. Thus, the hag and the little hag are the "cow and calf" of a different layer of sky fables, but relating to the same fundamental ideas. This brings us all the way back to Balor's Strand, where we met the magical cow, the Glas Ghoibhneann, and its calf which were transformed into the Rockabill islands and which we interpreted as a conjunction of the moon and Venus at the time of winter solstice. The only candidate years we can find such an occurrence happening in the era in which Newgrange was erected are 3107 BC, 3099 BC and 3091 BC. Eight years after the last of these conjunctions, in 3083 BC, the last crescent moon does not sit with Venus until four days after the solstice, at which time the sun's light is no longer visible in the Newgrange chamber.

The transit of Venus across the sun, 8 June 2004

Of the three "conjunction" years identified, only one, that which occurred in 3091BC, fits the Baltray cow and calf story. On that morning, the slender crescent moon rises first, followed by Venus which is in turn followed, just under an hour later, by the rising sun. Critically, in that year, the moon's declination was slightly lower than that of Venus, which fits in with the cow-calf story and how the cow became the larger, more southerly island at Rockabill.

Does all this have any relevance to Newgrange, which we have connected so far with the winter solstice sunrise, Deneb and the Milky Way? Of course it does.

COUNTING KERBSTONES

There is a theory about Newgrange that suggests the kerbstones can be counted in such a way as to represent the eight-year period which brings Venus into alignment with the roof box.[31] Venus has a 584-day period in which it appears to go around the sun as viewed from earth. During this period, the planet appears once as a morning star and once as an evening star. Five of these 584-day periods are almost exactly equal to the number of days in eight years: 583.92 x 5 = 2,919.6 days; 365.24 x 8 = 2921.9 days. This eight-year cycle is the period suggested by the markings on the light box lintel at Newgrange, and at the time Newgrange was built Venus was only visible from the chamber once during this cycle.

The eight-year cycle can be enumerated using the kerbstones as follows: Newgrange has 97 kerbstones. There are three highly decorated stones in the kerb: K1, K52 and K67. Both K1 and K52, which is opposite K1 on the northwest side of Newgrange, contain vertical line markings which could suggest that these stones are in fact "double" stones.[32] The addition of an extra two "stones" brings the total count to 99, which is almost exactly the number of synodic lunar months in eight years, and is an important subunit of the Metonic cycle of the moon.

An alternative to using the "split" stones is to count the 97 kerbstones as lunar months and then count the passage and chamber stones as days. In this scenario, all passage stones are counted and all chamber stones except the back stone, onto which the sun casts its light at the solstice. The total number of "days" in this counting system is 59; 97 synodic months is 2,864.5 days. Adding the extra 59 days (two synodic lunar months of 29.5 days each) yields 2,923.5 days, which is equal to the 99 synodic lunar months which ties in very closely with eight solar years and the Venus cycle.[33]

The entrance kerbstone, K1, is marked with a triple spiral symbol similar to that in the rear recess of the chamber, which some researchers

The entrance kerbstone, K1, at Newgrange

have suggested is representative of the idea of something in triplicate, such as a triple conjunction – sun, moon and Venus.[34] The moon and Venus conjunctions of 3107 BC, 3099 BC and 3091 BC occurred at the time of winter solstice, so the three objects are unified by the fact they all shone into Newgrange on the same day.

Gillies MacBain, who has suggested the eight-year kerb-count theory, explains, "the triple spiral within proclaims the achievement – 'We did it. We tied together the three spirals (recurrent cycles), the sun, the moon, and Venus'."[35] The regular meeting of crescent moon and Venus is also commemorated, we believe, with the star and crescent, the emblem of Drogheda, as mentioned in Chapter 3.

It is likely that a meticulously constructed and accurately oriented structure such as the Newgrange passage and light box could be used to scrutinise the moon at those times at which it occupies the same approximate declination as sun does on the shortest day of the year. It is an astronomical fact, as stated before, that at certain times the moon will occupy the same location in the sky as winter solstice sun. In this scenario, it is the moon, not the sun, which would rise over Red Mountain and, four minutes later, shine into the passage and chamber, assuming it is dark. Of course, there is nothing to preclude observations of the moon being made from the chamber during daylight hours.

What would be the benefit of such observations? They would allow the Neolithic sky watchers to identify those moments during the 18.6-year "moon swing" period when the full moon is located on or near one of the nodes in the "solstice" positions. A full moon occupying such a position has a high likelihood of being eclipsed. Because the full moon is always located directly opposite the sun, and because the moon in this case is in the winter solstice position, the sun would be "standing still" at the time of summer solstice. Thus, the astronomers would have identified those critical times in the moon swing cycle when eclipses happen in conjunction with the solstices.[36] In much the same way, when the moon is at its own standstills, eclipses happen at the time of the equinoxes. The nodes, the points where the moon's path crosses the ecliptic, are always located 90 degrees, or a quarter of a sky width, from the places in the sky where the moon's path is at maximum separation from the ecliptic.

An as-yet-unpublished theory put forward by an American physician suggests a possible connection between the number of kerb and chamber stones at Newgrange and the number of lunar months between eclipses. John E. Gordon MD has found eclipse intervals may have been encoded into the structure of Newgrange, and that the highly decorated kerbstones K1, K52 and K67 may relate to a counting system which can be used to enumerate these cycles.[37]

Eclipses happen in several series. One important series is repeated after 18 years and 11 days and is known as the Saros Cycle, which we mentioned in Chapter 6. In Dr Gordon's counting system, each stone (kerb, passage and chamber) represents a synodic lunar month, the period from one full moon to the next. There are 97 kerbstones, 21 stones on the right side of the passage, 22 on the left side, and 17 in the chamber. Starting at the entrance kerb, K1, we count the entire kerb of 97 stones. Then we add all the stones in the passage and chamber, 60 stones, yielding a total of 157 stones. Then, without including K1 again, counting the kerb back to stone K67 again yields a total of 223. This 223 could represent the 223 synodic months of the 18-year Saros eclipse cycle.

This is just one of a series of counts giving eclipse-related numbers. Dr Gordon has found that "half a dozen counts of stones between the three most highly decorated curb-stones were consistent with lunar eclipse cycles".[38] Gordon says that during certain periods of about 87 years, over 90 per cent of eclipses visible from Newgrange happen at intervals of 6, 41 or 47 lunar months. All of these periods can be found by counting the stones. For example, the 47-month interval can be reached by counting the eastern half of the kerb, from the highly decorated K52 to the entrance stone, inclusive. Five times this interval is the 235-month, 19-year metonic cycle. It can also be counted between K52 and the stone in the chamber containing the famous Triple-Double Spiral, he says.

The highly decorated Kerbstone 52 at Newgrange including (inset) one of the three-hole "Orion's belt" star designs

WOMB OF THE MOON

The fundamental difference in the design of Newgrange, compared with Dowth South, is that it covers a much smaller area of sky, and there is a strong probability that its roof box aperture was utilised to watch very minute changes in the declinations of the moon. While Dowth may have been employed in conjunction with distant foresights to mark specific setting points of sun and moon, Newgrange functioned differently because it was not used in conjunction with the horizon, any observations most likely being made from a recumbent position in the chamber, looking along the passage and out through its narrow roof box opening.

While structures such as the roof box at Newgrange are very rare, the Newgrange aperture is not unique in Irish archaeology. Another Stone Age cairn with a roof box which allows observation of both sun and moon is Cairn G at Carrowkeel in County Sligo.[39] Megalithic researcher Martin Byrne says that the cruciform chamber of Cairn G can be illuminated by light from both the sun and moon through its narrow light slit above the entrance. Furthermore, the chamber points towards an ancient megalithic monument called Maeve's Cairn on a hill called Knocknarea, which means "Hill of the Moon".[40] This is the direction of the most northerly setting of the moon, the major standstill, something which Byrne said showed the builders had a "sophisticated understanding of the cycles of the moon",[41] and which, yet again, shows a concern with the moon swing and eclipses.

Byrne also points out that the peninsula on which Knocknarea mountain is located is called Cuil Irra, which means "the remote angle of the moon".[42]

The likely association of Newgrange and the moon is further suggested by the name of a place which sits in line with the location where the sun and moon rise before shining into the chamber. A line from Newgrange across Red Mountain finds Bellewstown Hill, which has an association with the hag, the moon, and which is sometimes referred to as Sliabh na Callaighe, incidentally also the name by which the Loughcrew Hills are known.

Moonrise over Skerries

The very name associated with Newgrange and the Boyne monuments, Brú na Bóinne, suggests by itself a concern with the moon. Bóinne/Bóann is the illuminated cow, the moon, and the assortment of monuments in the Boyne Valley is dedicated to her. The word Brú is also very interesting, having a meaning which could relate to the notion of a "rebirth ritual" coincidental with the solar and lunar functions of Newgrange.

Brug na Bóinde, as it is written in the *Dindshenchas*, has traditionally been translated as the "house", "mansion" or "palace" of the Boyne. Brug was probably pronounced in ancient times with a guttural *g*, later softened to *gh*, as in Brugh, which is pronounced with a silent *g*. Brú is a different representation of the word, and is the spelling which has been used by the academics[43] as well as being the version used at the nearby Brú na Bóinne Visitor Centre, which serves as the point of access to Newgrange and Knowth for tourists. This word, Brú, means "womb"[44] or "belly" and can also mean "breast" or "bosom".[45] Thus Brú na Bóinne could mean "womb of the bright cow", or more specifically, "womb of the moon".

This is not such a far-fetched notion. Many researchers, including *Uriel's Machine* authors Knight and Lomas, have indicated that the layout and design of the Newgrange passage resemble the "female reproductive organs".[46] They concluded that the "organic quality" of the building appeared to be "deliberate rather than a consequence of engineering *naïveté*."[47] Another author, William Battersby, goes as far as to suggest the whole ridge on which Newgrange sits "gives the impression of a large image of a pregnant woman".[48]

The structure of Newgrange can be visualised in such a way that we can envisage the exterior of the entrance being the vulva, the chamber itself representing the uterus. At winter solstice, the sun, which is always represented in Irish sky mythology as being male, penetrates the womb-like, "feminine" structure of Brú na Bóinne and we can hypothesise that some sort of rebirth or fertility ritual may have been associated with this event. One author suggests that, to the ancient "Star Temple people", the "divine child (innocence) was created by the penetration of a rainbow or beam of light into the dark womb of the void mother".[49]

Bearing in mind the probable solstice eclipse prediction capability of Newgrange, it is tantalising to imagine a solar eclipse occurring at winter solstice sunrise being visible from inside the passage. In this way, the union of male and female would be happening on two levels – once in the sky, where, as was the case in the Dowth legend, the male sun and female moon are joined; and once on the ground, where the male sun is unified with the womb of Newgrange.

Of further interest to the idea of Newgrange being a womb is the fact that the designs on the entrance kerbstone, K1, can be mirrored in such a way as to imitate the female reproductive system. Additionally, a phallus-shaped stone was found in an oval quartz feature uncovered not far from the entrance to the "passage-womb" by Professor O'Kelly. George Eogan, who excavated Knowth, suggested that phallic stones such as that found at Newgrange, along with one he found himself at Knowth, could have been involved in fertility rites.[50] The Newgrange phallus was 24 centimetres long, and was made of highly polished sandstone.[51] It is worth noting that the phallic object found by O'Kelly was located in an oval setting, suggesting an egg shape, and that this setting was covered with water-rolled quartz pebbles,[52] suggestive of some association of this peculiar feature with the moon.

Brennan linked the egg-shape of Newgrange and the quartz façade with "the surface of a large egg".[53] He further stated, "The egg-shaped mound, concealing the womb-like cave, penetrated by a shaft of light on the day of winter solstice, symbolises the creation of the universe through the reconciliation of opposing forces."[54] Those opposing forces were heaven and earth, light and darkness, matter and spirit.

A COMPLEX CALENDAR

We have seen that Newgrange is much more than a solar construct. To create something on this scale, using hundreds of thousands of tonnes of stone and earth, may have taken generations of people. There can be little doubt that the calendar utilised by these people was much more complicated than a simple solar calendar, based around the days of solar standstill and the equinoxes. Their method of time-keeping was the most accurate and faithful of all, far more precise than the wristwatches of today, which need batteries or constant winding to keep them in time. Their calendar was complex, based around sun, moon and planets, with the stars as a background "grid" of sorts, used to track the movements of these bodies with a high degree of accuracy.

This is probably why Newgrange was referred to as the "rath with the many lights". That quote is from the *Agallamh na Senórach,* the "Colloquy with the Ancients", said to have been written by St Patrick and found in *The Book of Lismore.* Three sons of the king of Ireland go to Brú na Bóinne, wishing to gain the favour of the Tuatha Dé Danann. A cheerful man comes towards them, and the three ask him from whence he came. "Out of yonder brugh chequered with the many lights hard by you here", the man replies.[55] The man, it transpires, was none other than Bodhb Dearg, the Tuatha Dé Danann chief who helped in Aongus's quest to find his swan maiden Caer.

Newgrange is referred to as the "Brugh of the many lights" because it accepts light from more than just the sun. While some ancient sites are said to have "a light" in them, Newgrange is associated with numerous lights because of the fact that bodies like the moon and Venus, the cow and calf, also shone into its stone chamber.

One suggestion that emerges from the lore of the Boyne Valley is that Newgrange and its associated monuments were regarded as earthly reflections or embodiments of regions of the sky, something which Graham Hancock says was prevalent at places like the pyramids of Giza and the great temples of Ankor Wat in Cambodia.[56] The *Dindshenchas* poem about Brú na Bóinne opens with the following two quatrains:

> Bright is it here, O plain of Mac ind Oc!
> wide is thy road with traffic of hundreds;
> thou hast covered many a true prince
> of the race of every king that has possessed thee.
> Every bright wonder hath adorned thee,
> O clear shining plain with scores of hosts,
> O lucent land of grass and waggons,
> O virgin mead of birds and milking-places!

While we are not supposed to see the Bend of the Boyne monuments as an actual reflection of the sky, the above quatrains appear to be describing the sky as much as they portray the ground, leading us to think of the Brú as something which has major concerns with the night sky.

"Mac ind Oc" is Aonghus, but what it actually means has been the subject of some debate. It has been pointed out that if it was supposed to mean "the son of the youth" then it was grammatically incorrect.[57] But it may have meant "son of the virgin", which is given as *Mac na hÓige* in the MacCionnaith dictionary. This may be a reference to the way in which Aonghus was said to have been conceived. The Dagda, chief of the gods, desired Bóinn, the moon goddess, who was said to have resided at the Brú with her husband, Elcmar, which was another name for Nuadu, the silver-handed Orion god we met in the chapter about Tara. The Dagda sent Elcmar on a journey and cast a magic spell so that the night disappeared and nine months seemed like just a single day and a night. In the interim, Dagda and Bóann lay together and Bóann bore him a child. The child was referred to as Mac Óg because he was "begotten at the beginning of a day and born between that and the evening".[58] Elcmar returned, ignorant of what had taken place.

In the *Dindshenchas* poem, Aonghus's plain is described as being "bright", having been adorned with "every bright wonder". This sounds like a description of the night sky. We are told, "Wide is thy road with traffic of hundreds", which reminds us of the Milky Way, the "road" of the white cow, which is made up of countless hundreds of stars. The "clear shining plain" contains "scores of hosts", the Irish word for "hosts" being *slúag,* which can mean "fairy host",[59] or a flock of over 500. The Irish for fairy is *Sídheog,* which is derived from the early Irish word *síde* which can also describe a fairy mound; hence Newgrange is sometimes called the *Síd* of the Brugh.[60]

The reference in line eight of the *Dindshenchas* poem to birds and milking-places brings us back once again to the Milky Way, the bright band of which seems to have been a major preoccupation of the astronomers, as we saw in Chapter 7. The birds in this case are probably Cygnus and Altair, the swans of the Cygnus Enigma, although the duality of this ancient verse means we can envisage the plain of the Brú being the actual sloping fields at Newgrange adorned with the whooper swans. The "milking places" are the points, described previously, where the ecliptic, the path of the sun, moon and planets, crosses the Milky Way. There are two points where this happens, one in the upraised hand of Orion, between the constellations of Gemini, the Twins, and Taurus, the Bull. The other is located between the constellations of Sagittarius, the Archer, and Scorpius, the Scorpion, on the opposite side of the sky to Orion. Cygnus appears to be flying in the direction of this crossing point on its flight along the Milky Way.

It is at these two "milking places" that the moon appears to yield the milk which forms the bright band known as the Way of the White Cow. In Chapter 1, we saw how the magical cow, Glas Ghoibhneann, was milked by a jealous woman using a sieve, and although the Glas could yield an almost never-ending supply of milk, it ran through the sieve.

THE DOG STAR

We have shown how Newgrange was associated with sun, moon, Venus and the Milky Way, hence the reason for its description as being the Brugh with many lights, with "every bright wonder" having adorned it. But, apart from the other planets that would occasionally have been visible from its inner vault, there was one other significant object which was transiting the Newgrange sky window at the time it was built.

This object was none other than the brightest star in the night sky: Sirius, the so-called "Dog Star". As we outlined in Chapter 1, Sirius shared the same rising place as the winter solstice sun back in the Neolithic. In Chapter 4, we saw how Sirius was setting in the direction of Tara viewed from Millmount.

Newgrange would have been the prime location from which to view both the rising of Sirius and the slow displacement of this star due to precession. Because the hill of Red Mountain provides an elevated horizon, a false horizon of sorts, by the time Sirius clears the crest of the hill, it is already at an altitude which takes it out of the haze and atmospheric compression which can prevent even the brightest stars from being seen at the exact moment of their rising.

Richard and I have experienced for ourselves the frustration of watching star, planet and moon risings out of the sea. Any cloud towards the horizon makes it much more difficult to see risings, even those involving the sun. Any breaks in cloud are invariably best seen when they are overhead, or at the very least at an elevated altitude. When we look towards the horizon, we are looking horizontally through cloud and atmosphere. This makes our chances of seeing the exact moment of the rising of a star or other heavenly body more remote. We have gained evidence of this from our repeated attempts to see winter solstice sunrise at Baltray, and the equinox sunsets from Millmount. Year after year, we found our observations hampered by weather, even though some years we were visiting Baltray two or three days in succession around the time of solstice and Millmount for three days at equinox.

Even when cloud is not a factor, we still have to contend with the atmosphere. Again, because we are looking horizontally through the air, we are looking through a much greater "slice" of the atmosphere than if we were looking at the zenith overhead. This apparent compression of the atmosphere towards the horizon causes a lensing effect, which distorts and displaces bodies such as the sun and moon. Our observations of moonrises out of the Irish Sea were fascinating. We sometimes missed the "first flash" of the moon because it was so dim. For the first few minutes, the moon appeared to be squashed, so that it took on the shape of a flattened tennis ball.

Star risings and settings are also notoriously difficult to see when you have no elevated false horizon between you and the actual horizon. Even Sirius, which is the brightest star in the entire night sky, can vanish from view before the actual moment of its setting.

All of this was negated by the careful positioning of Newgrange, facing the ridge of Red Mountain. By the time Sirius is visible, rising over the hill, it is out of the "obscure" zone and is already more than 15 minutes off the actual distant horizon.

The people who erected Newgrange would doubtlessly have considered Sirius a very important star. It lies just on the edge of the Milky Way, which was also known as the *Síog na Spéire*[61] (the "streak of the sky"), or the *Earball na Lárach Báine*[62] (the tail, trail or remnant of the 'milky site'?)[63] in Irish.

At Newgrange, just as we found at Baltray, the Dog Star seems to have been held in high regard. Connections already established with Bóann's

Evening sun at Newgrange

faithful lapdog, who drowned with her at Inbher Colpa, are strengthened by a local story associated with the place where Sirius set as viewed from Newgrange in the Stone Age. This place is a hill called Realtoge, which is the anglicised form of *réaltóg,* meaning "star" or "a small star".[64] This hill is the point where the sun set at winter solstice. The word *réaltóg* is derived from *reultan,* meaning stars, which itself is derived from the early Irish word *retla.*[65]

On the western slope of the hill of Realtoge is a ringfort. Author William Battersby pointed out that there is an interesting legend connected with this fort: "In three separate cases in the Schools Survey Folklore in 1937, gold is mentioned as being hidden in the rath on Realtoge Hill, in one case it was stated to be guarded by a dog."[66] Battersby suggests an association between the gold of the Realtoge story and the sun, even though the metal gold "was not known in the age of Newgrange".[67] The idea suggested by the legend is that the golden sun sets behind the Realtoge rath, and that at night time during certain periods of the year, Sirius, the Dog Star, would set in the same place, thus the dog "guards" the gold. This is probably another example of the durability of local myths, and commemorates something which happened for a relatively short period more than five millennia in the past.

In 3150 BC, the declination of Sirius was $-23°$ 2' 43.1'", enabling it to be visible from the Newgrange chamber.[68] However, due to the effects of precession, it would not have been visible in the "chamber of the many lights" for long after Newgrange was built. Just 200 years later, in 2950 BC, Sirius's declination, $-22°$ 19', would have taken it out of the sky box because the Dog Star's elevation was too great at that time.

Engravings on a kerbstone at the rear of Newgrange, the already mentioned K52, could be interpreted as being representations of Orion's Belt and Sirius. On the right-hand side of the stone, there are three sets of three circular holes, known in archaeological terminology as "cup marks". Each of these sets of holes is contained within a double oval-shaped cartouche. There are a number of other cup marks on the stone, the most noticeable of which is one contained inside the vertical stripe in the centre of the stone. Is this Sirius, sitting on the axis of the site, which runs through the entrance kerbstone, K1, up the passage, and out the other side of the kerb in the centre of K52?[69]

Of significance to the Sirius alignment was the discovery by Professor O'Kelly of three dog skeletons inside Newgrange. Some 116 dog bones found in the chamber were said to have belonged to at least three individuals.[70] One of the partial dog skeletons was found in the east recess, one in the west recess and one just outside the end recess.[71] O'Kelly speculated that the skeletons belonged to "stray dogs that were unable to get out of the tomb", and suggests a "recent origin for the bones".[72] It is highly unusual, however, that one dog was found associated with each of the three recesses. This would be less likely the result of chance – that three dogs entered the chamber over time and were unable to exit again. Had dog remains been found in parts of the passage, it would seem more plausible to suggest that they had died there. Perhaps they were buried there as part of some sky ritual? The fact that there were three dogs reflects a possible connection with Orion's Belt, which points towards the Dog Star.

On the exterior of Newgrange, the triple cup mark emblems on Kerbstone 52 all show the circular holes in short, straight lines, mimicking Orion's Belt. The left-hand side of K52 contains three spirals, in a different configuration than on K1 and C10, but again we are reminded of the probable duality of meaning attached to the symbols.

An imaginary line through K52, C10 and K1 points to many things in the sky. It lines up with the "triple conjunction" of sun, moon and Venus at winter solstice 3091BC, all three of which would have been visible from the observation chamber. It also aligns with the rising place of Sirius around the same time, a star whose rising is heralded by the triple stars of Orion's Belt. In each case, this sacred sky line passes through three sets of tri-spiral petroglyphs, another unlikely coincidence.

While the ability of the sun, moon and planets to occupy part of the sky where they would be visible from the interior of Newgrange was not affected by precession over long periods of time, it is clear that other sky objects which were of obvious concern to the megalithic engineers held sacred positions in the sky which were skewed over relatively short periods of time.

It would seem like an implausible conjunction of coincidences that Deneb, Sirius and the Milky Way held a unique precessional importance at the time Newgrange was built, only for the fact that the astro-myths and the sky-ground architecture confirm that they were part of a grand cosmic scheme. The relatively fleeting moment in the cycle of precession during which important stars were doing apparently significant things would not be repeated for 25,800 years, around the twenty-third millennium AD, nearly 23,000 years from now. There can be no doubt the competence of the astronomer engineers allowed them to make an accurate estimation of the precessional time scale, the largest sky cycle of them all.

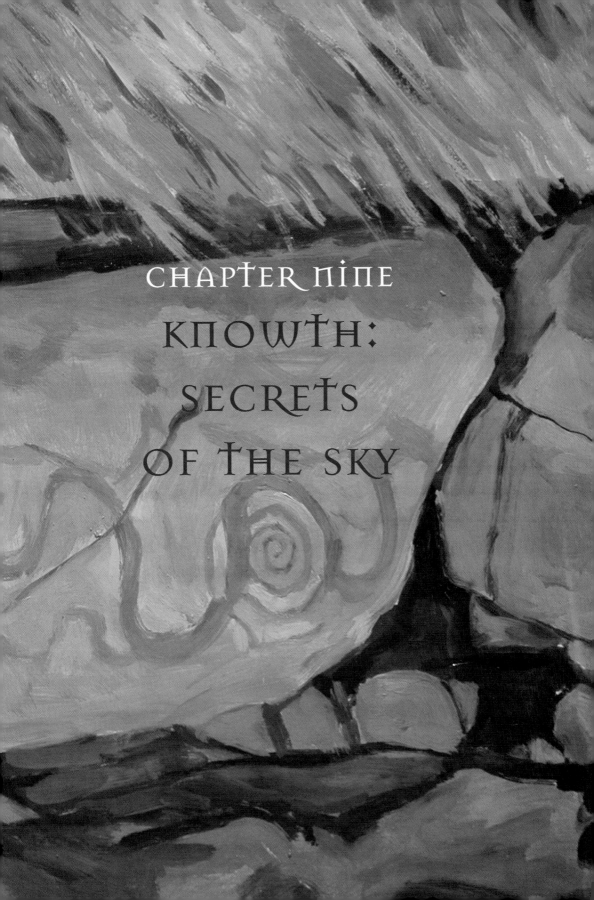

CHAPTER NINE

KNOWTH: SECRETS OF THE SKY

When George Eogan began excavations at Knowth in 1962, he could scarcely have realised he was setting out upon an epic journey of discovery. On 18 June that year, as he put trowel to sod in the green field at Knowth,[1] Eogan was embarking on a remarkable voyage through many complex, interwoven layers of time going all the way back to the fourth millennium before Christ. Over the next four decades, he would reveal one of the most multifaceted ancient sites in Europe and one of the finest archaeological treasures in all the world.

At the outset of his grand adventure, George Eogan felt the weight of duty on his shoulders. He was aware of the great magnitude of the task, both in terms of the large scale of Knowth and the huge significance of being responsible for its excavation. "From the beginning, we were conscious of the responsibility that we assumed," he said, revealing that at any one time there were "20 workmen and 12 students" taking part in the excavations.[2]

Knowth, Newgrange and Dowth are the best-known megalithic structures in Ireland, yet they constitute just a tiny fraction of the 1,400 megalithic "tombs" known to exist in the country.[3] Newgrange is the most famous of the trio, and up until Eogan began digging, Knowth was the poor relation of the Boyne trio. It had not yet yielded its secrets.

The first forays into Knowth's hidden enigmas were both tentative and modest. The humble objective of the early programme of archaeology was not to find any chambers or passages in the main mound, but rather to probe the possible existence of other smaller passage-mounds adjacent to the large one.[4] By the time his work at Knowth was complete, Eogan had uncovered 17 of these "satellite tombs", and indications that two or three more may have existed. As exciting new discoveries came to light, it became clear that Knowth's monuments constituted a "microcosm of Irish archaeology".[5] Eventually, a programme of work which would last years was planned.

In 1967, Eogan and his team discovered one of two passages at Knowth, on the western side, followed by the uncovering of the eastern passage in 1968. The western passage is a long, narrow corridor flanked by dozens of upright stones. George Eogan found that many of these massive orthostats were decorated, some exquisitely so. There were some stones which had been so well protected from the elements and the damp over 5,000 years that certain petroglyphs were as fresh as if they had been carved yesterday.

This was one thing which struck me in the summer of 2000, when I had the great pleasure of a personal tour of Knowth with Professor

Western view of the Knowth complex

Eogan, who was more than happy to take me around the site and show me its finer details. I was struck by Professor Eogan's obvious excitement at showing me the adorned orthostats which he had first set eyes on in the afternoon of 11 July 1967, not long after Martin Colfer, a workman from Slane, had become the first man in recent history to peer into the western passage.[6] So proud was Professor Eogan of this wonderful stone tunnel which he had unearthed, he even held an electric lamp so that I could take photos of the orthostats.

On another visit to Knowth that summer, Richard and I gained a rare opportunity to see the eastern passage and chamber. A visit to the eastern chamber takes the breath away, in more ways than one. And it's not for the faint-hearted or anyone suffering with claustrophobia, as George Eogan discovered when crawling on hands and knees up the passage for the first time on 1 August 1968. Some of the orthostats were leaning inwards; there were obstructions in the passageway and some of the capping stones were cracked. "Not knowing that there was so much more to come, I continued in astonishment, and with increasing trouble from inward-leaning orthostats. These touched at their tops, producing an inverted-V cross-section . . ."[7]

Eventually, Eogan was forced to continue on top of the orthostats and eventually found "the most amazing sight of my life" – he had discovered the eastern chamber, with its great corbelled roof and three recesses, very like its companion chamber at Newgrange. One big difference between the chambers was the presence of an enormous stone basin in the right-hand alcove.

On our visit in the summer of 2000, we took the route through the inverted V which was formed by the sloping orthostats. At the end of the stone corridor, one is forced onto hands and knees, and eventually you have to crawl like a worm with your belly to the floor to get in through the last gap. Being a fairly thin fellow, I was able to get through, but nonetheless there was a moment of blind panic brought about by the sudden feeling that I was going to become wedged between these two giant stones. People of a larger size may, I fear, never get to see the great chamber of Knowth. (That said, it is off-limits to tourists anyhow.)

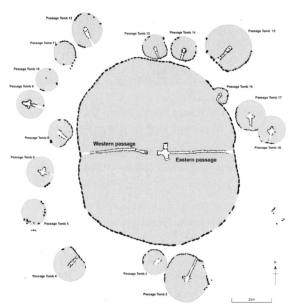

Ground plan of the Knowth complex
(Image: © Matthew and Geraldine Stout)

The giant basin in the northern recess weighs three hundred pounds, according to one author, and has a symbol carved onto its concave upper surface which is described as "a sunburst".[8] The same author implies that another carving, on the outer rim of the giant cauldron, is "an ikon (sic) of the Great Mother in the act of uniting the universe".[9] Presumably, this mother figure is the earth/river/moon/illumination goddess, Bóann, or the hag of the Boyne Valley. The basin stone is so massive it would almost certainly have been in place before the passage and chamber were constructed. Such a humongous object could not simply be rolled up the passageway and it certainly would not have fit through the gap between certain orthostats in the passage.

The western passage contrasts starkly with the cruciform eastern structure, being a simple stone tunnel formed of upright orthostats capstones, with a bend about three quarters of the way in and a sillstone near the end which seems to demark a simple chamber of sorts, which is actually just the end of the tunnel. One curious feature of this "chamber" is the fact that the rectilinear carvings on the rear stone seem to mimic those on the entrance kerbstone outside, something George Eogan pointed out to me during our visit into the dark chamber.

Over time, Eogan's dig at Knowth became the mother of all archaeological projects. In time, he would unearth not just the two great passages of the main mound and numerous satellite passage-mound structures, but many diverse features spanning huge epochs of time. These included standing stone gnomons, quartz stone settings, a rectangular house predating the passage-mound phase, a circle of post holes near the eastern chamber entrance, an iron age ditch dug into the main mound behind the kerb stones, a batch of underground tunnels or souterrains, some incorporated into the earlier passage structures, and even a Norman fortification on top of Knowth.

Some interesting finds turned up too, not least an exquisite flint macehead, which is presumed to have been ceremonial but whose real function remains an issue of contention. Other objects uncovered included a curious grooved phallic stone measuring 25 centimetres in length, made from sandstone and marked with a series of "arched grooves" and, near the thick end, "three arcs".[10] This penis-shaped stone shares a similarity to the undecorated phallus found at Newgrange, both being found near the entrances to the chambers. The Newgrange phallus was found in an ovoid quartz feature, while the Knowth phallus was found "in a small scoop in the old ground surface".[11] The area outside the western passage where the Knowth phallus was found was notable for a feature which consisted of a spread of quartz and other stones, but Eogan points out that the absence of these stones under the fallen gnomon stone indicates that this feature is more likely to have been formed from material slipping off the mound rather than being a "deliberately laid entrance feature".[12] Is it possible Knowth was also embellished with quartz, just like Newgrange?

All of this has added to the complexity of the already convoluted Knowth, a monument which appeared to overshadow the greatness of Newgrange by virtue of its multifarious facets. There are more kerbstones at Knowth – 127 in total – and the number of stones containing decoration is immense.

Inside the western passage at Knowth

Eogan describes Knowth's art as one of its "characteristic legacies" and points out that Knowth "possesses Europe's greatest concentration of megalithic art".[13]

At Newgrange, three of the kerbstones are lavishly decorated. At Knowth, the number of sumptuously decorated stones numbers in the dozens,[14] with many more petroglyphs being found on passage stones and lintels, roof corbels and even on mobile stone objects. The main tumulus contains more than three hundred decorated stones, while elsewhere on the Knowth site, there are

Kerbstone 13, one of the more highly decorated stones at Knowth

"80 pieces of decorated stone".[15] One noted scholar of megalithic art, Dr Muiris O'Sullivan, said of Knowth's kerb art, "the overall production marks the emergence of a remarkable school of art, emphasising grandeur of scale, boldness of expression, and simplicity of design".[16]

While George Eogan considered the Knowth art to be "wholly non-representational"[17] and Dr O'Sullivan reckoned the "pseudo-scientific literature" of the 1980s to be far-fetched,[18] some authors and researchers view Knowth as a place where study of the heavens was obviously undertaken. William Battersby, admittedly a non-academic writer, viewed the great kerb of Knowth in the context of the sky, suggesting that constellations or star pictures could have been placed on stones.[19]

What becomes apparent when one looks at Knowth in the context of the other megalithic sites of the Boyne and in the broader perspective of the sky myths, in tandem with petroglyphs contained on some of its stones, is that the monument was clearly inspired by the cosmos. The extent of this inspiration is open to dialogue and further study, but even a cursory glance at the symbolism of the stone carvings would suggest a genesis which is uniquely interrelated with the cosmos.

NO EQUINOX ALIGNMENT?

One difficulty with the proper interpretation of Knowth's astronomical function is the incorrect assertion that its passages face directly due east and west, to accept sunrise and sunset at the equinoxes, when day and night are of equal length. It's a beautiful theory, especially in light of the fact that Knowth has two passages on opposite sides, which could be envisaged as representing the two halves of the year.

Some diagrams of Knowth appear to show passages pointing almost exactly due east and due west. One could easily be forgiven for forging the mistaken conviction that Knowth shares an equinoctial function with another megalithic site, Cairn T, up on the top of Carnbane East at Loughcrew. Professor George Eogan hinted at such an alignment: ". . . the orientation of Site I suggests that there could have been two ceremonies at different times, the vernal equinox on 20 or 21 March and the autumnal equinox on 22 or 23 September."[20] During one of my visits to Knowth, Professor Eogan told me personally that the orientation of the passages was only approximately equinoctial, and confirmed in the case of the western passage that the sun shone in as far as the bend in the passage at least a week after the autumnal equinox.

Closer study of the ground plan of Knowth shows that neither passage is aligned precisely on due east or west.[21] However, the exact orientations in degrees were not given by the archaeologist. Martin Brennan was among those who held onto the notion that Knowth's passages had an equinoctial arrangement, something which appeared to be borne out by observations he made of the gnomon stone outside the western passage entrance. Brennan contended that on the autumn equinox, the sun would align with the standing stone and shine deep into the passage.[22] His diagram indicates that the shadow of this "coarse yellow quartso-sandstone"[23] gnomon aligns with the central vertical line of kerbstone 74, the entrance kerbstone of the western passage, at the equinox.[24] Brennan was unable to observe the assumed equinox sunrise alignment of Knowth East "because of obstructions".[25]

It seemed that there was a complete and satisfactory astronomical theory for the Brú na Bóinne trio of passage complexes. At Newgrange, the sunrise on the shortest day illuminated the chamber. At Dowth, the focus was the winter sunset, and at Knowth, two passages pointed out sunrise and sunset on the equinoxes.

But several factors made Knowth's position in this solar stone system doubtful. Eyewitness accounts, relayed by the archaeologist, suggested the western passage was at the very least a week out of line with the equinox. The ground plans did not provide definitive evidence of an equinox alignment. Then there was the fact that both passages had been disturbed significantly by what George Eogan referred to as "early Christian structures", souterrains and other stone buildings which had been incorporated into the entrances of both passages. This is what made the passages so difficult to access in the days when they were first discovered back in the 1960s. One photograph of the entrance to Knowth West in the early days of excavation clearly shows the entrance to a small, narrow, low stone passageway, part of the Early Christian re-modelling of the ninth and tenth centuries AD.[26]

On top of all this, it appears through anecdotal evidence that Martin Brennan did not have access to Knowth while formulating his theories about its alignments. Even if he had access, he would have found the east tunnel impossible to study, in part because of the Early Christian structures and in no small way due to the fact that the outer part of the east passage is bent and was clearly altered and damaged during the modification of the entrance area over a millennium ago. The outer portions of both east and west tunnels – about four or five metres in each case – were destroyed by the construction of a huge defensive ditch around the inside of the kerb of Knowth in the Late Iron Age.

As was the case at the entrance to the cruciform northern passage at nearby Dowth, the opening of the cross-shaped eastern passage at Knowth was seriously disturbed during later building phases. At the time Knowth East was discovered in July 1968, George Eogan slid down a hole which had been found on the eastern side of the mound and was pretty gobsmacked to find he was "at the junction of an elaborate complex of four passages".[27] One of these was a souterrain, which, Professor Eogan would tell me at Knowth in 2000, ran off up towards the top of the mound. Two others also consisted of dry-stone walling and were also souterrains. The fourth consisted of orthostats and was the original neolithic passage, leading to the grand chamber with its huge basin stone.

It was during a visit to Knowth with Victor Reijs in September 2000 that Richard and I first became aware of a serious doubt over the Knowth equinox theory. Victor was taking measurements, attempting to find out the orientation of the passages. We gave him what help we could. He measured the azimuth of the western passage using GPS (Global Positioning System), which required myself and Richard to assist in lining Victor up outside the passage with a distant horizon feature. Victor then drove to that distant feature and took a second measurement. We guided him into position using giant binoculars on a tripod on the top of Knowth.[28]

Reijs concluded that the minimum azimuth of Knowth West was around 259°. This is a massive 11°, or in layman's terms 22 sun-widths, *south* of west. He made a compass measurement also, which, when calibrated to a true measurement, yielded an azimuth of 260.6°, seeming to confirm that Knowth West was orientated a long way off the due west alignment (270°) needed for a sun show at the equinox.

The Reijs measurements would later be supported by survey data from the prominent archaeoastronomers Frank Prendergast and Tom Ray. Their survey revealed an azimuth for Knowth West of 258.5° and for Knowth East the bearing was 85°. This amounted to a skew of 23 sun widths for the western structure and nine solar diameters for the eastern opening.[29] The equinox solution for Knowth, first put forward by Brennan and repeated in many texts, lay in tatters. The extreme length and narrow width of the passages at Knowth make them very accurate as apertures for tracking down a particular sunrise or sunset. It was not conceivable that a sunrise five degrees off east could penetrate into the eastern chamber, and it was now totally incongruous to suggest that a beam of sunlight could reach the bend in Knowth West at the equinox, given that the passage pointed 23 sun diameters south of that point on the horizon where the sun would set on the equinoxes.

The measurements confirmed what George Eogan had told me directly. The western passage was way off the equinox mark. Although the sun did shine in there, it was on what could be considered to be a spurious date – 18½ days before vernal equinox and 18½ days after autumnal equinox. In other words, 2 or 3 March and 8 or 9 October.

THE SCRIBNER SOLUTION: A LUNAR CALENDAR

Knowth held onto her secrets, but only briefly. With the Reijs data at hand, retired Connecticut doctor Charles Scribner examined the orientations of both passages and came up with a solution: he proposed that the megalithic structure went far beyond the simple orientation of passages to easily found equinox points half way between the solstice points.

Scribner's solution to the complex, and baffling, Knowth quandary relied on an assumption that the people who built the megalithic monument counted the passage of time in lunar months. Gillies MacBain, the Tipperary cattle breeder who put forward the eight-year kerb-count theory for Newgrange, believed that the lunar time theory was "not a big assumption" and that "it would be most anachronistic to expect them to have evolved any division of time other than the natural one".[30] MacBain pointed out that the megalithic builders lived close to the furthest tidal reach of the Boyne, and would have been aware that the tides "faithfully kept lunar, not solar time".[31]

The Scribner analysis of Knowth hypothesises that Knowth's inner passages accepted the light of the sun on two significant lunar dates. (That may sound contradictory, but all will be explained.) The theory further suggests that the structure was concerned with the "movable feast" of Easter, or by whatever name its prehistoric equivalent was known.

There was considerable controversy in the early Irish church over the paschal date, a disagreement which was not resolved until 716 AD.[32] The paschal controversy split the Irish church into two opposing camps, the "Romans" and the "Irish" or "Hibernian'" groups, both governed by separate synods.[33] Easter was essentially a pagan festival, and part of the controversy surrounded the "transformation of a pagan calendar into a Christian one".[34] Issues which proved divisive for the various paschal debate parties included the actual date of spring equinox and the "permitted 'lunar limits', namely at what 'age' (what day of the lunar month) could the moon be on Easter Sunday".[35]

Despite the wrangling, all of the disputants were agreed on one thing – their formula was based upon the first full moon following the vernal equinox. We already know the Irish megalithic builders could reckon the exact day of equinox, as evidenced by the solar aperture at Cairn T, Loughcrew. We also know, or at least believe on the basis of evidence already presented in this book, that the Stone Age builders were not adherents to a simple solar calendar, but rather a more complicated solar-lunar calendar and on a broader scale a system of time-keeping which reckoned the movements of the planets and even the slow turning of the sky caused by precession into their grand calendar.

The "Scribner Solution" to Knowth recognises two significant dates around the time of vernal equinox – "vernal equinox plus six days" and "vernal equinox minus 18½ days".[36] These are the two dates, respectively, when the sun shines into Knowth's eastern chamber and as far as the bend of the western chamber. While direct alignments on the equinox sunrise

A partially eclipsed moon photographed in the Boyne Valley.
The megalithic builders were adherents to a complicated solar-lunar calendar

and sunset would have suited adherents to the "fixed feasts" theory, especially given the apparent direct alignment of Newgrange on winter solstice sunrise, the offset alignments of Knowth appeared to make no sense whatsoever. Until, that is, Charles Scribner stepped in to explain the real significance of these dates.

The day on which the sunrise penetrated deep into Knowth East, at the time when it was constructed, was exactly three synodic lunar months before summer solstice, six synodic lunar months before autumn equinox, and nine synodic moon months before winter solstice. Thus, the exact dates of the other three great festivals of the year could be determined if one watched the moon. This required the Neolithic astronomers to observe the moon on the day when the sun was shining into the chamber of Knowth East every year. If, for example, that moon was at first quarter phase, counting three further first quarter moons would bring them to the summer solstice; the sixth first quarter moon would mark autumnal equinox; and the ninth would mark winter solstice.

The odds of this being a coincidence are lengthened by the fact that the dates in question are specific to 3300 BC, the time Knowth was built. Because the lengths of the seasons vary in a slow cycle over long periods of time, this unique solar–lunar timepiece could not function today.

The probability of fluke is even further decreased when Knowth West is factored into the equation. At Knowth West, the sun shines deep into the passage 18½ days before vernal equinox. In the Neolithic, the day on which this occurred was exactly 13 synodic moon months before the following spring equinox. Again, an observer using the structure to calculate the date of equinox would watch the phase of the moon at the time the sunset was casting its rays into the bend of the passage deep in the corridor of Knowth West, and count 13 same phases of the moon to bring him/her to the following spring equinox.

Gillies MacBain describes how someone using Knowth West might calculate the "movable feast" of pagan Easter the following year: "Observe the sun reaching the passage of Knowth West – the one that is still open – in early spring. There are now 13 moons until the following year's vernal equinox. Now, after dusk falls, observe the day of the moon. If full moon is to follow in two days' time then the following year's 'Paschal' full moon, the one that defines Easter, will be two days after March 21st or wherever your vernal equinox is falling in that year of that era".[37]

Examination of the inner portion of Knowth's western passage provides an immeasurable strengthening of the whole case. This inner section is believed by some to have been the undifferentiated passage of an earlier, small structure erected before the main mound. The bearing of this smaller inner section of the passage is 278°.[38] This portion of the passage, if it was at some time a minor passage-mound, would accept the light of the sun on a date that is ten and a half days after the equinox. This date is precisely 12 synodic moon months before the following spring equinox. So both passage phases would seem to have been concerned with solar dates which were certain numbers of synodic months ahead of the spring equinox of the next year.

At some juncture, observations at Knowth West will demonstrate conclusively the proposed original intent outlined in the Scribner Solution. Up until the time of writing this book, the only photograph published widely showing sunlight in the western passage at the equinox was taken by me, on 22 September 2000. That picture shows diffuse sunlight which is clearly focused on the left side of the passage looking out, suggesting the sun is to the right of where it should be in order to shine directly down the length of the passage as far as the basin stone which sits on the floor near the junction of "new" passage and "old". Although I witnessed the sunlight penetrating into the depths of the passage in early October 2006, I have not yet had the chance to photograph this event. Perhaps that opportunity will present itself in time.

Sunlight in the western passage at Knowth on the autumn equinox

On the eastern side, the situation is much more complicated. Due to efforts to conserve the complex of Early Christian structures, a large wall consisting of a concrete slab now hinders any possible observations. The bend in the outer part of the eastern passage found during excavations has been preserved, whether for right or for wrong, and it is now impossible for any light entering through the modern doorway to penetrate the full length of the passage. And that is an enormous pity. At 40.4 metres long, the eastern "tomb" was much longer than that at Newgrange, which measures 24.2 metres.[39] The corbelled roof of Knowth East, similar to the waterproof ceiling found at Newgrange, measures 5.9 metres high, almost identical in height to Newgrange (6 metres).

The axis of Knowth East, which points towards 85 degrees, is directed towards Dowth. Brennan never suspected this because he thought this passage pointed due east, while a cursory glance at a map shows Dowth is offset by a few degrees from the east–west line. This apparent alignment of Knowth with Dowth is a further indication that its orientation was not a fluke. All of the three major mounds of the Bend of the Boyne have passages pointing to other sites of significance. At Dowth, one passage points to Newgrange, the other to Tara. At Newgrange, the passage points towards the Fourknocks complex. And at Knowth, Dowth is the target.

Another astronomical significance Knowth shares with its sister sites is a kerb count which can be interpreted in the light of the lunar cycles. There are 127 kerbstones at Knowth. The kerb has a couple of gaps, including a large space which has been filled by one of the smaller mounds, satellite site 17, which is joined to the main mound. The total number of known kerbs at Knowth is 127, which is an important lunar number; 127 is half of 254, the total number of sidereal lunar months in a 19-year metonic cycle of the moon.[40] It could be another of those incredible coincidences, but in light of the kerb count theories already expounded for Dowth and Newgrange, it is less likely to be so.

The sidereal month marks the return of the moon to the same background stars. Using the sidereal month would appear to be a better method of marking time, simply because it is easier to watch the moon's movement against the backdrop of the stars than it is to watch it returning to the same phase. Evidence presented thus far suggests the Boyne Valley builders made use of both synodic counts and sidereal reckonings.

The kerb count hypothesis developed by Gillies MacBain suggests that the satellite site, Site 16, which is conjoined with the main Knowth mound, was critical to what he termed the "pendulum swing" count. Site 16 was in place before the main mound was constructed, and was in fact disturbed by the construction of Knowth Site 1.[41] Despite this, it was not destroyed, and the orientation of its passages may add fuel to the fire of an astronomical solution for Knowth.

One whole count of the Knowth kerb, starting at kerb 1, which forms part of the southeast passage of Site 16, finishes at kerb no. 127, which is located on the north-western side of Site 16. 127 sidereal months is nine and a half years, or half the metonic cycle. Site 16 appears to have two passages, so to speak. The original passage points towards the south south-west, while the secondary portion, which was probably added on when Site 1 was built, points to the south-east. This secondary portion has an azimuth of approximately 130°, and assuming there was no hindrance or obstruction it is likely that the sunrise on winter solstice would penetrate into this passage.

MacBain points out that one count around the 127 kerbstones from the winter solstice aligned Site 16 back to Site 16 again would take you from one phase of the moon at midwinter back to the opposite phase of the moon at midsummer. Another circuit brings you back to midwinter again with the moon in the same position as it had been two counts previously, 254 sidereal months or exactly 19 years ago.

The original passage of Site 16 was most likely aligned to the direction of major standstill south setting moon. A more complicated development of the MacBain theory hypothesises that Knowth could also be used to calculate and observe the major and minor standstills – the "moon swing" discussed in the chapter about Dowth.

This would require the observer to pay close attention to certain phases of the moon which coincide with equinoxes and solstices. These phases are the new moon (dark moon), the full moon and the quarter moons. The MacBain theory suggests that a "dark" new moon occurring on the day the sun shines into the chamber of Knowth East warns of a major standstill full moon occurring on the date of summer solstice the following year.

Josephine Coffey, another amateur, carried out a valuable and thorough investigation into what she termed "Some Moon Rhythms", and applied the extrapolated data to the interpretation of Knowth's lunar functions. One of the details Coffey's study disclosed was that the "major standstills happen when the sun is at an equinox position".[42] "There's no preferred time of year for the Metonic cycle to start or end – the Metonic cycle is really a kind of yardstick; you can start it anytime – but as we've seen, the extreme moons in the nodal cycle are always near either the vernal or autumnal equinox."[43] Coffey thinks it's more likely the celebration of the extreme moon was held at spring equinox rather than autumn because "the spring extreme moon always rises in the early morning – in the dark", while the autumnal moon rises in the afternoon, "when it would be more difficult to see."[44] Coffey also revealed that the metonic cycle – the cycle apparently enumerated by Knowth's kerb – and the moon swing cycle – the one apparently recorded at Dowth – are intrinsically connected. "Although the nodal cycle (at 18.6 years) is different from the Metonic cycle (at 19 years), because the major standstills happen when the sun is at an equinox position, not infrequently one extreme moon is a Metonic cycle away from the next."[45]

What could be concluded from the above is that the builders of Knowth and Dowth, who were undoubtedly part of the same community, utilised differing methods to evaluate, enumerate and predict the same thing – the standstills, or "lunistices" of the moon. Furthermore, because of the fact that the moon swing and the prediction of eclipses were uniquely tied, as Thom pointed out, it is highly likely that all three of the large Brú na Bóinne mounds formed part of a unified system which had as a common goal the foretelling and recording of eclipse phenomena.

THE CALENDAR STONE

A number of the kerbstones at Knowth appear to contain counting systems, some with symbols which could be interpreted as representations of the moon. One of these stones is Kerbstone 52, which was dubbed the "Calendar Stone" by Martin Brennan.

This stone contains carvings which can be categorised simply as follows: a spiral, a waved line, a series of C-shaped crescents and some circles. Brennan correctly asserted that the petroglyphs on this stone constituted a lunar count. This leap of faith on Brennan's behalf required some elements of the stone to be interpreted as representational art. He theorised that the series of 22 C-shaped petroglyphs represented the early and late phases of the moon, while the circular patterns depicted the full moon and the almost-full phases.[46]

The total number of crescent shapes in the lunar count pattern is 22, while the circular forms number seven, making a total count of 29, which is, roughly speaking, the number of days in a synodic period of the moon, i.e. the period that marks the return of the moon to the same phase again.

Kerbstone 52, the "Calendar Stone"

Three of the crescent shapes merge with the spiral symbol, something which Brennan maintained represented those days when the moon is at its "new" phase in the same part of the sky as the sun, and therefore invisible.

Running along the length of the stone in the centre of these lunar symbols is a waved line, featuring a series of undulating arcs that look like a continuous series of U shapes and inverted U shapes all joined together. Brennan postulated that "each turn of the wavy line represents one month".[47] The waved line appears to have 31 of these undulations, with an additional flourish on the left end of the line which could be interpreted as an additional count, bringing the total to 32 or a possible 33. All of these numbers, 31, 32 and 33, have possible lunar interpretations tied in with synodic moon counts.

What the Calendar Stone demonstrates is that the ancient astronomers were acutely aware that the moon's cycle did not fit neatly into the sun's year and that the solar year did not contain an exact number of full synodic months. 12 returns of the moon to its full phase was 11 days short of a solar year; 24 returns was 22 days short of two solar years, while adding an additional synodic lunar month to get 25 months was longer than two solar years by eight days. The difference between the lunar count and the solar eventually evens out after 19 sun years, which, as stated already, is almost the exact number of days as 235 synodic moon months or 254 (double the number of kerbstones) sidereal moon months.

The period which is most likely the main focus of the Calendar Stone is five solar tropical years, which is just five days shorter than 62 synodic months. The tally of 62 is reached by counting the 31 waves on the Calendar Stone twice. (This is reminiscent of the 254-month kerb count which required the kerb stones to be reckoned twice.)[48]

A supplemental addition of two turns at the end of the waved line could represent a count of 33, which is one third of 99, the eight-year cycle which brings Venus and the moon back together, a period which we examined in Chapter 8 and which formed the basis of the 99-kerb count at Newgrange.

The Calendar Stone demonstrates a competent knowledge of the lunar movements, something which would have been forged over long periods of time. It shows that the sky watchers of the Stone Age knew the length of the lunar month in days, while demonstrating also that they could determine the longer metonic intervals based on counts of whole periods of lunar months.[49]

But as with all the Neolithic stone devices, kerbstone 52 probably functioned on multiple levels. It can also be used to calculate the number of days in the year, albeit in a slightly convoluted fashion. There are 29

Knowth (background) with two of its satellite mounds

moons in total, 22 crescents and seven circular moons which are really double circles, potentially signifying an extra count. There is a folk tale still in existence from Brittany to Scotland, recounted by Charles Scribner,[50] which says if you count the stones more than once you will not get the same number. The numbers and arrangements at Stone Age sites were chosen so that there were several ways of counting them. Thus, the Calendar Stone can be counted as a 62-month metonic interval, or a 99-month eight-year Venus–moon interval.

Counting the moon circles on K52 as doubles brings us to a total moon count of 36 (29 plus 7). If we double 36 (and the stone already suggests doubling with the waved line: 2x31=62) we get 72, and add the solar spiral, we get 73. Five times 73 is equal to 365, the exact number of days in the year. Every fourth year, add the solar spiral to get 366.

Another obscure but pertinent facet of the Calendar Stone is the fact that if you sit with your back towards it and look out at the horizon, you will find yourself peering at the Hill of Tara, which is visible in a gap between two of Knowth's satellite mounds.

There are many other stones at Knowth which feature crescents and circles which are probably lunar symbols. A stone on the north-west of the kerb, K93, features a series of crescents and circles, a spiral and a waved line in a different configuration than those on the Calendar Stone. One interpretation of these markings identifies a 27-month count, analogous with a sidereal lunar month count.[51] The addition of a double circle on the top left of the stone yields a count of 29, signifying that the stone could also be used to enumerate the synodic moon month. K93 can also be used to count the number of days in the year.[52]

The lunar symbolism at Knowth is stark, as is the solar imagery. It is to be expected that both should be interspersed, a calendar based purely on either the sun or moon proving impossible to maintain without reference to the other. Brennan, and other writers such as N.L. Thomas, believed certain stones to be solar calendar calculators. Thomas held that some stones were purely solar, such as kerbstone 65, while others, such as kerbstone 15, were intricate sun calendars.[53] This kerbstone contains a large motif consisting of rays emanating from a cup mark, something Brennan identified with a sundial. He called the people of the ancient Boyne Valley the "master diallers of the New Stone Age".[54] Crescents and circles are present on numerous stones at Knowth, some in lavish groupings, such as the "opposed C" shapes on kerbstone 86 and on kerbstone 5.

THE THREE GODDESSES

The mythology of Knowth suggests a lunar influence. The *Dindshenchas* myth about Knowth ascribes the site to a noble woman called Bua, or Buí, recalling that she was buried there and the mound was built over her:

> A hill had Bua in the midst of Bregia,
> where the noble woman was laid,
> in that spot yonder:
> the name of that hill is Cnogba.[55]

Cnogba is the original Irish name for Knowth. It means Cnoc Buí, the hill of Buí:

> But though easiest to utter
> of its names be perfect Cnogba,
> yet its more proper style is Cnocc Bui
> down from Bua daughter of Ruadri.[56]

Buí, while being the Irish word for yellow, is also a hag goddess who is considered by folklorists to be the equivalent of the Cailleach Bhéarra,[57] the moon personage who was said to have formed the cairns at Loughcrew and other ancient sacred sites such as Monasterboice from her womb of stones. It has been suggested that the different colours of cattle in Irish myth could be associated with the symbolism of the various phases of the moon. One author suggests, "Thus we get the white cow (*bó finn*); the *bó ruad* (red cow), the *bó donn* (brown) and the *bó orann* (dark)."[58] The Cnogba legend appears to add another colour to the moon – yellow. The moon can appear to have a yellow tinge when it has just risen above the horizon. This is especially noticeable when the moon is full.

The *Dindshenchas* story does not explicitly state that the hag Buí was "buried" at Knowth, stating instead:

> it is there her body was hidden:
> over her was a great hill built up.[59]

The legend is certainly accurate in referring to the Knowth mound as "a great hill". Its construction would have been a monumental task akin to the construction of Dowth, which, according to the *Dindshenchas*, was built by all the men of Erin. George Eogan tries to paint a picture for us of the scale of this monumental task: "The building of the Knowth tombs and the acquisition of materials constituted a formidable task, particularly when stones had to be taken to the site. The tombs used up to about 1,600 large stones, varying in weight from nearly a ton to several tons. In addition, the main mound consumed hundreds of tons of loose stones and other materials such as sods, boulder clay, and shale."[60]

Like its sister sites at Dowth and Newgrange, Knowth represented architectural endeavour on a gargantuan scale. Was all this work carried out simply so that the remains of certain select individuals could be interred in the inner chambers? Or was Knowth something much broader than this, an expression of sacred sky–ground temple building encompassing a belief that there was, indeed, something "in the great beyond"? Its multiplicity of lavish symbolism, its enormity of scale, its complexity of design and its endurance against the harsh ravages of time suggest that Knowth was at the pinnacle of a far-removed epoch of enlightenment and optimism, a time when men and women living ordinary lives were transformed into demigods, people who had a divine sense of the inseparable connection between heaven and earth. The Knowth community was part of the greater "Bend of the Boyne community", probably working in collaboration on the various sites, including the many smaller mounds which dot the landscape between the three great mounds.

If the triplicate moon goddess is represented by the three recesses of Newgrange and the white quartz oval setting outside its grand chamber, perhaps the lunar hag/witch of Knowth is also symbolised by the huge triple-alcove chamber of Knowth East, and the circular quartz setting found outside the entrance in front of the kerb.

The excavator found a total of seven "settings" on the eastern side of Knowth. The principal example lay directly in line with the passage and was 4.2 metres in diameter.[61] It consisted of some milky quartz and some rolled stones. While the quartz setting found near the entrance of Newgrange was a convex shape, described as a "low mound" by Professor O'Kelly,[62] the Knowth setting was concave, described by George Eogan as "dished or saucer-shaped".[63] Were these sanctified ceremonial features, associated with some moon ritual carried out at certain critical moments in the moon's cycles? As stated earlier, an invisible or "dark" moon associated with the sun at the time the eastern chamber is illuminated acted as a warning for the impending major standstill. Looking out of Knowth's Eastern chamber, across the "sacred moon bowl" feature towards certain moon rises, an observer would also be looking directly at Dowth, the site whose central purpose was observation of the moon swing and eclipse prediction.

A spectator sitting in the end recess of Knowth East, looking out towards Dowth, would find themselves with their back towards Orthostat 47, a stone with mysterious carvings which one planetary cartographer has said represent the oldest known map of the moon. Dr Philip Stooke, of the University of Western Ontario, Canada, normally makes maps of asteroids. He studied the carvings on Orthostat 47 and concluded that they constituted an ancient attempt at lunar cartography. "I was amazed when I saw it. Place the markings over a picture of the full moon and you will see that they line up. It is without doubt a map of the moon, the most ancient one ever found," Dr Stooke told the BBC's online science editor David Whitehouse in an interview in 2001.[64]

Dr Whitehouse visited Knowth and had the exclusive pleasure of a face to face encounter with the "Moon Stone" in the same year. After being ushered into the chamber by Professor George Eogan, Whitehouse asked, "It is a map of the moon?"

"It could be," came Professor Eogan's reply. "Certainly, the moon is here," Eogan said, pointing into the recess containing the huge ornamental stone bowl.[65] There, on the large upright stone behind the basin, is an intricately carved stone on which Dr Whitehouse could see "stars and cresents. They are undoubtedly images of the moon".[66]

Boldly engraved on this stone, Orthostat 54, are images of the star and crescent, the sky symbols we think are represented in the myths by the cow and calf, the Glas Goibhneann and her offspring, the hag and the little

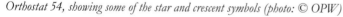

Orthostat 54, showing some of the star and crescent symbols (photo: © OPW)

hag, the moon and Venus, the heavenly pairing which formed the inspiration for so much of the sky stories and the cosmic architecture of the Boyne Valley. The almost pristine 5,300-year-old petroglyphs provide us with a manmade picture of the star and crescent that was the basis of at least some of the inspiration behind numerous sites, including Baltray, Colpe, Millmount, Tara and Newgrange. It is an image which persists today in the "star and crescent" emblem of Drogheda town, home of Amergin's mound, the mythical poet astronomer who could tell the ages of the moon.

Sadly, the sun and moon no longer shine into this beautiful primeval "star chamber". Perhaps some day in the future they may be able to do so. When and if that happens, Knowth East could teach us some very important things about the astronomers of the Boyne Valley.

George Eogan has speculated that St Patrick did not light his Easter fire on the Hill of Slane, as is commonly held to be the case. Eogan believes it is possible that Patrick lit the paschal fire at Knowth:

> Slane is not specifically mentioned in the early lives of the saint, although it appears that on his return to Ireland, Patrick landed on the east coast. Muirchú, in his *Life* of the saint, states that the landing place was Inver Colpa, the mouth of the Boyne, and that from there he moved inland and in the evening arrived at the "burial place of the men of Fiacc" where he and his companions pitched their tents and celebrated Easter.[67]

Eogan speculates that this "burial place" could have been Brugh na Bóinne, and states that there is no archaeological or historical evidence that Slane was an important site at that time.[68]

We have shown that an observer inside the equinox chamber at Cairn T, Loughcrew, would be looking directly at Sláine's mound on the Hill of Slane at sunrise on the equinox. Certainly the astronomical evidence would indicate that Slane was important in the far-off New Stone Age.

But there is something uniquely symbolic about the eastern chamber that resonates with Professor Eogan's speculation about Knowth and St Patrick. The sun shines into this chamber on "vernal equinox plus six days". Accounts of St Patrick's life indicate that he lit the Easter fire at Slane in the year 433 AD, on 26 March. Assuming a date of 20 March for the equinox, this would put the date of Patrick's paschal fire at "vernal equinox plus six days".

George Eogan has given us much food for thought. He has revealed Knowth to the world. Knowth, in turn, has given up some of its secrets. Yet some remain hidden, to be unlocked by bright minds some time in the future. It is a multifarious site far too complicated to be interpreted fully in one short chapter. Exploration of its astronomy deserves an entire book, and will no doubt provide grounds for dozens of research projects for many years to come. For now, we must leave Knowth, which is a jewel in the crown of the Boyne Valley, and turn our attention to the nearby hill of Slane and the wider cosmic landscape . . .

CHAPTER TEN
COSMIC GRID: LINES ACROSS THE LAND

When Saint Patrick arrived at the Boyne Valley in 433 AD to announce the Christian message to the people of the "Island of the Setting Sun", he must surely have realised he was right at the heart of a very sacrosanct and incredibly ancient pagan landscape. Whether it was at Slane hill or nearby Brú na Bóinne that torch was put to tinder and a fire was kindled "which in Éire shall not be extinguished for ever",[1] Patrick was surrounded in every direction by the abundant remnants of a vast and extraordinary pre-Christian monument assembly.

At the summit of the hill of Slane, the place traditionally associated with Patrick's paschal fire, lies the great motte of Sláine, the mythical Fir Bolg king said to be buried at that spot. From here, a sweep of the land from horizon to horizon finds ancient remains and eminent places of old in almost every direction.

To the east lies Drogheda, the location of Amergin's mound, and Inbher Colpa, the meeting of the waters where both Amergin, and Patrick, landed, at the same spot on the southern shore of the Boyne river. Slightly south of east lies the Bend of the Boyne assembly, with Newgrange and Knowth visible almost in line with each other. To the south lie the hills of Skryne and Realtoge and of course Tara, the ancient capital of Ireland. Looking in a southwesterly direction, the eye is led towards Tlachtga, the site of an ancient earthworks known as a multivallate ringfort.[2] Towards the west lies Teltown, in Irish Tailteann, the site of numerous old earthworks and the place where, in myth, Lugh held Ireland's harvest games in honour of his foster mother. Teltown was also the mythical location where the Tuatha Dé Danann kings were routed by the Milesians.[3] In the distant west, rising up from the grey horizon, the peaks of the hag, the storied hills of Loughcrew, reach up to touch the bottom of the sky.

Towards the northwest is Sliabh Breagh, the site of a conglomeration of ringforts and barrows. Occupying the northern horizon are the hills of Dunmore, the mythical site of three giants' graves, and Mount Oriel, once the site of a great stone cairn,[4] while immediately to the east of these is the Black Hill. Looking in a north easterly direction from Slane takes us in the direction of Monasterboice, another site associated with the lunar hag and once the location of a stone circle.

FIERY HILLS

When Patrick came to Slane, if indeed Slane was the site of the paschal fire, he followed the equinox line from Drogheda to the hill where Sláine was buried. He would have unwittingly found himself at the centre, the metaphorical crossroads, of an ancient system of astronomical alignments

The ruins on the Hill of Slane lit up with the aurora borealis (Northern Lights) forming a spectacular backdrop

laid down almost four millennia previously. From Amergin's Millmount, the sun at equinox appears to sink below the horizon at the hill of Slane. The paschal fire was lit after sunset.[5] So a unique sequence of events which had one foot in pagan prehistory and the other foot in the earliest Christian times, unfolded. First, the giant fiery orb of the sun appeared to sit on the peak of Sláine's hill as the day waned in the west around the time of vernal equinox. Six days later, with the sun moving north along the horizon as the days grew longer, Patrick kindled the Easter fire after dusk, its flame on the hill of Slane probably being visible at Millmount, which overlooks Inbher Colpa, the place where both Amergin and Patrick were said to have landed in Ireland. The blazing Easter fire may also have been visible from the equinox chamber at Cairn T, over 20 miles to the west of Slane.[6] Inside this chamber, the sun on the dawn of the equinox rises over Slane, which is visible in the distance looking out through the passage.

The lighting of a fire at the time of Easter/equinox was very much a pagan tradition, something which was prevalent on the mountains and hills not only of Ireland, but all across Europe, in early times.[7] Many hills have sacred fire traditions associated with them. Some of the fires were kindled on the feasts of Bealtaine and Samhain, while others were set at the time of the pre-Christian "Easter", the moveable feast discussed in Chapter 9. The hill of Tlachtga had a Samhain fire festival ritual strongly attached to the onset of winter.[8]

The Hill of Tara was the central focus of the prehistoric paschal flame ritual, and it was here that one of the main ceremonies of the great "Easter" assembly was the "striking forth of 'new fire'" to mark the

Samhain fires: an ancient ritual still living

"birthday of the year".[9] The law at the time of Patrick's arrival stated that no fire should be lit "on any hearth in Éire" until the "druid spark should be drawn by friction from the sacred wood on the royal heights of Tara".[10] Breaking this law was punishable by the death penalty. So when the High King, Laoghaire, and his kinsmen and subjects beheld the flame "across the darkness of the March night", the challenge of St Patrick drew angry words from the dismayed monarch: "Who is it that has dared to do this impiety in my kingdom? Let him die the death."[11]

As the fire on Slane blazed, "the whole sky above Bregia brightened with a lumination fairer than that of day; the Boyne rolled waves of gleaming light . . ."[12] At this crucial moment, with the King on Tara hill looking towards the new flame of Christianity on Slane, Laoghaire was looking along the sightline of an extraordinary alignment which was both immensely astronomically significant and extraordinarily symbolic at that particular juncture.

Standing at Tara, peering towards Slane, an observer is looking across Realtoge hill. Beyond Slane on the far horizon is Mount Oriel, near the village of Collon in County Louth. The happenstance linear configuration of four hills, all natural landscape features, is just that – a chance alignment. But all of these hills had distinguished places in the astronomical master plan, the cosmic grid, first spoken of in the early chapters. Tara was the capital of Ireland and is the location of many diverse archaeological remains. Realtoge marks the position of winter solstice sunset viewed from Newgrange. Slane was important in both pre-Christian and Christian times. And Oriel was once topped with a mound which was said to have possibly been the burial place of some ancient chief.[13] Today, Oriel retains the remnants of a prehistoric complex, and there are at least five known barrows on or near its summit. There is mention in local folklore of a possible "heap of stones" on Oriel hill which were taken by a Lord Mazareene to "drain his land".[14]

One link between Tara at one end of the alignment and Oriel at the other is found through the word "hostage". At Tara, we find the cross-quarter and minor-standstill-aligned Mound of the Hostages or Duma na nGiall. Mount Oriel takes its name from an ancient kingdom, known as Oriel, in which the hill was located. Oriel comes from the Irish *Oir-ghialla,* which translates as "golden hostages".[15] Intriguingly, St Patrick was brought to Ireland as a slave by an "Irish raiding party" which may have been led by Niall of the Nine Hostages.[16]

CROSS IN THE SKY

But the most fascinating aspect of the line from the "pagan paschal" Tara fire through the "Christian paschal" Slane fire towards Oriel is related to what was happening in the sky at that critical moment when the new flame was lit atop Slane by Patrick and his first priest, Cianán. Taking our computer sky software back to 433 AD, six days after the equinox, looking towards the northern horizon, we see that something astonishing happens.

With our view centred on 16 degrees,[17] we look at the arrangement of the constellations on the northern horizon. An observer, such as King Laoghaire, standing on Tara looking towards Slane would see, just as darkness falls and the stars begin to appear, that the stars of the cross-shaped Cygnus constellation are visible in the sky just above Oriel.

This could be mere chance, were it not for the fact that the star which marks the centre of the cross of Cygnus, the one called Sadr, is exactly in line with the row of hills as darkness falls. Was St Patrick drawing the King's eyes towards the cross in the sky, a potent symbol central to his new message for Ireland? The paschal fire was lit at the junction of two major sky–ground alignments, the equinox line of Millmount–Slane–Loughcrew and the Cygnus line of Tara–Realtoge–Slane–Oriel. Sadr marks the "junction" of the sky cross.

The imagery is stark. The "pagan" cross representing Aonghus, the "son of the virgin" with a powerful winter solstice link, is replaced by the "Christian" cross, representing Christ, the "son of the virgin", whose birth we celebrate four days after winter solstice.

What we are being presented with is compelling religious iconography, specifically the Celtic Cross, a symbol crafted in the Neolithic as part of a "wish fulfilment" and rebirth rite, in which the "son of the virgin", who has experienced rebirth among the stars, was a beacon of hope for the people of the Stone Age, whose material corpses may have undergone immolation in order to free the spirit for its transference to the otherworld.[18] This powerful icon, the cross with light at its centre, was first presented at Newgrange, where the beam of the sun penetrated into the heart of the crucifix-shaped chamber, at a time of year corresponding with modern Christmas, when we celebrate the birth of the new son / new sun.

The imagery of the cross of the divine son, inaugurated first by the megalithic culture, was replicated by Saint Patrick, who in lighting the paschal fire atop Slane was drawing the eyes of the pagan king towards the firelight at the centre of the cross. The Celtic Cross icon was later sculpted from huge blocks of stone at places such as Monasterboice, which is just over six miles from Newgrange. Muiredach's Cross, a 5.5-metre high monument, is the finest surviving example of a Celtic Cross in Ireland,

Muiredach's Cross agaust the night sky

and is lavishly decorated with biblical scenes. A second cross at Monasterboice, known as the West Cross, is around 7 metres tall.[19] Both are within metres of the round tower, and only ten minutes' drive from the Brú na Bóinne complex.

One history of Patrick tells us that "the 'Light of the World' had, indeed, come forth from the Stone Sepulchre".[20] Is this a glimpse at the true nature of Sláine's mound on the top of Slane hill? Was it once a passage-mound just like Newgrange? Could it be a reference to Knowth, where the sun shone into the heart of the cross-shaped eastern passage six days after the vernal equinox?

The rising of Cygnus as it gets dark at the time of the paschal fire is a very time-specific event, as the sky software illustrates. A week earlier and Cygnus appears in the sky lower and further north, while a week after the date of the Easter fire, it is higher and further east.

Another curious astronomical oddity involves the Millmount–Slane alignment. In the New Stone Age, when it is likely Millmount was first constructed, and possibly the mound on Slane, the setting autumn

Sunset over Slane

equinox sun found itself on the edge of the Milky Way in the constellation Scorpius, just under the constellation Ophiuchus. The sun was on the right-hand side of the river, just as the hill of Slane is right of the river viewed from Millmount.

THE SNAKE-KILLING KING

There is a long-standing folk tradition associated with St Patrick which asserts that he was responsible for banishing snakes from Ireland. The constellation Ophiuchus represents the serpent-bearer, the mythical Aesculapius who grasps the snake with both hands.[21] Aesculapius was the "god of medicine", a healer physician of great renown.[22] His Irish equivalent would probably be Diancecht, the Tuatha Dé Danann chief who fashioned a new hand made of silver for the wounded King Nuadu. Diancecht is associated with the killing of a "great serpent" which had endangered an area around the River Barrow in the southern part of Leinster.[23] Diancecht was also said to have possessed a special healing well in Sligo called Tiopra Sláine, and it is possible that there once was a well in the area around the Hill of Slane in Meath with the same healing association.[24]

One further symbolic connection between the constellation Ophiuchus and the whole St Patrick saga is that the shape of the serpent bearer constellation, minus the head and tail of the serpent, resembles the bishop's mitre worn by the saint. Patrick was known by the Irish as "Adze Head", which is a probable reference to his mitre.[25]

209

Also noteworthy with regard to the Millmount–Slane alignment is the fact that the sun was sitting on the edge of the heavenly Boyne, the Milky Way, on *both* equinoxes. Standing at Millmount around the autumn equinox, looking towards the sunset, a viewer would see the sun striking the top of Slane, with the invisible Milky Way to the left of the sun's position. On the ground, Slane is to the right of the river Boyne. The reverse of this occurs at the vernal equinox, when a viewer on Slane would see the sun rising over Millmount with the invisible Milky Way to its left, mimicking the position of the river on the ground, which is to the left of Amergin's mound as viewed from Slane. Also of significance in this regard is the fact that the sun was located in Taurus, the bull star grouping, recalling the connection between Millmount and the Black Bull area of Drogheda encountered in Chapter 3.

The first bishop of Slane was called Erc, a name which means "speckled", which is an adequate description of the freckled appearance of the Milky Way. Grippingly, Erc was also an early Irish word meaning "cow" and this brings to mind the indissoluble association between the Milky Way and the cow. One story about Bishop Erc recalls that the "wonder-working saint of God's people" had a custom of remaining immersed in the waters of the Boyne "up to his two arm-pits", praying constantly from morning until evening.[26] One image conceivably implied by this story is of a man in a river with arms outstretched, symbolic of the Cygnus constellation.

Erc's Grave with the sun at the meridian lining up exactly with a groove across the top of the stone

There are two large stones in the old graveyard on the Hill of Slane which are said to be Erc's grave, or at least part of a structure which was once his tomb.[27] One researcher who believes Slane to have been a very important epicentre of myth and culture over time is Seán Gilmartin, an amateur folklorist who has walked the length and breadth of Ireland recording local folk tales and myths in his own database of Irish lore. Gilmartin points out that the "house-shaped shrine"[28] of St Erc features some interesting alignments. Both of the triangular shaped stones are marked along their narrow edges by deep grooves, possibly man made. A sightline along the groove on the easternmost stone seems to point towards the sun's position at the meridian, while a sightline along furrows on both stones points towards the northern pole of the sky, marked by the star Polaris. Gilmartin has observed this directly, and indicates that there may have been markings on both stones which facilitate the position of the observer's head in order that a comfortable and correct observation of the phenomena be facilitated.[29]

SACRED SIGHTLINES

Information already presented about the Millmount–Slane–Loughcrew line and the Tara–Slane–Oriel line, along with evidence from many other sites in the Boyne area, would seem to infer that ancient megalithic sites were laid out along sacred lines on the ground. These lines form a "grid" of sorts; not a grid consisting of parallel and perpendicular lines forming squares, but rather a grid with lines at different angles which present an impression of some sort of complex sky–ground arrangement of intersecting pathways, each with its own fundamental purpose. Many of the rows or arrangements of sites line up with specific sky events which can be connected with the sites involved in the arrangement, whether through place name meanings, myths, legendary figures associated with the sites, or a combination of these things.

One example is the Millmount–Rath Maeve–Carbury line, which is a solstice line, commemorated at Millmount by Amergin, whose iconography is imbued with setting sun symbolism. But it is also a Dog Star line, immortalised by Bóann's lapdog, Dabilla, and furthermore it is an Orion line, perpetuated by the stories of the kings of Tara touching the Lia Fáil. Above and beyond all these, the Millmount–Tara–Carbury alignment is a Milky Way/river line, connecting the source of the Boyne with its estuary, two places which are 35 miles apart.

Another interesting alignment is the Site Q–Clogherhead summer solstice line, which points towards a hill commemorating the hound (Leo), which housed the summer sun in the Neolithic. Adjacent to Castlecoo Hill is Callystown, from the Irish *Baile na gCailleach,* town of the Hag, indicating that lunar observations were probably also a feature of Site Q.

Early on in this research project, Richard Moore showed me a map from a book about Ireland which appeared to show alignments of sacred ancient sites which radiated from Uisneach, the ancient heart of Ireland and the location of the "navel stone" or "stone of divisions".[30] The map illustrated alignments of sites which were separated in some cases by 50 miles or greater. Furthermore, some of the lines of ancient sites appeared to point towards significant astronomical events such as the midsummer and midwinter sunrises.

Author Michael Dames relates that, "Solsticial sunrises and sunsets and quarterdays, as seen from Uisnech, relate to an array of mountain peaks, hilltops and striking water features. Significant solar sunrise alignments link sacred sites in the four provinces to the fifth, Uisnech."[31] He further states, "Seen from Mide, the energies of the four provinces could be woven by enlightened observation into a web of radial and concentric 'place-events'."[32]

A number of these sacred sightlines encompass sites which are important to our own investigation of the ancient astronomers. The 46-degree line emanating from the hill of Uisneach, County Westmeath, and

Map showing the main megalithic and ancient sites discussed in this book

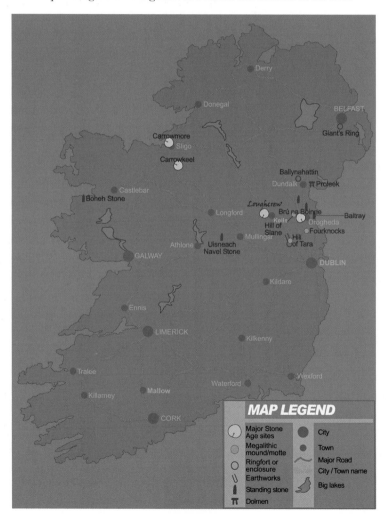

passing through the Loughcrew hills, the hag's peaks, finds Slieve Gullion, which itself it topped by two Stone Age passage tombs which are associated with the same Cailleach or hag, the lunar witch.[33] Dames tells us that the "apron" from which the hag dropped her stones at Loughcrew is "the divine womb, translated into the language of dress".[34] Although neither Gullion nor Uisneach are intervisible, both can be seen from Sliabh na Callaighe, again recalling the statement by Thom first encountered in the Baltray chapter that the megalithic builders could range in sites which were mutually invisible. The Uisneach-Loughcrew–Gullion line points towards the midsummer sunrise, according to Dames.

Another line from Uisneach, the centre of Ireland, passes through Teltown, the location of the Lughnasa games, and finds Sliabh Breagh in Meath and Dunany Point on the coast at Louth. This linear arrangement of sites is associated with sunrise on the May (Bealtaine) and August (Lughnasa) cross-quarter days. Dunany is the anglicised form of Dún Áine, the fort of Áine, whose name in ancient times meant "lustre" or "brightness",[35] and who might have had an association with the moon. At Dunany, we come across the "Mad Chair" of Dunany, which is a large, water-worn stone "somewhat bigger than, and roughly resembling a large chair, about 50 yards out in the beach . . . and covered at high water."[36] This chair could be analogous with the "Hag's Chair" at Cairn T on Loughcrew, another large stone which resembles a chair. The cross-quarter Uisneach– Dunany sun line could be associated with a minor standstill moon because of the proximity of their rising positions.

Local folklore suggests that Áine, "who had her fort on the brow of Dunany head, now washed away by the sea",[37] was trying to build a causeway from Ireland to England or Scotland.[38] The reef in front of the headland was believed to have been this causeway which she had attempted to construct, but "becoming tired of the work, she sat down on a chair-shaped stone and went mad".[39] Some people connect Áine with Dana, the "mother of the gods", while others say she was the Cailleach Bhéarra, the same lunar deity associated with Loughcrew and Gullion and other places such as Monasterboice.[40] Another folk tale recalls a magical calf which galloped past Dunany point, and jumped over Dundalk Bay and the Cooley Mountains after his rider said the words "High Over All". This is a possible reference to the magical calf associated with Baltray and other sites.

Lying along the Uisneach–Dunany line is the peak of the hill of Oriel. Also on this line is Sliabh Breagh, the only peak on the original range of hills called Sliabh Breagh which still retains that name. On its peak is a complex of low mounds and circular forts that suggest it was a place of import in former times. So striking is the number of remains that one author has suggested that "the earthen ramparts, which can be seen today at Slieve Breagh, are, in so many respects, a facsimile of the remains on Tara".[41] That author, Elizabeth Hickey, further suggests that Sliabh Breagh is Dun na nGed, the royal seat of King Domnall, a descendant of Laoghaire, who was king when Patrick lit the paschal fire.[42]

While Oriel sits on both the Tara–Slane line, or at least an extension of it, and also on the Uisneach–Dunany line, Sliabh Breagh is very significant because it has a direct association with the Newgrange–Fourknocks alignment outlined in Chapter 7. An extension of the line from Fourknocks through Newgrange eventually intersects the barrow complex on Sliabh Breagh. This is easily witnessed by drawing a line on a map (a custom which Richard and I became experts at!) from Fourknocks to Sliabh Breagh, which will neatly cross Newgrange on its way. An observer situated atop Sliabh Breagh would thus see the winter solstice sun rising over both Newgrange and Fourknocks. An observer situated with their back to the heavily decorated Kerbstone 52 opposite the entrance to Newgrange would find themselves looking towards Sliabh Breagh for sunset on the summer solstice. Of further interest is the fact that the Sliabh Breagh–Newgrange–Fourknocks line also passes through the centre of Duleek village, said to have been the location of Ireland's earliest stone churches, built by St Cianán, the first priest of Patrick who was said to have been involved in the lighting of the paschal fire. Duleek was also once the location of a motte, but this was destroyed for gravel in the eighteenth century.[43]

Sliabh Breagh is roughly north of the Hill of Tara, from where an observer positioned at the southern end of the banqueting hall, looking north along its axis, would perceive a few of the peaks of the Slieve Breagh range directly in line with this axis. One of these peaks is known as Sliabh Dubh, the Black Hill, which is sometimes known as Sliabh na gCearc,[44] the "hill of the hen", a possible reference to the fact that Cygnus dipped below the horizon there as viewed from Tara in the Neolithic.

In his own research in the early 1980s, Martin Brennan found lines of sites over long distances. His map of Ireland's ancient megalithic and Early Bronze Age sites showed two significant long-distance alignments. One of these lines stretched all the way from Carrowmore in Sligo, overlooking the Atlantic Ocean, through Loughcrew and Tara, to the hill of Howth in County Dublin, overlooking the Irish Sea. The Irish place name for Howth is Ben Edair, and folklore has it that a Tuatha Dé Danann chief was buried there.[45] There are archaeological remains at Howth including a dolmen (portal tomb) and two cairns. A second line identified by Brennan extends from Carrowkeel, in the Bricklieve Mountains in Sligo, through Loughcrew to Fourknocks.

ALIGNMENTS AT BRÚ NA BÓINNE

Of course, drawing lines on maps containing thousands of ancient sites is bound to yield apparent linear formations of sites, leading to the tentative conclusion that the finding of such arrangements is of no real consequence. However, many of the sites in question are the chief locations of Irish prehistory, culture and legend. Statistically, the chances of these principal sites lining up accidentally are remote. The probability of chance alignment becomes even more distant when major sites line up towards noteworthy astronomical happenings, and remoter again if a myth connects the sites and the sky event.

An example of this would be Baltray and Rockabill, which are intimately connected through the midwinter sunrise event and the myth which not only unites the two sites, but which appears to describe, in elaborate mythical symbolism, the actual sunrise occurrence.

In the Boyne Valley, there is evidence aplenty of a stringent and systematic arrangement of archaeological sites and landmarks which is suggestive of a cosmic grid on the ground which forms an exclusive interrelationship with the heavens. Examination of this Boyne grid appears to indicate that each site is just one piece of an enormous whole, and, in many cases, taking away a single element will render the entire system inoperable. Such an arrangement is indicative of a time-sensitive genesis of the sites – either they were all built around the same time, or the sites that came later were positioned strategically in relation to those that were built earlier.

Rockabill consists of two very small islands in the sea. It is not known whether there were any megalithic remains on these islands, but it is logical, given their propensity for using distant landmarks as foresights, to assume that the New Stone Age builders would see Rockabill as something of a golden opportunity – a revered landmark suspended in that sacred space between the sky and the earth, a natural signpost to the stars. While Baltray shares a very definite midwinter alignment with Rockabill, both astronomically and mythologically, the sites up on the Fourknocks ridge share an equinox alignment with Rockabill, lying as they do directly due west of the islands. We know from evidence presented in Chapter 7 that the Fourknocks I chamber points to the Baltray standing stones, while the megaliths of Balor's Strand also point back towards Fourknocks, consequently indicating a purposeful arrangement of both sites. Our gut feeling about Baltray is that it has a Neolithic origin, which would make it a contemporary of Fourknocks. Were they built at the same time, by the same community?

Fourknocks sits on two major alignments of significance which connect it with the wider archaeological landscape. One is the Newgrange–Sliabh Breagh line which is a pointer for winter solstice sunrise and summer solstice sunset. The other is the line which extends from Fourknocks through Loughcrew to Carrowkeel, identified by Brennan. Because of its unique astronomical and mythological Cygnus link, the Newgrange–Fourknocks arrangement leads one to conclude that they were both concurrent, which in turn would lead to the inclination that Baltray is contemporaneous with both. This conclusion is supported by the fact that the alignment of Fourknocks towards the rising of the swan stars also points towards Baltray.

Newgrange, sitting precisely on the Fourknocks–Sliabh Breagh line, lies directly due south of the Black Hill at Collon. This is the hill that marked summer solstice sunset from Millmount. The Millmount–Slane–Loughcrew equinox line crosses the Tara–Realtoge–Slane–Oriel Cygnus line at

A map showing the known and suspected alignments in the Bend of the Boyne. For more information about the alignments, see http://www.astroarchaeology.org/boynevalley.html (image: © Michael O'Callaghan)

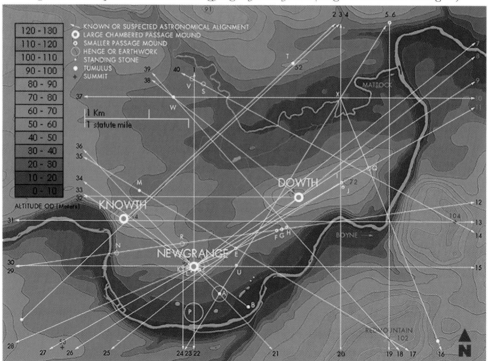

Slane. Realtoge is connected with Newgrange through the winter solstice alignment. The disparate arrangement of lines crisscrossing the land lends credence to the sense that a map of the Boyne region is effectively like a piece of cosmic graph paper. Is it all just the result of happenstance?

Even on a local level, sites appear to be strategically set out, so that the "cosmic grid" appears to operate on a much smaller level, functioning across shorter distances. In the Bend of the Boyne area, we have looked at some alignments, such as the Dowth South to Tara line, the Dowth North to Newgrange line, the Newgrange to Fourknocks line and the Knowth East to Dowth line. But examination of the complex layout of smaller sites in the loop of the Boyne throws up some interesting results.

One of the first alignments in the area investigated by us was the apparent solstice line from Knowth towards a small passage tomb site at Townley Hall known simply as Site T. Using magnetic compass measurements, we found that Site T was situated so that an observer situated there would see winter solstice sunset over Knowth, while an observer at Knowth would see summer solstice sunrise in the direction of Site T. This small passage-tomb was excavated by Professor G.F. Mitchell in the period 1960--61,[46] and has a short undifferentiated passage which could accept a wide range of azimuths, roughly centred on summer solstice sunrise.

Another Boyne Valley "sky line" involved Site E, a small passage tomb to the northeast of Newgrange. An observer at mound E would see the summer solstice sun rising over Dowth. This alignment was observed directly by Anne-Marie Moroney in the year 2000.

Brennan suggested an observer situated at Mound B, down on the floodplain of the Boyne to the southeast of Newgrange, would see the summer solstice sun setting over Newgrange. Richard Moore has observed this phenomenon directly, on a number of occasions. Brennan further indicated that an observer at mound A, another satellite mound sitting on the sloping fields in front of Newgrange, was situated in such a way that an astronomer standing at Site A would see the major standstill moon setting over Newgrange.

A largely destroyed site, probably another passage-mound, known as Site U, is due east of Newgrange and therefore falls into an equinox configuration with Newgrange. Three further satellite sites known as F, G, and H, could be part of a Samhain/Imbolc cross-quarter alignment with Newgrange.[47]

It has to be borne in mind that all of these Bend of the Boyne sites are located within short distances of each other, which reduces the accuracy of any suggested alignment. This is why there seems to have been a preference for more distant foresights, as suggested by Alexander Thom. However, even Dr Jon Patrick, who surveyed the Boyne Valley sites in the early 1970s, concluded that "there is evidence that some lines are deliberately orientated on solar phenomena".[48] He also indicated some lunar alignments.[49]

At Loughcrew, there is evidence of local alignments also. An example of this would be Cairn I on Carnbane West, where the end recess of its complex chamber receives sunlight at the beginning of September, a forewarning of the equinox.[50] Sitting in the chamber of Cairn I, looking out through the entrance, the stone heap of Cairn T is visible in the centre of the view. As the Samhain/Imbolc cross-quarter sunrise enters into the chamber of Cairn L, the sun is rising directly over Cairn M.[51]

There may have been a particular concern with Fourknocks, indicating longer-distance alignment was probably a key factor in the situation of the cairns. It has been shown that the preference for "tomb" openings at Loughcrew is for alignment towards the eastern aspect.[52] This may reflect

The Cosmic Grid

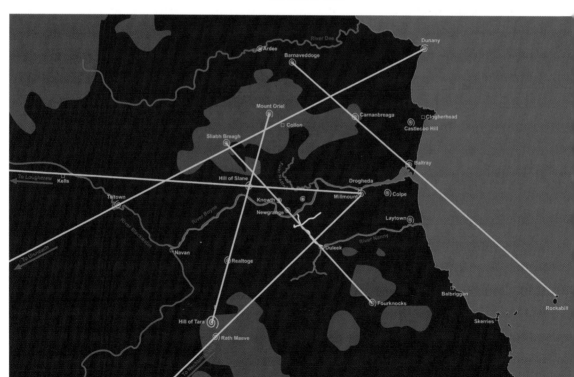

"a general cosmological concern and also a deliberate alignment to other passage tombs, particularly Fourknocks to the southeast".[53]

In Britain, there is some evidence of ancient megalithic structures being aligned over great distances, some of which point towards major sun and moon events.[54] The discovery "that ancient sacred sites were arranged in straight lines" was first announced in 1921 by Alfred Watkins in a paper to Hereford's Woolhope Society, and later published as a book, called *Early British Trackways*.[55]

Watkins found that the straight lines "extended for many miles and coincided with prehistoric tracks, laid down in times when people found their way across country by travelling straight from one landmark to another next in line".[56] The trackways contained not only Neolithic sites, but also stone crosses, crossroads, holy wells, churches, sacred trees, meeting points and other features.[57] Several of these trackways, which Watkins called "leys", formed astronomical alignments, some of which were "orientated to the Stone Age solstice points".[58] One author has said that "virtually every megalithic site is astronomically aligned and linked to other sites over vast distances, even across large bodies of water".[59]

It is clear that the megalithic cosmologists saw the eminences and landscape features on their horizon as natural foresights to aid them in their astronomical study. In some cases, they named these natural features in accordance with whatever astronomical event occurred in that direction. What is also apparent is that monumental structures were often erected on significant landscape features, such as hills and peaks, sometimes on eminences overlooking rivers, and there was a proven ability among the Stone Age builders to align sites over huge distances that were not intervisible, something pointed out by Alexander Thom in the early 1970s and confirmed in Ireland's case by Michael Dames and others.

The "cosmic grid" signifies a potent and palpable link between heaven and earth, something which was central to the belief system of the early communities on this island who long ago established that the path to the netherworld was one which opened when the sky touched the ground, metaphorically, at key moments in the calendar.

If there was a "cosmic grid" on the ground, surely the cunning star gazers of the New Stone Age had some kind of graph paper in the sky, a map of the stars, so to speak, which would form the backdrop for the movement of the sun, moon and planets? We believe they did, and that their star groupings, their constellations, were the basis of a plethora of star myths embedded in the huge body of mythic literature which comes to us from the earliest times.

CHAPTER ELEVEN

STAR STORIES: SKY MYTHS OF THE ANCIENTS

R. MOORE 2002

The surviving monumental architecture of ancient astronomical study in Ireland serves as a visceral reminder of a time long ago when dark nights and clear skies ensured the countless scores of twinkling lights in the sky provided the dramatic basis for a striking narrative. That narrative was the story of the stars. The vast black chasm of the night sky formed the backcloth of the stage against which this stellar drama unfolded.

An assessment of the various movements of the sky, whether at a cursory level or at a highly proficient intensity, reveals many interesting things about the rituals of the heavenly bodies, and their "dance in the bright heavens".[1] The stars themselves appear to move inexorably across the darkness, rising in the east every night and setting in the west, in a seemingly never-ending movement, each one of the myriad points of light moving in simultaneous unison with the others. None of the stars, these curious "bright things"[2] which adorn the abyss of night, appears to move out of place, each one apparently fixed to the giant invisible dome of the cosmic chasm. They float across the heavens in perfect synchronicity.

The early Irish astronomers would doubtless have perceived with even a superficial observation of the sky some relatively basic concepts: that some stars were bright, others were dim; that most stars appeared to rise in the east every night and set in the west; that there were some stars in the northern region of the sky which did not set below the horizon at all; that the stars rose slightly earlier every night and set a little earlier too; that the moon and planets move against the fixed stars.

The inexorable movement of the stars across the sky can be captured with a camera by leaving the shutter open for a period of time. The stars "float across the heavens in perfect synchronicity."

Observation over a somewhat longer period would have yielded more information: that the same stars are visible at certain times of the year, so stars that are visible in the winter of one year will also be visible at the same time of night the following winter; that the sun appears to drift slowly against the stars, following the same path through the sky year after year; that the moon's wanderings are more complicated than those of the sun; that the sun, moon and planets appear much higher in the sky when located against the background of some star groupings and much lower in the sky against others; that the bright band of the *Bealach na Bó Finne* rotates in the sky, sometimes flattening out on the entire horizon; that the sun, moon and planets cross the Milky Way at two locations in the sky.

These are all phenomena which would not require the observer to be a highly qualified and experienced specialist. Such heavenly occurrences are observable today and can be perceived easily by amateur star gazers.[3]

It is likely that sky knowledge was transmitted anecdotally. The oral tradition was very powerful in Ireland, and knowledge has been transmitted in the form of stories over vast intervals of time. This is evident from folk memory in the Boyne Valley, which recalls that Venus shone into the chamber of Newgrange once every eight years.

There is an apparent dearth of reference to the stars in the immense corpus of myths which this country possesses. In fact, one could easily draw the conclusion, on a perfunctory perusal of the literature, that the ancient myth-makers did not have constellations or a zodiac. There are occasional references to sun, moon and stars but nothing which would create the impression of a wealthy astronomical knowledge. It is clear that the sun and moon were important to the megalithic culture. In Old Irish, there is a "surprisingly extensive vocabulary" relating to the sun and moon,[4] with five names for the sun and six for the moon, "all native concepts".[5] Yet, the proficient astronomy practised in the Boyne Valley, and elsewhere in Ireland, would have required a considerable stellar knowledge, as the course of the sun, moon and planets can be more accurately observed and understood if they are viewed in relation to the fixed background stars.

At some point during the formation of their complex cosmic calendars, the Neolithic stone architects must have endeavoured to group the stars into patterns, and to give those patterns names. This is something which is common to many ancient cultures around the world: "Historically, stories and pictures have always gone hand-in-hand with observation of the stars as an expression of Man's relation to the universe."[6]

In previous chapters, we outlined the imaginative machinations behind sky myths relating to the sun and moon and some of the ancient Irish constellations. The "Pleasant Plain" of the sky was the mythic otherworld, the ultimate destination of the Neolithic soul, a place where the material world was cast away and the spiritual dimension became manifest in the glorious vault of heaven adorned with "every bright wonder".

The formation of constellations, star groups based on creatures, heroes and imaginary beings, helped enormously in the development of serious astronomy such as that practised in the Bend of the Boyne. Folk memory, going back many generations into the depths of the Paleolithic,[7] would have carried specific knowledge about some very basic concepts central to the development of a solilunar calendar. Such knowledge included realisation of the fact that the sun appears to follow a track or pathway among the stars, and more specifically among a number of "groups" of stars.

It is our contention, and a central tenet of this book, that the myths do, in fact, contain an ancient astronomical knowledge, and that some of the remarkable and sometimes unapproachable tales can be interpreted in the light of the night sky and the bodies of the heavens.

THE TÁIN IN THE SKY

We have already examined the bull constellation, which may have been the basis of some of the early stories. We met it first at Millmount, where the area known as Black Bull lay to the east, in the direction of the rising vernal equinox sun. The bull and seven stars of the Dowth *Dindshenchas* legend is linked with the position of the equinox sun in Taurus back in the New Stone Age. A central theme of the epic legend the *Táin Bó Cuailnge* concerns the capture of the "Brown Bull of Cooley". Does this epic mythical narrative relate to the Stone Age, a time when the sun was housed in the bull constellation on the vernal equinox? The *Táin* has long been held to be an Iron Age myth, something which in written form is only as early as the twelfth century AD, but which in verbal form stretches back into the depths of time. Thomas Kinsella, one translator of the *Táin*, said ". . . it is held by most Celtic scholars that the Ulster Cycle, with the rest of early Irish literature,

Was the Brown Bull of Cooley in fact Taurus?

must have had a long oral existence before it received a literary shape . . ."[8] Is it a fantastical notion to suggest that the basis of this epic related to the sky events of the Neolithic?

Hank Harrison, who has studied European megaliths and mythology extensively, says that Cúchulainn (Sétanta) is an "Iron Age Celtic warrior in a Neolithic milieu" and that "clearly the original bards wanted the two ages to be connected".[9] The time frame of the *Táin*, says Harrison, is "wide sweeping".[10] He goes further, pointing out that "either the Sétanta myth is Neolithic and survived all incursions, or the outsiders were converted to a style of worship reflected in the Star Temples".[11]

If the Sétanta story is from the Neolithic, it is possible stories about twins come from an earlier period, around the period 6000–5000 BC, during which period the vernal equinox sun was housed in Gemini, the twins constellation. One such Gemini story is the birth of Macha's twins at Armagh, who were said to have been delivered beside a chariot, a concept that is compatible with the arrangement of the sky, where the twins stand adjacent to the chariot. The name of the coastal area of Meath between Bellewstown, Laytown and Mosney was formerly called Eamhain (twins), the "ancient, pagan paradise of the Irish",[12] perhaps having a similar genesis in the early Neolithic.

The division of the year according to solstices and equinoxes would have required precise knowledge of the position of the sun in relation to the background stars, something that is not directly observable,[13] and it is probable that these stars were grouped into constellations at a very early age, before a single stone was set down in the Boyne Valley.

The formation of such an archetypal "zodiac" in ancient Ireland was probably brought about by the realisation that some of the star groupings of this early zodiac housed the sun at specific important moments in the yearly calendar. "On the zodiacal band, there are four essential points which dominate the four seasons of the year. They are, in fact, in church liturgy the *quatuor tempora* marked with special abstinences. They correspond to the two solstices and the two equinoxes."[14]

The Irish for zodiac is *cros na mearbhall,* meaning "cross/crossroads of confusion/wandering".[15] Does this describe the wandering, the apparent confusion, of the nomadic planets as they venture along the Ecliptic? It is a remarkable description, especially given the apparent dance of the planets, many of which perform perceptible "loops" in the sky watched against the background stars.[16] All of the so-called "exterior planets", i.e. those outside of the orbit of the Earth, perform this movement, known to astronomers as a "retrograde loop".[17] Another Irish word for zodiac is *uairchrios,* which could mean "hour belt" or "turning circle".[18] The idea of the zodiac relating to time and a slowly turning circle brings to mind many notions, including that the constellations of the zodiac were used to track the movements of the sun, moon and planets, and therefore to measure time. But greater than that is the suggestion implied by the translation "turning circle" that the belt of the zodiac was slowly revolving as a result of the precession of the equinoxes, something only manifestly perceptible over huge periods of time.[19]

The word *cros* as crossroads is fascinating, and we can extrapolate from this notion that the zodiac, viewed as a road or pathway along the sky, crosses the other road, the "way of the white cow", the Milky Way pathway associated with the illuminated moon/river goddess, Bóann. Perhaps these crossing points were seen as gateways, portals to the otherworld which opened when the solstice or equinox sun was located in the river.[20] These "crossing points" or crossroads, were very special places in the sky, as we will see.

It just so happens that at the time the Neolithic culture was beginning to flourish at places like Loughcrew and the Boyne Valley, the vernal equinox sun was housed in Taurus, having drifted slowly out of the upraised hand of Orion, in the middle of the Milky Way, after the year 4500 BC. So, leading up to the time Newgrange, Knowth and Dowth were constructed, the equinox coincided with one of the "crossroads" of the sky. At the time the mounds were being built, the equinox sun had drifted towards the edge of the cosmic river. As stated in Chapter 10, this resulted in an interesting phenomenon involving the Slane–Millmount equinox line, which saw the sun on the edge of the sky river at the equinoxes viewed from both mounds, something which was reflected by what was happening on the ground, where the mound being viewed at equinox was located on the correct side of the Boyne River.

Much of the mythical tradition surrounding bulls could be associated with memory of the Neolithic, when the "first point" of the zodiac, the vernal position, was housed in Taurus. The early Irish word for bull is *tarbh,* which bears some similarity to the Greek name.

In the Neolithic, the summer solstice sun was positioned under the giant "hound" constellation, the Irish version of Leo. The autumn equinox sun found itself in the grouping which we know today as Ophiuchus, which is not officially a member of the modern 12-constellation zodiac. This is the serpent-bearing constellation which we linked with St Patrick, the serpent-banisher, in Chapter 10. And finally, at winter solstice in the Neolithic, as the sun was shining into the chamber of Newgrange, it was located in the constellation Aquarius, which represents the water bearer. This is curious because of the connection already established between Newgrange and the river. Of further curiosity is an inscription associated with Aquarius on an old document containing an Irish zodiac in the library of Basle, Switzerland. Beside the male figure are the words *Leprosus Lunaris,* which mean, literally, "Lunar Leper".[21] This description immediately brings to mind the extraordinary tale of the drowning of Bóann, first encountered in Chapter 1, in which we are told the lunar deity was deformed by the rising waters of Nechtain's Well, losing an eye and being sadly mutilated before being washed along the new-formed Boyne to the sea at Rockabill. That tale has strong links to the winter solstice, at which time in the Neolithic the sun was housed in Aquarius, or whatever name the constellation had in Irish. The waning last crescent at the time of winter solstice signalled that the disappearing moon was about to vanish, joining the sun in Aquarius.

Deichtine, the mother of Cúchulainn, has a strong connection with the constellation Aquarius. One translation of her name could be "tenth chain link", based on *deich,* the Irish word for ten, and *tinne,* a word which means a "chain" or "link".[22] The tenth link in the "chain" of the zodiac, if Taurus is assumed to be the first in the Neolithic period, is Aquarius.

ORION: GOD OF MANY NAMES

In the *Táin,* the dramatic and convoluted tale detailing "How Cúchulainn was Begotten" saw Deichtine driving a chariot for her brother Conchobhar, the King of Ulster. They were chasing birds away from the plain of Armagh. The story relates how there were nine scores of birds with a silver chain between each couple, and each score had "two birds out in front . . . with a yoke of silver between them".[23] They eventually reached Brú na Bóinne, where they sought shelter at nightfall during a snow shower. Deichtine helped a woman deliver her baby in a store-room. The child later died, and Deichtine's grief was great. Thirsty for a drink, Deichtine unwittingly swallowed a "tiny creature" from the cup. That night, a man came to her in a dream and declared that he had brought her to Brú na Bóinne in order to lie with her there, and that she would bear a son who was to be named Sétanta. This mysterious figure who lay with Deichtine at Newgrange was none other than Lug mac Ethnenn, otherwise known as Lugh Lamhfada, whose symbolism has strong connections with the sun and Orion.

The tale is interwoven with some strong astronomical imagery. The swans with the silver chain between them are probably Cygnus and Aquila, two bird constellations which are seen to fly along the Milky Way in the direction of the southern crossroads of the sky, where the ecliptic crosses the Milky Way between Scorpius and Sagittarius. The narrative indicates that the season is winter, because it is snowing, and the appearance of Lugh to Deichtine in a dream at Newgrange could be interpreted as the meeting of the sun with Aquarius, which must happen in order for the sun to shine into Newgrange in the Neolithic.

In Chapter 4, we connected Lugh, the long-armed master of many arts, with Orion. So how is it possible that Lugh was the sun also? Lugh has long been associated by folklore experts with the sun, a tradition which is enriched by narratives such as that which described him as having the countenance of the sun.[24] His name may have an association with light, although this is argued by scholars, some of whom equate the word *lug* with light or brightness, others saying the word may be derived from the Celtic word *lugio*, meaning "an oath".[25] His name may also have an association with the word "fire",[26] but the general consensus is that he is a god of light,[27] as the following passage, from the Tuatha Dé Danann tale about the "Fate of the Children of Tuirenn" attests:

> Then arose Bres son of Balor, and he said. "It is a wonder to me that the sun should rise in the west today, and in the east every other day."
> "It were better that it were so," said the druids.
> "What else is it?" said he.
> "The radiance of the face of Lug Long-Arm," said they.[28]

The second part of his name, Lámhfhada, means "long-armed" or "long-handed", but this could portray the notion that Lugh's weapons had a long range rather than the concept of him having a long limb.[29] In fact, we are told that his title "testifies to an ability to hurl a weapon a long distance . . ."[30] It is this image, of a huge god-like figure casting weapons from his powerful arm, which brings to mind the constellation Orion, which in one form could be seen as a giant warrior with his upraised arm appearing to "throw" the sun, moon and planets along the zodiac. Thus, it is possible for Lugh to be interpreted as the constellation Orion, figuratively slinging the sun along the ecliptic from his upraised arm. This is a familiar image, one which we explored already in Chapter 3, where we saw that Amergin and the Milesians arrived at Inbher Colpa when the sun was in Orion's hand. And, as we saw in the Tara chapter, Lugh wore the Milky Way around his neck, something which Orion seems to do in the sky. The early Irish, we are told, also knew the constellation under another name, *Caomai*, the "Armed King".[31]

In the *Táin* story about Deichtine, we are told that Lugh comes to her in a dream at Newgrange. The light of the sun penetrates into the "womb of the moon" in midwinter, at which time the sun is housed in the water-bearer constellation Aquarius, having been "flung" across the sky, from the "crossroads" above Orion, along the "turning circle" of the zodiac, down to the tenth sign of the zodiac, the "tenth link", Deichtine. Is it possible that the name Lugh Lámhfhada meant, literally, "light of the long hand"? The Welsh equivalent of Lugh Lámhfhada was Lleu Llaw Gyffes, whose name meant "light of the steady hand".[32]

The winter solstice sunrise line from Newgrange, which passes over Bellewstown, the hill associated with the lunar hag, eventually meets a place near the coast at County Dublin called Lusk. This village, called Lusca in Irish, is "coextensive" with a mythical location called Luglochta Loga, the "garden of Lugh".[33] In some tales, Lugh is the foster son of Manannán mac Lir, the Irish sea deity, who had a magic currach or sea vessel called the "Ocean Sweeper", one of the "many magical gifts" which Lugh brought from the "Land of the Living".[34] Could this have been the magic boat on which the sun travelled every morning as its rising position changed along the horizon out of the Irish Sea? It was said to have been located at Brugh na Bóinne.[35] Lusk's association with Lugh is not surprising in light of the fact that both the winter solstice sun and the constellation Orion rose in the direction of Lusk viewed from Newgrange in 3150 BC.

We are told of Lugh that when he was a youth, the Tuatha Dé Danann "placed him in charge of Duach, 'The Dark', king of the Great Plain (Fairyland, or the 'Land of the Living' which is also the Land of the Dead)."[36] As ruler of the great plain of the sky, the Lugh constellation (Orion) finds himself with one of the great crossroads of the sky above his head, and in one configuration he appears to have his hand held aloft, as if reaching out for the sun and the planets as they pass above him.

Lugh is son of Cian, another chief character in the early myths of Ireland, and grandson of Balor, the Fomorian sun god we met first at Baltray. Not only was Lugh the grandson of Balor, but he would eventually become Balor's killer, something which, according to the myths, was long foretold in a "druidic prophecy".[37] As a result of this prediction, Balor imprisoned his infant daughter Eithne in a high tower to prevent her ever having contact with any man. The story goes that Cian's magical cow, the Glas Ghaibhleann (the same cow we met first at Baltray) was stolen by Balor. In order to exact some measure of revenge, Cian "seduces Balor's daughter, Eithne".[38] From this union, three children were born, although two were drowned on the orders of Balor, while one alone escaped. That child was Lugh.

In the tale of the Second Battle of Mag Tured (Moytura), a great war took place between the Tuatha Dé Danann and the Fomorians. It was during this apocalyptic battle that Lugh confronted Balor. The giant baleful, poisonous eye of Balor was opened so "that I may see the babbler who is conversing with me".[39] When Balor's eye was exposed, Lugh "cast a sling-stone at him, which carried the eye through his head while his own army looked on".[40] The story relates how the sling-stone "fell on the host of the Fomorians", killing 27 of them.[41]

Twenty-seven, or "thrice nine" as it is given in the myth, is a lunar number, which we discussed in previous chapters. It takes 27 days for the moon to return to the same place in the sky, a sidereal month. Clearly, the Second Battle of Moytura is a figurative account of a sky phenomenon, most likely an eclipse of the sun. Lugh cast his sling-stone, the moon, at Balor, the sun. The narrative relates how the fatal blow was delivered by Lugh just as he and Balor met, indicating the probability that the solar eclipse happened above Orion.[42] That Lugh is Orion is further hinted at in the build-up to the final meeting of grandfather and grandson. The text describes how "Lugh escaped from his guardians with his charioteer, so that it was he who was in front of the hosts of·the Tuatha Dé".[43] In the sky, the constellation Orion takes the form of a giant warrior-like figure, often represented with one hand stretched out, carrying a shield or weapon, and the other hand raised above his head, immersed in the Milky Way. This is Lugh, with his upraised arm firing off sling-stones along the ecliptic. Above Orion is the constellation Auriga, a star grouping which is almost completely contained within the band of the Milky Way. Auriga represents the charioteer, while the "hosts" of the Tuatha Dé could symbolise the multitude of stars of the Milky Way.

A description of the weapon with which Lugh vanquishes Balor reveals that it is a magic stone known as a *tathlum,* which means "concrete ball".[44] Such a weapon was, according to ancient tales, made "out of the brains of dead enemies hardened with lime".[45] The defeat of Balor with the "brain ball", cast by Lugh, is remembered in an ancient poem, of which here are the first and last stanzas:

> A tathlum, heavy, fiery, firm,
> Which the Tuatha Dé Danann had with them,
> It was that broke the fierce Balor's eye,
> Of old, in the battle of the great armies.

> To the hero Lugh was given
> This concrete ball – no soft missile –
> In Mag Tuireadh of shrieking wails,
> From his hand he threw the tathlum.[46]

The only object travelling along the ecliptic above the elevated arm of Orion that fits the description of the *tathlum* is the moon, its darker seas

Venus, the Caillichin, located between the bull (Taurus) and the chariot (Auriga)

representing the brains, the brighter areas the "cement" or "lime". The *tathlum* is another of the "native concepts" involving the moon, others portraying it as the hag or veiled woman, and the magical/illuminated cow.

There is a theme in the epic battle tales indicating a continuity of succession involving the constellation Orion, the idea that perhaps, over time, new myths were forged to replace older ones. The Moytura legends typify this idea. Nuadu had his hand chopped off in the first battle of Moytura and was eventually restored as king when his silver arm was fashioned, as outlined in Chapter 4. In the second battle of Moytura, Nuadu handed over authority of his army to Lugh just before being slain by Balor.[47] The symbolism is stark. Nuadu, the silver-handed sky king/constellation, was killed by Balor, the sun deity, presumably at a time when the sun was located above Orion so therefore the constellation was invisible because it was lost in the glare of the sun. At the same time, Lugh kills Balor with a sling-stone, perhaps symbolising a total eclipse, during which Orion and all the other stars would suddenly become visible on the ground. It is possible that a total eclipse above Orion was seen as a spectacular heavenly phenomenon and new mythology grew up around that occurence.

Incidentally, Nuadu's name might have meant "catcher",[48] again symbolising the idea of the upraised arm of Orion grasping the sun, moon and planets and releasing them along the path of the zodiac.

What can be extrapolated from the battle tales is that one of the central themes was the passing of Nuadu, the former King, and the coming to power, the accession to the stellar throne, of Lugh. Like his predecessor, Lugh became a powerful figure at the zenith of the ancient pantheon.

But even someone as great and renowned as Lugh must eventually wane, and the theme of succession continued with the eventual coming of Cúchulainn, whose supernatural conception was brought about by a mysterious and magical coming together of Lugh and Dechtine at Newgrange.

CÚCHULAINN: HERO OF THE SKY BATTLES

There are many attributes associated with Cúchulainn which equate him firmly with the constellation Orion, and some of these characteristics liken him to his supernatural father, the long-throwing god of light. In fact, they appear to share a common divine origin, and it has been suggested that Cúchulainn and Fionn mac Cumhaill, whom we will discuss later, may be Lugh's doubles.[49]

Cúchulainn's chief weapon was the *gae bulga* or *ga bolga,* a magical javelin that he sometimes threw with his feet while standing in water. *Ga* is a word which can mean "a shaft or ray of light",[50] while *bolga* means "a notch" or "a gap", but could be associated with the word *bolg,* meaning "stomach",[51] because of the damage it could inflict on the abdomen of the enemy. It was often described as a barbed spear. The climactic duel of the *Táin* saw Cúchulainn battle with his friend, Ferdia, at a river ford, an epic confrontation which ended after three days when Cúchulainn sent the *gae bulga* up the stream and into Ferdia's body, "so that every single joint filled with barbs".[52] In Chapter 1, we saw how Cúchulainn killed his son Connla at Baltray using this same magical spear.

But Cúchulainn, like his father, was also adept with a sling-shot. There are numerous accounts of his deeds with the sling-shot in the *Táin.* So adept was he with this weapon that it is reported he "could catch the shot from his sling before it hit the earth".[53] In one incident, the warrior hero fired a small stone at some birds, killing eight of them, before flinging another, bigger, stone with which he brought down 12 more.[54] The different sized stones in this account probably represented the planets, some of which appear to be brighter and larger than others.

Even as a boy, Cúchulainn, then known as Sétanta, was performing wonderful deeds, recounted in the star stories of the *Táin.* The most infamous of his boyhood deeds led to him becoming known as Cúchulainn, the "hound of Culann". The narrative is focused around a feast being held by Culann, a smith of great renown, for Conchobhar, the king of Ulster, and his people. Culann possessed a fierce hound, a dreadful beast which had the "strength of a hundred",[55] and he offered to loose it from its chain to keep watch and guard the cattle. Conchobhar told him to do so, forgetting that he had invited the young Sétanta, who was just six years old at the time, to the feast. Seeing Sétanta approaching, the dog sprung to its feet, barking so loudly that he might have been audible throughout all of Ulster. The mightly hound "sprang at him as if he had a mind not to stop and tear him up at all, but to swallow him at the one mouthful".[56] Armed only with his hurling stick and ball, the young hero struck the ball so fiercely that it went down the hound's throat and through his body, tearing out its entrails.

This is a sky myth. Sétanta is Orion, his hurling stick held aloft in his upraised arm, and the ball is the moon. The hound, as we related originally in Chapter 3, is the old Irish version of Leo, the large Zodiac constellation which represents the lion. The story relates to that time during the moon's nodal cycle when the ascending node is located above Orion. Sétanta (Orion) hits the ball (moon) with his hurley (held aloft above Orion) towards the hound (Leo), where it enters the animal at the front and exits its underbelly. As a result of this amazing deed, Culann mourned the loss of his great hound, but Sétanta offered to be his hound until a replacement could be reared from the same pack. "And I will guard all Murtheimne Plain. No herd or flock will leave my care unknown to me," Sétanta said. He was then given the name Cúchulainn, meaning "the Hound of Culann".[57]

In one of the many man-to-man contests of the *Táin*, Cúchulainn battled with Lóch, at a ford where "men drove some cattle over". This ford is synonymous with the crossing-point above Orion, where the cattle (moon and planets) cross the Milky Way. During the duel, Cúchulainn was attacked by the shape-shifting "war" goddess, Morrígan, who attacked him in the form of an eel, a grey she-wolf and a hornless red heifer. Morrígan

An illustration showing Sétanta (Orion) killing the hound (Leo) with the moon

first wrapped herself around his feet in the guise of an eel, causing him to fall backwards. This is interesting because of the fact that another great sky river, the constellation Eridanus, begins at the foot star of Orion, Rigel, and travels downwards into the southern hemisphere of the sky. In this way Cúchulainn/Orion could perhaps be seen to stand in the river, with the eel wrapped around his feet. Cúchulainn was renowned for his ability to fight in the shallow waters of river fords. Immediately preceding his epic combat with Ferdia, Cúchulainn suggested they fight in ford water. Ferdia agreed, but knew Cúchulainn had the upper hand "because Cúchulainn destroyed every hero and high warrior that ever fought him in ford water".[58] From this, we see that the Cúchulainn constellation is associated with two fords – that of the river flowing beneath his feet, and that of the Milky Way river, the fording point of which is located above his head.

After Cúchulainn smashed the eel's ribs, the cattle stampeded "eastward",[59] perhaps a reference to some planets passing to the left above Orion. Morrígan came back at him as a "rough, grey-red bitch-wolf",[60] and then she bit him in the arm "and drove the cattle against him westwards".[61] In revenge, the hero "let fly a stone from his sling and burst the eye in her head",[62] apparently repeating the great feat which his father, Lugh, had accomplished at the second Battle of Moytura when he mortally wounded Balor in much the same fashion. Finally, Morrigan came as a red heifer with no horns and "led the cattle dashing through the fords and pools".[63] The mighty warrior fired off another stone at the red heifer and broke her legs. The red heifer can be equated with a total eclipse of the moon, during which the white cow becomes a blood red colour. This wounding of the cow brings to mind once again the story of the drowning of Bóann, an episode during which her leg and arm were broken.

After defeating the Morrígan in her different guises, Cúchulainn chanted some verse which hints further that he was the great warrior constellation in the sky:

> I am alone against hordes.
> I can neither halt nor let pass.
> I watch through the long hours
> Alone against all men.[64]

Eventually, Morrígan appeared to Cúchulainn in the guise of an "old hag", milking a three-teated milch cow.[65] A great tiredness had fallen on Cúchulainn, who had defeated Lóch by sending the *gae bolga* upstream. The weary warrior thirsted greatly, and begged the *cailleach* (hag) for a drink. She allowed him to drink from each of the three teats. After he drank from the first, her eye was healed, after the second teat, her head became whole again, and finally after the third teat, her leg was repaired. There is no doubt that this lunar hag shares the same sky myth origin as the Cailleach Bhéarra, the lunar hag we met in previous chapters.

It is not difficult to equate Cúchulainn with the giant warrior constellation of the sky. He is described as a "huge high hero . . . vast as a Fomorian giant".[66] He carried two spears, a shield and a sword,[67] just as the constellation Orion appears to do. The narrative of the *Táin* is enriched with allegorical references to the heavens, and Cúchulainn, the "hound of Culann", takes his place at the centre of the plot as the sky hero who has strong associations with river fords, with cattle, with hounds and with the illustrious feats of a giant warrior which could only be attributed to a mythic personage whose origin and inspiration is drawn from that most brilliant man-like constellation.

Cúchulainn's association with fords can be attributed to the fact that Orion is allied with two sky rivers, the Milky Way which runs past his shoulder, and the Eridanus constellation which begins at his foot. His association with hounds is fascinating. Not only did Sétanta kill the giant hound of Leo, but as a sky warrior he is flanked by two dogs, the large dog and the small dog, both of whom straddle the Milky Way. The bright "Dog Star", Sirius, the most luminous of all stars, follows closely at Orion's heel, and is pointed out by Orion's belt. The small dog is marked by another bright star, Procyon, further to the east.

In one episode, Lugh Lámhfada came to aid his son whose wounds were grievous. Lugh offered him "succour . . . from the *síde*",[68] and allowed his offspring three days and nights of heavy sleep, while he cleaned his wounds. Lugh then made a chant, which included the following interesting lines:

A fair man faces your foes
In the long night over the ford . . .
Your vigil on the hound fords
A boy left on lonely guard
defending cattle and doom . . .[69]

Cúchulainn is the guardian of the "hound fords", defending the cattle. The Milky Way river is flanked on either side by the dog stars, while the Cúchulainn constellation guards the crossing point where the cattle have their passage over the river. Interestingly, there is an old Irish word, *ellach*, which means both "cattle" and "conjunction".[70] The many meetings of planets at the fording point of the Milky Way no doubt led to the creation of sky stories.

It is also interesting to note that Cúchulainn's father Lugh had an invincible lapdog which went by the name Failinis.[71] This "hound of mightiest deeds" was "irresistible in battle".[72] The whelp Failinis had to be procured for Lugh by the sons of Tuireann in reparation for killing Lugh's father, Cian.[73] This hound was said to have shone "like the sun on a summer day" – perhaps Lugh's hound was Leo, and not Canis Major.

Just before the incident in which Cúchulainn received succour from his father, he had witnessed a great army as evening drew in. The narrative states that, at nightfall, "Cú Chulainn saw far off, over the heads of the four great provinces of Ireland, the fiery glitter of the bright gold weapons at the setting of the sun in the clouds of evening."[74]

The stellar origin of *Táin* stories about warriors and heroes is left in no doubt with another passage, this one not concerning Cúchulainn, in which Fergus MacRoth surveys the plains of Meath from Slemain Mide[75] for signs of the Ulster army:

> Not long was he there when he heard a noise and a tumult and a clamour. It seemed to him almost as if the sky had fallen on to the surface of the earth . . . He saw a great grey mist which filled the void between heaven and earth . . . He seemed to see a flock of varied, wonderful, numerous birds, or the shimmering of shining stars on a bright, frosty night, or the sparks of a blazing fire.[76]

Cú Chulainn saw far off, over the heads of the four great provinces of Ireland, the fiery glitter of the bright gold weapons at the setting of the sun in the clouds of evening.

What were these wonderful visions that Fergus had atop Slemain hill in Meath? The narrative explains:

> The shimmering of shining stars on a bright night that he saw there, of the sparks of a blazing fire, were the fierce, fearsome eyes of the warriors and heroes from the beautiful, shapely, ornamented helmets, eyes full of the fury and anger with which they came, against which neither equal combat nor overwhelming number prevailed at any time and against which none will ever prevail until the day of doom.[77]

Along with fords, cattle and hounds, Cúchulainn is also often associated with chariots and his friend, the charioteer Laeg, whom we first met in Chapter 2. Above Orion in the sky is the "charioteer" constellation, Auriga, as mentioned previously. Auriga is mostly contained within the borders of the Milky Way, and is located above the crossing point over Orion.

A central theme of the *Táin* is the quest for the brown bull of Cooley and the epic battle between the brown and white bulls. Also above Orion, with the end of its horns embedded in the Milky Way and with one horn connected to the charioteer constellation, is Taurus, the bull. Above and to the left of Orion is Gemini, the twins, whose heads are marked by the bright stars Castor and Pollux, and whose feet appear immersed in the Milky Way. Are these the twins of Macha, who according to myth were born alongside a chariot? These twins gave their name to Emain Macha, the "Twins of Macha", which is now known as Armagh.[78]

Another of Cúchulainn's fights takes place at the "Ford of the Fist",[79] a possible reference to that point where the hand of the warrior constellation intersects the ecliptic. At another point, he is described by a character called Dubthach the Dark:

> His wild shape I see,
> and his heap of plunder –
> nine heads in one hand,
> and ten more, his treasure.[80]

Is this the metonic cycle encoded in myth, the 19 heads in Cúchulainn's hand representing the 19 full moons required to complete the cycle?

FIONN MAC CUMHAILL: SON OF THE SKY

Along with Cúchulainn, the most celebrated hero of Irish myth and lore is the giant Fionn mac Cumhaill, another great warrior, who is associated strongly with a "cult of wisdom" in the Boyne Valley.[81] His name means "bright son of the hazel" and he is descended, on the maternal side, from Nuadu.[82] Fionn, like Cúchulainn, was adept at hurling, and was good with a spear too, in one tale killing a charging sow with this weapon.[83] His father's name, Cumhal, "signifies the 'sky', and is the same word as Camulus, the Gaulish heaven-god identified by the Romans with Mars".[84]

Fionn's association with the hazel marks him out as a likely manifestation of Orion. In Chapter 4, we saw that Fionn gained his wisdom from the Salmon of Knowledge, which swam in the well of Segais. Not only did the Orion Nebula set in the direction of Nechtain's Well viewed from Millmount, but the entire Orion constellation set in the direction of the Hill of Allen, which was said to have been "one of the two chief places of abode of the celebrated Finn MacCoole".[85] His place of burial is said to be Slieve Gullion, a cairn on its summit recalled as being his final place of rest.[86]

Fionn is also associated with fights at fords. In the story about "the Death of Finn", the great hero and "his fifteen hundred warriors went to Ath Brea on the southern Boyne, and they arrayed themselves in battle-order upon the bottom of the ford in a mass of shields and swords and helmets."[87] He is also connected with the bull constellation. In a tale reminiscent of the Bressal story we discussed in Chapter 6, Ireland is afflicted by a plague for a year, during which "Finn fed the men of Ireland and put seven cows and a bull in every single farmstead in Ireland".[88]

Fionn is often accompanied by his two dogs, Bran and Sceolang, perhaps represented by the large and small dog constellations straddling the Milky Way. His standard, according to some of the later literature, is "the likeness of the golden sun half-risen from the blue floor of the sea".[89] Is Fionn, as Orion, alike to his progenitor, the silver-handed catcher, Nuadu? The image of the warrior constellation with the sun in his hand is powerful, representing a special moment in the year when the god-man of the sky clutches the orb of the sun with the sky river as a backdrop. It reminds us of Amergin, who set foot on the shores of the Boyne at the time the sun was in Orion's hand.

The Ulster King, Conchobhar, had three houses, one of which was called *Tête Brec,* which means the "Twinkling Hoard". In this house, javelins, swords and shields were kept, and "the place twinkled with the gold of sword-hilts and the gold and silver glimmering on the necks and coils of grey javelins, on shield-plates and shield-rims . . ."[90] Included among these items was *Nuadu's Cainnel,* "a bright torch", bringing to mind an image of the Olympic torch-bearer which is a nice mimic of Orion with the sun in his hand.

Fionn mac Cumhaill possessed a spear that never missed its target; it was forged in the otherworld and had beaten into it "the heat of the sun and the light of the moon and all the stars", as mentioned in Chapter 4. Along with this magic spear, he had a renowned sword, and he was a superb athlete. One common folk tale holds that the giant Fionn killed a serpent "in virtually every body of water in Ireland",[91] a trait reminiscent of Cúchulainn's slaying of the eel in the battle against Lóch.

There are natural landmark features scattered across Ireland which were said to have been cut by his sword, while there are a plethora of standing stones in various places which were said to have been thrown into their resting positions by the giant. These include an alignment of five standing stones known as "Finn McCool's fingers", located near Cavan town. The two standing stones at Barnaveddoge in County Louth, mentioned in Chapter 1, are said locally to have been thrown there by Fionn mac Cumhaill and his wife from Slieve Gullion far to the north. The Schools Folklore collection even indicates that the Baltray standing stones were thrown there by Fionn.

There is a fitting astronomical explanation for the abundance of stories connected with standing stones being thrown by Fionn. As Orion, Fionn mac Cumhaill throws the sun and moon from his hand along the ecliptic. At certain times during the solar and lunar cycles, such as at the solstices and the lunistices, the rising and setting sun and moon are marked by specific standing stones and stone alignments. These stories of marvellous superhuman stone-throwing feats are merely allegorical, suggesting a connection between the stones, the astronomical events they mark, and the giant hero who "threw" the sun and moon from his hand. It is appropriate, in light of the above, that it has been suggested by some that "Fionn was in fact Lugh living one more life".[92]

OISÍN IN TÍR NA NÓG

The theme of mythical succession involved in the Orion tales continues with Fionn's most valiant and illustrious son, Oisín, whose odyssey into Tír na nÓg, the land of eternal youth, is one of the famous Irish folk tales. Known as the "Lay of Oisín in the Land of Youth", the tale recalls how Oisín ventured into the otherworld sky realm, alternatively known as *Tír Tairngire,* the Land of Promise,[93] with the beautiful Niamh of the Golden Head. One version of the tale states that, on his way there, travelling due west, he slew a giant and upon arrival in the Land of Youth was granted Niamh as a companion. Once in Tír na nÓg, Oisín found he was unable to escape, and married Niamh. They made love for what seemed like 300 days, in some versions of the tale 365 days, producing two sons. Oisín longed to return to his own country, and eventually Niamh relented, but she warned him not to set foot on the earth of Ireland. She gave him "an enchanted horse on which he could visit his old haunts and estates".[94]

On returning to Ireland, Oisín found a changed landscape. "The countryside seemed to have undergone changes that would have taken decades to complete".[95] Eventually he came upon some men who were trying to move a rock from the middle of the road. The men told him that time in the otherworld "passes differently from that in the mortal world . . . A day there may count for a hundred years in this."[96]

For their calendar, the ancients used the stars, the moon . . .

Oisín offered to move the stone, saying that only a true warrior of the Fianna could move the rock without getting down from his horse. "Strangely," the tale recalls, "Oisín found the rock heavier than he imagined it would be . . . As he leant forward to get a grip on the sides of the stone, the strap that secured his saddle snapped. At the same time, the snorting steed moved forward a little and Oisín found himself tumbling to the ground. Instinctively, he thrust out a foot to save himself, touching the ground for only an instant. The moment the sole of his boot touched the earth of the human world, Oisín felt a tremor run through his entire body . . ."[97] The men stared at him as the son of Fionn mac Cumhaill "aged before their eyes. In a moment, he had become an old man with shaggy hair and a white beard . . ."[98]

The mythical motif of a colossal man in the sky whose foot touches the earth is reminiscent of the King putting his foot on the Stone of Destiny, discussed in Chapter 4. That was another sky myth, involving the "bright knee" star, Rigel, setting in the general direction of Tara viewed from Millmount.

Another familiar motif linking Oisín with the Orion heroes of Irish myth involves his curious slaying of a hound. This hound, according to folklore, was just one of a litter of pups born to a bitch belonging to Saint Patrick. When the pup grew up, Oisín took it into the forest, where the young hound killed an enormous blackbird. His success led the hound to go wild, and so fierce did it become that Oisín decided he must kill it. The story recounts how Oisín "took a metal ball and accurately flung it into the hound's gullet, choking it",[99] a tale very similar to Sétanta's famed killing of Culann's hound.

It is clear that many of the central gigantic warriors and kings of the Irish myths were inspired by the huge, high hero of the sky. Precession of the equinoxes and significant sky events such as total eclipses or multiple planetary conjunctions associated with Orion may have led to the changing of the identity of this sky giant over time, a theme explored extensively in this chapter, and exemplified in the story of the Second Battle of Moytura, in which one kingly Orion, Nuadu, passed away, and another, Lugh, arose to power.

Amergin, the "gigantic, sword-wielding champion", who put his foot on the shore of the river on the ancient cross-quarter feast day of Bealtaine, did so at the time when the sun was located in Orion's hand, and went on to rout the reigning Tuatha Dé Danann, killing one of its kings, whose name meant "son of the sun".

The great deeds of the sky kings and warriors of old have been commemorated in the narratives and dialogues of stories fashioned so long ago that it is remarkable they have endured over so many centuries. It is our conviction that some of the ancient astro-myths come from the same time as the remarkable stone monuments were constructed in the Boyne Valley, many of which have also survived the unkind passage of time. In addition to myths and monuments, there are countless place names which have lasted similar lengths of time, living on intact to help us in the reconstruction of the astronomical masterplan which revealed itself slowly to us during the course of seven and a half years of research leading up to this book.

At this juncture, an appropriate question might be, "Is this the end of the road?" And the answer would be a firm "no". *Island of the Setting Sun* is a journey. It was always intended to be a like a great adventure, travelling down the Boyne Valley, venturing back through time, looking at stars and stories and heroes of old. We have yet to reach our destination along the road on which this remarkable journey has taken us.

For the ancients, cunning and knowledgeable, wise and inventive, curious and perceptive, have left us more than a vast legacy of myths and monuments. It is possible they have presented us with something much bigger than anything we have explored so far.

. . . and the sun

And so we set out on the last leg of our journey along the road to revelation and realisation . . .

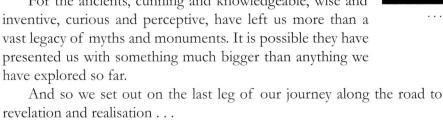

241

CHAPTER TWELVE

THE HIGH MAN:
RETURN OF
THE KING

Peace mounts to the heavens,
The heavens descend to earth,
Earth lies under the heavens,
Everyone is strong . . .[1]

In the spring of 1999, not long after I had become acquainted with the artist Richard Moore, he showed me something so incredible that I laughed at him and thought him demented. In a room in his Drogheda home, surrounded by massive paintings which hung on every available wall, he produced an Ordnance Survey map of the Boyne Valley region. There, among the many roads straddling the counties of Meath and Louth, was an enormous figure which resembled a man.

This "man" appeared to be standing, so to speak, in the Boyne river, with one leg entering the water at Slane and the other at Drogheda. He had a face, and hair, and he even appeared to have a belt. Towards the east, his arm reached out, apparently holding something resembling a shield or a weapon. The outline of this giant human figure was made up of roads, many of which appeared to be strangely straight, some of these straight parts stretching for miles.

I remember the night he showed it to me for the first time like it was yesterday. I could tell he was excited about it. Initially, the thought never entered my head that this was anything other than a curious oddity which he wanted to point out. That was, until he said something about the area in which it was located. This territory, he told me, was called the Barony of Ferrard.

"Okay," I said, wondering where all this was leading.

"Ferrard means Fear Ard, the High Man," he replied.

What a curious coincidence. There was this shape which looked like a man in an area called "High Man". I remember saying something dismissive like, "That's very interesting, Richard, and now I'd like to look at the carvings at Knowth because there's some very interesting petroglyphs which look like they could be crescent moons . . .", urging him to drop the fantasy and get with the programme.

But he was not to be swayed from his task. "It's interesting that one of his legs enters the Boyne at Drogheda, where Amergin 'Bright Knee' is buried," he said, pointing at the map.

"Hang on a second," I retorted. "Surely you don't think this is anything more than a coincidence?"

He looked me straight in the eye and said, "Well, the figure is there." I got the impression he was under the illusion that this giant road figure might be something more than an accidental arrangement of roads. I remember getting annoyed with him for engaging in such a fantasy, and dismissed the entire notion.

That was early 1999. That was at the beginning of a period of research which was to last seven and a half years and continues to this day. That was before I knew anything about Irish sky warrior myths and place name stories and the serious astronomy which was practised in the Boyne Valley in remote times. Today, we maintain a healthy scepticism about this giant road figure, which we've come to know as "The High Man". We have formed the opinion that it could well have been something which was laid out intentionally, perhaps in ancient times, but the evidence for this is overwhelmingly circumstantial.

The High Man could represent an effort, on a gargantuan scale, to create an Orion-like image on the ground. It does bear striking similarities, although it is far from being an exact copy of the constellation on the ground. The *Fer Ard*[2] may characterise an ancient enterprise which endeavoured to create a sort of "Heaven's Mirror", alike to the Egyptian "image of heaven", the "sanctuary of the Cosmos".[3] The *Táin* hints at this: "Not slight the thing he judged it to be, but as though it was the firmament itself that fell on the man-like face of the world . . ."[4] Is the man-like earth a reference to the High Man?

Whether or not this is the case, and whether there was an effort to recreate the stellar realm on earth, we cannot know for certain. What we have discovered is a raft of incidental data, a body of information derived from myths, place names, archaeology and the stars which supports the notion that the High Man might have been laid down as part of some ambitious astronomical master plan, and on a scale hitherto unknown on the face of this earth.

What we propose to do in this chapter is to present the information we have uncovered and to allow you to make up your own mind after considered contemplation.

AN FEAR ARD

Measuring 12 miles from head to toe, the incredibly human-like figure looms large on a very sacred and historical landscape. In the context of the Irish mythological and archaeological environment, the high hero finds himself in the most eminent area of the entire country. He has his legs planted in the Boyne, Ireland's foremost river in ancient times. He lies on an area rich in archaic myth and abundant in tales of giant legendary heroes. Within his boundaries lie Newgrange, Knowth and Dowth, the most celebrated monuments, rich in astronomy, legend and art, the primary

High Man key: 1. Millmount; 2. Legavoreen; 3. Cloghpatrick; 4. Mell; 5. Blackstaff; 6. Tullyosker;
7. Skeaghmore; 8. Finvoy; 9. Ballynagassan; 10. Annagassan; 11. Stagrennan; 12. Mellifont; 13. Louth Hill;
14. Fennor; 15. Hill of Slane; 16. Sliabh Breagh; 17. Rathbranchurch; 18. Rathbran Beg; 19. Rathbran More;
20. Leabby Cross; 21. Dunmore; 22. Belpatrick; 23. Mount Oriel; 24. White Mountain; 25. Corracon;
26. Creevagh; 27. Smarmore; 28. Kilpatrick; 29. Hurlstone; 30. Kildemock; 31. Garrett's Fort;
32. Rath Guth-aird; 33. Bohernamoe; 34. Silver Hill; 35. Yellow Hill; 36. Artnalevery; 37. Glack;
38. Áth Banlachta; 39. Feeross; 40. Ballabony; 41. Greatwood; 42. Crowmartin; 43. Drumbo;
44. Drumgoolan; 45. Ardpatrick; 46. Louth/Lugmag; 47. Summerhill/Mullach Oscair; 48. Grange

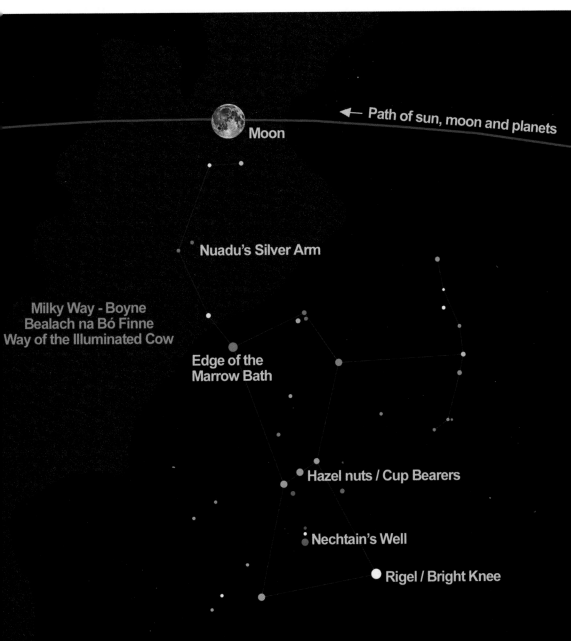

← Path of sun, moon and planets

Moon

Nuadu's Silver Arm

Milky Way - Boyne
Bealach na Bó Finne
Way of the Illuminated Cow

Edge of the
Marrow Bath

Hazel nuts / Cup Bearers

Nechtain's Well

Rigel / Bright Knee

Dog Star

Opposite: The "High Man" map
This page: Orion with its terrestrial equivalents

remnants of a culture which saw a unique interrelationship between sky and ground celebrated in a massive, monumental vision.

The name of the territory in which the giant road figure is located is said to have been derived from Fir Ard Cianachta, a third-century tribe which inhabited the area stretching from the river Liffey as far as Dromiskin in County Louth.[5] However, the name *Fer Ard* is probably much older than this:

> If, as has been suggested by D'Alton, the earthwork of the Millmount, Drogheda, be part of the great cemetery of the Boyne, the occupation of south Louth by that prehistoric race of mound builders is established, and also the connection of the plain of Ferrard with whatever poetry and legend the romantic imagination of our ancestors wove of this dim twilight of the early gods.[6]

In one translation of the *Táin*, the journey of Deichtine and Conchobhar from Emain Macha to Newgrange takes them across certain named territories, including Fir Ardae.[7]

An ancient territory adjacent to *Fer Ard* was called *Crích Rois* or *Fir Rois. Rois,* the genitive form of *Ros,* is a word which can mean a wood or copse, or a promontory or peninsula.[8] *Ros* can also mean "Judgement", as in the example *Lá an Ruis,* "the Day of Judgement". *Crích* means "end",[9] but can also mean "furrow", "boundary furrow" or a "region, territory or land".[10] This territory was located to the north of the High Man, and was situated mostly in the mid-Louth area.[11] It would correspond, interestingly, with the area above Orion where the ecliptic crosses the Milky Way. This *Fir Rois,* "Wood of the Man", was also known as the "wood of the Badb",[12] a female figure who often appears in the guise of a striped grey crow. Badb is the equivalent of the Morrígan, who came to Cúchulainn as a three-teated cow and allowed him milk from each. This Morrígan, meaning "great queen", is synonymous with the lunar deity Áine or Dana, who we met at Dunany,[13] and is yet another form of the Cailleach Bhéarra, the Glas Ghoibhneann and Bóann.

A curious place name located just above the High Man's head is Áth Banlachta, which means the "ford of the white milking place", or possibly the "ford of the milking place of the woman".[14] This place is synonymous with a crossroads today known as Ballybailie, which could signify the "town of the milking place".[15] A monument nearby was called Lios Glas, the word *lios* meaning a fort, enclosure or rath, and *glas* possibly indicative of the Glas Ghoibhneann, the magical cow we first met at Baltray.

The star watchers of remote times may well have seen the fording point above Orion as a point of completion or finishing. By the time of the Milesians, the sun was located above Orion at the beginning of the bright half of the year at Bealtaine. Thus, the point of passage across the Milky Way, perhaps seen as a wood or forest, marked the beginning and the end of cycles of time. *Crích Rois* may have translated as "furrowed wood", which might indicate the suggestion that the Milky Way was seen as a giant trough or furrow running past Orion. Abundant place name evidence certainly indicates that idea, as we will see.

There is no doubt that the territory of Crích Rois, and by association the *Fer Ard* region, is very ancient. It has been suggested that Crích Rois is contemporary with the settlement at Brú na Bóinne,[16] placing it right back in the Neolithic:

> Certainly Crích Rois as it appears in the oldest tales has an air of great antiquity. It is a formed territory with recognized boundaries, its monuments already ancient, its origin a myth . . . It seems, in a word, the hoary survivor of an earlier age.[17]

There are many other names associated with the region in which the High Man is based. It was part of Mag Breg, or Bregia, the "beautiful plain" mentioned in the *Book of Invasions* and the *Táin*.[18] This plain stretched all the way from the Boyne region to the Dublin mountains, and leaves its name still on the range of hills called Sliabh Breagh, which stretches from Meath across to the coast at Louth, crossing the abdomen of the High Man on the way.

CÚCHULAinn AS THE HiGH mAn

In the time of the *Táin*, the area containing the High Man was known as Mag Muirthemne, which means the "plain hidden by the sea", from *Muir*, "the sea", and *teimen*, meaning "concealment".[19] This is the plain belonging to Cúchulainn:

> He is the Hound
> Who calls Murtheimne
> Plain his own.[20]

In one part of the *Táin*, Cúchulainn comes out to display his noble shape to the women. The story recounts how he came out during the day "because he felt the unearthly shape he had shown them the night before had not done him justice".[21]

The women are forced to get up on each others' shoulders to see him. Is that because his daytime shape is a giant man spread out across miles of landscape? The narrative hints that his nighttime shape was "unearthly", perhaps a reference to the fact that the hero was to be found among the stars. He is, we are told, a boy "who checks sword with shield for cattle and women",[22] and is described as having blood on his belt, a possible reference to Orion's Belt, and a "hero-halo" round his head.[23]

It is our contention that Cúchulainn was Orion, and that much of the *Táin* is a coded astro-myth, relating to events in the sky. Could it be that Cúchulainn's plain, Muirthemne, contained a giant replica of the Orion constellation, laid out across a huge area? Elaborate, poetic descriptions of the high hero lead us to believe that he may have been a giant of both the sky and the ground. He is described as having seven jewels in each eye and he has a red tunic. The seven jewels represent each of the seven bright stars of Orion, the shoulder of which is marked by the bright red star, Betelgeuse.[24] The prophetess Fedelm describes Cúchulainn to Queen Medb:

> A giant on the plain I see,
> Doing battle with the host . . .
> I see him hurling against that host
> Two gae bolga and a spear
> And an ivory-hilted sword . . .
> He towers on the battlefield
> In breastplate and red cloak.[25]

Is this "giant on the plain" the High Man, towering on the battlefield? Later, Fergus leads Ailill and Medb and the Connacht Army around Muirthemne. Queen Medb asks Fergus "what kind of road is this we're taking? – straying to the south or north, crossing every kind of land." Fergus replies, "I take these turnings as they come, not to bring the host to harm, but to miss the mighty man who protects Muirthemne Plain".[26]

At the climax of the *Táin*, with Cúchulainn about to meet his death, there are some remarkable descriptive passages which indicate that Muirthemne might have been the otherworldly stellar realm around Orion, replicated on the ground on the "plain of concealment". The story, retold in the "Death of Cúchulainn", relates how Cúchulainn "came against" the men of Ireland, who were led by his enemy, Erc, son of Cairbre. Erc (meaning "speckled"), "saw him in the chariot, and his sword shining red in his hand, and the light of his courage plain upon him, and his hair spread out on the edge of the anvil, under the smith's hand, and the Crow of Battle in the air above his head".[27] This "crow of battle" is the Badb, there to remind Cúchulainn of his imminent death. She is located above his head, where the moon would be located if it was crossing the Milky Way above Orion. On the ground, the area above the High Man is called the "wood of the Badb". The tale continues:

> Cúchulainn came against them in his chariot, doing his three thunder feats, and he used his spear and his sword in such a way, that their heads, and their hands, and their feet, and their bones, were scattered throughout the plain of Muirthemne, like the sands on the shore, like the stars in the sky . . .[28]

Cúchulainn tied himself to a pillar-stone using his "breast belt", so that he could die standing up instead of sitting down. "Then the Grey of Macha came back to defend Cúchulainn as long as there was life in him, and the hero-light was shining above him."[29] A warrior called Lugaid lifted Cúchulainn's hair from his shoulders and chopped his head off. "Then he cut off Cúchulainn's hand . . . and then the light faded away from about Cúchulainn's head, and left it as pale as the snow of a single night."[30] Was this light above Cúchulainn's head the radiance of the sun, or the moon?

It might well have been. Another name for the territory in which the High Man is located was *Lugmag*,[31] meaning "The Plain of Lugh".[32] This name is retained to this day as Louth (*Lú* in Irish), the name of the county in which the greater portion of the High Man figure is situated. Interestingly, this county is said to have been Lugh's territory, just as Mag Muirthemne was Cúchulainn's plain.

LUGH AS THE HIGH MAN

Lugh's name survives in the name of a village, also called Louth, to which the ancient title of Lugmag was said to have applied.[33] In this village, there was a mound called Móta Luga,[34] said to have been the ancient centre of a sun-worshipping cult. Fascinatingly, this village, named after Lugh, sits

The motte at Louth, nestled among the trees. Folklore says Louth was once the centre of a sun-worshipping cult

above the High Man figure in a position corresponding to the place where the sun passes the fist of Orion.

However, the High Man road figure does not have an arm upraised, reaching out and grabbing Louth village. Instead, he appears in two alternative moulds – one with both his arms reaching out holding onto his shield; the second, with one arm grabbing the shield and the other by his side, holding a sword or some other weapon. While this may lead to the impression that the High Man does not mimic the constellation, there is tantalising place name evidence which corresponds with the notion of the ground warrior with his arm in the Milky Way. In addition, it is likely that Orion was seen in different poses, sometimes with his arm by his side, others with it raised above his head.

Lugh's name also survives in the name of a hill called Louth Hill in the southern part of the warrior figure, which may correspond with the location of the Orion Nebula, our Nechtain's Well of Chapter 4. On the lower slopes of Louth Hill is an ancient barrow, the only prehistoric remnant still apparent in the area.[35] Just below Louth Hill, in the valley of the Mattock River, lies Mellifont Abbey, the first Cistercian foundation in Ireland, founded in 1142.[36] The name Mellifont means "fountain of honey",[37] or "honey well"[38] and the name Mell may have been associated with the area before the arrival of the Cistercian monks.[39] It has echoes of *Mag Mell,* the Pleasant Plain we first met in Chapter 2, that otherworldly

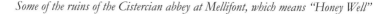

Some of the ruins of the Cistercian abbey at Mellifont, which means "Honey Well"

place analogous with the region of the sky containing Orion. In Irish, it is *Mag Meall,* which is described as the "old Irish Elysium".[40] Mellifont, the "honey well", marks the approximate location of the Orion Nebula, Nechtain's Well, on the High Man shape.

Another remnant of Mag Mell is the townland of Mell, which straddles the lower leg of the High Man just where it meets the Boyne at Drogheda. Intriguingly, the Irish word for honey, *Meall,* also means "the calf of the leg".[41] Of further interest is the fact that the *Fer Ard's* leg enters the Boyne at the place anciently called Inbher Colpa, meaning "the estuary of the calf of the leg". Oddly, the estuary resembles the shape of the tibia (shinbone). Is this what the legend of the monster's shinbone discussed in Chapter 2 was about?

Inbher Colpa is overlooked by Millmount, which effectively marks the bottom of the leg. This is the burial place of Amergin, the "bright-kneed" astronomer poet whose chant about the ages of the moon and the place of the sunset occurred as he placed his foot on the shore of the Boyne at Inbher Colpa. Millmount is in a townland called Legavoreen, meaning the "hollow of the little road"[42] and possibly even "bottom of the little road".[43] Between Millmount and Colpe, on the southern shore of the Boyne, is a townland called Stagrennan, which is locally explained as Teach Grianan, meaning "summer house"[44] or "house of the sun". If Amergin was Orion, he was the "house of the sun" on the day he was said to have placed his leg on the shoreline of the Boyne. The imagery fits neatly with the locations and the legends.

FIONN MAC CUMHAILL AS THE HIGH MAN

The area containing the High Man may also have been associated with Fionn Mac Cumhaill, the giant stone-throwing warrior who was a later counterpart of Lugh. As well as the fact that some of the ancient sites in the region are associated with Fionn, there is a townland near the top of the High Man's shield called Finvoy, which comes from *Fionnmhaigh,* meaning "Fionn's Plain". *Fionnmhaigh* may also denote a "white" plain, and one meaning of Fionn is "pleasant", bringing to mind the heavenly *Mag Mell* which has the same meaning, "pleasant plain".

A grandson of Fionn Mac Cumhaill was Osgar, who was the strongest of the Fianna, a mythical band of warriors and hunters led by Fionn. According to local tradition, Osgar's grave was located at a place called Tullyosker, which is a hill north of Drogheda, located about a mile and a half east of the right leg of the High Man. Local folk belief holds that the townland of Tullyosker is derived from a "great giant who was called

Osgar" who was "guarding the harbour of Drogheda".[45] Is this again the High Man, his leg planted in the Boyne at the harbour of Drogheda? Osgar left his name also in a townland immediately east of Louth village called Summerhill in English, but in Irish Mullach Oscair, the "hill of Osgar".[46]

Osgar's grandfather, Fionn Mac Cumhaill, may be remembered also at a place called Fennor, which is located just south of Slane where the High Man's left leg enters the Boyne. The area's name may be derived from *Fenard*,[47] which could signify "High Fionn", or even "high hero", if *Fen* is a derivative of the early Irish word *fian*, meaning hero,[48] from which we get the Fianna.

Fennor is said by place name authorities to be derived from *Finnabhair*, meaning "fair-browed" or even "bright beam", and often associated with a "whitish spot".[49] As well as being associated with the location where the High Man's left leg enters the Boyne, the name Finnabhair was also connected at one time with Drogheda, where his other leg meets the water.[50]

Yet another connection with Fionn is through two townlands to the west of the High Man's "belt", which are called Rathbran More and Rathbran Beag, signifying "the rath of big Bran" and "the rath of small Bran". Bran was the name of one of Fionn's great hunting dogs, and local folk memory says the area derives its name from Fionn's famous canine.[51] The townlands suggest a connection with the dog constellations, one large and one small, which are located to the left of Orion,[52] the idea being that they follow their master across the sky. One story suggests that Fingal, a giant based on Fionn Mac Cumhaill, rested at Rathbran with his dog while in pursuit of a giant.[53] Another local tradition maintains that Fionn Mac Cumhaill "was the owner of the dog tied in Rathbran souterrains" when they were on their way from Newgrange.[54]

One of the many straight roads making up the High Man figure, this one at Rathbran Beag

A nearby townland bearing the same name is Rathbranchurch, which is the location of the Sliabh Breagh barrow cemetery. This is the ancient complex that is located on the winter solstice line through Newgrange and Fourknocks, and one fact of major interest here is the Neolithic alignment along the same line of sight which would see Sirius, the Dog Star, rising on the horizon in the direction of Fourknocks. Here we see a direct link between the large dog in the sky and the large dog, Bran, on the ground.

SAINT PATRICK AS THE HIGH MAN

The *Fer Ard* commemorates another great Irish figure, whose legacy lives on as much in myth as it does in history. Saint Patrick landed at the same spot at Inbher Colpa as Amergin had done more than 2,000 years previously,[55] apparently mimicking the great Milesian bard. We can imagine that Patrick, like the great astronomer poet, also placed his foot on the shore at Colpe, the "calf of the leg", where the High Man's leg meets the water of the bright cow river. From there, Patrick journeyed to Slane, following the "equinox journey" towards the place where he would light the Easter fire. Slane marks the place where the High Man's other leg meets the Boyne.

Local tradition holds that, from Slane, Patrick journeyed up towards Leabby Cross, a route that would have taken him up the back leg of the Fer Ard. The area just north of the Leabby Cross is known as Belpatrick, a townland which derives its name from Buaile Phádraig,[56] meaning the "belt of Patrick". *Buaile* is a word which, as we saw earlier, can relate to a milking place or an enclosure for the summer grazing of cattle on upland areas,[57] but which is connected to the constellation Orion through the phrase *Buaile an Bhodaigh,* meaning "enclosure or belt or the enlightened".[58] This was a native Irish phrase referring to Orion's Belt, which is remarkable because the townland of Belpatrick is located just above the road that forms the belt of the High Man. In the townland of Belpatrick is the Dunmore hill, a summit of 239 metres from which, according to local lore, the "moat of Granard" in County Longford, over 50 miles away, can be seen.[59] The Dunmore hill is said locally to contain the "graves of three giants",[60] signifying perhaps the three belt stars of the sky giant. On the summit of Dunmore are some archaeological remains, including a barrow, a ring-barrow, and an enclosed barrow group.[61]

Leabby Cross, sitting in the shadow of this hill north of the western end of the belt, establishes another link with the giant. Leabby is derived from the Irish word *Leaba,* meaning "bed" or "graveyard", according to local folk memory.[62] However, the word *Leaba,* from the old Irish *lebaid,* is strongly associated with stone monuments, particularly cromlechs or dolmens, and giants. "Leaba is the name of several places in Ireland, which are by the common people called *Leabthacha-na-bhfeinne* [Labbaha-na-veana], the monuments of the Fenii or old Irish champions."[63] These are the same mythical warriors of whom Osgar was a champion.

From Leabby Cross, it would appear that St Patrick journeyed northwards, probably along the "back" road of the Fer Ard,[64] to a place now called Kilpatrick, from the Irish Cill Phádraig,[65] meaning "church of Patrick". There is a possibility Cill Phádraig means the "wood of Patrick". One branch of historical tradition surrounding Patrick in Louth suggests that he was "struck with the suitability of the place for a life of prayer and contemplation" and that he wished to establish his "primatial see" there.[66] After a "short struggle" with the druids, he took possession of Louth,[67] the area originally named Lugmag and the location of Lugh's mound. Not far from the current location of Louth village, he founded a church at a place now known as Ardpatrick, meaning "Patrick's height". This is the area that corresponds with the point in the sky where the sun would be located above Orion. Patrick has also left his memory at the side of the "calf" road at Mell outside Drogheda, where a stone at the side of the road is said to contain the marks of his knees to this day. We discussed this place, Cloghpatrick, in Chapter 3.

TOWNLANDS

It is abundantly clear that a number of central mythical Irish characters have a significant attachment to the *Fer Ard* region, and some with specific connections to places on the High Man figure which suggest they may have been inspired by the Orion constellation. Further to all this, there is a significant body of suggestive evidence that the High Man may have been the result of the exceptional brilliance of an ancient design.

We have seen from previous chapters that the Milky Way ran past Orion, its glimmering hoards of stars passing through the chariot constellation, the horns of the bull, the feet of the twins and then through Orion's arm, past his shoulder and then onwards down between the two dog stars. The territory above *Fer Ard,* the "furrowed wood" of Crích Rois, also known as Fir Rois, the "wood of the man", suggests a connection with the Milky Way. As we explored in previous chapters, the *Dindshenchas* describes the Boyne River in two poems entitled "Boand I & II". It could be inferred from information already presented that the *Dindshenchas* Boyne poems refer not only to the river which runs from Kildare through Meath and out to the sea at Inbher Colpa, but the river that runs across the sky, the Milky Way. The *Dindshenchas* poem refers to the Boyne as the

"Great Silver Yoke" and the "White Marrow of Fedlimid". Both of these descriptions can be connected with the Milky Way and the area west and northwest of the High Man which correspond with where the Milky Way would be located if the *Fer Ard* was Orion.

Two place names stand out as exemplary instances in which the ground seems to match the sky according to the *Dindshenchas* poem. One is called Silver Hill, located just west of the town of Ardee, which marks the top of the High Man's head. Silver Hill corresponds with the edge of the "Great Silver Yoke" which runs past the shoulder of Orion. The Celts knew the Milky Way as *Arianrod,* the "silver street".[68]

The second place name is Smarmore, to the south of Ardee, located at the shoulder of the High Man, just over two miles from Silver Hill. Smarmore is the anglicised version of *smioromair,*[69] which means a "trough/furrow of marrow". In the *Táin*, it is specifically referred to as *Imorach Smiromrach,* with an even more remarkable meaning – "edge of the marrow bath".[70] The development of native sky myth concepts and motifs may well have included the evolution of the idea that the shoulder of the constellation Orion touched the edge of the furrow of "white marrow" in the sky.

Smarmore was the location of a curious incident in the *Táin* in which a warrior called Cethern was healed of grievous wounds. There, it is said, Cúchulainn prepared a bath of "marrow-mash", which consisted of the flesh and bones and skins of cattle which he brought there at the request of Fingin.[71] The *Táin* specifically places the scene of this healing in "Smirommair . . . in Crích Rois".[72] The *Táin* hints elsewhere that the "furrowed wood" was to the north of the High Man: "Then they all went past Cúchulainn and set up camp in Crích Rois."[73]

Many place names in the Crích Rois area, the wood of the Badb, provide us with further tantalising connections between sky and ground. Of primary interest is a place called Mag Lamrigi, which may represent the plain of the hand or arm. *Lam* is possibly a form of *lám*, the old Irish for "hand", while *rigi* could be a version of *righidh*, meaning "forearm".[74] Of major significance to this interpretation of rigi is the fact that *Righe Mná Nuadhad,* meaning "forearm of the wife of Nuadu" was another name given to the Boyne[75] in the *Dindshenchas*. Mag Lamrigi has survived to this day in the form of a townland about five miles northwest of Ardee called Flowery, which is a likely corruption of *Fiodh Lamhraighe,*[76] *Fiodh* meaning a "wood". Does Lamrigi mean "hand of the king"? Another similar Irish word is *lamrach* or *lamraigh*, meaning a "ford".[77]

One thing the High Man is missing is an arm reaching up to grab the sun (Louth village). The *Fer Ard* does appear to have an arm down by his side, carrying some sort of sword or club or other weapon. Having said that, the great mythical heroes upon which the High Man is based were probably seen in different guises and manifestations. This is certainly true of Cúchulainn, one of the many mythical Irish characters who were shape-shifters, who at one point in the *Táin* is advised by his charioteer Laeg to go to a meeting with Queen Medb "with your sword at your side".[78]

There is a tenuous link between a king's hand, the moon and *Fiodh Lamhraighe* in mythology. The king was Conchobhar, and the story relates to his death, which was brought about when a brain-ball, one similar to the *tathlum* discussed in Chapter 11, finally fell out of his head, killing him. The King is said to have gone into a rage on hearing of the death of Christ on the cross. "'He attacked the wood around him so that he made a plain of the wood, .i. Mag Lamrigi a Feraib Rus'; 'clear will be the track of his sword over the slanting plain of Laim'."[79] Another recounting of the tale seems to indicate the Milky Way: "On the bare slopes of Lamraige . . . hosts of fair bands did homage to thee . . ."[80] The King's exertions forced the brain-ball to fall from his head. "Through the strength of the fury that seized him the ball bounded from his head, and a portion of his brain followed it . . . Coill Lamhruidhe in Feara Rois is the name of that wood-thicket".[81]

Adjoining *Fiodh Lamhraighe* is a townland called Crowmartin, signifying *Craobh Mhártain,* the "wood of Martin". In this townland is a motte, 37 metres in diameter, known locally as "The Mount".[82] Local tradition indicates that there is gold hidden in the walls of the Crowmartin mound,[83] a story which, as we saw at Réaltoge, may indicate that the mound could mark a significant sunset, perhaps from another important site in the region. Another local folk tale holds that light can be seen "in the centre" of Crowmartin moat at night.[84]

One author has suggested that a similarly sized nearby moat, on the summit of Stormanstown, was the "Sliabh Slea where King Conchubhar is buried".[85] The profusion of townland names in the area which denote a wood or forest give rise to the notion that this might indeed be the wood where Conchobhar made his plain. These include Greatwood, just west of Crowmartin, Crevadornan, Creevagh near Smarmore and Feeross, a part of the townland Charlestown. Feeross is the English rendition of *Fiodh Rois,* which "assures us that we are here in Fir Rois country".[86] Of course, it may yet be possible that some of the names relating to woods might imaginably refer to forests and woods that might have existed in these areas in former times. But further toponymic corroboration suggests otherwise.

Another of the very straight roads of the High Man at Grange.
This one forms the "back leg" of the warrior heading towards Slane

Another townland a few miles northwest of Ardee is Artnalevery, which "has a good chance of being Ard na Lamhraighe",[87] possibly meaning the "height of the King's hand". An adjoining townland is called Glack, which in Irish is *glaic,* which refers to the fist or the hand or even a hilt, the handle of a sword.[88] Glack often means "the hollow of the hand" in Irish place names.[89] Immediately west of Louth village, which might mark the point where the High Man's hand grasped the sun, is Drumgoolan, from the Irish *Droim Gualann,*[90] meaning "ridge of the shoulder". Two miles northeast of Louth immediately adjacent to Summerhill, the "hill of Osgar", is Grange, a word which is said to derive from *grainseach,* meaning "a place for grain",[91] but which may derive from the Irish word *grian,* meaning "sun".[92]

If all of this seems like a very tentative and far-reaching effort to connect sky and ground, all doubt should be cast aside by the place names in the area of Crích Rois which relate to the Milky Way or something associated with it.

Immediately west of Ardee is Bohernamoe, the anglicised form of *Bóthar na mBó,* meaning "road of the cow", one of the Irish names for the Milky Way.[93] The Silver Hill is located in this townland. Adjacent to Fiodh Lamraighe is a townland named Ballabony, from the Irish *Bealach Bóinne,* the "way of the white cow", another Irish name for the Milky Way.

Further inland, about seven miles or so west of Tallanstown, is a townland called Drumbo, located in Monaghan. It is tempting to think that it means *druim bó*, the "ridge of the cow", indicating perhaps a furrow of cow marrow, but according to place name literature it is more likely to derive from "*Druim-beo*, ridge of the living beings, as in Tir-na-mbeo."[94] This is the "land of the Ever-Living Ones" equated with Magh Mell, the "pleasant plain where the triumphant king is living".[95] Once again, we see that the region around Orion was probably held as being the place to which the soul journeyed after death. The *Dindshenchas* poetry also refers to the Boyne as the "roof of the Ocean". Because both Boyne and Milky Way have a similar derivation, involving the bright cow, it's likely that the *Dindshenchas* is describing the sky and the ground at the same time.

The natural landscape of the area representing the Milky Way takes on a very mottled appearance because of the array of drumlins which are scattered across the area. Drumlins are elongated ridge-hills formed by glaciation. The Irish for drumlin is *druim,* meaning "ridge",[96] hence *druim-beo.* Drumlins can be found in huge clusters, called drumlin fields.[97] Does the drumlin field northwest and west of Ardee represent the hosts of stars in the "speckled Milky Way", the twinkling hoard, the silvery marrow, the spray of milk droplets from the magic cow, the sparkling waters of the heavenly Boyne in the land of eternal youth?

This is one example of how the natural landscape augments the High Man figure. Features already extant were factored into the creation of this mirror of the heavens. The road figure is bounded to the south by the Boyne River, the *abhann bó finne,* while its northern extreme is demarcated by the river Dee at Ardee, which marks the top of the giant warrior's head. More about Ardee later.

LANDMARKS

So far, we have looked at the legendary figures which may have inspired the High Man, and the formation of an early Irish star grouping which we know today as Orion. We have looked also at toponymic and mythological evidence linking the area northwest of the High Man with the Milky Way. The body of substantive information already presented is plentiful, but there are more toponyms, and a host of monuments, which play a part in the ultimate presentation of the High Man as a complete theory.

Consider, for instance, the village of Collon, located on the eastern end of the "belt" road. The Irish name for this village is *Collann,* meaning the "place of the hazels" and signifying a place where hazel trees grew. Folklore states that the name is derived from the hazel woods which formerly grew on the "Ferrard Hills".[98] These hills include the Dunmore, upon which there are said to be three giants' graves, and Mount Oriel, which marks the end of the Tara–Realtoge–Slane alignment discussed in Chapter 10. Oriel and Dunmore are the highest peaks of the Ferrard Hills, and the entire Sliabh Breagh range which runs from inland Meath as far as the Louth coast. The Ferrard Hills command a view of the entire road figure, all the way from its pinnacle at Louth village to its foundation at the Boyne. In fact, it is only on the Ferrard peaks that an observer can grasp the true sense of the enormity of scale of the figure.

Northwest of the *Fer Ard* peaks are two more hills with interesting names. One is called Corracon, the "hill of the hound", which is from *corr* and *con*, meaning "round hill" and "hound". Is this the hound of Culann, the smith, the dog killed by Sétanta, or indeed Cúchulainn himself? Is the name Culann related to Collon, the place of the hazel? Fionn Mac Cumhaill, one of the mythical high giants, has a name which means, literally, "white son of the hazel". There are the remains of three barrows on Corracon.[99] According to folk memory in the immediate area, this hill contained a "remarkable quarry of quartz stone" with "stones which sparkle like diamonds".[100] These stones were, according to the folk archives, quarried and used in the construction of the grotto in the grounds of Oriel Temple, a monastery on the Black Hill in nearby Collon.

Perhaps the bright quartz of this hill gave rise to the name of another peak on the same ridge, called White Mountain, *An Sliabh Bán,* in the townland of Smarmore, the "edge of the bath of marrow". As we saw in Chapter 8, one Irish name for quartz is *clocha geala,* "bright stone", perhaps "moon stone". White Mountain is the location of a couple of barrows, plus a ringfort called Lismore,[101] from *lios mór,* meaning "big fort".

A straight road running from Mount Oriel towards Collon village

A mile and a half northwest of White Mountain is a townland called Hurlstone, the location of a curious menhir which has a large, circular hole in it. This 1.7 metre high monolith is located behind the High Man's neck, in his long mane of hair. One tale in the locality says that a solider or warrior is believed to have "thrust his head" into it. He was unable to retract his head until it was either chopped off, or, according to another tale, contracted by a blacksmith.[102] Is this a cryptic reference to the High Man, whose neck lies nearby?

The Hurlstone is referred to in the *Táin* as the *"Liaa toll i Crich Rois"*, the "pierced stone in the furrowed wood". This is where Cethern received the wounds which required healing in the bath of marrow at nearby Smarmore. The "hosts" (stars?) pitched camp at Smarmore.[103] There, they placed Ailill's dress and shawl and diadem over the *Lia Toll*, and Cethern fell into the trap of thinking it was Ailill himself. He drove at the stone so that "his fist went through it after the sword".[104] This story links nicely with the High Man's arm, because the Hurlstone is located just above the shoulder of the figure, where an imaginary arm reaching up for Louth might begin.

Furthermore, there is a scene in the *Táin* which describes Cúchulainn as having his back to the Hurlstone: "Then they (Fergus and Etarcumul) went their way in two chariots to Delga, to come up to Cuchulain where Cuchulain was between Fochain and the sea. There it is that he was that day, with his back to the pillar-stone at Crich Rois . . ."[105]

The town of Ardee and the river flowing through it mark the top of the head of the High Man. Ardee is derived from the Irish *Baile-Átha Fhir Dhiadh*,[106] meaning "the town of the ford of Ferdia" and is said to have been the location of the climactic three-day duel between Cúchulainn and Ferdia in which the latter was killed by the giant hero's *gae bolga*. The exact location of this ford is locally placed "about 80 perches W. of Ardee".[107] Curiously, Ferdia is referred to in local lore as "the Fear-dhiadh", probably meaning "divine man"[108] or "god man" or even "man of fire".[109] A grave mound located adjacent to the river Dee at the Ford of Ferdia marked the place where the god man was said to have been buried after he was killed by Cúchulainn. It was still in existence in 1836, but all traces of it have disappeared.[110] This mound was located between the High Man's head and the townland of Bohernamoe, the "road of the cow". The battle between the two great heroes took place at a river ford, so it is appropriate that the location of the battle is located on a ford of the Dee in addition to being positioned in the "furrowed wood" on the ground, the reflection of the Milky Way.

Further east, just yards from the top of the High Man's forehead, is another mound, known under various names in the district as "The Priest's Mount" and "Dawson's Fort", but whose name was previously "Castle Guard".[111] This "real name" is the "rendering in English of the sound of the Irish name, 'Caiseal Guth-aird', i.e., the stone fort of the high voice."[112] Castle Guard, which was likely to have been known originally as Rath-guthaird,[113] was described by Thomas Wright in *Louthiana* as being "of an amazing Magnitude", its perpendicular height being "nearly 90 feet".[114] Because it was described by Wright as having a "double Ditch",[115] it was assumed to be a "royal rath . . . the dun of a king".[116] It is also recorded in the *Seanchus Mor* that Rath-guthaird was the place "where the stone of Patrick is at this day, in Glenn-na-mbodhur . . ."[117]

This Glenn-na-mbodhar, the "glen of the deaf", was "so called for the reason that were all the men of Erin round about it and loudly uttering their cries of war, yet might none in that glen hear either shout or halloo".[118] One is drawn to the idea that the origin of the title "rath of the High Voice" may provide an allegorical tie with the High Man, being located at his forehead, not too far from the figure's "mouth", which, if it could speak, would perhaps leave many people deaf in Glenn-na-mbodhar!

THE SLEEPING ARMY AND THE BLACK PIG

Just one and a half miles south of the mound of the High Man's voice, right on the mouth of the *Fer Ard,* is a curious little church in ruins which has a gable end wall which is said to have "jumped"[119] two or three feet from its foundation during a "terrible hurricane".[120] In a field just half a kilometre from Kildemock's "Jumping Church", in a townland called Hacklim is a ringfort, known locally as Garrett's Fort.[121] Famous as the tale of Kildemock's jumping wall is, the legend attached to Garrett's Fort is equally renowned[122] and is uniquely attached to the legendary heroes and the mythology of the High Man region.

The legend of Garrett's Fort is a messianic myth of sorts, foretelling a future time when a hero is "expected to return to interfere again in the affairs of

Kildemock's famous Jumping Wall, located at the mouth of the High Man, with the full moon in the background

the world".[123] The central belief of the story is that, in an underground chamber of some kind, located beneath the rath, *Gearraid Iarla,* the "eighth Earl of Kildare",[124] is lying in with an enchanted army, waiting for a six-fingered hero to draw a sword from its scabbard and rouse the sleeping army which will "come forth to fight for Ireland".[125] While the monument known as Garrett's Fort is "featureless and forlorn",[126] nothing more than a "circular area enclosed by much-degraded earth and stone bank",[127] it may well have contained an underground chamber such as the one mentioned in the legend.[128]

In addition to the fact that the Earl of Kildare would appear to have had only the most tenuous link with the area,[129] there is a "distinct tradition that Fionn MacCumhail had his 'castle'" at Hacklim.[130] Indeed, such a tradition was also extant in Scotland, where Fionn and his army were said to have been *"fo gheasaibh"*, "under a spell" in a cave near Inverness.[131] Whether the Hacklim rath is the mythical dwelling place of *Gearraid Iarla* or Fionn MacCumhaill, the story about their release at the end of time is "just one form of a very old and universal folk theme, that of the enchanted hero reserved for a future day of deliverance".[132]

The story of the coming of the enchanted army is apocalyptic in nature, seemingly connected with the end of time. Garrett, or Fionn,

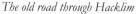

The old road through Hacklim

the "enchanted warrior", will "ride out for the last great fight of all to win Ireland's freedom"[133]. There is a belief that "this warrior may be a memory of the tales of Angus Og and the other mighty lords invisible who are to come thronging out of Brugh and join Lugh Lamh Fada in his triumphant return from Tír na N-og."[134]

While there are sporadic instances where the location of the enchanted army seems to have been confused, by and large folk memory throughout County Louth places it at Hacklim.[135] The hero tale, forged in the imaginations of those long-dead, "seems to correspond to some deep longing of unredeemed humanity".[136]

Who is the mysterious individual who will rouse Garrett and his army at the end of time? "At the entrance of the cave hangs a sword, and if a six-fingered man should find the entrance and have courage to draw the sword from its scabbard, the spell will be broken, and the warriors will waken and ride out to battle."[137] There's a striking similarity in the above passage to the myth about King Arthur, who drew the "sword from the stone" as the sign of his rightful sovereignty as King of Britain.

So who is the "right man"[138] who will rouse the sleeping army of Garrett's Fort? Is he the digitally deformed individual Cúchulainn, who was said to have had seven fingers on each hand?[139] Will the Hound of Culann ride out with his father from the sky, Lugh of the Long Arm, to engage in the final battle, to bring glory to Ireland in the last days?

Not all versions of the Garrett's Fort tale involve a man drawing a sword from its sheath.[140] In one rendition, contained in the schools folklore archive from Collon, it is said that Garrett's army is awaiting a "bugle call". Because of its proximity to the mouth of the High Man, it is not difficult to conjure up an image of this giant warrior figure stirring the enchanted soldiers with his mouth, perhaps using a bugle, or maybe using his *guth-aird,* his "High Voice".

The end-times prophecy of the messianic Hacklim hero is associated with another curious apocalyptic foretelling which we have not yet been able to unravel completely, but for which we might have a reasonable explanation. It involves a "Black Pig", said to be buried under stones at Kildemock, who will be seen again in conjunction with the beginning of a war.[141] A man called William Curran, of Funshog, near Ardee, is quoted in the schools folklore collection as having said that this pig "of enormous size" was "seen before the Great War", presumably World War I. Folklore surrounding this Black Pig is widespread in Louth, and in the schools collection alone there are dozens of mentions of it. In Ardee, it was recorded that, "It is also said the black pig will run again at the end of the world".[142]

Garrett's Fort was said to have been "in the 'race of the Black Pig' which will come before the Bugle sounds".[143] Countless places in Louth have an association with the Black Pig. The course taken by the Black Pig is called the "valley of the black pig – over which, it is prophesied, a great slaughter will be perpetrated, but is to end where the pig was killed."[144]

The Black Pig may be associated with Lugh Lamhfada's father, Cian, who took the form of a pig to avoid the attention of his "three mortal enemies", the three sons of Tuireann, who were trying to kill him.[145] Lugh had sought help when receiving news that the Fomorians had "landed at Es Dara". The king of Ireland had refused to help him battle against the invaders, so Lugh requested of the three sons of Cainte to "assemble the men of the fairy-mounds to me from all the places in which they are."[146] The sons of Cainte, who included Lugh's father, Cian, set out on their task, two brothers, Cu and Cethen heading southwards, and Cian going northwards, "until he reached Mag Muirthemne".[147]

At the plain of Muirthemne, Cian perceived the three sons of Tuireann, and without the help of his brothers to take them on in battle, he hit himself with a druid's wand and turned into a pig, joining a large herd of swine on Mag Muirthemne. Brian, one of the three sons of Tuireann, turned his two brothers into "sleuth-hounds"[148] who immediately went on the trail of the "druidical pig" that Cian had become. Brian threw a spear at the pig (Cian). "The wounded man-beast screamed in a human voice" and pleaded with the three sons to allow him to return to his human form.[149] They agreed, before crushing him to death "with the stones that lay about" and then they burned and mutilated his body and tried to bury him deep in the ground. They had to bury him seven times, because the first six times "the earth rejected it".[150]

Lugh had, in the interim, met the Fomorians in battle and defeated them. He was troubled by the absence of his father from the battle and went looking for him. He came to Muirthemne and at the spot where Cian had turned into a pig, "the earth spoke to Lugh and told him the fate his father had met".[151] Lugh unearthed Cian's remains and reburied them, placing a tombstone over them.

One possible location for the murder of Cian was said to be at Cortial Lough in the parish of Louth (which is north of the High Man figure), because of the association of that place with the Valley of the Black Pig.[152] A century ago, local tradition held that the black pig was killed "somewhere in the district" and that the red colour of the soil was due to the "stain of his blood".[153]

Another tradition says the black pig is buried near Clogherhead, at a place called Mayne, where a motte still extant is known as *Mota na muice duibhe*, the "Mote of the black pig".[154] In Collon, folklore holds that he came from Ardee to Belpatrick, and "stayed for a few days" in a fort at Dunmore, before going by Leabby Cross to a fort called "Croch an Alluis" and finally going down the Mattock River to Carrickanane fort, where he remains to this day.[155] "When he begins his course again Ireland will be free," states the story. There was once a well at Belpatrick (the belt of Patrick?) called the Black Pig's well because of a tradition that he drank out of the well in the course of his race. Numerous places in the area of the High Man are associated with the Black Pig, which may well be connected with the tradition of Lugh's father being killed on Mag Muirthemne. The territory of Fir Ard Cianachta may well have been named after Cian.

The often-stated direct relationship between the rousing of the enchanted army and the return of the Black Pig implies that both events are connected. Cian took his human warrior shape again just before Brian killed him, at Mag Muirthemne, the plain of Cúchulainn, who may be the mythical end-times hero who will waken the sleeping army and come forth with his father Lugh, and also his grandfather, Cian, "in his triumphant return from Tír na N-og" at the time of the breaking of the world.[156]

FiERY WEAPONS

Having done our best to unravel the end-times tales associated with the High Man, we must move on from Garrett's Fort and mention a few more places which might have associations with the *Fer Ard* figure.

The village of Dunleer indicates the end of the High Man's arm, where his wrist or hand is located. There are two traditions explaining the toponymic origin of Dunleer, one of which says the town was called *Dún Leirse,* meaning "town of sight", from the belief that St Bridget had her sight restored here after praying to God at a well "about five perches to the east of the road leading to Drogheda".[157] The other tradition holds that Dunleer is derived from *Lann Léire,* meaning "Church of Austerity",[158] although it is possible that *Léire* is the name of a district,[159] and a more remote possibility is that *Léire* is related to the name of the king of Ireland, Laoghaire,[160] who was challenged by St Patrick with the Easter Fire at Slane.

Lann Léire is mentioned numerous times in the *Annals of Ulster.* In the year 923, the annals record "The plundering of Fir Arda and Lann Léire and Fir Rois in the same month."[161] Saint Patrick is said to have mentioned Léire as being, along with Lerga, one of the "limits of Fir Rois territory".[162] Lerga has been identified with Largey, a townland near Drumconrath in County Meath,[163] which might well mark the limit of where the bright band of the Milky Way might have been seen to run past the High Man's shoulder. Dunleer, on the other hand, is located towards the eastern extremity of the figure. That Lerga is located in the "drumlin field" corresponding with the Milky Way is further hinted at by Saint Benen, who, speaking with St Patrick, referred to the *"Firu Roiss"* region as being "from the parts that are mountainous to Lére (i.e. Laind Leire) . . ."[164] While the exact derivation of Léire is foggy, looking up the Irish-English dictionary, we see there is a word *léire* which means "a person of sturdy build", or a "fine tall" person.[165]

How *Lann Léire* became Dunleer is not known. However, it may have another meaning, closely tied with the *Fer Ard*. *Lann* is an old Irish word meaning a "squama",[166] which is a thin, plate-like structure, and can specifically refer to the "blade of a sword".[167] *Lann* has also been linked to the Old Irish word *lamn,* modern *lamhan* or *lamhainn,* meaning "glove".[168] Does Dunleer mark the point where the High Man's hand grasps a sword or weapon? Fascinatingly, *lann* can also mean the "hollow" of a shield,[169] which is the part of a shield which accommodates the hand.

During Cúchulainn's epic "struggle fit for giants"[170] against Ferdia which marks the climax of the *Táin,* the two use copious different types of shields, including "two equally matched shields for feats", "two hard shields", "two full-firm broadshields" and "two full-great long-shields".[171] They threw weapons at each other from twilight until midday, and the story recounts how "they overcame their various feats with the bosses and hollows of their feat-shields."[172]

Ironically, Ferdia was killed because he manoeuvred his shield to protect himself from the *gae bolga,* first lowering it, and then, after Cúchulainn threw his short spear at Ferdia, raising it again. But the spear had already pierced Ferdia's heart. Cúchulainn then finished him off by sending the *gae bolga* through the water, "down the stream", under Ferdia's raised shield.[173]

The High Man figure appears to stand in the Boyne River, which marks its southern extremity. Is he a facsimile of the giant hero warrior Cúchulainn, standing in the ford? Curiously, Drogheda takes its name from Droichead Átha, which means "bridge of the ford" or "bridge over the ford". While there are fording points still extant on the Boyne at Drogheda, perhaps its name had a dual meaning, one signification relating to the actual fording points, the other to the fact that the High Man's leg enters the ford at Drogheda.

It is not beyond the realms of possibility that the Lerga mentioned previously is an off-shoot of *Fiodh Lamhraighe.* In this sense, the approximate bounds of the High Man would be the "wood of the hand of the king" to the west, and the "hollow of the shield of the sturdy/tall one" in the east. Both names are related to hands. Are these the hands of Tuatha Dé Danann king Lugh Long-Arm, who gave his name to County Louth, one grasping the sun at Louth village, the other reaching out for a shield?[174]

On the shield itself there is a curious townland called Skeaghmore, which is the location of a barrow known locally as "Kelly's Mote".[175] The first time we saw this place name, we thought it might perhaps be derived from *sciath mór,* meaning "big shield". However, official sources assert that it originates from *An Sceitheog Mhór*[176], meaning "thorn bush". Folklore about the origin of this name is completely absent from the Schools Folklore collection because Skeaghmore was located on the nearby Drumcar estate, and most of the residents interviewed for the folklore archive were not indigenous to the area and therefore knew nothing of its myths and stories.

A mile or so south of Skeaghmore is Briarhill, from *Cnoc na nDriseog*, "hill of the thorn/briar". Further north, near the tip of the shield is a place called Ballynagassan, from *Béal Átha na gCasán*,[177] meaning the "mouth of the ford of the paths/tracks/passes".[178] *Casán* is a word which is also spelt *cosán*,[179] which, as well as meaning a path or a track can mean a "sloe-bush".[180] Sloe is another word for blackthorn,[181] and can also refer to the fruit of the blackthorn. "In Ireland a blackthorn stick was regarded as providing protection against harm."[182] Fighting sticks, known as shillelaghs, were made from blackthorn, which was esteemed for its hard wood.[183] At the top of the shield is a seaside village called Annagassan, from *Áth na gCasán,* the "ford of the passes", where three rivers flow into the sea,[184] or possibly "ford of the blackthorn bush".

The "shield" or weapon of the High Man is the area which has the least toponymic and mythological evidence still extant to support it. Might his weapon have been some sort of walking stick, made from *sceach/ hawthorn*, like that of St Moling, which is said to have grown into a thorn bush in County Kilkenny?[185] Is the *Sceitheog Mhór* like the hawthorn staff which was said to have miraculously sprouted blossoms and leaves after Joseph of Arimathea struck it into the ground at Glastonbury, England?[186] St Joseph came to Glastonbury on Christmas Day in the year 63 AD, and "prayed for some miracle to convince [the unbelievers] of the truth of his words. As he struck his staff into the ground, his prayer was answered – the staff immediately shot forth leaves and blossoms."[187]

Patrick was the owner of a celebrated staff, known as the *Bachall Isu*, the "Staff of Jesus".[188] This miraculous staff was, according to the *Annals of Loch Cé*, said to have been "in the hand of Christ Himself".[189] The annals further record that the *Bachall Isu* was burned by the Saxons in Dublin in 1538. The staffs of St Joseph and St Patrick are similar through their connection to Jesus. The miraculous staff of Joseph which sprouted flowers at Glastonbury was "said to have the type of thorns with which Jesus was crowned".[190] The tree which sprouted from Joseph's staff was reportedly cut down by Cromwell's soldiers during the English civil war, but many people had taken cuttings from the tree and it is believed a thorn bush present in the grounds of Glastonbury Abbey until 1991 was a cutting from the original tree, planted in secret.

There is a tradition in Glastonbury that St Patrick may have been buried there. His remains are said by some to be interred at Glastonbury Abbey, the first church constructed in the British Isles in 63 AD, along with those of King Arthur and Queen Guinevere.[191] In one corner of Glastonbury Abbey, adjacent to a "still-used St Patrick's Chapel", there was a large thorn tree, "one of three in Glastonbury supposedly grown from the original that sprang from the staff of Joseph of Arimathea".[192]

Fascinatingly, Glastonbury is another place where there was apparently an effort to create a humongous starscape on the ground. The so-called "Glastonbury Zodiac" was discovered by Katherine Maltwood in 1927.[193] Maltwood proposed that a giant zodiac of constellation figures, a "counterpart of the heavens",[194] was laid out at Glastonbury 5,000 years ago, and that these shapes and figures could be seen today in aerial photographs and on Ordnance Survey maps and, in many cases, the ground constellations were delineated by old roads, prehistoric earthworks and water courses.

Another place which may commemorate the *Fer Ard* as St Patrick with his *Bachall Isu* is called Blackstaff, located just to the east of the "staff" near its southern point. Also at the bottom end of the staff is a townland called Carntown, which was formerly known in Irish as Sgáilleich,[195] which could be derived from the Irish word *scál,* meaning "champion".[196] It is interesting with regard to Patrick and his staff that there are places in County Louth which are said to bear, to this day, the impression of his staff and his knees. One such example is at Chanonrock, north of Louth village.[197]

While it may be short of evidence to substantiate it, the High Man's weapon/shield was definitely part of the area of the *Fer Ard.* In the townland of Dysart, which is immediately adjacent to the shield just southeast of Skeaghmore, is an old church, dedicated to the saint "Metheal Chaol, virgin of Disert".[198] This *Metheal Chaol,* also rendered Maur Caoil and more usually Borchoill, "is evidently a corruption of Meitheal Chaoil where Dysart is stated to be – *i bhfirarda* – i.e. in Ferrard, in which Dysart Parish is situated".[199]

Ferrard, as a barony created by the English, was clearly a much earlier Irish territory. As stated earlier, *Fer Ard* is believed to have derived from Fir Ard Cianachta, a third century tribe, but the tradition of Cian is likely to be much older than the third century. Place name author P.W. Joyce said the Sliabh Breagh range of hills, which run across the midriff of the High Man, were known as *Ard-Cianachta,* the "height of the territory of

Keenaght", and that the inhabitants were called "*Feara-Arda-Cianachta,* or more shortly, Feara-Arda . . . i.e. the men of the height, from which the modern name Ferrard has been formed."[200]

There are a couple of place names above the High Man which relate to bulls, an indication perhaps that the bull constellation, which we know today as Taurus, lies above Orion in the sky. One is Loughantarve, from *Loch an Tairbh,* the lake of the bull, which is located near the village of Knockbridge, just over two miles northeast of Louth village, and immediately adjacent to the townlands of Grange and Summerhill previously mentioned. This is the place in the Táin where the Brown Bull of Cooley "set his brow against the hill" after killing the white bull, Finnbennach.[201] This happened at Ath da Ferta, but the name of the place became known as Etan Tairb,[202] *etan* probably deriving from *éadan,* meaning "forehead". Before the *Táin,* there was an interesting episode in an older tale, *Táin Bó Regamna,* at Ath da Ferta which may have significance to our investigation of the High Man.

Cúchulainn and Laeg saw a chariot at Ath da Ferta, and "a red woman was in it . . . a big man beside the chariot . . . he drove a cow before him."[203] Of particular import here is the fact that the part of the sky which corresponds with Ath da Ferta would see the moon (cow) passing between the horns of Taurus (bull), one of which is attached to Auriga (chariot), and all this above Orion (the big man?). Cúchulainn tells the man that the "cow does not like being driven by you", to which the woman replies that it is none of Cúchulainn's business.[204] Cúchulainn tells the woman she is dangerous, after which the woman says, "Dolluid will be henceforth the description of the Grellach". Interestingly, the *Dindshenchas* says that Grellach Dolluid is the place where "Dollud son of Cairpre Nia fell thereat by Cuchulainn's hand."[205] Loughantarve/Ath da Ferta corresponds with the area of Taurus just above the hand of Orion.

Also at Knockbridge is a standing stone in the townland of Rathiddy called Clochfarmore, meaning "stone of the big man", which was according to legend the stone to which Cúchulainn tied himself at the time of his death.[206] It was here that the Badb, the grey crow, rested upon Cúchulainn's shoulder as a portent of his imminent demise. Again, the astronomical imagery fits the mythology. Badb, as one form of the lunar goddess, rested upon Cúchulainn's shoulder at a place which represents the location in the sky where the moon passes between the horns of Taurus. Three miles west of the "stone of the big man" is a townland called Carrickadooan, which is from the Irish *Carraig an Damháin,*[207] "rock of the young bull".

FROM SKY TO GROUND

The transference of the shapes of the sky onto the bare face of the earth involved the creation of a giant man, flanked by landscape features and place names of antiquity which preserve the sanctified region of the stellar realm where warriors and gods played out their surreal epics. There, in the sky, above Orion, is the mighty bull, the Donn Cuailnge, preserved in the skyscape to this day, his mighty form mythically conveyed on the ground at some unknown juncture in the past.

One could hypothesise on the basis of an array of data already presented in this book that, at that great unknown point in the past, probably as long ago as the New Stone Age, communities on the east coast of Ireland were making an indelible link between heaven and earth. They constructed, concocted and imagined a huge system, involving large monuments, horizon markers and landscape features, to somehow transcribe that cosmic connection into a readable system which would endure the centuries. Did they, could they, have tried to replicate Mag Mell on the ground using their monuments, their place names and their original roads? Whatever track or trodden ways existed long before the advent of tarmacadam were no more than narrow paths across the land. The Irish word for road is *bóthar*, meaning a "cattle track".

The roads that form the High Man are sacred highways, paths between consecrated places which uniquely embodied the concept, spoken of many times throughout this book, of a "duality and interpenetration of ground and sky, earth and heaven – matter and spirit". They are the paths to perfection, their associated monuments, like Tara, the "secret place(s) of the road of life".[208]

How old are these roads? Is it possible to tell? Surely one can simply pick up a road map of any area and pick out such a shape from the roads? These are interesting questions. There is no hard archaeological data immediately to hand which would make or break a case for the antiquity of the *Fer Ard* roads. What we do know is that the High Man was present on one of the earliest accurate maps of Louth, drawn by George Taylor and Andrew Skinner in 1778, at a time when there were much fewer roads to pick from than today.[209]

When we first announced the High Man to the world in 2004, there was some commentary on the internet which suggested that finding a shape like our giant hero on an Ordnance Survey map by choosing roads selectively was not such a difficult thing to do. As a result, we issued a challenge to the naysayers to do just that – find a giant warrior on your local road map which has toponymic and mythological evidence to substantiate the idea that it is more than just an accidental formation. To this day, no-one has responded successfully to that challenge.

Even in folklore, there is some indication of the antiquity of Ferrard's roads. The Schools Folklore project collected local traditions, folk customs, memories and beliefs under numerous headings, which included "local roads". The tradition held in the Collon area at the time the schools collection was compiled indicates that the old roads were indeed the ones which were straight for miles. One local person interviewed in 1938 said that the former roads of Collon "were all very hilly and ran quite straight with scarcely any turns".[210] Another native indicated that a lane across the "chest" of the High Man was "one of the first roads made". A Mr Kells from Corlis, Collon, said, "There are old roads in our district and some of them are still in use". Mr Johnson from Glenmore, Collon, spoke about the Collon–Tenure road, the White River road, the Monasterboice Road, the Drogheda Road and the Glenmore Road, and said, "All these roads were made very, very, long ago. Some of these are still in use." He added there were no accounts of when these roads were made, and that before bridges were made rivers were crossed by fords.

The Slighe Midhluachra, one of the five great roads mentioned in Chapter 4 which radiated from the Hill of Tara, likely ran through the Ferrard area, and may well have formed part of the High Man figure which is present today. "There is reason to think that the great highway of Slighe Midhluachra passed near by" to Garrett's Fort.[211] In fact, the Brown Bull of Cooley's journey after his victory over the Finnbennach took him along the "Midluachair road" from Etan Tairb, towards Cuib and then Druim Tairb, the "Ridge of the Bull", where he died.[212]

Some of the giant Orion warriors of Irish myth may have been connected with roads. The creation of the "Parallel Roads", which are horizontal markings left by ancient glacial lakes in Glen Roy, Scotland, are attributed to Fionn's sword.[213] Lugh was described by Julius Caesar as ". . . the inventor of all arts, the guide for every road and journey . . ."[214] And as Oisín returned from Tír na nÓg, "even the roads seemed somehow changed: where there had been no more than grassy tracks, leading off into the forests or mountains, they now seemed well paved and better laid-out with stones and proper borders".[215] Is this the transformation which came over the roads of *Fer Ard* during the course of the centuries?

We do not know how old the routes and thoroughfares of the High Man really are. They may have a hoary antiquity. Whether or not it was the end product of some dynamic and dramatic stellar blueprint, a primordial contrivance of remote times, the *Fer Ard* is present in the landscape today, a "high man" bearing compelling comparability to the High Man of the firmament, Orion, who has watched over us since the earliest ages.

The transmogrification of man to hero, hero to demigod, demigod to deity, deity to constellation, and the adaptation of that constellation onto the ground, may well have been a cardinal ingredient in the archaic belief system, a doctrine that recognised man's destiny as being ultimately fixed among the stars.

The mythical evidence certainly points to that conclusion. The High Man, both the constellation and its telluric reproduction, ostensibly symbolised some of the great champions, luminaries and divine beings of Irish mythic lore, from Cian to Lugh to Cúchulainn to Conchobhar, from Fionn Mac Cumhaill to Oisín to Osgar, from Amergin to St Patrick, from Nuadu to Bressal. Of these, the greatest surviving commemoration is reserved for Lugh, the many-gifted lord of light, Cúchulainn, his divine offspring, Amergin, the sun-holder, and St Patrick, the staff-bearing bringer of light of Christian times.

It is with the simulacrum of these divine giants with the light above their heads that we conclude our comprehensive and epic journey through time and myth. Having endured the ages in impassive slumber, the High Man has been suddenly stirred into life, his behemothic shape once again revealed to the world. His revelation comes at an interesting and thought-provoking time.

For once again, in this, the modern age, the sun has returned to the hand of Orion for one of the important festivals of the ancient Irish year. In the early Neolithic, the celestial High Man grasped the sun at the vernal equinox. In the Bronze Age, at the time of Amergin, the effects of precession had pushed the circle of the year westwards against the zodiac and Orion held the sun at Bealtaine. Now, in the twenty-first century, the age of the computer and the nuclear bomb, the starry High Man seizes the sun on the summer solstice, the day on which the sun reaches its annual zenith.

It is coincidental astronomical moments such as this, when there is a concordance between sun and stars, that mark out the waning of epochs and the dawning of ages. The Irish invasion legends portray numerous epic changes, some of which coincided with major sky events. The sun now reaches its vertex above Orion at the place where it crosses the river of the heavens. Are we about to endure another monumental, perhaps catastrophic, changing of the ages? Have we reached the time when the Black Pig will run again? Is the many-fingered hero about to rouse the sleeping army?

Whatever happens, we are hopeful that this new interpretation of myth, archaeology, landscape and starscape will aid the preservation of the monuments and myths which have persisted since antediluvian times. We may consider ourselves children of an enlightened age, but it is clear from the destruction we wreak that the age-old sacred attachment to the earth, which engendered a deep deference for all things natural, has been slowly eroded.

We are the products of ancestral continuity, whose progenitors walked the fertile plains of Ireland and discerned the harmony and disharmony of the sky, the celestial dance of the ages, and how the grand cycles of time influenced the banal intricacies of life on the ground. Those ancestors perceived the great cycle of precession. They knew that at a certain juncture in the future, Orion would grasp the sun on the summer solstice. That day has arrived. The phenomenon will last for the next century, but after that it will be another 25,800 years before it comes around again. Modern man has all but lost the ability to tell the time by the sun, moon and stars. The cosmic connection, exemplified by the megalithic monuments of the Boyne, which marked the pinnacle of prehistoric achievement, has been broken. Perhaps now it is time to re-establish that interconnection, for our own sakes and for the betterment of this wonderful place we call home.

Out of the obscurity of prehistory, a light has emerged . . .

EPİLOGUE
·OΠ ΤHE BRİΠK

One of the most mind-blowing facets of this exploration of ancient Ireland is the fact that a sizeable proportion of the myths and monuments contrived and created in the remote yesteryear abide to this day. It is an outstanding testament to the creators, and to the countless generations of people who have lived between then and now, that we are furnished with such a huge corpus of stones and stories from prehistory.

However, in recent history our record on the preservation of the past, particularly relating to the safeguarding of the monuments, has not been good. Throughout much of the period of research for this book, the heritage headlines have been dominated by the debate over the Irish Government's proposal to route the M3 motorway through the Tara–Skryne Valley, running through the heart of one of Ireland's most sacred and celebrated prehistoric and early historic landscapes.

Those against the plan feel it is inappropriate to route a motorway through a sensitive archaeological and rural area. Those who support it, who are sadly in great numbers, wish to have the ability to travel between their homes in Meath and their jobs in Dublin in a much shorter time than they can with current infrastructure. Meanwhile, there is no rail connection between Meath's main town, Navan, and the capital, and plans to construct one seem to be on the long finger.[1]

The M3 debate typifies the polarised opinion currently held in Ireland about the value of our monuments, our heritage and our landscape. But the threat to our ancient heritage is much broader than one single motorway project. Throughout the Boyne region, the area upon which *Island of the Setting Sun* focuses, there are developments and proposed construction schemes which are eroding and altering the ancient landscape.

In 2003, the new M1 motorway and Drogheda bypass cut a huge slice through the Hill of Rath, severing the leg of the High Man. Drogheda has seen its population rise considerably, and its urban area now occupies areas that were, only five years ago, green fields. The town continues to spread westwards, towards Brú na Bóinne.

The western boundary of the town, currently delineated by the M1 motorway, is just three and a half miles from Newgrange, and less than half that distance from Site Q, the easternmost surviving monument of the Bend of the Boyne complex. Town authorities are predicting that the population of Drogheda will rise from its current level of around 30,000 to 70,000 in the next decade.[2] In the six years since we photographed the summer solstice sunrise at Site Q, the development of Drogheda has been such that now a large retail scheme dominates the view along the axis of the henge's openings towards Castlecoo Hill.

A municipal incinerator has been granted planning permission for an area called Carranstown, near Duleek, just three and a half miles from Newgrange. Also in the pipeline is a power-generating factory in the same area. A huge cement factory at Platin, adjacent to the site of the proposed incinerator, has been given planning permission to boost its capacity by 40 per cent, with additional permission for the construction of a chimney stack 125 metres high. The twin stacks of the cement factory are already visible from Brú na Bóinne.

Further down the Boyne Valley, a new motorway bypass of Slane village is proposed, which will bridge the Boyne River at one of its most breathtakingly picturesque points, between the village of Slane and the great passage-mound complex of Knowth.

In Ardee, the once rural scene around the Castleguard mound has taken on a very urban feel. It is now flanked by new roads and all the time the residential development taking place in the area creeps closer and closer. The site of Ireland's Stonehenge at Carn Beg outside Dundalk is located in an area which is under intense development.

Intensive agricultural activity has wiped out entire archaeological sites and complexes. Many remain as mere crop marks, barely visible remnants of archaeological remains which were intact up until the twentieth century.

As long ago as the year 2000, the Heritage Council was warning that one in ten of Ireland's archaeological monuments were being wiped out every decade. At that time, the Heritage Council estimated that one third of these sites had been lost.[3] More have been wiped away since.

The so-called "Celtic Tiger" economy, which has transformed Ireland from a sluggish, backward economy into one of the richest nations in the world, has demanded a heavy price from our heritage. There has been huge controversy in this country surrounding land rezoning deals and bribery of politicians and council officials, with tribunals of inquiry still investigating such matters a decade after they first came into the public spotlight.

The Department of the Environment, which is the division of government that sanctions large infrastructural projects such as the M3 motorway, is the same branch of government which is charged with looking after our heritage. That's a contradiction which wouldn't be allowed to exist anywhere else in the world.

We stand on a threshold. Our heritage is teetering on the brink. A radically different approach to the development of this country is needed, one that is sensitive to the natural and archaeological landscape. Otherwise, many things might be lost which cannot be regained.

In a letter to a leading Irish current affairs magazine in April of 2006, I wrote the following, which sums up our feelings on the issue:

> We are a long way off a complete comprehension of the things that were set down in the Irish landscape around 5,000 years ago. Many of the stories and the sites themselves have survived five millennia. It is doubtful that the motorcar will last another 50 years, never mind 5,000. What will become of our motorways then? In the meantime, we are in danger of losing the unique connection with the landscape which has been an important part of who we are since the earliest times.[4]

BIBLIOGRAPHY

Note: CLAJ = County Louth Archaeological and Historical Journal

Allen, Richard Hinckley (1963) [1899], *Star Names: Their Lore and Meaning*, Dover Publications.

Allen, W.P. (1943), "Some Notes on the Old Fortifications of Drogheda", reprinted from the *County Louth Archaeological Journal*.

Barry, Thomas (1904), "Castle Guard, Ardee", *CLAJ*, Vol. I, No. I, p. 43.

Bassett, G.H. (1998) [1886], *Louth County Guide and Directory*, published by County Louth Archaeological and Historical Society.

Battersby, William (1997), *The Age of Newgrange: Astronomy and Mythography*, self-published.

Battersby, William (1999), *Knowth: 10 Ages*, self-published.

Benigni, Helen, Carter, Barbara and Ua Cuinn, Éadhmonn (2003), *The Myth of the Year: Returning to the Origin of the Druid Calendar*, University Press of America.

Beresford Ellis, Peter (1996), "Early Irish Astrology: An Historical Argument", *Réalta* (Journal of the Irish Astrological Association), Vol. 3, No. 3.

Best, E. (1955), *The Astronomical Knowledge of the Maori*.

Bhreathnach, Edel and Newman, Conor (1995), *Tara*, Government of Ireland Stationery Office.

Boylan, Henry (1988), *A Valley of Kings: The Boyne*, O'Brien Press.

Boyle O'Reilly, John, "Letter to Father Anderson, Drogheda, November 7th, 1884", printed in *The Cry of the Dreamer and Other Poems*, edited by Peggy O'Reilly and Breeda Tuite.

Bracken, Gerry, "The 'Rolling Sun' Spectacle of Boheh", http://www.carrowkeel.com/sites/croaghpatrick/reek3.html (Retrieved 25 March 2006).

Bradley, John (1997), *Drogheda: Its Topography and Medieval Layout,* Aspects of the history of Drogheda Number 1, Old Drogheda Society.

Brennan, Martin (1980), *The Boyne Valley Vision*, The Dolmen Press.

Brennan, Martin (1994) [1983], *The Stones of Time*, Inner Traditions International.

Buckley, Victor (1988), "Ireland's Stonehenge – a lost antiquarian monument rediscovered", *Archaeology Ireland*, No. 2, pp. 53–54.

Buckley, Victor M. and Sweetman, P. David (1991), *Archaeological Survey of County Louth*, The Office of Public Works.

Campbell, Joseph (1959), The Masks of God: Primitive Mythology, vol. I.

Casey, Christine, and Rowan, Alistair (1993), *The Buildings of Ireland: North Leinster*, Penguin Books.

Charles-Edwards, T.M. (2000), *Early Christian Ireland*, Cambridge University Press.

Coffey, George (1977) [1912], *New Grange and Other Incised Tumuli in Ireland*, Dolphin Press.

Coffey, Josephine (2000), "Some Moon Rhythms", http://www.global-vision.org/ireland/stones/sunmoon/index.html Retrieved 23 September 2006.

Collins, Andrew, (2006), *The Cygnus Mystery*, Watkins.

Concannon, Mrs Thomas (1931), *Saint Patrick: His Life and Mission*, Talbot Press.

Condit, Tom (1997), *Ireland's Archaeology from the Air*, Country House.

Conlon, Larry (2000), "The Holy Wells of County Louth", *CLAJ*, Vol. XXIV, No. 4, p. 469.

Connolly, Susan and Moroney, Anne-Marie (2000), *Ogham: Ancestors Remembered in Stone*, Flax Mill Publications.

Cooney, Gabriel (2000), *Landscapes of Neolithic Ireland*, Routledge.

Corcoran, Moira (1986), "Drogheda Folklore", *Journal of the Old Drogheda Society*.

Cotterell, Arthur (1996), *The Encyclopaedia of Mythology*, Anness Publishing Ltd.

Cross, Tom P., and Slover, Clark Harris (editors) (1996) [1936], *Ancient Irish Tales*, Barnes and Noble.

Curran, Bob (2000), *Complete Guide to Celtic Mythology*, Appletree.

Cusack, Mary Frances (1995) [1868], *An Illustrated History of Ireland from AD 400 to 1800*, Senate.

D'Alton, John (1997) [1844], *History of Drogheda, Volume II*, Buvinda Historical Publications.

Dames, Michael (2000), *Ireland: A Sacred Journey*, Element Books.

Danaher, Kevin (2004) [1964], *Irish Customs and Beliefs*, Mercier Press.

Davidson, Norman (1985), *Astronomy and the Imagination: A New Approach to Man's Experiece of the Stars*, Routledge & Kegan Paul.

Davies, John (2000), *The Celts,* Cassell & Co.

De Santillana, Giorgio, and von Dechend, Hertha (1977), *Hamlet's Mill: An Essay on Myth and the Frame of Time*, David R. Godine.

Department of the Environment and Local Government (2002), *Brú na Bóinne World Heritage Site Management Plan.*

Dinneen, Rev. Patrick S., M.A. (1927), *Foclóir Gaedhilge agus Béarla*, Irish Texts Society.

Dolan, J.T. (1904), "Early Legends of Louth", *CLAJ*, Vol. 1, No. 1.

Dolan, Joseph (1929), "Louth Ordnance Survey Letters", *CLAJ*, Vol. VII, No. 1, p. 57.

Downey, Margaret (compiler) and McCullen, John (editor) (1999), *From the Nanny to the Boyne: A Local History of the Villages and Townlands on the East Coast of Meath*, East Meath Co-Operative Society Ltd.

Drogheda Strategy Report, 2006, http://www.louthcoco.ie/downloads/Reports/DevelopmentPlans/GreaterDroghedaArea/policycontext.pdf

Duffy, Joseph (1972), *Patrick in his Own Words,* Veritas Publications.

Duncan, David Ewing (1999), *The Calendar: The 5000-Year Struggle to Align the Clock and the Heavens – and What Happened to the Missing Ten Days*, Fourth Estate.

Dunn, Joseph (1914), *The Cattle-Raid of Cooley (Táin Bó Cúailnge)*, David Nutt, London

Ekirch, A. Roger (2006), *At Day's Close, A History of Nighttime*, Phoenix.

Eogan, George (1986), *Knowth and the Passage-Tombs of Ireland*, Thames and Hudson.

Eogan, George (1991), "Prehistoric and Early Historic Culture Change at Brugh na Bóinne", *PRIA*, Volume 91, C, Number 5, p. 119.

Eogan, George, and Roche, Helen (1994), "A Grooved Ware wooden structure at Knowth, Boyne Valley, Ireland", *Antiquity* 68, pp. 322–330.

Evans-Wentz, W.Y. (1911), *The Fairy-Faith in Celtic Countries*, Section III, Chapter VIII.

Fenwick, Joseph (1997), "A panoramic view from the Hill of Tara, Co. Meath", *Ríocht na Midhe*, Vol. IX, No. 3.

Folklore Commission schools archives.

Frazer, James George (1963) [1922], *The Golden Bough: A Study in Magic and Religion*, Collier Books.

Frost, Gregory (1986), *Táin*, Ace Fantasy Books.

Garry, James (1990), "Townland Survey of County Louth: Mell", *CLAJ*, Vol. XXII, No. 2.

Geoffrey of Monmouth, *History of the Kings of Britain*, translated by Aaron Thompson, http://www.yorku.ca/inpar/geoffrey_thompson.pdf

Gibbons, Fiachra (2001), "Stones that could be Britain's pyramids", *The Guardian*, 29 May.

Gilroy, John (2000), *Tlachtga: Celtic Fire Festival*, Pikefield Publications.

Graves, Robert (1999) [1948], *The White Goddess, A Historical Grammar of Poetic Myth*, Faber and Faber.

Gregory, Lady Augusta (2004a) [1902], *Lady Gregory's Complete Irish Mythology*, Bounty Books.

Gregory, Lady Augusta (2004b) [1904], *Gods and Fighting Men*, Bounty Books.

Gwynn, Edward (1906), *The Metrical Dindshenchas*, Hodges, Figgis & Co. Ltd. (Royal Irish Academy Todd Lecture Series Volume IX).

Hancock, Graham (2001), *Fingerprints of the Gods*, Century Books.

Hancock, Graham and Faiia, Santha (1998), *Heaven's Mirror: Quest for the Lost Civilization*, Michael Joseph.

Harbison, Peter (2003), *Treasures of the Boyne Valley*, Gill & Macmillan in association with the Boyne Valley Honey Company.

Harrison, Hank (1992) [1970], *The Cauldron and the Grail*, The Archives Press.

Havill, Georgiana (1997), "King Arthur Meets the New Age", *New York Times*, 5 January.

Heifetz, Milton D. and Tirion, Wil (1996), *A Walk Through the Heavens: A Guide To Stars and Constellations and their Legends*, Cambridge University Press.

Herity, Michael (ed.) (2001), *Ordnance Survey Letters Meath*, Four Masters Press.

Herity, Michael and Eogan, George (1996) [1977], *Ireland in Prehistory*, Routledge.

Hickey, Elizabeth (1988), *The Legend of Tara*, Dundalgan Press, Dundalk.

Hickey, Elizabeth (2000), *I Send My Love Along the Boyne*, published by Áine Ni Chairbre (first published in 1966 by Allen Figgis & Co.).

Hicks, Ronald (1975), *Some Henges and Hengiform Earthworks in Ireland: Form, Distribution, Astronomical Correlations, and Associated Mythology*.

Hicks, Ronald (1985), "Astronomical Traditions of Ancient Ireland and Britain," *Archaeoastronomy*, Volume VIII, p. 72.

Hughes, A (2003) [1893], *The History of Drogheda*, reprinted by the Publications Committee of The Old Drogheda Society.

Irish Countrywomen's Association Togher Guild (1993), *Togher Through the Years: Reflections & Reminiscences, a History of Togher Parish*.

Johnston, L.C. (1826), *History of Drogheda, from the earliest period, to the present time*, printed by Patrick Kelly, Drogheda.

Joyce, P.W. (1869), *The Origin and History of Irish Names of Places, Volume I*, The Educational Co. of Ireland.

Joyce, P.W. (1879), *The Origin and History of Irish Names of Places, Volume II*, The Educational Co. of Ireland.

Joyce, P.W. (1910), *The Origin and History of Irish Names of Places, Volume III*, The Educational Co. of Ireland.

Joyce, P.W. (1997) [1894], *Ancient Celtic Romances*, Parkgate Books.

Kearns, Hugh (1993), *The Mysterious Chequered Lights of Newgrange*, Elo Publications.

Keating's History of Ireland, Irish Texts Society, II.

Kelly, Eamonn P. (1996), *Sheela-na-Gigs: Origins and Functions*, Country House.

King, Heather A. (1999), "Excavation on the Fourknocks ridge, Co. Meath", *Proceedings of the Royal Irish Academy*, Vol. 99C.

Kinsella, Thomas (1969), *The Táin*, Oxford University Press.

Knight, Christopher and Lomas, Robert (1999), *Uriel's Machine: The Prehistoric Technology that Survived the Flood*, Century.

Knight, Peter (1996), *Ancient Stones of Dorset*, Power Publications.

Kondratiev, Alexei (1998), "Danu and Bile: The Primordial Parents?" *An Tribhis Mhor: The IMBAS Journal of Celtic Reconstructionism*, Vol. 1, No. 4, Bealtaine 1998.

Kondratiev, Alexei (1999) [1998], *Celtic Rituals: An Authentic Guide to Ancient Celtic Spirituality*, New Celtic Publishing.

Lacey, Brian (2003), *Pocket History of Irish Saints*, The O'Brien Press.

Lawless, Nicholas (1908), "Killaine in Slieve Breagh", *CLAJ*, Vol. II, No. 1, p. 27.

Leask, H.G. (1933), "Inscribed stones recently discovered at Dowth Tumulus, Co. Meath", *PRIA*, Vol. XLI, Section C, No. 5, p. 164.

Lenehan, Larry (1995), "Wintering Waterfowl at Newgrange, Co. Meath", *Irish East Coast Bird Report 1995*.

Lippard, Lucy R. (1983), *Overlay: Contemporary Art and the Art of Prehistory*, Pantheon Books.

Louth Ordnance Survey Letters (Reprinted from *County Louth Archaeological Journal* Vols. IV, V & VI).

Lynch, Ann (1982), "Astronomy and Stone Alignments" in S.W. Ireland, *Archaeoastronomy in the Old World*, edited by D. Heggie, Cambridge, p. 205–13.

Lynn, Chris (2003), *Navan Fort: Archaeology and Myth*, Wordwell.

Mac Airt, Seán, and Mac Niocaill, Gearóid (1983), *The Annals of Ulster*, School of Celtic Studies.

Macalister, R.A.S. (1938-1956), *Lebor Gabála Érenn, The Book of the Taking of Ireland*, Irish Texts Society, Dublin.

MacBain, Alexander (1998), *Etymological Dictionary of Scottish-Gaelic*, Hippocrene Books.

MacBain, Gillies (2000), "The Secret of Dowth", *The Pulse of the Irish Passage Mounds*, Samhain.

MacBain, Gillies, "Finding Easter at Knowth", http://www.mythicalireland.com/ancientsites/knowth/herdayinthesun.html (Retrieved 9 July 2006).

McCionnaith, L., S.J. (1935), *Foclóir Béarla agus Gaedhilg, English-Irish Dictionary e*, Oifig Díolta Foillseacháin Rialtais (Irish Manuscripts Commission).

McEvoy, J.P. (1999), *Eclipse: The Science and History of Nature's Most Spectacular Phenomenon*, Fourth Estate.

Mac Coitir, Niall (2003), *Irish Trees: Myths, Legends and Folklore*, The Collins Press.

Mac Iomhair, Rev. Diarmuid (no date), *Kildemock and its jumping church*, published by the Ardee Sub-Committee of the County Louth Archaeological Society.

Mac Iomhair, Rev. Diarmuid (1950), "Townland Survey of County Louth: Hacklim", *CLAJ*, Vol. XII, No. 2, p. 126.

Mac Iomhair, Rev. Diarmuid (1962), "The Boundaries of Fir Rois", *CLAJ* Vol. XV, No. 2.

Mac Iomhair, Rev. Diarmuid (1964), "The History of Fir Rois", *CLAJ*, Vol. XV, No. 4, p. 321.

MacIvor, Rev. Dermot (1958), "The Legend of Gearóid Iarla of Hacklim", *CLAJ*, Vol. XIV, No. 2, p. 72.

MacKillop, James (1998), *Oxford Dictionary of Celtic Mythology*, Oxford University Press.

McMann, J. (1994), "Forms of power: dimensions of an Irish megalithic landscape", *Antiquity* 68.

McMann, Jean (1999), *Loughcrew: The Cairns, A Guide*, After Hours Books.

MacManus, Seumas (1990) [1921], *The Story of the Irish Race*, Random House.

McNally, Kenneth (1984), *Standing Stones and Other Monuments of Early Ireland*, Appletree Press.

Maltwood, K.E. (1982), *A Guide to Glastonbury's Temple of the Stars*, James Clarke & Co.

Mathews, John (1991), *Taliesin: Shamanism and the Bardic Mysteries in Britain and Ireland*, London: Aquarian.

Michell, John (2001) [1977], *A Little History of Astro-Archaeology*, Thames & Hudson.

Mitchell, Frank (1990), *The Way That I Followed: A Naturalist's Journey Around Ireland*, Country House.

Mitchell, Frank and Ryan, Michael (2003) [1986], *Reading the Irish Landscape*, Town House.

Mohen, Jean-Pierre (2002) [1999], *Standing Stones: Stonehenge, Carnac and the World of Megaliths*, Thames & Hudson.

Moore, Michael J. (1987), *Archaeological Inventory of Co. Meath*, Stationery Office, Government Publications.

Moroney, Anne-Marie (2000), *Dowth: Winter Sunsets*, Flaxmill Publications.

Morris, Henry (1907), "Louthiana: Ancient and Modern", *CLAJ*, Vol. 1, No. 4, p. 61.

Murphy, Anthony (2006), "Astronomical alignments in Boyne region", Letters to the Editor, *Village Magazine*, 6 April 2006, p. 49.

Murray, Fr. Laurence (1911), "The Burial Place of St. Fanchea", *CLAJ*, Vol. II, No. 4.

Murray, Laurence (1904), "Monasteries of Louth, Part I: Pre-Norman", *CLAJ*, Vol. I, No. I.

National University of Ireland Research Matters, Nollaig 2002, Volume 1, Issue 3, http://www.nuigalway.ie/press/ research_matters/ features3.html#tara

Ní Sheaghdha, N. (1967), *Tóruigheacht Dhiarmada agus Ghráinne*, Irish Texts Society, Series 48, Dublin.

North, John (1996), *Stonehenge: Neolithic Man and the Cosmos*, HarperCollins Publishers.

O'Brien, Jacqueline and Harbison, Peter (1996), *Ancient Ireland: From Prehistory to the Middle Ages*, Weidenfeld & Nicolson, London.

O'Callaghan, Chris (2004), *Newgrange: Temple to Life*, Mercier Press.

O'Donovan, John (ed.) (1990) [1856], *Annala Rioghachta Eireann: Annals of the kingdom of Ireland by the Four Masters, from the earliest period to the year 1616*, Dublin.

O'Grady, Standish Hayes (1892), *Silva Gadelica, I–XXXI*, London, p. 520.

Ó hÓgáin, Dáithí (2006), *The Lore of Ireland: An Encyclopaedia of Myth, Legend and Romance*, The Collins Press.

Ó hÓgáin, Dr Dáithí (1990), *Myth, Legend and Romance, An Encyclopaedia of the Irish Folk Tradition*, Ryan Publishing.

O'Kelly, Claire (1971) [1967], *Illustrated Guide to Newgrange*, John English & Co. Ltd..

O'Kelly, Michael J. (1989), *Early Ireland*, Cambridge University Press.

O'Kelly, Michael J. (1998) [1982], *Newgrange: Archaeology, Art and Legend*, Thames and Hudson.

O'Kelly, Michael J. and O'Kelly, Claire (1983), "The Tumulus of Dowth, County Meath", *Proceedings of the Royal Irish Academy (PRIA)*, Vol. 83c.

"One-third of Irish heritage sites now wiped out", *Irish Independent*, 26 April 2000, p. 3.

O'Rahilly, T.F. (1946), *Early Irish History and Mythology*, Dublin Institute for Advanced Studies.

Ó Riain, Flann (2000), *Townlands of Leinster and the People who Lived There*, Open Air.

Ó Ríordáin, Seán P. (1965) [1942], *Antiquities of the Irish Countryside*, Methuen & Co. Ltd.

Ó Síocháin, P.A. (1983), *Ireland: A Journey into Lost Time*, Foilsiúcháin Eireann, p. 112.

O'Sullivan, Anne (1965), *Book of Leinster* (Vol. 4), edited by Dublin Institute of Advanced Studies, Dublin.

O'Sullivan, Harold (1978), "The Grant of Arms to the Louth County Council", *CLAJ*, Vol. XIX, No. 2.

O'Sullivan, Muiris (1993), *Megalithic Art in Ireland*, Town House and Country House.

O'Sullivan, Muiris and Downey, Liam (2003), "Booley Huts", *Archaeology Ireland*, Vol. 17, No. 4, Winter, p. 34.

Ordnance Survey Letters Meath (2001) [1836], Four Masters Press.

Oxford Compact English Dictionary, Oxford University Press, 2000.

Patrick, John (1974), "Midwinter sunrise at Newgrange", *Nature*, 249, pp. 517–19.

Placenames (Co. Louth) Order, 2003, http://www.pobail.ie/en/IrishLanguage/ThePlacenamesBranch/PlacenamesOrders/file,3917,en.pdf, retrieved 17 August 2006.

Poynder, Michael (2000) [1997], *The Lost Magic of Christianity*, Green Magic.

Prendergast, F. and Ray, T. (2002), "Ancient astronomical alignments: fact or fiction?", *Archaeology Ireland*, Vol. 16, No. 2, Issue 60, Summer, p. 35.

Proctor, Mary (1924), *Legends of the Stars*, George G. Harrap & Co.

Quinn, Bob (2005), *The Atlantean Irish, Ireland's Oriental and Maritime Heritage*, The Lilliput Press Ltd.

Ray, Tom P. (1989), "The winter solstice phenomenon at Newgrange: accident or design?", *Nature*, Vol. 337, Issue 6205, pp. 343–345.

Rees, Martin (general editor) (2005), *Universe*, Dorling Kindersley.

Reijs, Victor (2003), "Some evaluation of measurements at Dowth", http://www.iol.ie/~geniet/eng/dowthmeasure.htm (Retrieved 16 May 2006).

Reijs, Victor, "Measurements on passages at Knowth", http://www.iol.ie/~geniet/eng/westknowthmeasure.htm (Retrieved 9 July 2006).

Rhys, John (1901), *Celtic Folklore: Welsh and Manx*, Oxford University Press.

Ridpath, Ian (ed.) (1996), *Norton's 2000.0 star atlas and reference handbook*, Longman, eighteenth edition, p. 136.

Ring, Evelyn, "Huge temple found under Hill of Tara", *Irish Examiner*, 12 November 2002.

Robinson, Aidan P. (1994), *Ancient Drogheda*, PRC Ireland Limited.

Robinson, J.A., Colhoun, K., McElwaine, J.G. and Rees, E.C. (2004), "Whooper Swan *Cygnus cygnus* (Iceland population) in Britain and Ireland 1960/61 – 1999/2000", Waterbird Review Series, The Wildfowl & Wetlands Trust/Joint Nature Conservation Committee, Slimbridge.

Roe, H.M. (1954), "The High Crosses of Co. Louth", *Seanchus Ard Mhacha 1*, No.1, pp. 101–14.

Rolleston, T.W. (1995) [1993], *The Illustrated Guide to Celtic Mythology*, Studio Editions.

Rolleston, Thomas (1998), *Myths and Legends of the Celts*, Senate.

Sagan, Carl (1995) [1980], *Cosmos*, Wings Books.

Scribner, Charles (1999), *Fates and Destinies: Translations from the Neolithic*, Hilltop Press.

Sjoestedt, Marie-Louise (2000) [1949], *Celtic Gods and Heroes,* Dover Publications.

Slavin, Michael (no date), *The Tara Walk*.

Slavin, Michael (1996), *The Book of Tara*, Wolfhound Press.

Slavin, Michael (2005), *The Ancient Books of Ireland*, Wolfhound Press.

Smyth, Daragh (1996), *A Guide to Irish Mythology*, Irish Academic Press.

Sobel, Dava (2005), *The Planets,* Fourth Estate.

Squire, Charles (1998) [1912], *Mythology of the Celtic People*, Senate.

Stout, Geraldine (1991), *Embanked Enclosures of the Boyne Region*, Proceedings of the Royal Irish Academy, Volume 91, C, No. 9.

Stout, Geraldine (1997), *The Bend of the Boyne: An Archaeological Landscape,* Country House.

Stout, Geraldine (2002), *Newgrange and the Bend of the Boyne*, Cork University Press.

Stout, Matthew (2000), *The Irish Ringfort*, Four Courts Press.

Summer Guide to Inis-na-Righ, The Hidden Island of the Kings, author unknown, 1987, A Stray Sod Publication.

Sweetman, David, M.A. (1982–83), "Reconstruction and Partial Excavation of an Iron Age Burial Mound at Ninch, Co. Meath", *Ríocht na Mide*, VII, 2.

Táin Bó Cúalnge from the Book of Leinster, translated and published on the internet as part of the CELT Corpus of Electronic Texts initiative by the History Department of University College Cork, http://www.ucc.ie/celt/published/T301035/index.html.

"Tara continues to yield up its secrets", http://www.nuigalway.ie/archaeology/Tara_Aerial-Photos.html

Taylor and Skinner Map, 28 September 1778, republished by the County Louth Archaeological and Historical Society, 1982.

Tempest, Henry G. (1911), "Louthiana: Ancient and Modern, Fort at Ballinahattin, Dundalk", *CLAJ*, Vol. II, No .4, p. 428.

Temple, Robert (1999), *The Sirius Mystery*, Arrow.

Thom, Alexander (1967), *Megalithic Sites in Britain*, Oxford University Press.

Thom, Alexander (1971), *Megalithic Lunar Observatories*, Oxford University Press.

Thom, Alexander (1955), "A Statistical Examination of the Megalithic Sites in Britain", *Journal of the Royal Statistical Society*, No. 118, pp. 175–98.

Thomas, N.L. (1988), *Irish Symbols of 3500 BC*, Mercier Press.

Tolkien, J.R.R. (1992), *The Lord of the Rings*, Grafton.

Vance, Rob (2003), *Secret Sights: Unknown Celtic Ireland*, Gill and Macmillan.

Walter, Denton P. (1996), "Cygnus", *Astronomy and Space magazine*, Vol. 4, No. 3, October, p. 17.

Warner, Richard (1990), "The 'Prehistoric' Irish annals: fable or history?", *Archaeology Ireland*, Volume 4, Number 1, p. 30.

Waters, Ormonde D. (1965), "Some Notes on Rath-Colpa", *Ríocht na Mídhe*, Vol. III, No. 3, pp. 260–1.

Whitehouse, Dr David (1999), "Ancient tomb captured both sun and moon", http://news.bbc.co.uk/2/hi/science/nature/313720.stm

Whitehouse, Dr David, "Encounter with the Moon Stone", http://news.bbc.co.uk/2/hi/science/nature/1205638.stm

Wilde, William (2003) [1849], *The Beauties of the Boyne and Blackwater*, Kevin Duffy (first published in 1849 by McGlashan & Gill, Dublin).

Williamson, Hugh Ross (1962), *The Flowering Hawthorn*, Hawthorn Books, New York, Flyleaf.

Wood, Florence & Kenneth (1999), *Homer's Secret Iliad, The Epic of the Night Skies Decoded*, John Murray Ltd.

Wright, Thomas (2000) [1748], *Louthiana: or, an Introduction to the Antiquities of Ireland*, Dundalgan Press.

Websites

http://groups.yahoo.com/group/irish-stones

http://www.astronomy.ca/3340eclipse

http://www.bluhorizonlines.org/discover/discover.html

http://www.dunleer.com/back_history.htm

http://www.excavations.ie/Pages/Details.php?Year=&County=Louth&id=578

http://www.hilloftara.info

http://www.iol.ie/~geniet/eng/azimuth.htm

http://www.iol.ie/~geniet/eng/dowthmeasure.htm

http://www.iol.ie/~geniet/eng/westknowthmeasure.htm

http://www.jncc.gov.uk/pdf/UKSPA/UKSPA-A6-16.pdf

http://www.mythicalireland.com

http://www.ngdc.noaa.gov/seg/geomag/jsp/struts/calcDeclination.

http://www.radical-astrology.com/irish/miscellany/irishzodiac.html

http://www.rockhoundingar.com/quartz/experiments.html

http://www.savetara.com

http://www.taraskryne.org

http://www.tarawatch.org

NOTES

CHAPTER ONE: BALOR'S STRAND

[1] Buckley and Sweetman (1991).

[2] We are very grateful to Dominic Hartigan for permission to visit the stones, and would always encourage anyone wishing to visit ancient sites on private land that they seek the assent of the owner first. The standing stones are a national monument, and, as such, should be treated with the utmost respect and care.

[3] Mitchell (1990), p. 258.

[4] Buckley and Sweetman (1991), p. 75, state that "The NMI topographical file records three stones at the site, but only two are now visible".

[5] Ibid.

[6] Michael O'Kelly (1989, p. 228) speculates that some standing stones may have acted as boundary markers.

[7] The stones are now in Leinster. The provincial boundaries have changed since ancient times.

[8] Murray (1911), p. 432.

[9] *Ordnance Survey Letters Meath*, p. 46. In modern times, only one peak of this range of hills is now called Sliabh Breagh, in County Meath. Parts of the hill were known as Sliabh Dubh (Black Hill) and Sliabh na gCearc (Hill of the Hen), according to O'Donovan.

[10] Mac Iomhair (1962), p. 159.

[11] Ibid.

[12] Cross and Slover (1996), p. 174.

[13] Kinsella (1969), p. 44.

[14] Mitchell (1990), p. 258.

[15] Ibid.

[16] Cross and Slover (1996), p. 175.

[17] See Thom (1955).

[18] Thom (1971), p. 36.

[19] Buckley and Sweetman (1991), p. 75.

[20] The Paps of Jura is a mountain range which dominates the southern part of the island of Jura, which is the island pointed towards by the Ballochroy stone.

[21] Ibid.

[22] Ibid.

[23] Mitchell (1990), p. 258.

[24] McNally (1984), p. 45.

[25] Victor Buckley, private communication.

[26] The story was taken from the archives of Skerries Historical Society 1948–1995. We are indebted to Andrew Kieran for bringing it to our attention.

[27] This celebrated cow of mythology and folklore was described as a "grey white-forked cow", who gave an inexhaustible supply of milk (Dinneen (1927), p. 543).

[28] Balor was actually a king of the Fomorians, not the Tuatha Dé Danann.

[29] Ó hÓgáin (1990), p. 43.

[30] Rolleston (1995), p. 29.

[31] Ó hÓgáin (1990), p. 43.

[32] Curran (2000), p. 112.

[33] Cotterell (1996), p. 103. Cotterell describes Belenus (Beli to the Welsh) as a "Celtic sun god".

[34] The name Traig Baile is also said to be derived from Baile Binnbérlach, an heir to the throne of Ulster who was said to have died on the strand after being told, falsely, that his lover Ailinn had died.

[35] Ó hÓgáin (1990), p. 240. Goibhniú was the smith of the Tuatha Dé Danann.

[36] A study of astronomical alignments in southwest Ireland revealed that a considerable number of stone circles had significant solar or lunar orientations, while a few others could have been aligned on Venus. (Lynch, Ann (1982), pp. 205–13. Cited in O'Kelly (1989) p. 231).

[37] The maximum elongation of Venus occurs when the planet is at the greatest angular distance from the sun as seen from Earth.

[38] A synodic period of Venus marks the time it takes Venus to return to the same position in the sky relative to the sun. It is 583.92 days long.

[39] Diametrically opposite. If the sun is setting in the northwest, the full moon would be rising in the southeast.

[40] A 19-year cycle of the moon which marks the return of the same phase of the moon to the same background stars. The metonic cycle will be dealt with in detail in later chapters.

[41] Thom (1971), p. 11.

[42] Smyth (1996), pp. 22–3.

[43] In *The Secret Doctrine*, H.P. Blavatsky tells us the following about the Egyptian goddess Isis: "Isis was the moon, the bed of the River Nile, or the Mother Earth, for the parturient energies of which water was a necessity, the lunar year of 354–364 days, the time-maker of the periods of gestation, and the cow marked by, or with, the crescent new moon." Blavatsky, H.P., *The Secret Doctrine*, Volume 1, Book 2, Chapter 9.

[44] We are talking here about a synodic lunar month, the time it takes the moon to return to the same phase, i.e. full moon to full moon.

[45] Thanks to Gillies MacBain, a member of the Irish-Stones eGroup and a cattle breeder. He says that a useful rule of thumb states, "Don't let out the bull till a little after St. Patrick's Day, or you might be up at night over Christmas . . ."

[46] Wilde (2003), p. 24.

[47] In the grounds of Newbury Hall. We are grateful to Mr Robinson for permission to visit and photograph the well.

[48] Wilde (2003), pp. 24–5.

[49] Ibid., p. 25.

[50] Ó hÓgain (1990), p. 49.

[51] Ibid.

[52] Ibid.

[53] McCionnaith (1935), p. 824.

[54] De Santillana and Von Dechend (1977), p. 188.

[55] Ibid., p. 256.

[56] Hancock and Faiia (1998), p. 96.

[57] See Chapter 11.

[58] Squire (1998), p. 48.

[59] Ibid.

[60] Kondratiev (1998).

[61] Ibid.

[62] Ibid.

[63] There is a "navel stone", a "stone of divisions" at Uisneach which is said to represent the same divisional idea. See Chapter 10.

[64] Squire (1998), p. 186.

[65] Kondratiev (1998).

[66] O'Sullivan (1965).

[67] Rolleston (1998), p. 168.

[68] Ó hÓgain (1990), p. 241.

[69] Ibid.

[70] Ibid.

[71] O'Rahilly (1946), cited in MacKillop (1998), p. 257. We will later meet the "Bean Gabhán", wife of the Gobán Saor, at Drogheda in Chapter 3.

[72] MacKillop (1998), p. 253.

[73] Ó hÓgain (1990), p. 44.

[74] Buckley and Sweetman (1991), p. 75.

[75] Roughly located at northwest, northeast, southeast and southwest.

[76] Connolly and Moroney (2000), pp. 19, 21. Ogham markings were often added to stones at later periods.

[77] The Baltray-Fourknocks alignment will be discussed further in Chapter 7.

[78] Thom (1971), p. 9.

[79] Cooney (2000), p. 106.

CHAPTER TWO: COLPA

[1] Cusack (1995), p. 58.

[2] Also written Matha and Matae.

[3] Gwynn (1906), *The Metrical Dindshenchas, Part II.*

[4] Cross and Slover (1996), p. 598.

[5] Squire (1998), p. 54.

[6] Looking at a map of the Boyne at that point, it does bear a resemblance to a shinbone, with the "knee" at Baltray.

[7] *Annals of the Four Masters.* The annals state that the Milesians came to Ireland in "The Age of the World, 3500". The last annal before annal M1, "The first year of the age of Christ", is annal M5194. Subtracting 3500 from 5194 gives 1694 BC. It is possible the date of the Milesian arrival is actually 1700 BC, based on the fact that the compilers of the *Annals of the Four Masters* favoured 5200 BC as the date of creation. See Warner (1990), p. 30.

[8] Cross and Slover (1996), p. 21.

[9] Ibid. p. 21.

[10] Squire (1998), p. 124.

[11] Ibid. p. 123

[12] Ibid.

[13] In various sources spelt also Mile, Miled, Milidh, Milesius.

[14] Squire (1998), p. 123.

[15] Ó hÓgáin (1990), p. 296.

[16] Rolleston (1998), p. 130.

[17] Ibid. p. 130.

[18] Squire (1998), p. 121.

[19] Ibid.

[20] Cross and Slover (1996), p. 14.

[21] Squire (1998), p. 121.

[22] This site is known as the Grianán Aileach and is located in County Donegal.

[23] In Chapter 11, we will see that an alternative account holds that Lugh Lámhfada succeeded Nuadu, not Mac Cuill, Mac Cecht and Mac Gréine.

[24] Squire (1998), p. 122.

[25] Cross and Slover (1996), p. 15.

[26] Rolleston (1998), p. 133.

[27] Cross and Slover (1996), p. 15–16.

[28] Ó hÓgáin (1990), p. 297.

[29] Rolleston (1998), p. 130.

[30] Cusack, (1995), p. 76.

[31] Squire, (1998), p. 125.

[32] Ibid. p. 126.

[33] Ibid. p. 127.

[34] Ibid. p. 128.

[35] Ibid.

[36] Downey and McCullen (1999), p. 31.

[37] D'Alton (1997), p. 2.

[38] Squire (1998), p. 123–4. (Quoted from De Jubainville: *Cycle Mythologique*). Curiously, Squire omits the line "[Who knows] the place in which the setting of the sun lies" quoted in other sources. Robert Graves (1999, p. 201) translates the line as: "Who but myself knows where the sun shall set?"

[39] Waters (1965), pp. 260–1.

[40] Mac Cuill means "son of the hazel", Mac Cecht could possibly mean "son of the Plough", while Mac Gréine means "son of the sun".

[41] Squire, p. 69.

[42] Scribner (1999). I have been unable to get my hands on a copy of this book, but the author kindly sent chapters from the book by e-mail.

[43] There were other concepts involving the Milky Way, which will be explored in later chapters.

[44] MacKillop (1998), p. 404.

[45] Mathews (1991), p. 55. This translation, according to John Mathews, is "based on the original Irish, and on the translations of R.A.S. MacAlister, Eleanor Hull, T.P. Cross and C.H. Slover".

[46] There are stories which hint at a heavenly setting for Magh Mell, the Pleasant Plain. One story relates how a woman of the Sidhe comes from the otherworld to call Connla, son of the King of Tara, Conn, to Magh Mell. "I am asking him to come to Magh Mell, the Pleasant Plain where the triumphant king is living, and there he will be a king for ever without sorrow or fret". The woman tells Connla that the "Ever-Living Ones . . . are asking you to take sway over the people of Tethra . . ." She goes on, "Come now into my shining ship, if you will come to the Plain of Victory. There is another country it would not be worse for you to look for; though the bright sun is going down, we shall reach it before night". (Gregory (2004b), Part 1, Book 4.)

[47] Brennan (1994).

[48] Mellifont means "Honey Well", according to County Louth Ordnance Survey Letters.

[49] McCionnaith (1935).

[50] Although it is worth noting that Milton, in his description of the Creation, said that the Pleiades had "danc'd" before the sun. The Indians saw the Pleiades as "Dancers". See Allen (1963), pp. .394, 400.

[51] MacKillop (1998), p. 320.

[52] Ibid.

[53] Other likely Orion candidates in Irish myth will be identified in later chapters, in particular Chapter 11. In later chapters, we will also see the association between "Mag Mell" and the Milky Way.

[54] Chris Finlay, who is an experienced civil engineering technician, accompanied us on a visit to the mound around the time of Samhain 2001, and carried out some measurements at our request.

[55] Herity (2001), pp. 50–1.

[56] D'Alton (1997), p. 18.

[57] Waters (1965), p. 261.

[58] *Ordnance Survey Letters Meath*, p. 50.

[59] Cusack (1995), p. 60.

[60] Ibid. Rorye is also spelt Rudraige.

[61] A flint flake found at Mell in Drogheda in 1973 was found to be a man-made artefact dating to the Paleolithic, 300,000 years ago. However, its discoverer, the late Frank Mitchell, did not believe it to be evidence of human habitation here. Rather, because the flint object was rolled, it had been brought here by marine currents. See Harbison (2003), pp. 97–8.

[62] Johnston (1826).

[63] Boylan (1988), p. 154.

[64] Wilde (2003), p. 262–4.

[65] Boylan (1988), p. 154.

[66] "The Eight Pagan Holidays: The Turn of the Wheel of the Year", retrieved 8 November 2001: http://www.witchvox.com/holidays/beltaine/beltainehistory.html

[67] A gnomon is an object whose shadow is used to indicate the time of day.

[68] Philip David, personal communication.

[69] Wilde (2003), p. 262–4.

[70] Mathews (1991), p. 55.

[71] McCionnaith (1935), p. 151.

[72] It is described in Volume I of the *Dindshenchas* as follows: "Calf is its name, though it never sucked a cow". Thanks to Moira Griffith, a member of the group Sláine which is committed to the regeneration of old Irish wells, including those at Tara. The group has already restored one well at Tara, the White Cow Well.

[73] Sweetman (1982–83).

[74] Ibid.

[75] Ibid.

[76] Disarticulated is an archaeological term relating to bones which are found out of their natural arrangement.

CHAPTER THREE: mILLmOUNT

[1] Robinson (1994), p. 14.

[2] Casey and Rowan (1993), p. 232.

[3] Ibid, p. 232.

[4] Robinson (1994), p. 14.

[5] Johnston (1826), 28–9.

[6] Ibid.

[7] Ibid.

[8] Ibid.

[9] D'Alton (1997), p. 5.

[10] Cusack (1995), p. 66.

[11] *Lebor Gabala Erenn*, from *The Book of Leinster*.

[12] Allen (1943).

[13] Cusack (1995), pp. 77–8.

[14] There was some collapse on the southern side of the mound during the twentieth century.

[15] Hughes (2003), p. 139.

[16] Ibid. Hughes reports that during excavations in the mid nineteenth century, Cromwell's Mount was "found to be choke full of mortal remains of Cromwellian soldiery".

[17] Buckley and Sweetman (1991).

[18] Ibid.

[19] Moore (1987).

[20] Ibid.

[21] MacKillop (1998).

[22] *Metrical Dindshenchas*, Volume III.

[23] Cusack (1995), p. 60.

[24] Wilde (2003).

[25] Dolan (1904), p. 15.

[26] Ibid.

[27] The alignment is approximate. The day after spring equinox, the sun sets on the western slope of Slane, while on the second day it sets on the eastern slope.

[28] Thom (1971), .

[29] Brennan (1994), p. 47.

[30] Ibid.

[31] Ibid.

[32] We would later realise that author William Battersby, in his book *The Age of Newgrange*, had already noted this apparent alignment of the passage of Cairn T towards the Hill of Slane.

[33] Brennan (1994), p. 90.

[34] Ibid.

[35] Concannon (1931), p. 111.

[36] O'Donovan (1990), p. 497.

[37] Johnston (1826).

[38] http://www.excavations.ie/Pages/Details.php?Year=&County=Louth&id=578

[39] The setting position of today's summer solstice sun is about one degree, or two sun-widths, to the south, or left, of where it was in the Neolithic. Today's midsummer sunset still occurs at the Hill of Rath, a broad, gently sloping hill. In the Neolithic, the sunset position would be a bit further north. The Black Hill was called "Collon Hill" on the Taylor & Skinner Map of Louth of 1778.

[40] In Chapter 6, we will examine a possible link between a place connected with darkness and the summer solstice.

[41] Garry (1990), p. 153.

[42] McCionnaith (1935), p. 1546.

[43] The midsummer sun may have touched both the right slope of the Hill of Rath and the left slope of the Black Hill in the Neolithic, as viewed from Millmount. Perhaps the black in the name signified the sun's retreat southward every evening and that the darker evenings would be set to return after this time. Cúchulainn's link with Collon will be explored in Chapter 12.

[44] *Taylor and Skinner Map*, 1982.

[45] Conlon (2000), p. 469.

[46] Ibid.

[47] Bassett (1998), p. 79.

[48] Corcoran (1986).

[49] *Book of Invasions*.

[50] MacKillop (1998).

[51] Ibid.

[52] Allen (1963).

[53] See Chapters 11 and 12.

[54] Squire (1998), p. 123. (Quoted from De Jubainville, *Cycle Mythologique*).

[55] This passage is quoted from the foreword of MacManus (1990). The passage was contained in an article on "The Ancient Language, History and Literature of Ireland", which, according to the author, had been "kindly contributed for this volume – but which was unfortunately received too late for inclusion". Dr Hyde was the first President of Ireland, from 1938 to 1945.

[56] MacKillop.

[57] Ibid.

[58] Gobhann was also known as Gobhán Saor, and Goibniu.

[59] For a description of Drogheda's heraldic emblems, see D'Alton (1997), p. 138.

[60] The conjunction of the moon and Venus was considered very important in the Neolithic, and there is evidence the ancient sky watchers recorded the eight-year Venus cycle in the Boyne Valley. See Chapter 8.

CHAPTER FOUR: TARA

[1] Slavin (1996).

[2] Ibid., p. 161.

[3] Hickey (1988), p. 5.

[4] Slavin (1996), p. 11.

[5] Kelly (1996), pp. 28-9, 38, 43. Kelly (p. 5) describes sheela-na-gigs as "carvings of naked females posed in a manner which displays and emphasises the genitalia".

[6] Bhreathnach and Newman (1995), pp. 32–33.

[7] Ibid., p. 33.

[8] Ibid.

[9] Ring (2002).

[10] *National University of Ireland Research Matters*, Nollaig 2002, Volume 1, Issue 3, http://www.nuigalway.ie/press/ research_matters/ features3.html#tara

[11] "Tara continues to yield up its secrets", http://www.nuigalway.ie/archaeology/Tara_Aerial-Photos.html

[12] Bhreathnach and Newman (1995), p. 11.

[13] Using SkyMap Pro, we were able to ascertain that summer solstice sunrise in the year 3000 BC was located at 46° 16' azimuth (at the moment the entire disk of the sun is visible above the horizon; see note 97 below for an explanation of "azimuth"). Using a JavaScript tool provided by archaeocosmologist Victor Reijs on his website at http://www.iol.ie/~geniet/eng/azimuth.htm, we found that the direction of Millmount from the Mound of the Hostages was 49.96°. An observer at Rath Maeve, which is located approximately one mile south of Duma na nGiall on the Hill of Tara, would see the sun rise in precisely the direction of Millmount, the latter being located at 46.966° azimuth viewed from the former.

[14] Tolkien (1992), *The Lord of the Rings, Part II, The Two Towers*. Quoted from the chapter entitled "The King of the Golden Hall". At first glance, *The Lord of the Rings* may seem to be completely unconnected with Irish mythology, but there are many themes running through Tolkien's epic which can be seen in European mythology. During 2004 and 2005, some of the similarities between the book and Irish myths were explored on the forum at http://www.mythicalireland.com/forum

[15] Dames (2000).

[16] Michell (1989), p. 49.

[17] Ibid. Alfred Watkins published a book called *The Old Straight Track* in 1925 in which he presented the "complete case" for the system of prehistoric alignments, or "leys", as he called them.

[18] See Chapter 10 for more about the "cosmic grid".

[19] This event will be discussed in Chapter 6. Anne-Marie Moroney is author of the book *Dowth: Winter Sunsets*.

[20] The *Lebor Gabala Érenn*, referred to in previous chapters, is a collection of pseudo-historical accounts by different authors which detail a series of mythical invasions – seven in total – said to have occurred

in Ireland since the time of the biblical Noah's flood. The texts are preserved in the twelfth-century manuscript, *The Book of Leinster*.

[21] That Millmount is the burial place of Amergin is recorded in numerous historical sources. Some of these sources say the mound was built over his body. We think it's much more likely that the mound had been built in the Stone Age, and was contemporary with Newgrange, Knowth and Dowth. As to whether there even was a real man called Amergin, one can only guess.

[22] Macalister (1938-1956), Part IV, par. 363.

[23] Ibid.

[24] This line from Millmount to Carbury actually intersects the large henge site known as "Rath Maeve", which lies a short distance to the south of the main complex of earthworks and the Mound of the Hostages on Tara. Rath Maeve is up to 300 metres in diameter. For more about Rath Maeve and the other giant rings, see Chapter 5.

[25] The Boyne flows some distance west of Tara. At its closest, the river is 2.4 miles away.

[26] Gregory (2004b), Part I, Book II, Chapter I, "The Coming of Lugh", p. 26.

[27] Ibid.

[28] Ibid.

[29] In Irish, his epithet was "*Airgetlám*", meaning, literally, "silver hand".

[30] Cross and Slover (1996), p. 28.

[31] Ibid. p. 28. We will meet a slightly different version of this story in Chapter 11.

[32] Ibid., p. 29. In giving Nuadu his silver arm, Diancecht unwittingly became Ireland's first prosthetics engineer!

[33] Ibid.

[34] Ibid. p. 35.

[35] Lugh was known variously as the *Ioldánach,* which means to be skilled in numerous arts and trades, and *sáimh-ioldánach,* which means to be "skilled equally in all arts".

[36] North (1996).

[37] Battersby (1997).

[38] Ibid., p. 11.

[39] The story, called "The Wooing of Emer", is contained in *The Book of the Dun Cow*.

[40] Squire (1998), p. 185.

[41] Allen (1963), p. 117.

[42] Heifetz and Tirion (1996), p. 51.

[43] Skymap Pro, www.skymap.com

[44] Hancock and Faiia (1998), p. 30.

[45] *Foclóir* is the Irish word for "dictionary".

[46] Dinneen (1927), p. 1052.

[47] McCionnaith (1935), p. 924.

[48] Dinneen (1927), p. 78.

[49] Ibid., p. 77.

[50] Squire (1998), p. 62.

[51] In George Lucas's epic *Star Wars* film trilogy, Luke Skywalker had his hand chopped off by his father, Darth Vader, and it is later replaced with a robotic hand. We have been told Lucas's inspiration for this was the Irish battle of Moytura myth. There is another stark link also with the walker god in Luke's name, "Skywalker".

[52] Gwynn (1906), Part III.

[53] Slavin (1996), pp. 18, 130.

[54] A movement called British Israelism has put forward a theory that the original Lia Fáil was the Biblical Jacob's Pillar, brought to Ireland by the Old Testament prophet Jeremiah. This organisation believes the true Lia Fáil was later brought to Scotland, and then to England, where it is now the Coronation Stone at

Westminster Abbey. They believe the phallic stone at Tara is not the true Lia Fáil. Furthermore, there is a belief among the British Israelites that the Biblical Ark of the Covenant is buried at Tara, so much so that excavations were carried out by British Israelites at the Rath of the Synods in 1899. However, they did not find the Ark, only coins which were placed there each night by local tricksters.

[55] Slavin (1996), p. 157.

[56] Herity (2001), p. 85. Other versions of the story say the stone roared when the rightful king touched it or sat on it.

[57] Ibid.

[58] Allen (1963), p. 312.

[59] Ibid. Allen says it was the "Left Leg of the Jauzah". He adds (p. 307) that Al Jauzah has often been translated, erroneously in his opinion, as "Giant".

[60] Dinneen (1927), p. 1000.

[61] MacKillop (1998), p. 382.

[62] Mac Coitir (2003), p. 72.

[63] MacKillop (1998), p. 265.

[64] We will see how this native Irish concept of the Orion Nebula representing a well would be repeated in another sky–ground system in Chapter 12.

[65] Carbury Hill is, however, visible from Tara.

[66] Allen (1963), p. 307. Allen says the belt stars may previously have borne the name Jauzah, possibly "from another meaning of that word – Walnut".

[67] These hazel water-divining rods are also called *Virgula divina.*

[68] Slavin (1996), p. 18.

[69] Gwynn (1906), Volume III.

[70] Dinneen (1927), p. 463.

[71] Ibid., p. 680. It is worth noting that one Irish word for an astronomer or navigator is *luamhaire,* which is a probable extension of the word *luamh.*

[72] Lugh succeeded Nuadu after the latter was killed in the Second Battle of Moytura. Similarities between the two as Orion will be further explored in Chapter 11.

[73] Slavin (1996), p. 19.

[74] Squire (1998), p. 62.

[75] Gregory (2004), Part II, Book 1, Chapter I, "The Coming of Finn", p. 122.

[76] MacKillop (1998), pp. 265–6.

[77] Slavin (1996), p. 64.

[78] Ibid, p. 65.

[79] MacKillop (1998), p. 101.

[80] Gregory (2004), Part I, Book II, Chapter IV, "The Hidden House of Lugh", p. 54.

[81] Brennan (1994), p. 14.

[82] Ibid.

[83] MacKillop (1998), p. 22

[84] See in particular Chapters 11 and 12.

[85] Knowth is a maximum of 95 metres in diameter, according to George Eogan, while both Newgrange and Dowth have maximum diameters of 85 metres.

[86] This means that the chamber forms part of the passage and there are no recesses.

[87] Brennan (1994), p. 121.

[88] Ibid.

[89] Gilroy (2000), p. 9. Interestingly, the Samhain bonfire tradition continues to this day with the lighting in Ireland of the Hallowe'en bonfires on 31 October, the eve of Samhain, every year.

[90] Ibid., p. 13.

[91] Hickey (1988), p. 14.

[92] Ibid.

[93] MacManus, Seumas (1990), p. 55.

[94] *Ordnance Survey Letters Meath*, p. 86.

[95] Ibid., p. 85.

[96] Slavin (1996), p. 31.

[97] The declination of an object is its position relative to the celestial equator. Just like latitude and longitude on earth, modern astronomers have a system of longitude and latitude in the sky. Declination is similar to latitude, while right ascension is the equivalent of longitude.

[98] The azimuth is the angular position on the horizon at which an object is located relative to the pole. North is 0° or 360°; east is 90°; south 180°; and west 270°. In this case, the azimuth is a true bearing, not a magnetic one.

[99] This term was coined by Alexander Thom. We will discuss the "moon swing" cycle in more detail in Chapter 6.

[100] This would require a very dedicated team and the promise of good weather!

[101] An archaeological term meaning a stone which is set upright, from the Greek *orthostatês*, "standing upright".

[102] Mo Griffith, Sláine Well Group; personal communication. This group was responsible for the restoration of the "Well of the White Cow" at Tara, and is highlighting ancient wells in Ireland.

[103] Slavin, Michael, *The Tara Walk*, p. 8.

[104] Ibid., p. 18.

[105] Brennan (1994), p. 14.

[106] Moore (1987), p. 181.

[107] North (1996), p. 22. For more on Deneb, see Chapter 7.

[108] *Ordnance Survey Letters Meath*, p. 46.

[109] Fenwick (1997), pp. 3–4.

[110] Ibid., p. 4.

[111] Known as Fourknocks Site I to archaeologists.

[112] *Archaeological Inventory of Co. Meath*, p. 15.

[113] Bhreathnach and Newman (1995), p. 8.

[114] *Archaeological Inventory of Co. Meath*, pp. 28, 98.

[115] Ibid., pp. 160, 126.

CHAPTER FIVE: COSMIC CIRCLES

[1] 23 June. The feast of St John's Eve is considered the modern continuance of the ancient Summer Solstice festival, and in parts of Ireland today, bonfires are still lit a sundown to celebrate the longest day of the year. The actual date of Summer Solstice varies between 21 and 22 June.

[2] Wilde (2003), p. 211.

[3] Stout (1991).

[4] Ibid.

[5] Ibid. Rath Maeve is 275 metres, Irishtown 245 metres and Heathtown 200 metres.

[6] Stout (2002), p. 34. Stout says Dowth is unique, having a well-preserved bank width of c.20 metres, rising to an average height of four metres.

[7] Castlecoo Hill is one of the eastern peaks of the range of hills known as Sliabh Breagh in former times. It is located in the townland of Glaspistol at Clogherhead. It was formerly known as Caiseal Có, *caislean* meaning "castle" and the earlier *caiseal* meaning either "castle" or "stone fort". "No one attempts to assign a meaning for Có", according to the Louth Ordnance Survey Letters (Reprinted from *County Louth Archaeological Journal* Vols. IV, V & VI). However, we believe *Có* to be related to *cú*, an old Irish word meaning "hound" or "dog". The anglicised version, "coo", better reflects the Irish word *cú* than it does *có*, which would probably be anglicised "coe".

[8] Ibid. Stout does say that only one of the Boyne enclosures has yielded dating evidence resulting from archaeological work, that being the henge at Monknewtown, from which radiocarbon dates from charcoal indicated a construction date of 1860 BC. Michael J. O'Kelly (1989, p. 132) says the henge structures cover diverse periods from the Neolithic on into the Bronze Age.

[9] For a broader overview of precession of the equinoxes, see Chapter 7.

[10] Moroney (2000). Further astronomical influences on the major Brú na Bóinne sites will be explored in Chapters 6 to 9.

[11] Stout (1991).

[12] Stout (1991), p. 259.

[13] O'Kelly (1989), p. 132.

[14] Henge expert Ronald Hicks, Professor of Anthropology at Ball State University, Indiana, says (private communication, 6 September 2006) that most Irish henges have not been excavated, so it's impossible to tell whether there might be "any broad pattern" to the formations of post holes in the embanked enclosures. "They don't always appear in any sort of pattern (like a circle). In some cases they are only found in – or just outside – the entranceway. Sometimes they seem to be traces of a building that stood within the enclosure". Professor Hicks says "only a small fraction of henge enclosures have stone circles in their interiors".

[15] Ibid., p. 134.

[16] Ibid.

[17] Wilde (2003), p. 211.

[18] Moroney (2000). We will discuss this winter solstice alignment in more detail in Chapter 6.

[19] From Site Q, the Mound of the Hostages at Tara is located at 220°T; Stout (1991, p. 259) says the southwest opening is at 227°T. The T here stands for "true".

[20] O'Kelly (1989), p. 132.

[21] Hicks, Ronald E., personal communication, 2 August 2005.

[22] Hicks (1985), p. 72.

[23] Ibid. The interpretation of this myth will form the backdrop to our exploration of Dowth in Chapter 6.

[24] Hicks, Ronald E., personal communication, 2 August 2005. It is interesting to note here that Professor Hicks and Irish henge expert Geraldine Stout are acquainted and are aware of their differing positions on the openings. Hicks says that he would not stake his reputation on claiming the north-east entrance is contemporary with the construction of Site Q, and says that even an archaeological dig might not provide definitive evidence either way.

[25] Hicks, Ronald E., personal communication, 12 August 2005.

[26] Ibid.

[27] Stout (1991), p. 253. "Uncal" means a C-14 date which is uncalibrated. The rate of absorption of C-14 into the analysed material varies because of numerous factors. Uncalibrated dates can be corrected by such means as comparing them to more definite methods, such as tree ring dating (dendrochronology).

[28] Eogan and Roche (1994), pp. 322–330. A total of 33 "post-pits" were found, "which would have held 35 upright wooden posts".

[29] Stout (2002), pp. 33, 59.

[30] Eogan and Roche (1994), p. 322.

[31] Stout (1991), p. 27. There is a nine-metre-wide gap opening towards 104°T, which Stout says was "probably the original entrance". An aerial photograph revealed another possible gap on the western side of the monument (270°T) which is much narrower than the eastern entrance.

[32] O'Kelly (1971), p. 68.

[33] Ibid., p. 69.

[34] Stout (2002), p. 65.

[35] Ibid., p. 64.

[36] Herity (2001), p. 78.

[37] MacKillop (1998), p. 126.

[38] See Chapter 4.

[39] Gwynn (1906), Part I.

[40] Hicks (1985), p. 72.

[41] It appears to be connected only with the great megalithic cairn of Dowth, but the proximity of Site Q, and the association of both sites with solstices, suggests that both sites shared a similar cosmic purpose.

[42] Dinneen (1927),, p. 175.

[43] Ibid., p. 1030.

[44] Benigni, Carter and Ua Cuinn (2003), p. 47.

[45] Ibid.

[46] Ibid.

[47] Graves (1997), p. 241.

[48] Hicks, Ronald, personal communication, 12 August 2005.

[49] North (1997), p. 287.

[50] Ibid.

[51] Stout, Matthew, personal communication.

[52] Stout (2000), pp. 14 and 23.

[53] Stout, Matthew, personal communication.

[54] Stout (2000), p. 15.

[55] Ibid.

[56] MacCionnaith (1935), p. 623.

[57] Lippard (1983), p. 89.

[58] Buckley (1988), pp. 53–54.

[59] Wright (2000) [1748].

[60] Morris (1907), p. 61.

[61] Ibid., p. 57. The three monuments featured in that year's archaeological journal, those at Ballynahattin, Killing Hill and Balrichan, had all disappeared since Wright's 1748 account.

[62] Tempest (1911), p. 428.

[63] Wright (2000) [1748].

[64] Ibid.

[65] Morris (1907), p. 61.

[66] Ibid.

[67] Bracken, Gerry, "The 'Rolling Sun' Spectacle of Boheh", http://www.carrowkeel.com/sites/croaghpatrick/reek3.html (Retrieved 25 March 2006).

[68] Thom (1971), p. 11.

[69] Ibid.

[70] The rising and setting positions of stars change slowly over the course of time due to precession. We will explore this in more detail in Chapter 7.

[71] This in itself is a contradiction. Carn Beg means "small cairn" or "small stone heap". Being such a huge site, the Stonehenge would have been better situated in another adjoining townland, Carn More, the big cairn. Ballynahattin is translated as the "town of the furze". It must be pointed out that the townland boundaries as we know them today were first formally defined during the first Ordnance Survey of Ireland which was completed in 1842.

[72] Buckley and Sweetman (1991), pp. 70, 191.

[73] North (1997, p. 338), gives Petrie's diameter for the outer bank at Stonehenge as 102.74 metres.

[74] Curiously, one of Ireland's largest surviving embanked enclosures, the "Giant's Ring" near Belfast, is located in a townland called Ballynahatty, which is very similar to Ballynahattin.

[75] Geoffrey of Monmouth, *History of the Kings of Britain*, translated by Aaron Thompson, http://www.yorku.ca/inpar/geoffrey_thompson.pdf

[76] Ibid.

[77] Ibid.

[78] Dames (2000), p. 190.

[79] Wright (2000) [1748], Book III, Plate I. Wright says the stone circle is located at the top of a little hill.

[80] Ibid.

[81] Morris (1907), p. 59. Morris was quoting a song by Nicholas O. Kearney about the hill.

[82] Our thanks to Munich Reilly, Dermot Foley and the staff at Drogheda Library, who regularly requested the Folklore Commission microfiche reels for Louth from the County Library in Dundalk.

[83] According to Michael Dames (2000, p. 207), the hag's apron is "the divine womb, translated into the language of dress".

[84] McMann (1999), pp. 19–20.

[85] McNally (1984), p. 46.

[86] Coffey (1977), p. 61.

[87] Ibid.

[88] Ibid.

[89] Wilde (2003), p. 211.

[90] Ibid.

CHAPTER SIX: DOWTH

[1] Gwynn (1906), Part III.

[2] Because of damage caused to the western side of the cairn as the result of excavations in the 1840s, the mound appears higher and more rounded when viewed from the south, although when approached from the north, Dowth still seems a great deal higher than its more famous neighbour, Newgrange.

[3] Professor Michael J. O'Kelly, who excavated Newgrange, calculated that the cairn of material covering Newgrange contained approximately 200,000 tonnes of stone (O'Kelly (1998), p. 117).

[4] In the years 1847–48, to be precise, on the recommendation of the Committee of Antiquities of the Royal Irish Academy.

[5] Brennan (1980), p. 35.

[6] Boyle O'Reilly, John, "Letter to Father Anderson, Drogheda, November 7th, 1884", printed in *The Cry of the Dreamer and Other Poems*, edited by Peggy O'Reilly and Breeda Tuite.

[7] Ibid.

[8] Ibid.

[9] Brennan (1980).

[10] Coffey (1977), p. 70.

[11] O'Kelly and O'Kelly (1983), p. 148.

[12] Ibid.

[13] Leask (1933), p. 164.

[14] O'Kelly (1983), pp. 138–9, tells us that Governor Thomas Pownall wrote in 1769 that it was reported there was a "cove" (sic) under the tumulus, while Samuel Lewis in his *Topographical Dictionary* (1837, p. 496) reported it contained "subterraneous passages wherein a number of human and other bones have been found". Mention of subterraneous passages reminds us of Johnston's description of Millmount which we gave in Chapter 3.

[15] Stout (2002), p. 54.

[16] Ibid, p. 140.

[17] O'Kelly (1998), p. 21.

[18] O'Kelly (1983), p. 154. O'Kelly lists two publications by a T.N. Deane in her references.

[19] Ibid., p. 156.

[20] Ibid. pp. 150, 152, 156.

[21] *Irish Press*, 15 December 1980. Many thanks are due to Toby Hall, one of Brennan's research team in the 1980s, who has kept an archive of press material from that time on the website http://www.stonelight.ie

[22] Brennan's discovery was made on 14 December, a week before actual solstice. In his book *The Stones of Time* (1994, p. 83), there are photographs showing the sunlight in the chamber on 20 December of that year.

[23] *Irish Press*, 15 December 1980.

[24] The Cairn T discovery was trumpeted on the front page of the *Irish Independent* on 25 March 1980, with the main headline, "Golden secrets of our history".

[25] Moroney (1999).

[26] Ibid., p. 11.

[27] Ibid.

[28] This footage was shown to us by Hank Harrison, another member of Brennan's 1980 research team.

[29] Dubhadh has traditionally been translated as "darkness", although Dinneen's 1927 *Foclóir* gives it as "blackening". The word *Dubh* (old Irish *dub*) means "black".

[30] Slavin (2005), p. 37.

[31] Ibid., p. 50.

[32] Ó hÓgáin (2006), p. 45.

[33] Ibid. Ó hÓgáin says Bressal was a "fictional High-King of Ireland in prehistory".

[34] *The Annals of the Four Masters* seem to indicate that the cattle plague of Bressal occurred in the Iron Age, around the dates 209–199 BC. (See Warner (1990), p. 32.) However, we know that Dowth is a New Stone Age monument and we will see later in the chapter how the *Dindshenchas* myth correlates with an apparent astronomical purpose for Dowth related perhaps to sky events encoded in the *Dindshenchas*. It is impossible that Dowth was constructed in the Iron Age. If the Bressal of the *Dindshenchas* story dates from the Iron Age, it is probable that the story is a later rendering of a very similar, earlier tale.

[35] Gwynn (1906), Part IV.

[36] This particular phrasing is contained in the *Cnogba* version of the story. The *Dubad* version states, "that they might go by it to heaven".

[37] Ó hÓgáin (2006), p. 44.

[38] Gwynn (1906), Part III.

[39] Two versions of the myth are given in the *Dindshenchas*, once in the poem about *Dubad* (Dowth), and again in more detail in the poem about *Cnogba* (Knowth).

[40] According to the Oxford dictionary, solstice originates from the Latin *solstitium*, from *sol* "sun" and *sistere* "stop, be stationary".

[41] Astronomical twilight ends when the sun is 18 degrees below the horizon. At summer solstice, it is around 13 degrees below the horizon, and therefore is still able to contribute to sky illumination.

[42] This was mentioned at the beginning of Chapter 5.

[43] This axial tilt of the Earth is known as the Obliquity of the Ecliptic.

[44] See Chapter 5.

[45] This verse is contained in the *Cnogba* version of the account.

[46] MacBain (1998), p. 169. The old Irish word *fert* means "tumulus", while *cuilidh* means "secret place" or "treasury".

[47] Dineen (1927), p. 1301. *Urdubhadh* can mean "act of darkening, obscuring, eclipsing; eclipse, eclipsis *(gram.)*.

[48] Allen (1963), p. 396.

[49] Roughly between 3500 and 3000 BC.

[50] Temple (1999), p. 124.

[51] Archaeologist Gabriel Cooney (2000, p. 18) says the "largely non-representational character of the art in Irish passage tombs, would have facilitated an openness and multiplicity of meanings". Perhaps this could apply in special cases to representational art also?

[52] Prendergast and Ray (2002), p. 35. The inconsistency between magnetic north and true north in the Dowth plans was something which was earlier noted by Gillies MacBain in the Samhain 2000 issue of *The Pulse of the Irish Passage Mounds*, and was discussed in considerable detail on the Irish-Stones internet eGroup, run by Victor Reijs, of which Mr. MacBain and myself were members, in 2001.

[53] MacBain (2000).

[54] Prendergast and Ray (2002), p. 35.

[55] Ibid., p. 34.

[56] Reijs (2003).

[57] Ibid. Victor Reijs calculates the "likely average azimuth" of the sky window to be 219.5°.

[58] SkyMap Pro can be used to show reasonably accurate rise and set positions for the sun, moon and stars. In this case, I have assumed a date of c. 3200 BC, based on the likely construction date for Newgrange. The actual figure is 227° 38', more than 10.5° west of where the central axis of Dowth points to on the horizon.

[59] Reijs, Victor (2003).

[60] http://www.iol.ie/~geniet/eng/azimuth.htm We entered the data from maps, so any errors are ours!

[61] More alignments will be discussed in Chapter 10.

[62] The lunar standstills are like moon solstices. The most northerly and most southerly risings of the moon during its 18.61-year cycle are known as major standstills, a term coined by Alexander Thom.

[63] We assumed the date of 3200 BC for this purpose.

[64] Thom (1971), p. 18.

[65] O'Kelly (1983), p. 147. It would appear O'Kelly's source is Edmund Hogan's (1910) *Onomasticon Goedelicum, An index, with identifications, to the Gaelic names of places and tribes.*

[66] Gwynn (1906), Part II.

[67] Stout (2002), p. 65.

[68] MacKillop (1998), p. 343 says, "Recent scholarship suggests that Nechtan may be but a pseudonym for Nuadu Airgetlám", and (p. 177) that "Elcmar is a pseudonym for Nuadu Airgetlám".

[69] The figure is actually 10° 39' according to calculations for Dowth using the magnetic declination tool at http://www.ngdc.noaa.gov/seg/geomag/jsp/struts/calcDeclination.

[70] My calculations using SkyMap yielded an azimuth of 237° 55' for minor standstill south setting Moon, based on a lunar declination of −18° 44' for 3200 BC. It must be cautioned that the standstill azimuth yielded by SkyMap is based on a geocentric declination, and correction for topocentric declination due to parallax, giving a local azimuth, could skew the result.

[71] http://www.iol.ie/~geniet/eng/dowthmeasure.htm

[72] Ibid.

[73] My thanks to members of the Irish-Stones group who pointed this out to me when I was writing about Dowth North on www.mythicalireland.com in 2003.

[74] O'Kelly (1983), p. 152.

[75] Ibid., p. 154.

[76] Brennan (1980), p. 30.

[77] This azimuth is 238°. See note 67 above.

[78] O'Kelly (1983), p. 170.

[79] Smyth (1996), p. 144.

[80] This passage is contained in the *Cnogba* version of the Dowth myth.

[81] Curran (2000), p. 133.

[82] Ibid.

[83] Ibid., p. 157.

[84] Ó Síocháin (1983), p. 112.

[85] This stone is not to be confused with the rectangular stone basin in the centre of the northern chamber previously mentioned.

[86] O'Kelly (1983), p. 154.

[87] Calculated approximately by using a plan of Dowth South and a protractor, so this is a rough guide!

[88] The moon's maximum declination at that time was, according to SkyMap, +29° 18', which would have put its setting position at Dowth's latitude at 327°.

[89] Davidson (1985), p. 96.

[90] Scribner, Charles, personal communication. Thom (1971) points out that astronomers say its mean value is 5° 8' 43", but that the ancient stone erectors were aware of a slight oscillation in that value.

[91] Thom (1971), p. 17.

[92] Charles Scribner, personal communication. The value expressed to five decimal places is 27.32159 days.

[93] Thom (1971), p. 20.

[94] Charles Scribner, personal communication. The value expressed to six decimal places is 27.212222 days.

[95] This period is approximately 18 years and 11 days long.

[96] Thom (1971), pp. 18–19.

[97] Ibid., p. 19.

[98] Ibid., p. 23.

[99] Anne-Marie Moroney was kind enough to supply me with observation notes she made at Dowth South during the winters between 1997 and 2002.

[100] http://www.mythicalireland.com/astronomy/boynecalendars.html. Kerb counts are important in the overall evaluation of Newgrange and Knowth as well, as we will see in later chapters.

[101] http://www.astronomy.ca/3340eclipse/ and http://www.bluhorizonlines.org/discover/discover.html

[102] Ibid.

[103] Ibid.

[104] For information on the solar alignment of Cairn L, see Brennan (1994), pp. 110–111.

[105] Davidson (1985), p. 101.

[106] Thom (1971), p. 17.

[107] Gwynn (1906). From the *Cnogba* version of the *Dindshenchas* myth.

[108] Genesis 11:4, King James Bible. It is possible the "biblical" elements in the *Dubad* poem were added by the medieval scribes, many of whom were monks.

[109] Gwynn (1906). This is from the *Cnogba* version.

[110] Ibid., from the *Dubad* version of the myth.

CHAPTER SEVEN: NEWGRANGE I

[1] Herity (2001). This is quoted from "Clarence in *Dublin Penny Journal*, Vol. 1, p. 132?".

[2] Hickey (2000), p. 25.

[3] O'Grady (1892), p. 520.

[4] Hickey (2000), p. 25.

[5] Department of the Environment and Local Government (2002), pp. 62–64.

[6] Access to Newgrange is organised from the Brú na Bóinne Visitor Centre, which is located across the Boyne near Donore.

[7] Department of the Environment and Local Government (2002), p. 48.

[8] And the numbers entering the solstice draw have been increasing every year, thus lengthening the odds of having your name drawn.

[9] O'Grady (1892), p. 110.

[10] Joyce (1910), p. 388.

[11] In fact, the name Newgrange is often assumed to be the anglicised form of *uaimh na gréine*, meaning "cave of the sun", but there has been some debate over this. Geraldine Stout (2002, p. 86) says that the Cistercians divided the area into farms (granges) during the period 1142–1539 AD, and that place names

such as Newgrange, Sheepgrange, Roughgrange and Littlegrange "probably correspond with the location of these medieval monastic farms".

[12] Ray (1989), pp. 343–345. O'Kelly (1982) says that the moment of sunrise is 8.54 hours, and the "first pencil of direct sunlight" shines into the chamber floor at 8.58.

[13] I've been in the chamber a few times when the tour guides have turned off the lights to demonstrate how dark it really is in there. Despite the fact that ambient light is available in the passage, the chamber is in almost complete darkness for most of the year.

[14] Patrick (1974), pp. 517–19, and Ray (1989). Patrick says the sunbeam was just 17 centimetres wide, which is confirmed by earlier observations made by archaeologist Professor Michael O'Kelly who witnessed the phenomenon in 1967. Tom Ray says the width of the light beam "near the entrance" of the chamber is 34 centimetres.

[15] Patrick (1974) says that the two principal orthostats causing obstruction to the light beam are L18 and L20, L denoting "left", i.e. stones on the left side of the passage as one looks in from the entrance.

[16] Ray (1989).

[17] O'Kelly (1998), p. 177. O'Kelly points out the label "triple spiral" is incorrect, and that the symbol consists of three double spirals.

[18] O'Kelly (1982), p. 124.

[19] Ní Sheaghdha (1967).

[20] Cross and Slover (1996), p. 417.

[21] O'Kelly (1982), p. 126.

[22] O'Callaghan (2004), p. 42. O'Callaghan says, "No advanced dating device or technique has indicated that any of the bones and ash found within the mound have been dated to between 3200 BCE and 2200 BCE, when Newgrange was in use".

[23] Ibid., p. 47.

[24] Ibid, p. 123.

[25] O'Kelly (1971), p. 69.

[26] Ibid.

[27] This story is from the *Táin Bó Cuailnge* epic, and is explored further in Chapter 11.

[28] Ó hÓgáin (2006), p. 20.

[29] O'Kelly (1982), p. 46; also MacKillop (1998), p. 17.

[30] Lenehan (1995).

[31] Ibid., p. 75.

[32] Colhoun, Dr. Kendrew, I-WeBS National Organiser, BirdWatch Ireland, personal communication, 10 November 1999.

[33] Ibid. Colhoun indicated a population total of 16,000 was calculated during the five-yearly census of birds held in January 1995. In 2005, it was 14,079, according to Olivia Crowe of BirdWatch Ireland (personal communication).

[34] Lenehan (1995).

[35] Ibid., p. 76.

[36] Ibid.

[37] Ó hÓgáin (2006), p. 22.

[38] Walter (1996), p. 17.

[39] Gibbons (2001).

[40] Ibid.

[41] Ibid.

[42] Collins (2006), pp. xv, 202.

[43] Herity and Eogan (1996), p. 57.

[44] Cruciform chambers and tombs with numerous recesses are known in Iberia and more often in western France and Brittany, although George Eogan says they are "not a common Continental type". Eogan (1986), p. 208.

[45] Patrick (1974) says the range is 133°42'–138°24', while Ray (1989) says it is 133°49'–137°29'.

[46] Using the Reijs azimuth calculator (http://www.iol.ie/~geniet/eng/azimuth.htm) we found that Fourknocks I lay at 138° from Newgrange, just inside the range of azimuths covered by Newgrange as calculated by Patrick, and just outside the scope computed by Ray, although other ancient remains on the Fourknocks ridge lay firmly within.

[47] *Archaeological Inventory of Meath*, p. 15.

[48] Cooney (2000), p. 104. Cooney suggests that a post-hole found off-centre in the floor of the chamber may have contained a post holding up a roof structure.

[49] King (1999), p. 157.

[50] Harrison (1992), p. 71.

[51] Brennan (1994) says it is 17°, but Hartnett's 1957 plan shows the axis points to roughly 26° magnetic, which is the equivalent of 14° if we take off the 12° which separated magnetic and true north in 1957.

[52] The actual direction of the Baltray stones from Fourknocks is 15.37°, just over a degree off the axis we have calculated for Fourknocks. It must be borne in mind that this axis figure is approximate.

[53] Cooney (2000), p. 106.

[54] Walter (1996), p. 19.

[55] Collins (2006), p. 119.

[56] Ibid.

[57] Cooney (2000), p. 166.

[58] The pond at Monknewtown has an embanked form, according to Cooney.

[59] Mitchell and Ryan (1997), cited by Cooney (2000), p. 166.

[60] http://www.jncc.gov.uk/pdf/UKSPA/UKSPA-A6-16.pdf

[61] Ibid.

[62] Robinson, Colhoun, McElwaine and Rees (2004).

[63] Walter (1996), p. 17.

[64] Thuban was not precisely at the pole until around 2800 BC, being located about two degrees from the actual position of the northern pole of the sky in 3150 BC, the date when Newgrange was built.

[65] Hancock (2001), p. 263.

[66] Hancock and Faiia (1998), p. 144.

[67] Ridpath (1996), p. 136. There are 6,500 visible stars in the entire night sky.

[68] William Battersby, author of *The Age of Newgrange*, says that because of the slow change in its position, an alignment towards Deneb is not a clue to the date of that alignment.

[69] Ó hÓgáin (1990), p. 40.

[70] This is illustrated in many astronomy books showing maps and photographs of Cygnus. For example, see Rees (2005), pp. 350–1.

[71] Allen (1963), pp. 55–59. Allen (p. 56) says the constellation "is supposed to be represented by the bird figured on a Euphratean uranographic stone of about 1200 BC . . ."

[72] If that was the case, however, only Cygnus retains a significance to the Newgrange–Fourknocks system because Aquila set below the horizon at the time they were constructed.

[73] De Santillana and von Dechend (1977), p. 245.

[74] Best (1955), p. 45, cited in *Hamlet's Mill*.

[75] De Santillana and von Dechend (1977), p. 245.

[76] Collins (2006), p. 216.

[77] De Santillana and von Dechend (1977), p. 245.

[78] Ibid., p. 246.

[79] This is partly due to pollution and partly because stars are harder to see nearer the horizon because their light has to travel through more of the atmosphere because of the angle at which the light approaches the observer.

[80] Ekirch (2006), p. 339.

[81] The first time Richard and I saw this was in 1999, using a computer program called SkyGlobe.

[82] De Santillana and von Dechend (1977), p. 260.

[83] O'Kelly (1982), p. 68.

[84] Ibid., p. 72.

[85] Ibid., p. 73.

[86] Because of its description as the "white-topped Brugh", we are tempted to think Newgrange was once completely covered with white stone. However, the archaeological evidence shows there was no quartz under the cairn slip to the rear of the mound.

[87] Gregory (2004a, b). This quote is from *Gods and Fighting Men* (originally published in 1904 by John Murray, London), and is contained in Book IV, "The Ever-Living Living Ones", Chapter III, "Angus Og".

CHAPTER EIGHT: NEWGRANGE II

[1] Sagan (1995), p. 318.

[2] Ibid.

[3] This is the title of the introduction of Graham Hancock's 1998 book, *Heaven's Mirror*.

[4] Hancock and Faiia (1998), p. 37.

[5] Ibid.

[6] Gregory (2004b), *Part I, The Gods, Book IV, The Ever-Living Living Ones*, Chapter XIII, "His Call to Connla".

[7] Squire (1998), p. 252.

[8] Gregory (2004b), p. 62.

[9] For a good indication of this, refer to the Folklore Commission archives for Louth and Meath where such references are plentiful.

[10] http://rockhoundingar.com/quartz/experiments.html Retrieved 4 June 2006.

[11] The Dinneen dictionary gives *scáil* as "a shadow or reflection; *manes,* ghost, spirit, ka or astral body; a hue, tint or shade of colour".

[12] *Geal* means "white", but has its root in *ghel,* which means clear, shine, glow. MacBain, Alexander, *Etymological Dictionary of Scottish-Gaelic*, p. 190.

[13] Ibid., p. 191.

[14] Knight and Lomas (1999), p. 281.

[15] Ibid., p. 283.

[16] Brennan (1994), p. 168.

[17] Campbell (1959), Vol. 1, Chapter 9, "Thresholds of the Palaeolithic".

[18] Brennan (1994), p. 78. Michael O'Kelly (1982, p. 38) reports that a French visitor, called De Latocnaye stated in 1797 that treasure hunters "broke one of the basins and carried one that was in the centre to a corner . . ."

[19] Campbell (1959).

[20] Knight and Lomas (1999), pp. 291, 294.

[21] http://groups.yahoo.com/group/irish-stones/message/3579 Retrieved 5 June 2006.

[22] Ibid.

[23] Campbell (1959).

[24] It may be that the authors of *Uriel's Machine* did not compensate for Daylight Savings Time, hence the one-hour difference.

[25] Patrick (1974), pp. 518–519, cited in O'Kelly (1982).

[26] MacCionnaith (1935), p. 1281.

[27] Dinneen (1927). *Mochóir* means "an early-riser" (p. 754), while *Cailleach* means a "hag" or a "veiled woman" (p. 148).

[28] Ó hÓgáin (2006), p. 58.

[29] In other words, that she appears to have three separate identities. Suggested by Gillies MacBain on the Irish-Stones eGroup.

[30] Dames (2000), p. 207.

[31] This theory was put forward by Gillies MacBain.

[32] MacBain, Gillies, posted on the Irish-Stones list.

[33] Ibid.

[34] Kerb 52 also has three spirals, but in a different configuration.

[35] MacBain, Gillies, posted on the Irish-Stones list.

[36] It was Charles Scribner who first pointed this out as a probable function of Newgrange to me.

[37] Gordon, Dr John E., personal communication, January 2006.

[38] Ibid.

[39] Whitehouse (1999).

[40] Ibid.

[41] Ibid.

[42] Ibid.

[43] O'Kelly, Cooney.

[44] McCionnaith (1935), p. 1527; Dinneen (1927), p. 129. William Battersby (1999, p. 1) connects the word with "belly".

[45] Dinneen (1927), p. 129.

[46] Knight and Lomas (1999), p. 287.

[47] Ibid.

[48] Battersby (1999), p. 1.

[49] Harrison (1992), p. 71.

[50] Eogan (1986), p. 179.

[51] O'Kelly (1998), p. 76.

[52] Ibid., p. 75. There were 607 water-rolled quartz pebbles, according to O'Kelly, along with 612 bits of quarried angular quartz and 103 granite boulders.

[53] Brennan (1980), p. 18.

[54] Ibid., p. 19.

[55] Evans-Wentz (1911), Section III, Chapter VIII.

[56] Hancock and Faiia (1998).

[57] Ó hÓgáin (1991), p. 39.

[58] Ibid.

[59] Dineen (1927), p. 1062.

[60] O'Donovan, *Annals of the Four Masters*, cited in Stout (2002), p. 67. The word *Síd* is not unlike the word for silk, which is síoda, a possible reference to the Milky Way.

[61] One of the Irish names given to the Milky Way, according to the McCionnaith *Foclóir* (1935), p. 824.

[62] Ibid.

[63] Interestingly, there is a place in Scotland near Glenoe called Larach na ba Baine, which means the "Site of the White Cow". The story associated with the place says it was the spot where the cow first lay down to rest, perhaps a reference to the time when the Milky Way sat along the whole horizon. Glenoe means "speckled valley".

[64] Dinneen (1927), p. 884.

[65] MacBain (1998), p. 290.

[66] Battersby (1997), p. 18.

[67] Ibid.

[68] Patrick (1974) said the sun's light could penetrate into the chamber if its declination was in the range −22° 58' and −25° 53', and that for light to travel through the lightbox onto the stone at the back of the rear recess, the sun must be located in the azimuth range 133° 42' and 138° 24'.

[69] A line plotted from the centre of K1 through the centre of K52 on a ground plan of Newgrange appears to follow the right-hand wall of the passage and touches the chamber stone C10, the one with the famous triple spiral emblem.

[70] O'Kelly (1982), p. 215.

[71] Ibid.

[72] Ibid.

CHAPTER NINE: KNOWTH

[1] Eogan (1986), p. 9.

[2] Ibid., pp. 9–10.

[3] Ibid., p. 17.

[4] Ibid., p. 21.

[5] Ibid., p. 23.

[6] Ibid., p. 32. Colfer was the "smallest workman on the site" and agreed to peer in through a cavity which had been opened on the western side of Knowth on the afternoon of 11 July.

[7] Ibid., p. 34.

[8] Harrison (1992), p. 50. The symbol contains some concentric circles contained within arcs and is said by some to resemble a floral motif while others have said it looks like two hands holding a circle.

[9] Ibid.

[10] Eogan (1986), p. 179.

[11] Ibid.

[12] Ibid., p. 65.

[13] Ibid., p. 146.

[14] In fact, there are about 90 kerbstones which contain decoration.

[15] O'Sullivan (1993), p. 14.

[16] Ibid.

[17] Eogan (1986), p. 146.

[18] O'Sullivan (1993), p. 36. He says, "pseudo-scientific literature, especially that of the 1980s, draws heavily on archaeological research but is frequently almost paranoid about archaeologists. Prehistorians, for their part, find it difficult to cope with the claims of science fiction, which, operating according to different principles, has no difficulty in leaping chasms of logic".

[19] Battersby (1999), p. 41.

[20] Eogan (1986), p. 178.

[21] In Eogan (1986), figures 9 and 15 both show ground plans of Knowth, but the orientation of North seems to be slightly different in each.

[22] Brennan (1994), p. 104.

[23] Eogan (1986), p. 65.

[24] Brennan (1994), pp. 101, 107.

[25] Ibid., p. 107.

[26] Eogan (1986), Plate 6.

[27] Ibid., p. 33.

[28] Victor Reijs's results can be found at http://www.iol.ie/~geniet/eng/westknowthmeasure.htm (Retrieved 8 July 2006).

[29] Prendergast and Ray (2002), p. 35.

[30] MacBain, Gillies, "Finding Easter at Knowth", http://www.mythicalireland.com/ancientsites/knowth/herdayinthesun.html (Retrieved 9 July 2006).

[31] Ibid.

[32] Charles-Edwards (2000), p. 391.

[33] Ibid.

[34] Ibid., p. 392.

[35] Ibid.

[36] MacBain, Gillies, "Finding Easter at Knowth", http://www.mythicalireland.com/ancientsites/knowth/herdayinthesun.html (Retrieved 9 July 2006).

[37] Ibid.

[38] Reijs, Victor, "Measurements on passages at Knowth", http://www.iol.ie/~geniet/eng/westknowthmeasure.htm (Retrieved 9 July 2006).

[39] Eogan (1986), p. 36 and O'Kelly (1982), p. 21.

[40] Gillies MacBain first pointed this out to the Irish-Stones group in 2001.

[41] Eogan (1986), p. 82.

[42] Coffey (2000).

[43] Ibid.

[44] Ibid.

[45] Ibid.

[46] For Brennan's interpretation of the Calendar Stone, see *The Boyne Valley Vision*, pp. 97–99 and *The Stones of Time*, p. 144.

[47] Brennan (1994), p. 144.

[48] It is possible the waved line count involved counting an upswing and a downswing as two rather than one.

[49] Charles Scribner maintains that the Metonic Cycle can be reckoned without the need to know the number of days in the lunar synodic and sidereal months. The cycle could be identified by counting whole periods, i.e. by counting returns of the moon to the same background stars (sidereal) or to the same phase (synodic) and working out the difference in days between certain numbers of these returns and the end of the solar year (Scribner, Charles, personal communication).

[50] Scribner, Charles, personal communication.

[51] Brennan (1994), p. 148.

[52] For further discussion of this, see http://www.mythicalireland.com/ancientsites/knowth/lunarknowth.html

[53] Thomas (1988), pp. 44, 64.

[54] Brennan (1980), p. 67.

[55] Gwynn (1906), Volume III.

[56] Ibid.

[57] MacKillop (1998), pp. 63, 70.

[58] Smyth (1996), p. 23.

[59] Gwynn (1906), Volume III.

[60] Eogan (1986), p. 112.

[61] Ibid., pp. 46–47.

[62] O'Kelly (1982), p. 75.

[63] Eogan (1986), p. 47.

[64] Whitehouse, Dr David, "Encounter with the Moon Stone", http://news.bbc.co.uk/2/hi/science/nature/1205638.stm

[65] Ibid.

[66] Ibid.

[67] Eogan (1991), p. 119.

[68] Ibid.

CHAPTER TEN: COSMIC GRID

[1] Concannon (1931), p. 112. Concannon tells us it was actually Cianán, the first priest ordained by Patrick, who lit the fire from "the blessed flame".

[2] Gilroy (2000), p. 17.

[3] See Chapter 2 for an account.

[4] This is recalled in the Folklore Commission archives for Louth.

[5] Concannon (1931), p. 112.

[6] If, that is, anyone was inside Cairn T when the paschal fire was lit in the fifth century AD, nearly four millennia after the Loughcrew complex was built.

[7] Ibid., p. 110. Also Frazer (1963), pp. 712–715.

[8] Gilroy (2000).

[9] Concannon (1931), p. 110.

[10] Ibid.

[11] Ibid, p. 113.

[12] Ibid, p. 112.

[13] This was recounted by one of the locals in the Folklore Commission archives for Collon.

[14] Folklore Commission archives, Collon.

[15] Joyce (1879), p. 364.

[16] Ó hÓgáin (1990), p. 356.

[17] The direction of Slane and Oriel viewed from Tara.

[18] O'Kelly (1982), p. 197. The human skeletal materials recovered during the excavation of the Newgrange chamber "consisted of both unburnt and burnt material".

[19] Buckley and Sweetman (1991), p. 245. For more on the crosses, see Roe (1954), pp. 101–14.

[20] Concannon (1931), p. 112. It is also possible this is a direct reference to Jesus coming forth on Easter Sunday from his stone tomb.

[21] Proctor (1924), p. 81.

[22] Ibid.

[23] Ó hÓgáin (1990), p. 157.

[24] As reported anecdotally by a resident of the area.

[25] MacKillop (1998), p. 364.

[26] Wilde (2003), p. 176.

[27] Stout (2002), pp. 73–74.

[28] Ibid., p. 74.

[29] Gilmartin, Seán, personal communication.

[30] This map was from the book *Mythic Ireland* by Michael Dames, originally published by Thames & Hudson in 1992 and later republished as *Ireland: A Sacred Journey* by Element Books in 2000. The map can be found in the latter on page 198.

[31] Dames (2000), p. 201.

[32] Ibid., p. 186.

[33] Ibid. Dames points out that O'Donovan concluded that the hag of Loughcrew and the hag of Slieve Gullion were the Cailleach Bhéarra.

[34] Ibid., p. 207.

[35] Ó hÓgáin (2006), p. 7.

[36] Louth Ordnance Survey Letters.

[37] This is quoted from the "folklore" section of a booklet entitled *Togher Through the Years – Reflections & Reminiscences*, a history of Togher Parish compiled by members of the Irish Countrywomen's Association Togher Guild and published in 1993, p. 93.

[38] Dolan (1904), p. 19.

[39] Ibid.

[40] *Togher Through the Years*, p. 93.

[41] Hickey (2000), pp. 38–39.

[42] Ibid., p. 38.

[43] Stout (2002), pp. 96, 216.

[44] *Ordnance Survey Letters County Meath*, p. 46.

[45] Joyce (1869), p. 81.

[46] Eogan (1986), p. 21.

[47] Brennan (1994), p. 70.

[48] Cited in Brennan (1994), p. 71.

[49] Ibid.

[50] Ibid., p. 109.

[51] Ibid., p. 108.

[52] McMann (1994), pp. 525–44, cited in Cooney (2000), p. 162.

[53] Cooney (2000), p. 162.

[54] Some very interesting examples are to be found in Knight (1996).

[55] Michell (2001), p. 49.

[56] Ibid.

[57] Ibid.

[58] Ibid.

[59] Harrison (1992), p. 67.

CHAPTER ELEVEN: STAR STORIES

[1] A quote from Amergin. See Chapter 2.

[2] The early Irish word for star was *retla*, from *rét glé*, meaning "bright thing" (MacBain (1998), p. 290).

[3] Provided the observer has a good visible horizon, dark, unpolluted skies and is away from city lights. Also, the Milky Way horizon phenomena does not occur today in Ireland, as outlined in Chapter 7.

[4] Beresford Ellis (1996).

[5] Ibid.

[6] Davidson (1986), p. 24.

[7] There is little or no hard evidence of human activity in Ireland during the Paleolithic, which began about 2,000,000 years ago and ended with the Mesolithic, 10,000 years ago. Mitchell and Ryan (2003, p. 79) provide some discussion on the possible reasons for this.

[8] Kinsella (1969), *ix*.

[9] Harrison (1992), p. 65.

[10] Ibid.

[11] Ibid., p. 67. The "Star Temples" Harrison refers to are the Neolithic passage mounds.

[12] This is quoted from an article called "Eamhain – The Twins", from the 1987 *Summer Guide to Inis-na-Righ, The Hidden Island of the Kings*.

[13] Assessment of the position of the sun in relation to the background stars requires precise observation of heliacal risings – i.e. watching the stars vanishing in the light of dawn – in order accurately to evaluate the sun's position in the zodiac.

[14] De Santillana and von Dechend (1977), p. 62.

[15] MacCionnaith (1935), p. 1546; Dinneen (1927), pp. 271, 728.

[16] Perhaps this was what Amergin meant when he referred to the dancing cattle in Chapter 2.

[17] For a good explanation of why this happens, see Davidson (1986), Chapter 9.

[18] MacCionnaith (1935), p. 1546; Dinneen (1927), pp. 265, 1283.

[19] Hancock and Faiia (1998), pp. 50–52. Hancock says that, "In observational terms the one-degree shift brought about by precession over 72 years – an entire human lifetime – is barely perceptible, being roughly equivalent to the width of a forefinger held up towards the horizon."

[20] An idea explored in *Hamlet's Mill*, p. 244.

[21] http://www.radical-astrology.com/irish/miscellany/irishzodiac.html

[22] MacBain (1998), p. 367.

[23] Kinsella (1969), p. 22.

[24] Cross and Slover (1996), p. 57. See also Chapter 4.

[25] MacKillop (1998), p. 305, Ó hÓgáin (1991), p. 273. Ó hÓgáin says there is a tendency among scholars to connect his name to the Latin word *lux*, meaning light.

[26] Dinneen (1927), pp. 684, 670.

[27] Dinneen (1927), p. 684, describes him as the "Celtic god of light and genius".

[28] Cross and Slover (1996), p. 56.

[29] Ó hÓgáin (1991), p. 272.

[30] MacKillop (1998), p. 305.

[31] Allen (1963), p. 310.

[32] MacKillop (1998), p. 305.

[33] Ibid., p. 310.

[34] Rolleston (1998), p. 113.

[35] Cross and Slover (1996), p. 64.

[36] Ibid., p. 112.

[37] Rolleston (1998), p. 110.

[38] MacKillop (1998), p. 88.

[39] Cross and Slover (1996), p. 44.

[40] Ibid.

[41] Ibid.

[42] The lack of mention of a river in the story casts some doubt on this idea, because of the strong association between the Orion figures of Irish myths and rivers, mirroring the relationship seen in the sky.

[43] Ibid., p. 43.

[44] Squire (1998), p. 112.

[45] Ibid.

[46] This poem is quoted from Eugene O'Curry's *Manners and Customs of the Ancient Irish*, Lecture XII, p. 252, cited in Squire (1998), p. 113.

[47] Ó hÓgáin (2006), p. 387. Curiously, in other versions of the tale, it is Mac Cuill, Mac Cecht and Mac Greine who succeeded Nuadu, as we saw in Chapter 2.

[48] Ibid., p. 385.

[49] MacKillop (1998), p. 305.

[50] Dinneen (1927), p. 501.

[51] Ibid., p. 108.

[52] Kinsella (1969), p. 197.

[53] Ibid., p. 90.

[54] Ibid., p. 91.

[55] Gregory (2004a), "Cúchulainn of Muirthemne", p. 344.

[56] Ibid.

[57] Kinsella (1969), p. 84.

[58] Ibid., p. 194.

[59] Ibid., p. 135.

[60] Dunn (1914).

[61] Ibid.

[62] Kinsella (1969), p. 135.

[63] Ibid.

[64] Ibid., p. 136.

[65] Dunn (1914).

[66] Kinsella (1969), p. 195.

[67] Ibid., p. 141.

[68] Ibid., p. 143.

[69] Ibid.

[70] MacBain (1935), p. 150; Dinneen (1927), p. 392.

[71] MacKillop (1998), p. 200.

[72] Squire (1998), p. 97.

[73] More about the death of Cian in Chapter 12.

[74] Quoted from *Táin Bó Cúalnge from the Book of Leinster*, translated and published on the internet as part of the CELT Corpus of Electronic Texts initiative by the History Department of University College Cork.

[75] Identified with a place called Slanemore near Mullingar, County Westmeath, which would have been located in the ancient province of Meath.

[76] Ibid.

[77] Ibid.

[78] Kinsella (1969), p. 7.

[79] Ibid., p. 114.

[80] Ibid., p. 159.

[81] Ó hÓgáin (2006), p. 238.

[82] MacKillop (1998), p. 231.

[83] Cross and Slover (1996), p. 364. The tale is recounted in "The Boyhood Deeds of Finn".

[84] Squire (1998), p. 204.

[85] *CLAJ*, Vol. 1, No. 4, 1907, p. 18.

[86] Ibid., p. 16.

[87] Cross and Slover, pp. 428-9.

[88] Ibid., p. 433.

[89] MacKillop (1998), p. 232.

[90] Kinsella (1969), p. 5.

[91] MacKillop (1998), p. 232.

[92] Slavin (1996), p. 63.

[93] MacKillop (1998), p. 355.

[94] Curran (2000), p. 156.

[95] Ibid.

[96] Ibid.

[97] Ibid.

[98] Ibid.

[99] Ó hÓgáin (1991), p. 352.

CHAPTER TWELVE: THE HIGH MAN

[1] Squire (1998), p. 117. These are the first lines of the victory song of Badb/Morrigan, recorded in *The Book of Fermoy*. The words were sung from "the summits of all the high mountains in Ireland".

[2] The old Irish representation of *fear*, meaning "man", was *fer*.

[3] *Heaven's Mirror* is the title of Graham Hancock's book which explores the idea that ancient civilisations may have incorporated images from the sky into their architecture on the ground, sometimes on a huge scale, such as at Angkor Wat in Cambodia, which Hancock maintains is a copy of the constellation Draco, the Dragon.

[4] This is the same story dealt with in Chapter 11 where Fergus MacRoth was surveying the plains of Meath, except this is the translation given by Joseph Dunn. The chapter is entitled "Here Followeth the Array of the Host".

[5] O'Donovan (1990).

[6] Dolan (1904), p. 20.

[7] Gregory (2004a), "Cúchulainn of Muirthemne", p. 340. Such a journey, following a straight line from Navan Fort (Emain Macha/Armagh) to Newgrange, would pass through the head of the High Man, crossing exactly over his mouth.

[8] Joyce (1869), p. 443.

[9] MacBain (1998), p. 107.

[10] Dinneen (1927), p. 264.

[11] Mac Iomhair (1962); see also Mac Iomhair (1964), p. 321.

[12] Mac Iomhair (1964), p. 325, citing *Revue Celtique*.

[13] Dolan (1904), p. 19.

[14] From *Áth*, meaning "ford", *Bán*, meaning "white" and *lachtadh*, meaning "act of milking". Without the fada (accent) the word *Bán* is *Ban*, which means "woman".

[15] From *baile*, town, and *buaile*, milking place. I've seen it given as Baile Báilleach, but can find no meaning for Báilleach. Ath Banlachta is marked on a map in Mac Iomhair (1964). Mac Iomhair (1962) says it was called Ath Benlechta, the *lechta* (graves) referring to the graves of the women (*ban*) who were buried there. These women, according to the *Dindshenchas*, were killed by Cúchulainn. Also killed there was Mand of Muiresc, son of Daire, who "fell there by the hand of Cúchulainn".

[16] Mac Iomhair (1964), p. 325.

[17] Ibid.

[18] O'Sullivan (1978), pp. 95–96. O'Sullivan says that in the mid-fifth century AD, the territory of Fir Arda Ciannachta (Ferrard) was a sub-kingdom of Brega.

[19] Dolan (1904), p. 16.

[20] Kinsella (1969), p. 159.

[21] Ibid., p. 156.

[22] Ibid., p. 159.

[23] Ibid., p. 61.

[24] This name is of Arabic origin, and means "Armpit of the Central One".

[25] Kinsella (1969), p. 62.

[26] Ibid., p. 69.

[27] Gregory (2004b), pp. 532–533.

[28] Ibid.

[29] Ibid, p. 535. The Grey of Macha was a famous horse. Perhaps this was the moon in another guise, maybe located in the constellation Gemini, the twins, which are associated with Macha through the story of the birth of her twins. These twins were born, beside a chariot, after Macha had beaten two of the king's chariot horses in a race. It may also have been Pegasus, which was a magical winged horse.

[30] Ibid.

[31] Dolan (1904), p. 18.

[32] While the first element of Lugmag is considered to be the old spelling of Lugh, "there is no certainty as to the meaning of the second element" (Ó Riain (2000), p. 87). Mag is an Old Irish word meaning "plain" or "field".

[33] Dolan (1904), p. 18.

[34] O'Sullivan (1978).

[35] Buckley and Sweetman (1991), p. 54.

[36] Casey and Rowan (1993), p. 387.

[37] Ibid.

[38] *Co. Louth Ordnance Survey Letters.*

[39] Garry (1990), p. 150.

[40] Dinneen (1927), p. 694.

[41] Dinneen (1927), p. 724.

[42] Lawless (1908), p. 27.

[43] As reported locally.

[44] Downey and McCullen (1999), p. 61.

[45] *Co. Louth Ordnance Survey Letters.*

[46] Placenames (Co. Louth) Order, 2003, http://www.pobail.ie/en/IrishLanguage/ThePlacenamesBranch/PlacenamesOrders/file,3917,en.pdf, retrieved 17 August 2006.

[47] Ibid., under "Clogher".

[48] MacBain, *Dictionary*, p. 170.

[49] Joyce's *Irish Names of Places*, Vol. II.

[50] *Co. Louth Ordnance Survey Letters*, under "Clogher".

[51] Folklore Commission archives, Collon.

[52] One difficulty with this link is that the Rathbran Mór and Beag townlands do not correspond with the location of the dog stars in the sky.

[53] Battersby (1997), p. 23.

[54] Ibid., p. 26.

[55] Harbison (2003), p. 94.

[56] Placenames (Co. Louth) Order, 2003.

[57] O'Sullivan and Downey (2003), p. 34. The authors state that "it is possible (even probable) that a form of booleying was practised from Neolithic times onward."

[58] Beresford Ellis (1996).

[59] Folklore Commission archives, Collon.

[60] Ibid.

[61] Buckley and Sweetman (1991).

[62] Folklore Commission archives, Collon.

[63] Joyce (1869), p. 341. Joyce is quoting O'Brien. There is a suggestion in the folklore archives that traces of a graveyard were to be found at Leabby, while the *Archaeological Survey of Co. Louth* indicates a possible cemetery adjacent to the crossroads.

[64] Although the Folklore Commission archives indicate that the route taken by the saint on his "frequent journeys" took him along a boreen (little road) "round the foot of the hill [Dunmore]."

[65] Placenames (Co. Louth) Order, 2003.

[66] Murray (1904), pp. 23–24.

[67] Ibid., p. 24.

[68] Allen (1963), p. 480.

[69] *Louth Ordnance Survey Letters: Smarmore*, p. 58.

[70] Ibid.

[71] Ibid.

[72] Kinsella (1969), p. 212.

[73] Ibid., p. 165.

[74] Dinneen (1927), p. 899.

[75] And probably the Milky Way too.

[76] Mac Iomhair (1962), p. 153.

[77] Dinneen (1927), p. 629.

[78] Kinsella (1969), p. 138.

[79] Mac Iomhair (1962), p. 153.

[80] Ibid.

[81] *Keating's History of Ireland*, Irish Texts Society, II, p. 203, cited in Mac Iomhair (1962), p. 152.

[82] Buckley and Sweetman (1991), p. 284.

[83] Folklore Commission archives, Ardee.

[84] Ibid.

[85] Mac Iomhair (1962), p. 152.

[86] Ibid., p. 153.

[87] Ibid.

[88] Dinneen (1927), p. 539.

[89] Joyce (1910), p. 362.

[90] Placenames (Co. Louth) Order, 2003.

[91] Joyce (1910), p. 388.

[92] Hicks, Ronald (1975), *Some Henges and Hengiform Earthworks in Ireland: Form, Distribution, Astronomical Correlations, and Associated Mythology*, pp. 195–196. As noted previously, Grange is considered by some to be a word for a farm.

[93] The two rivers have the same origin in myth. The Eridanus, which is the river constellation starting at Orion's foot, has the same name as the Milky Way, which was known as Eridanus to the Greeks.

[94] Joyce (1910), p. 317.

[95] See Chapter 8.

[96] Dinneen (1927), p. 371.

[97] Mitchell and Ryan (2003), p. 46. Mitchell and Ryan refer to these "small ovoid masses" as "a swarm or field of small hills". They also say the word "drumlin" is "a blundered form of the Irish word for a small hill".

[98] Folklore Commission archives, Collon.

[99] Buckley and Sweetman (1991), pp. 51, 56.

[100] Folklore Commission archives, Belpatrick.

[101] Buckley and Sweetman (1991), pp. 56, 185.

[102] *Louth Ordnance Survey Letters*, for Hurlstone.

[103] From Dunn's translation of the *Táin*.

[104] Ibid.

[105] Mac Iomhair (1962), p. 158.

[106] *Louth Ordnance Survey Letters*.

[107] Ibid.

[108] Ó hÓgáin (2006), p. 212.

[109] Ibid.

[110] Buckley and Sweetman (1991), p. 42.

[111] Barry (1904), p. 43.

[112] Ibid.

[113] Ibid. The name probably changed when a Caiseal (Cashel), was built on top of the mound. Barry says, "It is very natural to think that on the erection of the Caiseal the name changed from Rath-guthaird to Caiseal-guthaird – a name it still bears."

[114] Wright (2000) [1748], Book I, page 10. Wright also included two drawings of Castle Guard in his work.

[115] Ibid. *The Louth Archaeological Survey* (Buckley and Sweetman, 1991, p. 285) says there are "no definite traces" of two banks surrounding the motte.

[116] Barry (1904), p. 44.

[117] Ibid.

[118] Ibid.

[119] Mac Iomhair, Rev. Diarmuid, *Kildemock and its Jumping Church*, p. 2.

[120] Burns (1775), cited in Mac Iomhair's booklet about Kildemock.

[121] Buckley and Sweetman (1991), p. 174.

[122] The story about Kildemock's jumping wall is present numerous times in the Schools Folklore Collection for Louth, even in the schools around Dundalk in the north of the county. The tale of Garrett's Fort was recalled in numerous accounts gathered by various schools in mid-Louth and other parts of the county.

[123] Rhys (1901), Volume II, Chapter VIII, "Welsh Cave Legends".

[124] MacIvor (1958), p. 72.

[125] Ibid.

[126] Ibid., p. 68.

[127] Buckley and Sweetman (1991), p. 174.

[128] MacIvor (1958, p. 69) says that a certain Joseph Dolan of Ardee "tried, in vain, to penetrate to the chamber or 'cave' that is supposed to exist below". If there is a souterrain underneath the fort, it would not be an isolated example. One such cave or souterrain underneath a circular monument is said locally to connect the giant henge monument, Site Q (detailed in Chapter 5) with the nearby Dowth Hall.

[129] Dolan (1929), cited in MacIvor (1958), p. 71. Dolan said there was "no record or tradition to connect the Fitzgeralds with ownership of land or any military operations in County Louth". There was however, a tradition "that a certain member of the Earl of Kildare's family, named Garrett, fought a battle against the O Neills of the north in this townland". (*CLAJ*, Vol. XII, No. 2, p. 126, cited in MacIvor (1958)).

[130] MacIvor (1958), p. 72.

[131] Ibid., p. 75.

[132] Ibid., p. 78.

[133] Dolan (1929), p. 57.

[134] Ibid., pp. 57–58.

[135] In the Schools Folklore archive, there is one mention of such an enchanted army in connection with Dunleer, and also one mention relating to Dundalk. However, the tale of the enchanted army of Hacklim was widely reported throughout the schools of Louth during the time the Folklore Commission records were collected.

[136] MacIvor (1958), p. 75.

[137] Dolan (1929), p. 58. This archetypal myth is also used in lots of fantasy/science fiction works, including *The Lord of the Rings*, where Aragorn goes through the Paths of the Dead to lead the dead army out with the sword of Andúril, although the sword plays a much bigger role in the film than it did in Tolkien's book.

[138] MacIomhair (1950), p. 126.

[139] Kinsella (1969), p. 158.

[140] In some versions, the sword is stuck in the wall of the cave.

[141] Schools Folklore archive, Collon.

[142] Ibid, Ardee.

[143] Ibid.

[144] "Louth Ordnance Survey Letters", p. 337.

[145] Dolan (1904), pp. 16–17.

[146] Cross and Slover (1996), p. 54.

[147] Ibid.

[148] Dolan (1904), p. 17.

[149] Ibid.

[150] Cross and Slover (1996), p. 56.

[151] Dolan (1904), p. 17.

[152] Ibid., p. 18.

[153] Ibid.

[154] *Louth Ordnance Survey Letters.*

[155] Schools folklore archive.

[156] Another tradition indicates that a son of Partholan, called Slainge, is buried in a cairn on top of Slieve Donard and that "he awaits a summons to return to life and rule over Eire". See *CLAJ*, Vol. I, No. 1, 1904, p. 15.

[157] *Louth Ordnance Survey Letters.*

[158] Joyce (1869), Vol. I, p. 323.

[159] Lannleire and Dunleer, http://www.dunleer.com/back_history.htm, retrieved 9 August, 2001.

[160] The Louth OS Letters says that the "accentuation given by the people precludes all pretensions" of it being related to Laoghaire.

[161] Mac Airt and Mac Niocaill (1983), p. 375.

[162] MacIomhair (1962), p. 155. Patrick is quoted as saying, "A blessing on Fir Cúle. I am pleased though . . . On Fir Ross without . . . From Lerga to Léire."

[163] Ibid., p. 155. Does Drumconrath derive from Druim Con Rath, the "hill of the rath of the dog"?

[164] Ibid., p. 166.

[165] Dinneen (1927), p. 655.

[166] MacBain (1998), p. 223.

[167] Dinneen (1927), p. 630. Also, the word *lannaire* means "swordsman".

[168] MacBain (1998), p. 223, Dinneen, *Foclóir*, p. 628.

[169] Dinneen (1927), p. 970.

[170] Dunn (1914), p. 20, "The Combat of Ferdiad and Cuchulain".

[171] Ibid.

[172] Ibid.

[173] Ibid.

[174] The obvious difficulty with this interpretation is that the actual High Man figure lacks, as previously stated, an arm reaching up towards Louth, instead having one with a weapon by his side. Many of the Irish mythical characters were shape-shifters, including Cúchulainn and Cian, and the myths hint that the stellar warrior was seen in different guises.

[175] Buckley and Sweetman (1991), p. 56.

[176] Placenames (Co. Louth) Order, 2003.

[177] Ibid.

[178] Louth Ordnance Survey Letters states it is "passes".

[179] Dinneen, *Foclóir*, p. 168.

[180] Ibid., p. 253.

[181] *Oxford Compact English Dictionary*, Oxford University Press, 2000, p. 1083.

[182] Mac Coitir (2003), p. 102.

[183] Ibid., p. 107.

[184] *Louth Ordnance Survey Letters*, under "Ballynagasson T.L.".

[185] Mac Coitir (2003), p. 55.

[186] Hall (1928), p. 180, from the chapter "Mystic Christianity".

[187] Williamson (1962), flyleaf.

[188] Cusack (1995), p. 114.

[189] Ibid., p. 115.

[190] Havill (1997).

[191] Ibid.

[192] Ibid.

[193] Maltwood (1982).

[194] Ibid., p. 5.

[195] *Louth Ordnance Survey Letters*, under "St. Peter's, Drogheda".

[196] Dinneen (1927), p. 953.

[197] Murray (1904), p. 24.

[198] *Louth Ordnance Survey Letters*, under "Dyzart".

[199] Ibid.

[200] Joyce (1869), p. 135.

[201] Mac Iomhair (1962), p. 147.

[202] Kinsella (1969), p. 252.

[203] Mac Iomhair (1962), p. 147.

[204] Ibid.

[205] Ibid. This Grellach Dolluid of the *Dindshenchas* has been identified with Girley, near Kells, County Meath, but in the location of the story involving the woman and the cow is significant because it takes place above "Cúchulainn's hand".

[206] Vance (2003), pp. 84–85.

[207] Placenames (Co. Louth) Order, 2003.

[208] Gwynn, Vol. I.

[209] *Taylor and Skinner Louth Map* (1778).

[210] This, and the following information about roads was taken from the Schools Collection for Louth.

[211] Mac Iomhair (1958), p. 79.

[212] Kinsella (1969), p. 252.

[213] MacKillop (1998), p. 232.

[214] Ó hÓgáin (2006), p. 311.

[215] Curran (2000), p. 156.

EPILOGUE

[1] For more information on the Tara-Skryne debate, see the following websites:
http://www.taraskryne.org/
http://www.tarawatch.org/
http://www.hilloftara.info/
http://www.savetara.com/

[2] Drogheda Strategy Report, 2006, p. 54. http://www.louthcoco.ie/downloads/Reports/DevelopmentPlans/GreaterDroghedaArea/policycontext.pdf

[3] "One-third of Irish heritage sites now wiped out", *Irish Independent*, 26 April 2000, p. 3.

[4] Murphy, Anthony, "Astronomical alignments in Boyne region", Letters to the Editor, *Village Magazine*, 6 April 2006, p. 49.

INDEX